Navigating the Sermon

for Cycle A
of the Revised Common Lectionary

A Compilation of "Charting the Course" Columns from
Emphasis: A Preaching Journal for the Parish Pastor
a Component of **SermonSuite.com**

CSS Publishing Company, Inc.
Lima, Ohio

NAVIGATING THE SERMON, CYCLE A

FIRST EDITION
Copyright © 2013
by CSS Publishing Co., Inc.

Published by CSS Publishing Company, Inc., Lima, Ohio 45807. All rights reserved. No part of this publication may be reproduced in any manner whatsoever without the prior permission of the publisher, except in the case of brief quotations embodied in critical articles and reviews. Inquiries should be addressed to: CSS Publishing Company, Inc., Permissions Department, 5450 N. Dixie Highway, Lima, Ohio 45807.

Most scripture quotations are from the New Revised Standard Version (NRSV) of the Bible. Copyright 1989 by the Division of Christian Education of the National Council of the Churches of Christ in the USA. Used by permission.

Scripture quotations marked RSV are from the Revised Standard Version of the Bible, copyrighted 1946, 1952 ©, 1971, 1973, by the Division of Christian Education of the National Council of the Churches of Christ in the USA. Used by permission.

Scripture quotations marked TEV are from the Good News Bible, in Today's English Version. Copyright © American Bible Society 1966, 1971, 1976. Used by permission.

Scripture quotations marked NIV are taken from Holy Bible, New International Version, copyright © 1973, 1978, 1984 International Bible Society. Used by permission of Zondervan Bible Publishers. All rights reserved.

For more information about CSS Publishing Company resources, visit our website at www.csspub.com, email us at csr@csspub.com, or call (800) 241-4056.

ISBN-13: 978-0-7880-2706-2
ISBN-10: 0-7880-2706-9

PRINTED IN USA

Table of Contents

Introduction — 7

Advent 1 — 9
School of rock(s) by William Shepherd

Advent 2 — 13
And now, introducing... by David Kalas

Advent 3 — 18
Watching and waiting by David Kalas

Advent 4 — 23
The road no one wants to travel by Wayne Brouwer

Christmas Eve / Christmas Day — 28
Beartivity by William Shepherd

Christmas 1 — 33
Search and preserve mission by William Shepherd

New Year's Day — 38
What you are not responsible for by R. Craig MacCreary

Christmas 2 — 43
Who's your daddy? by David Kalas

Epiphany of Our Lord — 48
Shine, Jesus, shine! by Wayne Brouwer

Baptism of Our Lord / Epiphany 1 / Ordinary Time 1 — 53
Divine debut by David Kalas

Epiphany 2 / Ordinary Time 2 — 58
Called before born by William Shepherd

Epiphany 3 / Ordinary Time 3 — 63
The day boy and the night girl by Wayne Brouwer

Epiphany 4 / Ordinary Time 4 — 68
Of simplicity and simpletons by David Kalas

Epiphany 5 / Ordinary Time 5 — 73
Internal medicine by Wayne Brouwer

Epiphany 6 / Ordinary Time 6 — 78
Heart condition by David Kalas

Epiphany 7 / Ordinary Time 7   83
Tall order by David Kalas

Transfiguration of Our Lord   88
(Last Sunday after the Epiphany)
Mountaintop experience by William Shepherd

Ash Wednesday   93
Called to a different life by Mark Molldrem

Lent 1   97
The day God got lonely by Wayne Brouwer

Lent 2   102
Far from the tree by David Kalas

Lent 3   107
The jar left behind by William Shepherd

Lent 4   112
Believing is seeing by Wayne Brouwer

Lent 5   116
No spring chicken by David Kalas

Passion / Palm Sunday (Lent 6)   121
The wrong anthem by William Shepherd

Maundy Thursday   126
Long table by David Kalas

Good Friday   131
Why did Jesus have to die? by Wayne Brouwer

Easter Sunday   136
Breaking boxes by Wayne Brouwer

Easter 2   141
Now it's time to preach by David Kalas

Easter 3   146
Read the manual by William Shepherd

Easter 4   151
Finding safety in the call of the wild by Wayne Brouwer

Easter 5   156
Between acts by David Kalas

Easter 6   161
Our known God by David Kalas

Ascension of Our Lord   166
Ground rules by R. Craig MacCreary

Easter 7   171
Invisible link by Wayne Brouwer

Pentecost Sunday   176
The counterproductive sermon by David Kalas

Holy Trinity Sunday   181
It was good by William Shepherd

Proper 7 / Pentecost 2 / Ordinary Time 12   186
Family privilege by Wayne Brouwer

Proper 8 / Pentecost 3 / Ordinary Time 13   191
Pick me! Pick me! by David Kalas

Proper 9 / Pentecost 4 / Ordinary Time 14   196
Covenant: the next generation by William Shepherd

Proper 10 / Pentecost 5 / Ordinary Time 15   201
Living in unsafe neighborhoods by Wayne Brouwer

Proper 11 / Pentecost 6 / Ordinary Time 16   206
That's the way by David Kalas

Proper 12 / Pentecost 7 / Ordinary Time 17   211
"X" marks the spot by William Shepherd

Proper 13 / Pentecost 8 / Ordinary Time 18   216
God in unexpected places by David Kalas

Proper 14 / Pentecost 9 / Ordinary Time 19   221
Hitting out of the rough by David Kalas

Proper 15 / Pentecost 10 / Ordinary Time 20   226
It could happen to you by William Shepherd

Proper 16 / Pentecost 11 / Ordinary Time 21   231
People you can count on by Wayne Brouwer

Proper 17 / Pentecost 12 / Ordinary Time 22   235
Choose your weapon by R. Craig MacCreary

Proper 18 / Pentecost 13 / Ordinary Time 23 — 240
School days, school days by William Shepherd

Proper 19 / Pentecost 14 / Ordinary Time 24 — 245
Life on the inside by David Kalas

Proper 20 / Pentecost 15 / Ordinary Time 25 — 250
Of grease and squeaky wheels by David Kalas

Proper 21 / Pentecost 16 / Ordinary Time 26 — 255
By what authority? by William Shepherd

Proper 22 / Pentecost 17 / Ordinary Time 27 — 260
On beyond perfection by Wayne Brouwer

Proper 23 / Pentecost 18 / Ordinary Time 28 — 265
Under the circumstances by David Kalas

Proper 24 / Pentecost 19 / Ordinary Time 29 — 270
Show me your ways by William Shepherd

Proper 25 / Pentecost 20 / Ordinary Time 30 — 275
Testimonies by Wayne Brouwer

Reformation Day — 279
Don't miss out on the coming reformation by R. Craig MacCreary

All Saints Day — 283
The church triumphant by Timothy Cargal

Proper 26 / Pentecost 21 / Ordinary Time 31 — 288
Help wanted by David Kalas

Proper 27 / Pentecost 22 / Ordinary Time 32 — 293
On high alert by David Kalas

Proper 28 / Pentecost 23 / Ordinary Time 33 — 298
Midterm exams by Wayne Brouwer

Christ the King (Proper 29) / Ordinary Time 34 — 303
Ride on in majesty? by R. Craig MacCreary

Thanksgiving Day — 308
God is so good by Bass Mitchell

About the Authors — 313

If You Like This Book… — 315

Introduction

Over forty years ago, CSS Publishing Company was founded by two pastors and a Sunday school superintendent who had a vision to assist pastors "on the front lines" in their efforts to share the gospel of Jesus with people over the entire United States. The lectionary was taking hold over the country in an effort to bring a common message to people, no matter where they worshiped.

Over the years, CSS has published many different products. Of the more than 1,700 publications that have been produced in the history of the company, *Emphasis: A Lectionary Preaching Journal* has been one of the most popular. In its history, thousands of pastors and their congregations have benefited from the commentaries and insights found within its pages.

Navigating the Sermon is a collection of commentaries from "Charting the Course," which is at the core of what **Emphasis** is about. For each Sunday in the Cycle A lectionary, the writers who contributed to these columns have provided thematic guidance drawing together the lessons for each Sunday in the church year. Not only have they provided one idea for each Sunday, but most days have multiple themes from which to choose.

We are excited to offer this new resource to the readers of **Emphasis**, both old and new, and pray that this book will be a blessing to you and an invaluable aid to your preaching ministry.

The editors of CSS Publishing Company

Advent 1
Isaiah 2:1-5
Romans 13:11-14
Matthew 24:36-44
William Shepherd

School of rock(s)

Christianity is, among other things, an intellectual quest. The curriculum to know God truly. The lesson plans interact creatively with other aspects of faith: worship is vain if not grounded in truth, while service is misguided if based on faulty premises. While faith certainly cannot be reduced to knowledge, it cannot be divorced from it, either.

The intrinsic intellectual character of faith creates certain problems. There is, for one thing, the danger that faith may be reduced to mere knowledge, and theology become ideology. As James notes, such faith, condensed to content and devoid of faithful action, is shared even with demons, who know that God is to be feared (James 2:19).

The danger of making an idol out of intellectual belief is naturally countered by the nature of the knowledge of God. The creator cannot be known comprehensively by the creatures; human minds cannot encompass the enormity of the deity. This inherent "unknowability" of God is symbolized often in the scriptures, in those passages where the human being is said to be unable to stand before the divine presence; no human being can see God and live (cf. Exodus 33:17-23; Judges 6:22; Isaiah 6:5). Here is the ultimate irony of faith: It is a quest to know that which is inherently unknowable.

The necessity and the limits of the human knowledge of God are examined in today's scriptures. In Isaiah, the nations know to come to learn from God. In Romans, the knowledge of God is compared to a garment and a weapon. In Matthew, limited knowledge provides the rationale for constant watchfulness.

Isaiah 2:1-5

The opening chapters of Isaiah contain prophecies against Judah and Jerusalem (Isaiah 1-12). Some of these oracles are quite harsh, but they are occasionally bracketed by predictions of salvation "in days to come" (Isaiah 2:2; cf. 4:2-6). The benefits are not to be limited to the Jewish people, because the "nations" will join in the pilgrimage to "the mountain of the Lord's house," for example, the Temple in Jerusalem. In this school on the rock, "the highest of the mountains... raised above the hills," the nations will come to learn from the Rock of Ages (2:1).

Isaiah's oracle is closely related to a passage in Micah (4:1-4), and there is some debate over whether one is quoting the other or both are using a common source. Many scholars think that the passage in Isaiah has been shaped by the subsequent events of the Babylonian Exile or the even later Persian period. However it may have developed, the material is undeniably ancient and is connected to the prophecies about Judah and Jerusalem in verse 5: "O house of Jacob, come, let us walk in the light of the Lord!"

However, it is the "nations" or Gentiles who are the focus of this prophecy about the latter days. The picture is of a vast procession to Jerusalem from all points on the map, a pilgrimage of Gentiles. As they walk, they recite a kind of liturgy, "Come, let us go up to the mountain of the Lord, to the house of the God of Jacob, that he may teach us his ways and that we may walk in his paths" (v. 3). Note that God is explicitly cast in the role of teacher. Isaiah further defines the nature of this teaching; it covers "instruction, and the word of the Lord" (v. 3). "Instruction" translates the Hebrew word *torah*, which covers a wide range of meaning: "teaching," "instruction," "law." However, in conjunction with "the word of the Lord," *torah* here would seem to refer to *the* Torah, the Mosaic Law. Isaiah would have seen no conflict between his prophetic word and the ancient law; later Jewish tradition would see the prophetic works as commentaries on Torah. The teaching the Gentiles are to receive in these "days to come" is identical with the tradition that has been passed down in Jerusalem all this time. The nations come to learn God's Word and God's Law.

This teaching will result in a universal rule of peace. God will not only be teacher, but also "judge" who will "arbitrate for many peoples" (v. 4). Whatever issues have separated these people will be resolved by one who is, by nature, fair and impartial. This arbitration will make weapons of war unnecessary, and so "they shall beat their swords into plowshares, and their spears into pruning hooks" (v. 4). The transformation of weapons into farming equipment is a fundamental economic change; rather than using their resources to fight one another, the nations will learn to feed one another. Having learned God's Torah, they shall not "learn war any more."

Romans 13:11-14

Paul's letter to the Romans picks up not only the eschatological language of Isaiah, but also the emphasis on learning. This may not be apparent from the brief passage we read in church, but the passage is part of a larger section that encourages the Romans to develop their knowledge of God (chs. 12-13). This section is framed on both sides by a call to a radical education: "Do not be conformed to this world, but be transformed by the renewing of your minds, so that you may discern what is the will of God" (Romans 12:2; cf. 13:14). Christians are called to renew and transform their *minds*; learning about God is presented as a primary task of faith. Only with this correct knowledge can faith be practiced; it is necessary to "discern what is the will of God" according to what has been learned.

In our passage, this transformation of the mind is expressed in baptismal imagery: "Put on the Lord Jesus Christ," Paul says (v. 14). To "put on Christ" reflects the actual practice of the early Christians; the baptismal candidate would be given a new white garment as a symbol of the new life in Christ. The expression became quite common (cf. Romans 6:3-4; Galatians 3:27; Colossians 3:8-10; Ephesians 4:22-25; James 1:21; 1 Peter 2:1). Any doubt about the connection to baptism is dispelled by Paul's exhortation to "put on the armor of light"; "light" was another metaphor for baptism (cf. Ephesians 5:8-9, 14; 1 Peter 2:9; 2 Timothy 1:10; Hebrews 6:4). The exhortation to transform one's mind by the teachings of Jesus is a reminder of the pledge to follow Jesus that is made in baptism; the disciple is, if nothing else, a student.

The student disciple learns to "make no provision for the flesh, to gratify its desires" (v. 14). Paul here makes a passing reference to his previous explanation of the power of the "flesh." This may be difficult for modern congregations, who often speak of "sins of the flesh" as if it were a matter of the body and not the spirit. Paul's use of "flesh" is quite different from this; for him, the "flesh" (*sarx*) is everything in the human being that rebels against God. The flesh is the root of idolatry and sin that malign arrogance that thinks it knows better than the one true teacher (cf. Romans 1:3; 2:28; 3:20; 4:1; 6:19; 7:5, 18, 25; 8:3-9, 12-13; 9:3, 5, 8; 11:14; 13:14). That Paul's use of the word "flesh" differs from the popular notion can be seen in that he includes "quarreling and jealousy" equally among more bodily sins (v. 13); churches that judge drunkenness and sexual sin harshly need to learn that the "flesh" can be manifested just as well in the petty conflicts that rage widely in their pews.

Paul's exhortation to learn from our baptisms and not from our flesh is intensified by his assessment of the moment. "For salvation is nearer to us now than when we became believers" (v. 11). Any Christian could say this; of course our time gets shorter as we get older. Paul's language intensifies the thought by drawing on conventions and metaphors associated with apocalyptic thought. He refers not to chronological time but *kairos*, a special "time" or "season" that is urgent and compelling. The *kairos* time is metaphorically just before daybreak, as Paul draws in the metaphors of waking/sleeping and darkness/light (cf. 1 Thessalonians 5:1-11; Matthew 24:42-44, 26:45; Mark 13:33-37; Luke 12:35-46, 21:36; Ephesians 5:8-16, 6:18). Paul exhorts the Romans to wakefulness in light of the coming dawn, when his gospel mission will find its completion (cf. Romans 8:18-23; 11:15). Even the vices he warns against are those associated with the darkness; Christians are to learn to walk in the daylight (v. 13).

Matthew 24:36-44

Matthew shares with Romans the metaphors and conventions of apocalyptic writing; in fact, Matthew 24 is often referred to as a "little apocalypse." In particular, Matthew emphasizes the necessity for keeping alert. His exhortation is not based on the certainty of Jesus' return, however, but on its uncertainty. Some things cannot be taught. That does not mean they cannot be acted upon.

The limits of knowledge are emphasized in the verse that sums up the chapter so far and leads to the next section: "But about that day and hour no one knows, neither the angels of heaven, nor the Son, but only the Father" (v. 36). "That day and hour" refers to the coming of "the Son of Man... on the clouds of heaven with power and great glory" (v. 30). Matthew does not seem particularly interested in what would become a burning question in later theology: How could the Son not know the day and hour? The limits of human (and even angelic) knowledge are clear.

Matthew uses two tightly woven illustrations to lead to his conclusion. The first refers to the days of Noah and the unexpectedness of the flood. With life going on as usual, no one expected a crisis (vv. 37-39). The second is a more generic picture, with pairs of people separated as they do their chores (vv. 40-41). Just as a few were gathered to safety with Noah in the ark, so some will be taken to safety on the Day of the Lord, while others, still engaged in the same occupations, will be left for judgment. As with Noah, there will be no warning when it happens. "Keep awake therefore, for you do not know on what day your Lord is coming" (v. 42).

Matthew expands his point further through the brief parable of the householder: "If the owner of the house had known in what part of the night the thief was coming, he would have stayed awake and would not have let his house be broken into" (vv. 43-44). Note once again that this is all a matter of what you know: "understand this," Jesus says (v. 43). In this case, what you know is what you don't know. Since there is no way to predict the time, the knowledge of your own ignorance is the incentive to stay alert. "Therefore you also must be ready, for the Son of Man is coming at an unexpected hour" (v. 44).

Application

The Englishman Who Went Up a Hill But Came Down a Mountain was about a surveyor who was sent to make maps of Wales. The townspeople were dismayed to find that his measurements showed that their hill was just a few feet short of a true mountain. Rather than have their mountain demoted on the maps, they decided to make up the difference. The movie shows a steady progression of villagers hauling dirt and filler and whatever else they could get their hands on up to the top of the hill that would soon be, officially, a mountain.

Isaiah pictures a steady stream of pilgrims to an artificially high mountain. In this case, it is God who has raised the mountain. The people merely respond to the invitation to ascend the mountain and learn. They are not required to bring anything with them, not even textbooks. God will instruct them in all they need to know.

It is not our job to build the mountain of God. Our job is merely to join the pilgrimage. We will not learn everything there is to know, but we will learn everything we need to know. What we don't know will remind us that our knowledge is not an end in and of itself. The point of all this knowledge is the transformation of our minds so that we are the people we are called to be... alert, awake, and ready for the day when God will call all the nations to the school on the rock.

Alternative Applications
1) Romans 13:11-14; Matthew 24:36-44. Common wisdom has it that those who are most interested in apocalyptic schemes about the end times are the least likely to care about the present. If you spent your days counting the days in Daniel, adding up the numbers in Revelation, and looking for Matthew's fig leaves, you are not going to be caring for the sick, the homeless, or the hungry, so they say. Pie in the sky by and by isn't a big seller at the food pantry.

In fact, however, such common wisdom is not born out by empirical study; groups that place a strong emphasis on the immediate hope of Jesus' coming also have proved to have strong social ministries (see Timothy P. Weber, *Living in the Shadow of the Second Coming*, 1983). Social awareness among millennial groups should come as no surprise, since the biblical tradition links eschatological awareness and moral exhortation. Both Paul and Matthew link the imminent return of Jesus with the imminent need to act accordingly. In effect, Paul says that the end is near, so get your act in gear. You know what time it is, and it is no time to sit on your hands. Matthew exhorts us to be alert on the basis that we cannot know when the end will come, and therefore we should keep alert.

There is thus a connection between the eschatological warning to "watch" and the moral command to "love." Advent for Christians is a time for watching, but it is never a time to sit back and watch disinterestedly. The kind of watch Paul and Matthew had in mind involved doing and not just looking. In fact, there is not much point in looking, if as Matthew says, you'll never see it coming. Watchfulness is manifested in living according to Jesus' teaching.

2) Matthew 24:36-44. Mainline clergy sometimes look with disdain on fundamentalist apocalyptic schemes, but they do so at their own peril. Books like the *Left Behind* series have made premillennial dispensationalism *the* dominant eschatology in America today, and the mainline pastor might be surprised at how many people in the congregation have been reading these books. Ignorance of this tradition, which for many people is not one interpretation among others, but simply "what the Bible says," can be hazardous for our preaching.

While there are plenty of good studies of the ins and outs of dispensationalism, I think it's important to answer claims about the Bible with the Bible itself. Foremost among these is Matthew's denial that it is possible to pinpoint the coming of the Son of Man. The touted "signs of times" have always been wrong and always will be, and to prove the point, one does not have to cite titles like *88 Reasons Why the Rapture Could Be in 1988*. One need only cite Jesus: "About that day and hour no one knows, neither the angels of heaven, nor the Son, but only the Father" (Matthew 24:36). The highly detailed fantasies about the last days found in these tracts are just that — fantasies — because the Bible itself takes a much more modest approach to the question. Quite simply, you can't know when it's going to happen, so there's no point in guessing. What you should be doing, instead, is living out the teachings of the one who will return to take us home.

Advent 2
Isaiah 11:1-10
Romans 15:4-13
Matthew 3:1-12
by David Kalas

And now, introducing...

In the United States, we're in the period between the election and the inauguration of the president. In our system, by the time they are inaugurated, our leaders are fairly familiar faces. Months of primaries and campaigning, debates and speeches, and conventions and commercials, all contribute to a fairly high degree of familiarity. We may wonder what kind of president someone will be, but we have certainly heard many promises, and we have had plenty of opportunities to get to know the candidate.

We experience a sense of newness when a president is inaugurated, but we do not experience a sense of permanence. We have seen other presidents before, and we will see still other, different presidents after. A given administration is, by design, a short-term thing.

Because of the design of our political context, therefore, it may be hard for us to imagine the political climate of ancient Israel at the time of John the Baptist. The present administration — Rome, with its occupying forces, its appointed governor, and its handpicked local "kings" — was certainly not elected. Even if the ever-hopeful people of Israel did not fear that the Roman rule was permanent, it surely must have seemed indefinite.

Meanwhile, there was this long-standing promise and hope of another ruler — a ruler sent by God, with a perfect and a permanent administration. But the timing of his inauguration was uncertain. For that matter, his very identity was uncertain. Who was he? What would he be like?

Far from the high-profile familiarity of our elected officials, Israel's promised leader was virtually anonymous. Unlike the constitutionally scheduled timing of our elections, inaugurations, and term limitations, the reign of Israel's promised leader could not be pinned down on the calendar.

That is the hopeful uncertainty of Advent. The season is a marvelous mixture of question marks and exclamation points. On the one hand, there are the magnificent promises of what the anticipated and anointed leader will be and what he will do. On the other hand, there is the complete mystery of who he would be and when he would come. That is the setting of the season and that is the context of the passages we preach this Sunday.

Isaiah 11:1-10

The people of ancient Israel did not know who their promised ruler would be, but they at least knew his family tree. "A shoot shall come out from the stump of Jesse." Jesse, of course, was David's father, and as such represented the source of the royal line that reigned in Jerusalem.

Obviously, it was all descendants of Jesse who reigned in Jerusalem during the entire life and ministry of Isaiah. Such a promise in New Testament times would have had a different feel, for David had no descendant on the throne in those days. For that matter, what throne there was in Jerusalem did not represent a sovereign Israel anyway. But there already was a member of Jesse's family tree on the throne at the time this promise was made. What, then, would be so spectacular about this promised branch grown from Jesse's roots?

The key lies in the image of a "stump." The promise of God's perfect future contains within it the imagery of a judgment in between: Namely, in order for a shoot to spring from Jesse's stump, Jesse's tree has to be cut down.

That imagery with which chapter 11 begins is a carryover from the imagery that concludes chapter 10.

Isaiah 10:28-32 sounds an alarm: The enemy is in the midst of Israel, ravaging the towns, threatening and terrifying the people. Then, in 10:33-34, the final two verses of the chapter, we find the promise that the Lord will "lop the boughs with terrifying power," that "the tallest trees will be cut down," and that "he will hack down the thickets of the forest with an ax, and Lebanon with its majestic trees will fall."

The promise in our lection that a "shoot shall come out from the stump of Jesse" follows next.

The larger theme of Isaiah 10 is God's guaranteed judgment on Assyria, so it's possible that the image of God chopping down tall, proud trees is a reference to that judgment. In the immediate context, however, between the threatening enemy of 10:28-32 and the image of Jesse's stump in 11:1, it seems that the tree-felling in 10:33-34 may be a reference to judgment on God's own people.

In any event, when chapter 11 opens, Jesse has roots, but no tree; just a stump. That imagery is the bad news. The good news is that there is still life there, and God will bring from those roots and that stump a new branch, and his reign will be perfectly glorious.

We have mentioned the American political context of presidential administrations. While almost every candidate promises greatness from his or her administration, history's sieve produces only a few great presidencies. Whether the hyperbolic promises of a candidate on the campaign trail or the *post facto* affirmation of a historian, no other human reign compares with this description found in Isaiah 11. This promised ruler will be characterized by wisdom, knowledge, justice, and righteousness, and his time will be marked by unprecedented peace — or at least a quality of peace only previously known to Eden.

Here is an opportunity to explore the person and work of Christ in terms that our people may not be accustomed to. The first five verses are descriptive of the person, and the remaining verses might be a way of describing his work. In the passage itself, there is no expressed connection between the promised ruler and the peaceable kingdom described in 11:6-9, yet the implicit connection is obvious: This marvelous ruler will be in place and a certain kind of realm will be the natural extension of his reign.

Romans 15:4-13

On this Sunday in December, most of the people in our pews are thinking about Christmas. We may talk deliberately about Advent, but they are thinking about Christmas. For weeks now, they have been seeing Christmas displays and hearing Christmas music in stores. Now, with so few shopping days left, they're thinking about Christmas. A reading from the end of Romans, therefore, with no reference to mangers or shepherds or wise men, may seem to them out-of-place.

Some themes are tied to a season — whether a season of the liturgical calendar (for example, the Transfiguration or the Ascension) or a season of an individual's life (for example, a wedding or retirement). On the other hand, some themes rise above the particularity of any season. They are for all seasons, and one of those themes is hope.

On any given Sunday in any given congregation, hope is an issue. In any life or heart or home, hope is relevant. This season of Advent gives us good opportunity to talk and to sing about hope. And Paul's words to the Christians in Rome give us good insight into hope.

It would be an interesting exercise — though perhaps more suited to a small group discussion than a worship service — to explore with our people the relationship that exists in their minds between the past, the present, the future, and hope. Our first instinct is to associate hope with the future, for by definition the future is the concern of hope. Yet, in reality, the degree to which we are hopeful about the future is usually a product of the past and the present.

Paul begins with the past — "whatever was written in former days" — and observes that "by the encouragement of the scripture we might have hope." Our first key to hope for the future is found in what may seem to some a surprising place: in the dusty pages of ancient writings.

Here is where a diminished view of scripture proves costly to our people. As the Bible declines from God's living word to exemplary stories and teachings, to great literature, to *persona non grata* in our culture, it has lost its capacity to give hope to people. If the words of scripture are no different than *Aesop's Fables* or Caesar's Commentaries, then I will sift through many pages before I find a scintilla of hope for my everyday life. If, however, those pages reveal God, his heart, his will, and his word, then those stories, teachings, and promises become vibrant with hope that speaks to my heart and applies to my life.

Paul moves on to reference "promises given to the patriarchs" that have been fulfilled in Christ. Promises fulfilled ought to foster hope the way that timely payments produce a good credit rating. We human beings have no basis for judging the probability of a promise from God apart from his past performance. If I tell you that I can throw a baseball through a tiny hole in a wall a hundred feet away, you might not be inclined to believe that guarantee. If, however, you've seen me do it twenty times in a row, then you have a different view. Likewise for us: our hope for the future is rooted in the promises of God, and our confidence in his promises is based upon what we have seen him do before.

That fact brings us to the real issue of hope. Paul quotes Isaiah's reference to the one in whom "the Gentiles shall hope." When push comes to shove, our hope is not vested in pages or in promises, but in a person. The Gentiles shall hope in him, and next Paul refers to the Lord as "the God of hope."

We have been thinking a bit about the American presidential election, and we are reminded just now of the political reality that people like to feel hopeful. The enthusiastic voters will tell you that the candidate they supported is the one who gives them hope. It is hope for the future, but hope vested in a person.

Most people, of course, are risky investments for much of our hope, but we are not directed to just any person. We are directed to "the God of hope."

Finally, Paul concludes with this compelling image: "that you may abound in hope by the power of the Holy Spirit." In our vernacular, we speak of hope in terms of volume. Hope is not an either/or proposition. For us — it is a matter of degree: a little hope, not much hope, no hope, very hopeful, and so on. Paul contributes to that understanding of hope with this large-scale statement — "that you may abound in hope."

Christians are not sentenced to tiny and distant hope. We do not cling desperately to small and weak shreds of hope. Rather, we are to abound in hope — like Niagara Falls abounds in water or the clear night sky abounds in stars.

Matthew 3:1-12

In our American political system, some favored member of the particular political party has the honor of introducing the presidential nominee at their convention. That introduction usually concludes with the bold proclamation that he or she is "the next President of the United States," which leads inevitably to a great ovation. And about half the time they're right.

In the New Testament, John the Baptist is the one who makes this introduction. After centuries of prophetic pictures and promises, the time — and the man — have finally come, and John is the one to "prepare the way" for him.

Artists, authors, advertisers, moviemakers — virtually anyone involved in communication — all talk about the relationship between message and medium. That relationship is a particularly interesting study in the case of John the Baptist.

As John is described here, he is the embodiment of rough, tough, and wild. Is it essential for one whose jurisdiction includes "the rough places" to be a little rough himself? The reference to "the rough places" comes from Isaiah 40:4, which follows immediately after the verse quoted in reference to John earlier in our lection (Matthew 3:2). Surely John's greeting to the Pharisees and Sadducees is rougher than you and I are inclined to be with the folks who come to hear us preach or to be baptized.

John's threat that "even now the ax is lying at the root of the trees" is reminiscent of the context of our Isaiah lection. John's word of judgment, however, may have a still more devastating and permanent quality to it. In the case of Jesse in Isaiah 11, you recall, there was a stump and roots still in place, which suggests that the tree was cut down somewhere at its trunk. In the case of John's threat, by contrast, "the ax is lying at the root of the trees." If the cut is made there, there's very little chance of anything growing back.

Finally comes the introduction. In the books we read and the pieces we write, the "introduction" comes first. But that's not the order in this writing. Here the introduction is a kind of climax. The introduction is the moment we've been waiting for. And in this case, the wait has been hundreds and hundreds of years — arguably since Eve's promised offspring in Eden (Genesis 3:15).

The people had come to John to be baptized, and John skillfully uses that connection to segue to the Christ: "I baptize you with water... but one who is more powerful than I is coming after me... he will baptize you with the Holy Spirit and fire." John's introduction of Christ is a kind of "you ain't seen nothin' yet" promotion. The coming attraction is greater. The coming baptism is greater. And the coming judgment is greater.

John illustrates the comparative greatness with this startling statement: "I am not worthy to carry his sandals" (or "untie the thong of his sandals" in Mark 1:7 and Luke 3:16). The picture is that of a servant — one who would stoop down and take care of the master's footwear. It is the most subservient imagery John could have used. Yet the extreme statement from this reputed prophet of God is that he is not even worthy to be subservient to the one who is coming.

If a person is invited to do something that they are not worthy of, then it is understood as a very great honor. If John the Baptist was not worthy to be Christ's servant, then we and our people might be invited to understand what a very great honor it is to be invited to serve him.

Application

In preparation, this may be the season and the Sunday for introductions.

The Advent season recalls the anticipation of Christ's coming, and this Sunday's lections introduce us to him. Isaiah's introduction is from far away: a promise about this one who would come, what he would be like, and the beauty of his reign. John's introduction has a greater sense of imminence, although it still has an anonymous quality to it. The figure who is about to appear from out of the shadows is, as yet, unidentified. Then Paul's introduction to Christ is *post facto*. The promises have been fulfilled — or at least have begun to be — and Christ has been revealed.

Perhaps the people to whom we preach this Sunday and this season might fall into the same camps as the original audiences for our lections. For some, like the people of Isaiah's day, Christ is unknown and far away. For others, like the crowds who came to hear John, Christ feels close but unfamiliar. For still others, like Paul and the Christians in Rome, Christ is known, and he becomes for us the source of our unity, praise, and hope.

Alternative Applications

1) Isaiah 11:1-10; Matthew 3:1-12; Romans 15:4-13. What can we expect? Advent is a season of expectation. The flipside of expectation, of course, is disappointment. Perhaps we might explore the expectations and the potential disappointments involved in this season of the year.

People want to know what they can expect from their new leader. That is central to how we do campaigns and elections in the United States. But it is not unique to modern democracies, for even back in the ancient monarchy of Israel, the people wanted to know what to expect from their new king (see 1 Kings 12:1-4).

In the wake of a recent election and in anticipation of an inauguration, we might be able to tap into our people's natural curiosity about their leaders. Let's explore what we can expect from this one "born to reign in us forever" (Charles Wesley, "Come, Thou Long-Expected Jesus"), whose coming we anticipate during Advent.

We can expect certain things from him in terms of his character. The first section of the Isaiah passage offers insight there. We can also expect a certain quality from his reign and his realm, as articulated in the peaceable kingdom part of the Isaiah lection. Beyond that, however, we must also expect judgment from him (see Isaiah 11:4 and Matthew 3:12). The reality of his judgment brings us to a different set of questions: What does he expect from us? Do we disappoint him?

The picturesque imagery in Isaiah gives us an Edenic view of what perfect coexistence in nature might look like. Closer to home, however, is Paul's word to the Romans, where peaceful coexistence is meant to characterize the church ("live in harmony with one another," "with one voice glorify God," and "welcome one another"). That is what he expects from those who live in his kingdom. John, too, gives us some sense of our king's expectations: "Every tree that does not bear good fruit is cut down and thrown into the fire."

2) Isaiah 11:1-10; Matthew 3:1-12. "The clothes make the man." We know how apparel affects appearance, and how appearance influences first impressions. What we assume about, and expect from, someone who is well groomed and well dressed is quite different from someone who appears unkempt and sloppy.

Our selected lections present us with an interesting juxtaposition of apparel. Not necessarily a contrast, but a fascinating comparison.

When John the Baptist appears on the scene, he is described as wearing "clothing of camel's hair with a leather belt around his waist." The image is rough and outdoorsy. His clothes reflect his surroundings and his lifestyle, and we find that his message and style are also rather rough.

In Isaiah, meanwhile, we are given a quick glimpse of Jesse's promised descendant: "righteousness shall be the belt around his waist, and faithfulness the belt around his loins." His clothing, too, reflects his style. In his case, what he "wears" is not the product of his surroundings but rather influences and determines the world around him.

Advent 3
Isaiah 35:1-10
James 5:7-10
Matthew 11:2-11
by David Kalas

Watching and waiting

When I was a boy, the father of my best friend accepted a job offer in another country. It meant that my friend had to move away — a long distance away — and that our opportunities to see each other would be few and far between.

I remember vividly the first day that he and his family were returning for a visit. I was so eager to see him! I was not content to sit in the house and wait for them to arrive. Instead, I started walking up the street. We lived on a cul-de-sac, so I knew from which direction they would be coming.

After a few minutes of walking, however, I came to an intersection. At this point, it was no longer certain in my mind whether they would be coming from the left or the right, so I couldn't go any further. I just had to stand there at that intersection, watching and waiting.

I tell you this: If I had known the exact path that my friend's family was going to take, I would have kept walking that route until we saw each other. That was the nature of my eagerness — indeed, my impatience — to see him again. In my boyish reasoning, I thought I could whittle down the wait, you see, by shortening their trip. My endeavor was to meet them part way.

In the big scheme of things, of course, my efforts were silly. They had a journey of so many hundreds of miles, and my endeavor was to shorten it by a few blocks. They had to travel many hours to get to our house; I was impatient to shave off the final two minutes.

In our three lections this week, we will be invited to consider a promised coming. In the Old Testament book of Isaiah, we read of a time that is coming: a most desirable time, marked by rejoicing, healing, great fertility, peace, and gladness. In the gospel story, we see John the Baptist wondering about the long-awaited coming. And in our epistle reading, we are encouraged to be patient for another promised coming: the second coming of Christ.

What is our posture and our practice as we await these promised comings?

Isaiah 35:1-10

It is standard fare in biblical scholarship to divide the book of Isaiah into two or three different sections. The first line of division is generally drawn between chapter 39 and 40. There, we observe, the messages and ministry seem to shift from the threat of impending judgment for eighth-century BC Jerusalem into the good news of restoration and promise for the Jews who were in exile.

Not all of the prophecies of hope and promise, however, are reserved for that latter section and perhaps later time. For here in chapter 35, Isaiah of Jerusalem offers a word from God that is glorious in hope and beautiful in detail.

In order to help them appreciate this oasis of hope, we should offer our congregations a glimpse of the desert of judgment that surrounds it. Chapters 13-24 feature almost uninterrupted messages and images of judgment. It is not exclusively judgment on Jerusalem; not at all. So many surrounding nations and empires are in God's sights, and so a global drumbeat of God's righteous judgment pervades those chapters. Then in chapters 25-27 we have an interlude of hope and promise. Chapters 28-35 include a mixture of gloomy forecasts and bright promises. The poetry and pictures of our text represent the grand culmination of the whole section. But then turn the page, and the Assyrians are at the door. Now the material is neither bad future nor good future; now the report is of a terrible present.

How lovely it is that the fabulous anticipation of chapter 35 should immediately precede the onslaught of chapter 36. For in the face of an intimidating human enemy, the people could cling hopefully to the assurance of God's good will and plan for their future.

God's good will and plan are laid out with characteristic thoroughness. Nature is depicted as fertile and bountiful. That's not simply to say that ordinarily fertile places will be green and lush; no, this is an encouraging image of redemption, for it is "the dry land" and "the desert" that shall "blossom abundantly," for "waters shall break forth in the wilderness."

Furthermore, in addition to those compelling images of beauty and bounty, nature shall also be declawed. The "burning sand" and the "thirsty ground" will be relieved, and God's people shall walk without fear or threat of lions or ravenous beasts.

Beyond the images of nature, this passage of promise also paints a picture of human healing. The "weak hands," the "feeble knees," and the "fearful hearts" are all addressed. Furthermore, the blind, the deaf, the lame, and the dumb shall all be healed.

Beyond the physical healing alone, the passage also anticipates a still greater gift from God. "He will come and save you" is the timely promise, followed by images of a people who have been "redeemed" and "ransomed"; a people, freed from sorrow, who will populate Zion with joy and gladness.

Finally, above and beyond the pictures of nature and of people, the passage offers a glimpse of God. The coming of the Lord is promised, with all his glory and majesty promised, as well as with his rescuing vengeance. It is all extraordinarily good news for a people who, on the next page, will be surrounded by the Assyrians.

James 5:7-10

I remember as a boy hearing a preacher observe how many of the African-American spirituals sang about heaven or going to heaven. "Songs about heaven," he said, "almost always come out of times of trouble. People don't write songs about heaven when they're quite comfortable on earth."

That is a point worth considering for many of us whose parishioners are, frankly, quite comfortable on earth.

The person who is unhappy in his job counts down the minutes until quitting time, the days until the weekend, the weeks until vacation, and the years until retirement. Because the present is unpleasant, the unhappy worker spends a great deal of energy focusing on the future. Likewise, the student who is counting the days until Christmas break or summer vacation. But it's a rare individual, by contrast, who counts down eagerly the days until vacation is over. When the present is comfortable, we don't feel so impatient for the future.

Accordingly, the encouragement from James may not resonate immediately with our people. "Be patient," he says, "until the coming of the Lord." That's fine, except that we weren't feeling impatient.

Comfort with the present is not our only problem. We may also suffer from a diminished understanding of the future.

We instinctively anticipate some future event that we fully expect to be good. The occasion that promises to be fun, exciting, relaxing, or enjoyable — these are the events for which we feel impatient. We are not impatient for that appointment with the dentist, the final exam in school, or the unpleasant conversation we must have with some underling or superior at work.

The fact that our people are not, generally speaking, impatient for the coming of the Lord may not only reflect our present comfort but also our dim view of the future. For if we were profoundly certain of the goodness of what was to come, then surely it would be natural for us to anticipate it — to shift our weight impatiently from one foot to the other, wondering how soon it was going to happen, how much longer we'd have to wait.

James frames the wait in terms of a natural process: the farmer waiting "for the precious crop from the earth." One essential difference between the farmer and us, however, is the certainty of the timetable. An experienced farmer knows which week he can expect to see sprouts, and how many weeks later he will be able to bring in a harvest. However, the "season" of the Lord's coming is not so clear.

That said, we recognize with the farmer that there is no virtue in a premature harvest. It might be encouraging to see the corn stalks up over our heads just two weeks after planting, but if the ears aren't fully developed, what's the point?

Likewise, we trust God's timing in the matter of Christ's return.

During these Sundays of Advent, we rightly give thought to the faithful waiting of those earlier generations of God's people, who did not know just when the Messiah would finally appear. We affirm with the apostle Paul, however, that Christ came "in the fullness of time" (Galatians 4:4) at his incarnation. So, too, we trust that the timing will be just right for his return. Therefore, we are patient "until the coming of the Lord."

Matthew 11:2-11

Lay the contents of all four gospels side by side and you will discover that surprisingly few items are common to all four. We do not find the Christmas story or the Transfiguration in all four. The Sermon on the Mount, the Lord's Prayer, and our favorite parables are not universally recorded. Neither is the calling of James and John, the raising of Lazarus, or the doubting of Thomas found in every gospel.

Few things from the thirty-some years of Jesus' life are found in all four canonical gospels. The bulk of the overlap is limited to just one week of his life — that final, eventful week in Jerusalem.

In light of that select and crucial intersection of the sets, we should be impressed to discover that the ministry of John the Baptist appears in all four gospels.

I don't know that our members — or, for that matter, our preaching — accord John such importance, but the gospel writers recognize his importance. And Jesus affirms John's importance in the most dramatic terms: "Among those born of women no one has arisen greater than John the Baptist" (v. 11).

Jesus' high praise for John comes at an interesting moment: doubt. In prison, we catch a glimpse of wavering just a bit from John's characteristic boldness and authoritative certainty. Perhaps when one's own future is so uncertain every other thing seems somewhat less certain, as well. Specifically, John was uncertain whether Jesus was "the one who is to come, or are we to wait for another?" (v. 3).

Jesus sends John's messengers back to him with a strong affirmation rooted in Jesus' own powerful deeds — "the blind receive their sight, the lame walk, the lepers are cleansed, the deaf hear, the dead are raised, and the poor have good news brought to them" (v. 5). Jesus' response is not a direct quote of the poetry in our Isaiah 35 lection, but the elements are all there. Isaiah anticipates the day when "the eyes of the blind will be opened" — check! — "the ears of the deaf unstopped" — check! — and "the lame shall leap like a deer" — check!

It is interesting to note that Jesus, who elsewhere bemoans and denies requests for a sign (see, for example, Matthew 12:38-42; 16:1-4), should point John to signs for the proof of Jesus' identity and the confirmation of John's faith. Of course, Jesus' response might rightly be understood as the fulfillment of prophecy, as we have noted above. Furthermore, the signs to which Jesus pointed in this episode were performed to bless, heal, and free people; in the cases where doubters (or even challengers) asked for a sign, it would have been an artificial and self-serving use of God's power.

The occasion of the message from John, meanwhile, prompts Jesus to speak to the crowds about him. He speaks playfully with the people as a way of making the point that John was a prophet, just as the people suspected. But, more than a prophet, John was also a fulfillment of prophecy ("the one about whom it is written").

Finally, the two-part ranking of John that Jesus offers — greater than anyone born of women, yet less than the least in the kingdom of heaven — suggests a certain understanding of history. Specifically, John the Baptist seems to be the very hinge of history — greater than all who had come prior to the kingdom and proclaiming the coming of that kingdom at hand (see Matthew 3:1-2; Luke 16:16).

Application

While my impatient, childish efforts to hasten my reunion with my boyhood friend were rather silly in the big scheme of things, there's no question that my heart was in the right place. He was coming to visit and I was excited.

Imagine, by contrast, if I had been blasé about the entire thing. Perhaps I would have been sitting at home watching television, only mildly aware that today was the day of his arrival. I expect that my welcome in that circumstance would have been comparatively weak and inadequate. Imagine that I had forgotten altogether that my friend was coming. Perhaps I would have gone over to another friend's house to play, and I would have missed his arrival altogether.

This season of Advent invites us to consider just what is our posture and our practice in regard to the Lord's coming. The heroes of the season are people like Simeon, whose expectation did not diminish with waiting; the Magi, who made every effort they could to greet and worship properly the newborn king; and John the Baptist, who leapt for joy in utero and who "prepared the way of the Lord" in his ministry.

Meanwhile, the terrible and tragic disappointments of the season include the antagonistic Herod, whose fear and paranoia led him to an unimaginable response; the all-head-but-no-heart scribes, who pointed the Magi to Bethlehem but did not go themselves; and the too-busy, too-crowded innkeeper, who could not accommodate the Lord's arrival.

Now it is our turn to wait for his coming. As we wait, whose response do our lives most resemble?

To what extent are we at the corner, watching and waiting, straining to see? Are we eager to meet him part way? Are we doing what we can to shave off even two minutes?

Conversely, to what extent are we indifferent and preoccupied? Are we not thinking about him because we are so distracted watching television, playing with our toys, or over at someone else's house altogether? Have we forgotten that this might be the day he comes?

Alternative Applications
1) James 5:7-10. "Here comes the judge." When you see a police car on the road, does it change how you drive? Perhaps you slow down just a bit or return both hands to the wheel. Perhaps we are less likely to take a sip of coffee, adjust the radio, or make a phone call when a police officer is driving right behind us.

Human behavior is typically altered by the presence of some official. The calisthenics are performed more crisply and energetically when the coach walks down our row. The worker is that much more focused and industrious when the boss is in view. The defender is more careful to avoid any illegal contact when the referee is nearby.

The phenomenon has other layers too. When our baby girl seemed to be having a medical emergency, we urgently called 9-1-1. We were in a panic but we were reassured when we heard the sound of the sirens because help was almost to us!

James assured his audience that another "official" was nearby. "See," James wrote, "the judge is standing at the doors!" The one who has the power and authority to make all things right is nearby. How shall we live in response?

If we are slouching or careless, then we should take his proximity as cause to straighten up and fly right. If we are troubled or oppressed, then our hope may rightly be renewed by his arrival. And if we are impatient for everything to be just so, then we will be encouraged to know that "here comes the judge!"

2) Isaiah 35:1-10; Matthew 11:2-11. "Mr. fix-it." We have a gentleman in our church whom we call when something needs fixing. Perhaps you have someone like him too. There are a lot of us who like to tinker, of course, and we can sometimes get the object in question working properly again. But this guy is amazing. From the copying machine to the furnace — from the small car to the big tractor to the kid's bicycle — from the sound system in the sanctuary to the drinking fountain in the hallway — he can fix it all.

It's interesting to observe how people feel about this guy. They cherish him. They depend on him. They count on him to make everything just so.

For all the marvelous breadth of Joe's repertoire, it's still small potatoes. He can't cure the church members who are suffering with cancer. He can't fix broken marriages. He can't relieve a region devastated by drought. He can't forgive sins.

Imagine how so many in this world would feel if only they knew the one who could! Imagine how they would cherish and depend upon the one who truly can fix anything and everything. Not this guy, but Jesus. And not only is he able to fix everything, he promises that "he will come and save you."

Invite your members to consider for a few moments the things they own that need to be fixed. Then go the next level: What things in their lives need to be fixed? Then one step further: What things in this world need to be fixed?

For most of the things on that first list, I would recommend someone like this guy. For everything else, however, I recommend Jesus Christ. There is no one like him.

Advent 4
Isaiah 7:10-16
Romans 1:1-7
Matthew 1:18-25
by Wayne Brouwer

The road no one wants to travel

Last winter, I had to attend a meeting in Ontario, Canada. The trip from our west Michigan home took approximately four hours with dry roads and little traffic. A strong storm blew in during the day and by the time I headed back, ice, sleet, blowing snow, and whiteout conditions made the driving nearly impossible. It was a drive I did not want to make on a road that no one wanted to travel.

There are other roads none of us wants to take. When my brother-in-law died suddenly and tragically, I did not want to travel down the road that would take us to his funeral. When someone I love dearly was locked in prison, I did not want to take the road that led me to a face-to-face confrontation with her. When one of my staff committed a social indiscretion requiring public discipline, I did not want to move ahead on a path that I knew would bring many people much pain.

Though I made my way down each of these difficult roads, there are others I have avoided. One road toward reconciliation with a friend of years ago still seems blocked to me. We all have roads we don't want to travel. A friend of mine, for instance, knows what his drinking is doing to his marriage and career, but he is not yet desperate enough to travel the road of admitting he is an alcoholic who needs to enter a treatment program. A graduate student I know enrolls in one program after another, fearing the road of permanent employment because he does not believe he has any skills. Another acquaintance won't allow anyone to date her, because years ago a man abused her and now she is skittish to travel any road that points in the direction of intimacy.

Nations come to crossroads as well, and their leaders read signs indicating a variety of paths to take. When Abraham Lincoln became president, he made it clear in which direction he would move the United States on issues related to slavery. A number of states could not see themselves traveling down that road and seceded, fighting desperately to move the country in another direction. In the 1930s, a group of Christians within the established churches of Germany banded together to form the Confessing Church, resisting at every turn the road that Adolf Hitler wanted the nation to travel.

The passages in today's lectionary are about signs that were posted at forks in the roads being traveled by familiar Bible characters. Each faced at least one road he did not want to travel, and after reading the signs, needed to make a choice about that road. Ahaz chose not to travel where God was pointing and refused even to look at the signpost lifted by Isaiah the prophet. Paul found himself traveling a road that he resisted long and hard, only to find that it was, in fact, the road of grace and hope. Joseph was planning to take the high road of moral rectitude, only to find that the sign of the angel pointed to a path mapped in ways he could not have understood, leading to an outcome only God could produce.

Each of us makes choices every day. Most are little ones but now and again we come to the crossroads that Robert Frost talks of in his marvelous and mystic poem "The Road Less Traveled." There we must make a decision — a truly religious decision. There we must read the signs and determine which road has been traveled before us by our Lord. There we must make a decision that will change the fundamental shape of our existence. Sometimes it is a road of trust in the darkness. Sometimes it is a road of repentance, a true U-turn. Sometimes it is a road of fear mixed with awe. But always it is a road of pilgrimage (as John Bunyan so powerfully put it in *The Pilgrim's Progress*).

Isaiah 7:10-16

Ahaz is in a tough spot. Assyria, the major power of the Fertile Crescent, is on a campaign of expansion and conquest that feels about as politically sensitive as that of an elephant seeking room to roll and romp in a savannah owned otherwise by grasshoppers. To the north, Syria and Israel have formed a feeble pact, knowing that they will likely die with a fight or without one. Either way, Assyria is taking over the neighborhood.

Ahaz stands at a crossroads with four possible roads to take. First, he could give in to the pressure from Syria and Israel and reluctantly join a fight he knows cannot be won. There are blood ties to consider, of course, because Ahaz is the grandson of great Israelite king Ahab and may still owe a little family allegiance to his northern neighbor. Furthermore, Israel and Judah, in spite of their differences, shared a common history that lifted them to a place that some might call a religious superiority complex. They were part of the old Israelite collection of desert wanderers who still told stories of defeating great nations like Egypt, Moab, Edom, the Philistines, and the ten nations of the Canaanites. Because of their unique and divine calling, they had once been the scourge of Yahweh among the nations of the Middle East. Perhaps it was time to rise again and fight a holy war.

Second, Ahaz could do an end run around Syria and Israel and send ambassadors to Nineveh (the capital of Assyria) promising tribute and loyalty in exchange for safety and self-rule when the Assyrian steamroller crushed Syria and Israel and obliterated everything in its path on its march toward Egypt. This may, in fact, be what Rezin and Pekah, the kings of Syria and Israel, feared. It would be tough enough for them to send the sons of their countries' women to sure slaughter on one front. But to also fight a rear guard action against Judah, if that little pipsqueak nation dared make an alliance with Assyria, would be too much. So the two bullies were staring down Ahaz before they scrambled for battle on the northern front.

Third, Ahaz could turn to Egypt for aid. This was a constant temptation for Judah. In fact, Isaiah will declare a mighty divine judgment against Egypt in chapter 19 and will tie to it God's divine displeasure on all in Judah who think that their southern neighbor is a safe and helpful ally (ch. 20).

Finally, Ahaz could simply stay aloof from the swirling chaos of world politics roiling around Judah. There were different reasons to make such a choice: hope that isolation in the hill country would provide safety while the big nations battled it out on the plains, fear of getting involved, or even a declaration of trust in a higher power.

Some might consider this fourth choice foolhardy and use it as a campaign slogan against what they would perceive as the mark of a weak and indecisive king. Yet it was precisely the counsel urged to Ahaz by Isaiah in this outdoor conference. Why? Because Judah needed to learn that it had a divine role still to play among the nations of the world. Its primary strength did not come through international alliances but from its religious reliance on Yahweh. Strong as the bullies to the north might seem, they would pass quickly from the scene. And powerful as Assyria was perceived among the nations of the Fertile Crescent, she too would soon slip and fall and her colors would fade from the map.

Standing at the crossroads, Ahaz could not easily make the right choice. Isaiah was dispatched by God to point Ahaz down the fourth road, and the prophet was commissioned to offer a divine sign nudging Judah in that direction. Ahaz likely knew Isaiah well. They were, perhaps, distant relatives (hence their mutual awareness of which "young girl" would be giving birth in a few months). In any case, Isaiah was certainly a widely respected religious leader in the ceremonial cult of the temple that remained tightly tied to the royal house.

Ahaz was afraid of both the choice he needed to make and also of God's leading in that decision. He knew the divine road would be difficult, so he piously pleaded to be left in the dark. But the sign was given anyway — a young girl (the Hebrew word does not necessarily mean virgin) that they both knew (probably Isaiah's own wife) would soon be pregnant; her child would be a male, and before he was two or three, Israel and Syria would have disappeared from the scene.

This was, in fact, the political outcome. Assyria obliterated both Syria and Israel within the next few years, and Judah was divinely delivered (see Isaiah 37). But Ahaz played almost no part in that process because he would not read the signs at the crossroad and vacillated in irreligious indecision.

Romans 1:1-7

When Paul wrote this letter he was completing his third mission journey (see Acts 19-20) and was spending the winter at the home of his friend Gaius in Corinth (Romans 16:23). While the bulk of Paul's time on his second mission journey was spent in Corinth (Acts 18), Paul's major stop on his third mission journey was Ephesus (Acts 19). While he was staying in Ephesus, the Corinthian congregation experienced a great deal of turmoil and sent a delegation to Paul seeking his advice. In response, Paul wrote at least four letters of concern and advice. Our New Testament letters 1 and 2 Corinthians are just two of these pieces of correspondence that Paul wrote from Ephesus.

After Paul's work in Ephesus was well established, he made a quick tour around the Aegean Sea, renewing his relationship with the congregations he and Silas had worked to found. His final stop before heading back to Palestine was Corinth. As he brought reconciliation and maturity to his relationship with that congregation, Paul looked forward to his next major mission push. It would send him further west, he thought — certainly to Rome and possibly to Spain (Romans 15:23-29).

Since two of the most difficult challenges to Paul's lengthy ministry with the Corinthian congregation were their resistance to his apostolic authority and their tendency to step back from his theology of divine grace, Paul wants now to ensure that these will be presented clearly to the church in Rome before he arrives there. Hence, when he learned that Phoebe, one of the church leaders from Cenchrea (Corinth's suburban port city), was traveling to Rome on business (Romans 16:1-2), he dictated a letter to Tertius (Romans 16:22) to be delivered by Phoebe to Paul's friends in Rome.

The opening of Paul's letter is informative in several respects. First, it is more focused on Paul himself than are most of his greetings. Rather than list those who share the ministry with him, he spends more time detailing his clear calling as a missionary to the Gentiles. Second, he briefly, but powerfully, ties together the historic Jewish religious faith with the new revelation of God in Jesus. In this way, Paul immediately addresses the two major issues that he has had to wrestle with in every one of his fledgling mission congregations: challenges to his authority as a divinely appointed teacher and attempts to pull apart his teachings into either a new form of Pharisaic asceticism or some version of Hellenistic hedonism.

Both of these themes will be developed much more fully in the body of Paul's letter. At this point, Paul's confirmation of each idea is simply Jesus. He indicates that Jesus is the one who called him to his special Gentile mission (vv. 1, 5); he points to Jesus as God's confirmation of the historic prophetic message (vv. 2-3); he identifies Jesus as the Messiah proven in power because of the resurrection (v. 4); and he declares Jesus to be the ensign under which the Christians in Rome find their identity (v. 6), just as the soldiers of Rome would march under the standard of the great Roman eagles.

In all of this, Paul is raising a sign at the crossroads of life. Whatever road any might be traveling, it always comes to a fork where the choice of paths leads to different outcomes. Paul is determined to point his friends in Rome down the Jesus trail. This will not be an easy way to go. It requires, first of all, that people admit their sinfulness and inability to do good, and the legitimacy of God's wrath against them (chs. 1-3). Further, it means that they will not be able to claim merit of their own in finding God's favor (chs. 4-11). Finally, it demands total sacrifice on their part (chs. 12-15).

This is the road no one wants to travel. But it is the only road of "good news." Down one road God wins the day by way of reasserting God's righteousness (1:16-17) as demonstrated and delivered in Jesus. Down all the other paths, no matter how wholesome they may seem, lies either a trap of divine judgment or one of self-destruction.

Matthew 1:18-25

Many of us start reading the gospel of Matthew at this point; we are not thrilled with the evangelist's list of names in the first seventeen verses. Yet without the genealogical records, the punch of this story is not as evident. The genealogies locate Jesus in both divine and human time. Matthew's three series of fourteen generations maps out the human landscape: Israel was created by God to be God's people in the land of covenant promise (Abraham through David; 1:2-6), Israel experienced times of both success and failure in Palestine (David through Jechoniah; 1:6-11), Israel was now reduced to the remnant of Judah that returned from exile and was waiting for the Messiah to come (Jechoniah through Joseph; 1:12-16). Thus, these are the days of expectation; the Messiah should come about now.

Furthermore, on the divine timeline, two covenants need fulfillment. God made a promise to Abraham that all of the nations of the earth would be blessed through him and his descendents (Genesis 12:1-3). Later, God made a promise to David that he would always have a descendent on the throne (2 Samuel 7). At the time of Matthew 1:18, the remnant of Israel was hardly significant to bless its few Palestinian neighbors, let alone the whole world. At the same time, even though the descendents of David's family kept their genealogical records intact by updating them with every baby born, they certainly were not kings or rulers.

So it is that Matthew's words in verse 18 are freighted with expectation. This is the right time and Jesus is the one who will bring together the fulfillment of each covenant. But Joseph does not know this. He cannot stand above the times to see the big picture, and he is not aware of God's plans. What God is doing in Mary, his youthful pledged bride, seems to him to be merely a nasty act of immorality on her part. How can she, the woman of his hopes and dreams, be pregnant when he has circumspectly maintained their propriety?

In order to bring Joseph on board, God sends an angel to stand at the crossroads of his life and point in a new direction, one Joseph would not otherwise have considered. God has performed a miracle in Mary's womb; the one who will be born will finally stitch together Israel's human time and God's divine time. The covenants and the covenant people will give birth, through Mary, to the Messiah of the covenant. God will again come close ("Immanuel").

Joseph has to make a choice. Before he went to sleep, he had been headed in one direction (v. 19). After the nighttime vision and the signpost presented by the angel, Joseph turned and went down another path (v. 24). And the rest, as they say, is history.

Application

The Sundays of Advent are signposts in our time. While the culture around us prepares for Christmas by way of parties and pageants and purchases, Christians are scanning the horizon for the dawn when every day of the year will be Christmas. The Messiah came once and brought convergence between the two great covenants of the Old Testament and the covenant people; then he left for a time, declaring that the nations needed opportunity to come on board with God's age-old plan.

Now the church of Jesus holds up the signposts of Advent Sundays each year to remind those in the family of Jesus of who they are and whose they are. And in a world that is constantly at crossroads of political tensions, ethnic antagonism, materialistic kingdom building, cultural elitism, individualistic isolationism, agnostic questing, and atheistic denial, there is constantly a need to raise high these signposts in the marketplaces and among the societies of our times. We are not counting down the remaining days of Christmas shopping; we are keeping vigil at the crossroads of life, giving people another opportunity to find the right road — the road of non-alignment among the political superpowers of our day (cf. Ahaz), the road of Jesus' good news among the religions of our world (cf. Paul), and the road of divine initiative and redemptive purpose among the cluttered calendars of our times (cf. Joesph).

This is not an enviable task. We are guides interrupting the paths of those who have already chosen their own roads and telling them that they need to change course. We are heralds of the way of the Messiah few desire. We point to the road less traveled in an age that follows gurus with stories of the trampled paths to success. This is the way of Advent: "Prepare ye the way of the Lord...."

An Alternative Application
Isaiah 7:10-16; Matthew 1:18-25. A focus on just the Isaiah and the Matthew passages may be used to reflect on the idea of "Immanuel." Ahaz had chosen to secularize his little kingdom, and he was not thrilled with the idea of a God who came too close. He did not want the sign that Isaiah offered, nor did he want a divine king who would compete with him for both the allegiance of the people and the values of the kingdom. In spite of his refusal of the sign, God gave him one anyway. In the sign of "Immanuel," the nearness of God was both a threat and a promise.

Similarly for Joseph, the nearness of God in the birth of Mary's son was both a threat and a promise. It would cause him embarrassment. It would cause Mary pain. It would cause conflict among the Jews. It would cause unrest in the world ruled by the god emperors of Rome.

But "Immanuel" is also a promise. Only God could deliver Judah and Ahaz in a time of overwhelming political odds against them. Only God could bring meaning back to a world that was drifting in the days of post-exilic Judaism. The God who had been too distant from the world, and the world that had been too distant from its God were now coming close in divine acts of deliverance. Nothing would ever be the same again.

Christmas Eve / Christmas Day
Isaiah 9:2-7
Titus 2:11-14
Luke 2:1-14 (15-20)
by William Shepherd

Beartivity

I live in a house with my wife, two cats, and about 200 teddy bears. So when I saw the Beartivity set, I could not resist.

You have to see it to believe it — a nativity scene like no other, carved and molded in exquisite detail: Mary Bear kneeling before the manger, her hands folded in prayer, her long white headdress shimmering against her black body. Joseph Bear kneeling beside her, the look on his brown muzzle somewhere between puzzlement and awe. Baby Jesus Bear lying face up in the manger, swaddling cloths laid across his lap. Hanging above them from bronze wires are two cherubic Angel Bears, complete with bronze haloes.

My wife's daughter said, "Mom, don't you think that's a little sacrilegious?"

"No more so than bathrobe Christmas pageants," she replied.

Actually, I think it more sacrilegious to etch the Nativity in stained glass, as if Mary, Joseph, Jesus, the shepherds, and the wise men were not real human beings who lived in a specific place and time but were disembodied archetypes of some imagined piety. If the incarnation is to have any meaning, Jesus must come as a real human child. A bathrobe Christmas pageant — or a Beartivity scene, for that matter — may well speak of the human Son better than a stylized portrait of a haloed infant in prayer. If God had wanted to reach bears, God would have come as a bear. Instead, God came as one of us, bathrobes and all.

Besides, stained glass takes all the fun out of Christmas. It's supposed to be a party!

Isaiah 9:2-7

The party begins in the book of Isaiah with a psalm of thanksgiving. It is a birth announcement of sorts, with elements of a royal succession oracle (the passage is often taken to be an oracle for the coronation of a king, but it is clearly addressed *to* God). The invitation to the party gives thanks to God while announcing the birth of a crown prince who will usher in a period of unprecedented peace.

The psalm is deeply embedded in its larger literary context. Isaiah 7:1—9:7 is a series of prophecies about a royal figure with an eschatological edge: "His authority shall grow continually, and there shall be endless peace for the throne of David and his kingdom. He will establish and uphold it with justice and with righteousness from this time onward and forevermore" (v. 7). Clearly we are dealing with a larger-than-life king, a type of all just rulers. Even the name given the child is symbolic; it is "Immanuel," "God with us" (7:14; cf. 9:6). The exact identity of Immanuel has long been a matter of debate, while the problems of chronology will never be fully resolved. The best guess is that Isaiah's prophecy originally referred to King Hezekiah, one of the bright lights of the Davidic line. Given the eschatological and messianic idealization that Isaiah applied to the king, Christians did not move far in transferring the accolades of Immanuel to Jesus. The Messiah is not made of stained glass, however, since the reference was originally to an actual king. Jesus comes to the job of Messiah with a real earthly type and predecessor, the historical Hezekiah.

Isaiah clearly sees the birth of Immanuel as set on the border between present and eschatological time. The contrast is between "the former time" and "the latter time," the time of judgment and the time of redemption (9:1). The opening of the psalm places the cause for rejoicing in the past — the coming of light to the people, the release from oppression, the birth of the messianic king (vv. 2-6). Only at the end do the verbs look to the future: "His authority shall grow continually... there shall be endless peace... he will establish it (peace) and uphold it... from this time onward and forevermore" (v. 7).

Throughout, it is God who acts while the people respond. God is responsible for the great light; the people merely look up to see it (v. 2). God has "multiplied the nation"; the people respond with joy (v. 3). God has broken the yoke of the oppressor, because God has given a child who will be named "Wonderful Counselor, Mighty God, Everlasting Father, Prince of Peace" (v. 6). These names probably reflect coronation names of Egyptian rulers and they represent the extraordinary gifts that God has given to the anointed ones. God has acted to share part of God's own nature with us. Immanuel, "God with us," is given "to us" (v. 6; cf. 7:14).

There is a note of force in God's action; the metaphors are mixed between military and agricultural. While God has tended to the people, giving them prosperity and growth despite darkness and oppression (vv. 2-3), God has done so as a general: "For all the boots of the tramping warriors and all the garments rolled in blood shall be burned as fuel for the fire" (v. 5). Like Joshua leading Israel to victory over Midian with only 300 soldiers and their trumpets, God has broken the yoke and bar of Israel's oppressor (v. 4; cf. Judges 7:15-25). The historical reference is to the Syro-Ephraimite war, with perhaps a look ahead to impending judgment on Assyria. The promise is that God will defeat all the people's enemies, in the person of a mighty warrior-king who will bring peace. "The zeal of the Lord of Hosts will do this" (v. 7).

The people's response to God's action is to throw a party. It will be like the joy of the harvest or joy over battle plunder carted home. The language is liturgical: "They rejoice before you..." (v. 3; cf. Psalm 13:6; 31:7). The proper response to God's action is to lift voices and sing to the Wonderful Counselor, Mighty God, Everlasting Father, and Prince of Peace.

Titus 2:11-14

Debate over Pauline authorship of the letter to Titus continues with the majority holding that it reflects the work of a posthumous "Pauline school," and a vocal minority asserting that it could be the work of an imprisoned Paul or by disciples supervised by him. There is nothing in this passage that could not be taken either way.

At any rate, it is clear that the author is writing to Gentile Christians who are in sore need of moral instruction, and this instruction is provided in a familiar form: the "household table" of moral conduct as espoused by Hellenistic philosophers (2:2-10). The Roman household consisted of what we would now call an "extended family" that included servants and slaves as well as blood relatives, each with its proper place. Our lection provides the theological basis for household behavior; it provides the *why* to the *what* of Christian morality.

The *why* of Christian virtue proves to be the *how* as well, since 2:11-14 is one long sentence in Greek that has as its subject, "grace." Grace, God's unmerited favor or "free gift," is the teacher of morality. Grace educates and civilizes these former pagans, the Gentile residents of Crete who have come to believe in Jesus Christ. The verb *paideuo*, which means "train, educate" (v. 12), reflects the ideal of Hellenistic philosophy that true knowledge, true learning, actually made one a better person. The difference here is that the force to become good is not the individual human will, but the power of God. Grace is a teacher, trainer, and coach.

This grace of God has appeared in Jesus Christ and brings salvation to all (v. 11; this could be a reference either to universal salvation, or undiscriminating salvation). Salvation is not devoid of moral content, since grace trains us in two directions (v. 12). First, it tells us to drop "impiety and worldly passions," all false conceptions of God, along with the immoral conduct that goes with them. Second, grace teaches us "to live lives that are self-controlled, upright, and godly." These three adjectives reflect three of the four cardinal virtues in Hellenistic philosophy: moderation, justice, and piety; again, pagan values are being adapted and transformed by Christian faith. Like any good sermon, the movement is from the familiar to the new. These virtues are now set in an eschatological context; Christians practice them "in the present age," implicitly looking for the "age to come" (cf. 1 Timothy 1:16).

Having made clear the ethical requirement, the letter goes on to give the theological foundation in "the blessed hope and the manifestation of the glory of our great God and Savior, Jesus Christ" (v. 13). It is clear that the actions of the present are rooted in the promises of the future. Less clear is how exactly to construe this complex clause. "Blessed hope" (or "hope that brings blessings") is probably to be equated with "manifestation," which refers to the future coming of Christ (though the same language can be used of the first coming of Jesus, cf. 2:11; 3:4; 1 Timothy 6:14; 2 Timothy 1:10; 4:1, 8; 2 Thessalonians 2:8). What is manifested is "glory" (though the expression could mean, "the glorious manifestation," as KJV). The glory belongs to "our great God and Savior, Jesus Christ." This expression could also be rendered, "of the great God, and our Savior, Jesus Christ"; in favor of the first option is that nowhere else is God said to accompany Jesus in his coming, while in favor of the second is that nowhere else in the Pauline corpus is Jesus equated with God (except perhaps Romans 9:5). A third option is that "Jesus Christ" may stand in apposition to "glory," so that the point is that Jesus defines God's own glory.

The grace that is manifested in Jesus teaches us proper behavior, because that is its very nature. The twofold action of grace corresponds to its twofold effect on the believer: "He it is who gave himself for us that he might redeem us from all iniquity and purify for himself a people of his own who are zealous for good deeds" (v. 14; cf. v. 12). Christians can renounce impiety and worldly desires, because Jesus has redeemed us from iniquity (the allusion is to Psalm 130:8). They can live lives that are self-controlled, upright, and godly because Jesus has purified them (alluding to Exodus 19:5; Deuteronomy 14:2 LXX, and Ezekiel 37:23). Thus we see that grace activates the virtues required by the "household table" in verses 2-10; a purified people has the ability to live in the present age while looking forward to the age to come, to be a part of the usual structures of society; yet for God's purposes, not the world's. Thus these Gentile Christians can become "a people of his own" (1 Peter 2:9).

The end result of this theological reflection is eminently practical: grace creates a people "who are zealous for good deeds," the kind spelled out in verses 2-10 and verse 12. In true Pauline fashion, good deeds do not make for salvation but the opposite. True salvation inevitably results in the moral life. The zeal of the Lord of hosts makes a people who are equally zealous — for good!

Luke 2:1-14 (15-20)

Luke's nativity scene is part of an introductory section that parallels and contrasts two prophets, John the Baptist and Jesus, with Jesus placed in the superior position. Luke's story is set in two historical contexts, biblical and secular. It takes place in the time and place of Emperor Augustus and Governor Quirinius (unfortunately, Luke's chronology seems off the mark here, since the census of Quirinius was several years later than Luke's timeframe). Yet the language and personnel are straight out of the Greek Old Testament: angels, prophets, biblical cadences. Again, we stand at the border of two ages.

Luke presents his pageant in three scenes. In Scene One, we find ourselves on the road with a great mass of humanity displaced at imperial whim (Luke 2:1-5). While there are historical problems with a census that would require such a mass pilgrimage (an event otherwise unknown), Luke's theological point is clear: earthly powers, even in Rome, actually work at God's bidding. Though the era of Augustus was widely known as an era of peace, Luke presents the true bearer of peace as an infant in an out-of-the-way village, born to transients. Augustus proves to be God's agent in making the Messiah's birthplace conform to the prophets.

Joseph is clearly identified as a descendant of the royal line, and he takes with him his fiancée, the pregnant Mary (the reader has already learned the miraculous details of her pregnancy, Luke 1:26-38). Since betrothal was a binding commitment, Mary would have to go with Joseph on such a trip, and Luke avoids calling her his "wife" in order to highlight the unusual nature of her condition. Their trip from Nazareth to Bethlehem probably took place on foot, because as the poor of the land, a donkey would have been beyond their means.

Scene Two takes place in the city of Bethlehem (Luke 2:6-7). The child's birth in less-than-ideal conditions is presented in unsentimental terms. Unlike many a Christmas pageant, there is no nasty innkeeper who refuses to take them in, nor cooing animals surrounding the feed trough. In fact, the "manger" may have been no more than a pile of feed on the ground, and the "inn" no more than an open area with a wall to keep the wind off the animals. Into such humility was the Prince of Peace born. His beginning foreshadows his ending as he is wrapped in bands of cloth to stiffen his limbs and placed in the feed trough, so he will be wrapped in a linen cloth and placed in a tomb where no one yet had been laid (Luke 23:53).

Scene Three takes place in fields outside Bethlehem before it moves to the manger (2:8-20). Shepherds become the first recipients of the good news of the birth of the Messiah. Like Joseph and Mary, they were among the poor in the land, because sheepherding was not a lucrative trade and shepherds were often reviled as shiftless or dishonest. Mary's prophecy has come true and God "has lifted up the lowly" (1:52). Shepherds are also appropriate witnesses to the Davidic messiah, since David himself began from such a position (cf. 1 Samuel 16:11; 17:15). The shepherds receive a visit from an angel, as did Zechariah and Mary (1:11, 26); indeed, the angel's words are the same as to Mary, "Do not be afraid" (2:10). Fear they might well have, since the angel exposes them to the "dawning from on high" (2:9; cf. 1:78). God's glory is manifested in the most unlikely of places, as the poor have good news preached to them (cf. 4:18).

The angel brings to the shepherds "good news of great joy for all the people" (2:10). It is hard not to see a hint of Lukan universalism in this proclamation, since by the end of Luke's story the gospel will indeed have spread to "the ends of the earth" (Acts 1:8). The good news is that "to you is born this day in the city of David a Savior, who is the Messiah, the Lord" (the echo of Isaiah 9:6 is certainly intentional). The rhetoric of "Savior, Messiah, Lord" stands in contrast with the reality of a babe on a pile of wheat, but the very humility of the situation is its own proof. "This will be a sign for you: you will find a child wrapped in bands of cloth and lying in a manger" (v. 12; again, the allusion to Isaiah 7:14 is probably intentional). The fulfillment of this small prophecy in verse 16 provides assurance that the rest of the angel's words will come to pass. If there were any doubt that the heavens had burst the bounds of earth, one angel is joined by a multitude in chorus: "And suddenly there was with the angel a multitude of the heavenly host, praising God and saying, 'Glory to God in the highest heaven, and on earth peace among those whom he favors!'" (vv. 13-14). The "favor" in the angel's song refers to God's attitude toward humanity, not any human accomplishment (the traditional KJV reading, "goodwill toward men" is based on a faulty Greek manuscript).

The shepherds respond with immediate faith: "Let us go now to Bethlehem and see the thing that has taken place, which the Lord has made known to us. So they went with haste and found Mary and Joseph, and the child lying in the manger" (vv. 15-16). The shepherds become the first human witnesses of the good news proclaimed by angels: "When they saw this, they made known what had been told them about this child" (v. 17). The story produces amazement and pondering (vv. 18-19), but the shepherds return to their fields convinced of what they have seen, "glorifying and praising God" (v. 20). The party has begun!

Application

Some preachers hold Christmas so tightly that you'd think they would be afraid of breaking it. They are rightly appalled by the commercialization of the holiday and seek to draw clear lines between the preparation of Advent and the twelve days of Christmas: no proleptic Christmas carols, no pageants in Advent, no "Christmas" parties sponsored by the church (okay, let's call them "holiday" parties instead!).

When merchants begin Christmas in October and close it down on December 26, what is a church to do? It's our holiday, after all.

However, I hate to see all the fun squeezed out of Christmas. I confess I love the hullabaloo, including Santa and tinsel and trees. I love Christmas movies, *Miracle on 34th Street* (the original, not the remake), *How the Grinch Stole Christmas* (ditto), *Holiday Inn* — not to mention Christmas classics like *Die Hard* and *Lethal Weapon*. And I love my Beartivity scene. If Christians can't have fun on Christmas, who can?

The good news is news of great joy. Christmas Eve is a cause for singing. Dour faces in the pulpit simply will not do. There is no need to denounce the secular holiday (let alone those people who only show up tonight and on Easter). Rather, sing the good news, because truly a human Prince of Peace has come to live among us. God has acted to take care of us by sending us a king who will make us into the people we were meant to be. If anything we preach on Christmas (not to mention Easter) is true, then the Messiah is still alive and with us today.

If that isn't cause for joy, I don't know what is.

Alternative Applications

1) Luke 2:1-14 (15-20). One reason I like my Beartivity scene is that it has no wise men. It is Luke's nativity scene, with no attempt to harmonize it with Matthew, which warms my biblical scholar's heart. Preachers should let each biblical writer speak independently. Don't let Matthew's wise men stumble over the shepherds on their way out of the barn. Not only does Matthew represent a completely different tradition, but also in his chronology, the wise men show up two years later. At any rate, he places Jesus in a "house," not a manger (cf. Matthew 2:11, 16). Let Matthew have Christmas Eve off. He can work later. Let Luke tell his own story.

2) Titus 2:11-14. The Christian life is something that God does before it is something we do. In Isaiah, the people respond to God's great actions. In Titus, Christian social morality is based on the teachings of grace; again, God acts, then we respond. Luke's shepherds follow the same pattern. They become the first human witnesses to the Messiah when they simply repeat what has been told them by the angels. The biblical pattern is clear: God makes us who we are to be, then we respond by being that people. It follows that the main job of the preacher is to tell Christians what God has done to make them who they are. What they are to do will follow, even without saying.

Christmas 1
Isaiah 63:7-9
Hebrews 2:10-18
Matthew 2:13-23
by William Shepherd

Search and preserve mission

"Practice random acts of kindness and senseless acts of beauty," says the bumper sticker. If the news media is right, we're more likely to encounter red-faced road rage on the highway than kindness or beauty. But random acts of kindness and senseless acts of beauty only make sense in a context where they are rare. If we expected warmth, courtesy, and compassion in our dealings with strangers, we wouldn't be so surprised when we get them. Nor would we feel the need to advertise our preferences on bumper stickers.

We tend to present God as the paradigm of kindness and beauty but that image stands in contrast to something darker. Whether it's human sin or the prospect of divine judgment, there is always a bleak side to the Bible's promise of God's love. Today's lessons all present a positive picture of God; yet each have a caveat lurking in the background. In Isaiah, God does great deeds in love, and yet human beings reject that love. In Hebrews, Jesus comes as a faithful and merciful high priest, tested as we are, but we hesitate to follow in his steps. In Matthew, God miraculously preserves the child of promise, while allowing evil to have full sway with other innocent children.

Isaiah 63:7-9

Sometimes the only sensible response to reality is the lament, "Oh, woe is me!" It is a perfectly appropriate thing to say at certain times. No one likes a constant complainer, but the reason is not the complaint *per se* but its lack of suitability; if every little thing is a cause for lament, the force of the lament is diluted. We feel we ought to save the lament for something truly lamentable (just as, I often say, preachers ought to save the word "wonderful" for something that is truly full of wonder and not use it to describe a routine church outing). When something truly lamentable happens and we all know what those things are, no need to list them — launching into a lament is a perfectly unlamentable thing to do. We have plenty of precedent for the proper lament. The Bible is full of them.

Isaiah 63:7—64:12 is one long lament. The prophet, on behalf of the community, appeals to God for mercy in misery. Interspersed with appeals for compassion are confessions of sin and hardening of heart. What is lamentable here is not just the sorry situation that the community has found itself in (Isaiah is not specific about the situation, but it may have to do with the Babylonian Exile), but also the sorry state of the community itself. "We have all become like one who is unclean, and all our righteous deeds are like a filthy cloth. We all fade like a leaf, and our iniquities, like the wind, take us away. There is no one who calls on your name, or attempts to take hold of you; for you have hidden your face from us, and have delivered us into the hand of our iniquity" (Isaiah 64:6-7). Such rebellion has put the community in a precarious situation: "We have long been like those whom you do not rule, like those not called by your name" (63:19). In fact, God has reserved the harshest sort of language for these people: "They rebelled and grieved his holy spirit; therefore he became their enemy; he himself fought against them" (63:10). Human sin has been unmasked as what it really is, enmity with God (cf. James 4:4).

Biblical laments often begin with recitations of God's great deeds, and this lament is no exception (cf. Psalm 106 or Nehemiah 9). The recitations heighten the contrast between God's grace and human rebellion. The prophet begins the recitation in the first-person singular but quickly moves to identify with the entire community, "the house of Israel": "I will recount the gracious deeds of the Lord, the praiseworthy acts of the Lord, because of all that the Lord has done for us, and the great favor to the house of Israel that he has shown them according to his mercy, according to the abundance of his steadfast love" (63:7). The opening line is wrapped in *chesed* (here translated as both "gracious deeds" and "steadfast love"), which is the emphatic first and last word in the sentence. In between, the prophet piles on the praise of God, citing "praise" or "praiseworthy acts" (*tehillah*), "reward" (*gemal*, the verb is used twice, though somewhat obscured in our translation), "compassion" or "mercy" (*rachamim*), and "great goodness" or "favor" (*rav-tuv*). The prophet puts a bit of the classic covenantal formula in God's mouth: "Surely they are my people" (cf. Leviticus 26:12; Deuteronomy 29:13), but adds ironically that they are "children who will not deal falsely" (63:8). I guess God can always hope!

The final verse in the lection presents a translation problem. The Hebrew text traditionally reads, "In all their distress he was distressed; the angel of the presence saved them" (cf. NRSV note). The NRSV text follows the Greek translation, which is based on a possible reading of the Hebrew, and takes the opening words with the previous verse, introducing a contrast between God's presence and that of a hypothetical angelic mediator. In favor of this reading is that "the angel of the presence" is not otherwise found in the Hebrew Bible (but cf. Exodus 33:12ff). However, the reading may have been changed precisely because it was so odd and also because it may have seemed inappropriate to speak of God's "distress." Either reading is possible. At any rate, it was at God's initiative, not to mention "love" (*'ahavah*) and "pity" (*chemla*) that the Lord "lifted them up and carried them all the days of old" (63:9).

Since the lectionary includes only the recitation and not the rest of the lament, today's reading is a bit deceptive. It makes it sound like everything is hunky-dory, when it isn't. The broader context of Isaiah's lament sets off God's great deeds in contrast with the human rebellion called "sin." The job of the preacher today may well be to create for the congregation the context in which the recitation makes sense; God's past deeds become the basis for the appeal for mercy in the present.

Why not just emphasize the positive and forget all that lamentable stuff (as the lectionary tries to do)? There are at least two reasons. One is that light is always set off by darkness, and God's grace truly shines only in contrast with its human opposition. The second reason is perhaps more important: The congregation, as a group and as individuals, may well have need to compose their own laments, when something truly lamentable happens to them. Isaiah's lament, understood in its entirety, gives them a model. The formula still works.

Hebrews 2:10-18

Contrasts and comparisons are basic forms of definition. The contrast helps define something by describing what it is not like. The comparison takes the opposite tack, describing something on the basis of its similarity to something else. The two methods work well together because they pull in opposite directions toward the same goal; one tries to connect, the other to disconnect.

The book of Hebrews is not a letter but a sermon that uses the basic rhetorical device of contrast and comparison to define Jesus as God's definitive word to humankind (cf. Hebrews 1:1-3). The sermon begins with an extended contrast between Jesus and the ministers of the old covenant, the angels. This is but preparatory to the comparison, however, because Hebrews is primarily concerned to make a connection. This primary connection is between Jesus and us.

Though he was by nature superior to the angels, Hebrews pictures Jesus as descending below his proper position. "We do see Jesus, who for a little while was made lower than the angels, now crowned with glory and honor because of the suffering of death, so that by the grace of God he might taste death for everyone" (Hebrews 2:9). This statement leads the preacher to consider further the connection between Jesus and human beings. Jesus became one of "many children" being led "to glory" (v. 10). Jesus can call us "brothers and sisters" because "the one who sanctifies [Jesus] and those who are sanctified all have one

Father" (v. 11). Like any good homiletician, the preacher cites scripture to prove his point; unlike modern preachers, the assumption is that Jesus as God's word is the speaker of the ancient text: "I will proclaim your name to my brothers and sisters, in the midst of the congregation I will praise you" (v. 12, cf. Psalm 22:22); "Here am I and the children whom God has given me" (v. 13, cf. Isaiah 8:18). Hebrews also quotes Isaiah 8:17, "I will put my trust in him," to make the point that the family resemblance is found through faith (v. 13). The preacher emphasizes the complete humanity of Jesus, because he shared "blood and flesh" (the NRSV reverses the original order) and was "like his brothers and sisters in every respect" (v. 17; later the preacher will make "sin" the one exception, 4:15). The reason for his solidarity with humankind is clear: "Because he himself was tested by what he suffered, he is able to help those who are being tested" (v. 18).

Thus Jesus' connection to humanity made him "a merciful and faithful high priest in the service of God" (v. 17). Here the preacher foreshadows the sermon that is to come, which will speak of Jesus as faithful (cf. 3:1—4:14) and merciful (4:15—5:10), and as "a high priest after the order of Melchizedek" (5:5, 10; cf. 6:20; 7:26-28; 8:1-3; 9:11, 25). The preacher uses the language of priesthood because he sees Jesus as making "a sacrifice of atonement for the sins of the people," that is, a once-for-all blood sacrifice that would remove the stain of sin from Jesus' brothers and sisters (v. 17; cf. chs. 8-10). This action would mean liberation not only from the fear of death and judgment (v. 15), but also from the power of evil itself, personified by the devil (v. 14). Jesus' own death is the sacrifice that frees his brothers and sisters from the negative effect of sin, which is ultimately death itself.

Thus Jesus is "the pioneer of their salvation"; he becomes both the "leader" of this troop of like-natured people, and the "author" of the next chapter in their lives (the word *archegos* in v. 10 can mean both "leader" and "author"). God was at work in Jesus, making him "perfect through sufferings" (v. 10). The expression "make perfect," *teleioo*, is used throughout Hebrews (cf. Hebrews 2:10; 5:9; 7:19, 28; 9:9; 10:1, 14; 11:40; 12:23) and can mean "to complete an activity, bring to an end, finish, accomplish"; in the Greek Old Testament, it is used of the consecration of priests (Exodus 29:9; Leviticus 16:32; Numbers 3:3). God brings about the accomplishment of Jesus' mission "through sufferings," that is, through his priestly act, his sacrificial death.

It may seem strange to be talking about death and sacrifice as we celebrate the birth of Jesus; we are by no means straying far from our biblical charter. As we will see, the Bible is not nearly as sentimental about the baby Jesus as we are.

Matthew 2:13-23

While we think of Christmas as a joyous celebration of new life, the shadow of death always hangs over it. The dark side of Matthew's infancy stories is that they so often point to the end of his story, the crucifixion. This is particularly the case in chapter 2 of Matthew (cf. 2:2, 3, 4, 16, 20). Jesus is associated with suffering and death from the beginning; part of the miracle of God's work is that Jesus is delivered from premature submission to fate. It waits for God's good time, but the cross is always overhanging Matthew's story.

Matthew's second chapter is concerned with the question, "Where can we find Jesus?" It gives various answers as the story moves along: Jesus is to be searched for in Jerusalem (in the words of the scribes, 2:1-6), in Bethlehem (2:7-12), in Egypt (2:13-15), in Bethlehem again (but fortunately he's not there, 2:16-17), and finally in Nazareth (2:19-23). Ultimately, the story shows Jesus' true location, which is in the hands of God. As Herod engages in a search and destroy mission, slaughtering the innocents to ensure his status as "king," God launches a search and preserve mission, successfully keeping the true king of the Jews from harm.

Jesus is to be found in accordance with scripture. This is confirmed by the abundance of "formula quotations," one of Matthew's favorite devices. Events are said to have happened "to fulfill what was spoken by the prophet" (cf. Matthew 2:5, 15, 17, 23). More importantly, Matthew models his story of Jesus' infancy on a particular story from the Hebrew Bible — the story of Moses. Like Moses, Jesus survives the decree of a wicked king that children must be sacrificed (Exodus 1:16-22). His salvation is miraculous (Exodus 2:1-10). There is a flight in fear (Exodus 2:15). After the death of the king, there is a return (Exodus 2:23; 4:19). Matthew sees the story of Jesus as being a work out of God's ancient story, and a literal fulfillment of the biblical text.

Matthew is also concerned with human action; in particular, the "higher righteousness" that goes beyond the usual and traditional observance of Torah (cf. 5:20). Joseph is a prime example of someone who observes this higher righteousness, because in each case, he does exactly what he is told. Matthew takes "exactly as he is told" literally, as the descriptions of Joseph's actions are simply direct repetitions of the angel's commands. By contrast, Herod cannot even observe the most basic precepts of Torah, let alone be open to the kind of direct revelation that Joseph is privy to. While there is no other record of Herod's slaughter of the innocents, such an action would have been quite in keeping with his character; the joke in Rome, in light of his ruthless disposal of his relatives for political gain, was that it was "better to be Herod's pig than his son." Such a man would hardly think twice about wiping out a town, if it threatened his rule.

Application

I hope you will give some real attention to the lections for the First Sunday after Christmas. They bring quite a different perspective from the usual Christmas Eve or Christmas Day sermon. Hanging over them is a shadow — the shadow of judgment, the shadow of Good Friday. While Christmas need not be turned into Lent, it would be nice for the preacher to make some connection between what our society observes as the most significant Christian holiday, and what is in fact the most theologically significant of events — the death and resurrection of the Messiah.

Such words might be more welcome this Sunday than you think. Face it, the day after Christmas is a letdown. We didn't get what we wanted, or if we did, it didn't measure up to our expectations. The children have already left the toys lying around, some never to be played with again, to judge from previous years. A few are broken or the batteries are dead. Not to mention the strain of having all those relatives at home. Alternatively, this is for some people the first Christmas without a significant relative or friend. For others, Christmas is always spent alone. For many, the holidays are a time of depression, sadness, and disappointment.

The message of the gospel is that Jesus meets us where we are, no matter where we are. Jesus meets us in the depths of depression as well as in the heights of elation. Jesus meets us in disappointment as well as exhilaration. He has been where we are, and he has conquered. No longer a baby, this full-grown Messiah suffered as we do, yet was able to bring his work to a completion. God was watching over him, even when he could not watch over himself.

As God watches over us, even at those times when we cannot bring ourselves to believe or behave. God continues to care for us with steadfast love.

Alternative Applications
1) Isaiah 63:7-9. Praise is the prelude to confession. Isaiah's lament begins deceptively, because it does not start out lamenting. As often with psalms of lament, it begins with a recitation of the great deeds of God. This forms the basis of the appeal for mercy: If God has done great things for us in the past, how could God refuse to show pity on us now? It is a clever and sensible rhetorical move for a prayer.

Those of us who wish to learn how to pray from the Bible will take this example to heart. When we feel low, perhaps the place to start is with praise. Recount God's blessings and the ways that God has come to our help in the past. Not only will it make us feel better, it will provide a sure foundation for the confession to follow. We can approach the throne of grace boldly knowing that God cares enough to turn our hearts back toward heaven.

2) Matthew 2:13-23. In a way, Joseph had it easy. He had an angel appearing to him, telling him what to. It was a simple matter to follow simple instructions. He proved himself righteous by doing exactly as he was told.

It's not so easy for us today. We hardly ever have angels telling us exactly what to do (and we'd probably want to check our medications if it happened more than once!). Moral decisions are not always clear-cut and dried. There are a myriad of decisions that we must make that are not particularly covered by the Bible and theology: "At what sort of job should I work? Who should I love? Shall I have children? Where shall I live?" The list goes on and on. Yet we expect God to give us guidance in these areas of our lives, as well as in the direct prescriptions of the biblical commandments.

If Matthew were to give us one answer for this problem, it might be: "Take and read, take and read." Matthew's approach to scripture moved beyond a simple assent to commandments (in fact, he left the commanding to extra-biblical angels). Instead, Matthew advocated an immersion approach to the Bible. He was able to piece out meaning from the biblical text that was not obvious on the surface, simply because he knew it so well. He could see in the events happening around him the working out of God's purpose, reading life in light of God's word.

Admittedly, this results in some strange interpretive moves. Modern readers are often confused by Matthew's formula citations, since they seem to indulge in more of a metaphorical than a literal interpretation. In one case, it's not even clear exactly what passage Matthew is quoting (Matthew 2:23). Matthew's midrashic use of scripture may seem beside the point to those who have learned to see the Bible in all its literary, historical, sociological, and religious complexity.

Nevertheless, Matthew has something to teach us here, even if we can't read exactly the way he read. Matthew's immersion in the Bible was an immersion in the gracious God behind that Bible. We, too, can learn to read our lives in light of the God of grace we encounter in scripture. The first step will be to immerse ourselves in that scripture, as Matthew did.

New Year's Day
Ecclesiastes 3:1-13
Revelation 21:1-6a
Matthew 25:31-46
by R. Craig MacCreary

What you are not responsible for

'Tis the season to measure up, sum up, and own up. While most sanctuaries will not be bursting at the seams on this day, few congregants can escape the meaning that catches up with us in the interim between Christmas and Epiphany. Certainly, in the days ahead the bills for the Christmas revelry will come due and many of us will find that there is more distance than we want between our resources and the Christmas we enjoyed. Many of us will find ourselves haunted by irresponsible behavior that will be making a regular appearance on our credit card statements for the next few months. Some of us will be wondering what we have left undone in the old year that will catch up with us in the new year. Others of us somewhat more optimistically will see the coming year as a blank slate to be responsibly filled by the resolve to do better this year than last. Perhaps it is a good thing that there are all of those football games on television on New Year's Day to help some of us escape from the heavy weight of all this responsibility. The revelers may be on to something, for if you think too much about it, New Year's Day can be even more overwhelming than Christmas and certainly something that has for the masses more *gravitas* than Epiphany.

Where is the good news in this? I feel my basic protestant genes kicking in. "Forgive us for the things we have left undone, do not overwhelm us with the things that we might do, save us from the consequences of having overdone." I hear voices from the past urging me on to ever greater heights of responsible behavior. "Clean your room" has been transformed into "clean the environment." "Clean your plate" has become "clean your plate of super-size portions and unnecessary food additives." "Clean behind your ears" has been replaced by "clean up your sexist, politically incorrect act."

This is not to say that something has not been gained here. As a matter of fact much has been gained, yet it also seems that something may have been lost as well. It seems that this emphasis on my activity, however warranted, has put some distance between me and God's activity. I suspect that if by some strange quirk I was actually able to keep all my new year's resolutions, the kingdom still may not be ushered in. Probably it would bring in a harvest of self-righteousness, a belittling of the less disciplined, and fear and trepidation at trying my hand at the next round of resolutions. Frankly, I would rather be watching football than having such thoughts on New Year's Day.

This is far from the renewal and hope that John Wesley found in his Watch Night service for the first Sunday of the new year that reads in part: "Dearly beloved, the Christian life, to which we are called, is a life in Christ, redeemed from sin by him, and through him consecrated to God. Upon this life we have entered, having been admitted into that new covenant of which our Lord Jesus Christ is mediator, and which he sealed with his own blood, that it might stand forever. On one side of the covenant is God's promise that he will fulfill in and through us all that he declared in Jesus Christ, who is the author and perfecter of our faith. That his promise still stands we are sure, for we have known his goodness and proved his grace in our lives day by day."

The flaw in much of our new year's thinking is that we focus more on what *we* have done or will do than on what *God* has done and can do. Like Wesley's service, each of the texts do not focus on human activity, indeed the texts suggest the futility of much human effort and the belief that divine actions form the basis for any hope we have in the year to come. The texts bring relief and clarity around what we are not responsible for in our lives. The Hebrew text speaks of the ebb and flow of life that God has set. The Revelation text reminds us that if there is going to be anything genuinely new under the sun it will come from the hand of God. The gospel lesson reminds us that getting past the final judgment has less to do with getting it right than receiving the God who has gotten close to us in some surprising ways.

Ecclesiastes 3:1-13

This passage must surely be one of the most recognizable and familiar pieces of scriptures. Few ardent secularists or eager atheists have gone far in their development without having been exposed to these words. Certainly it beautifully names one of the more familiar aspects of the human condition whatever one's theological orientation, "The words of the Teacher, the son of David, king in Jerusalem. Vanity of vanities, says the Teacher, vanity of vanities! All is vanity. What do people gain from all the toil at which they toil under the sun?" As a statement of human prospects it certainly seems quite a come down but it comes close to the frustrations of life that we all experience.

This passage is eloquent testimony to the truth that, whatever one's theological convictions or resources, none of us can completely avoid this part of life. Life is like that! From time to time we feel this truth more or less. One thing is certain: none of us can avoid these feelings.

However, many of us feel that somehow we have failed if we do have these feelings or if the reality of human futility emerges, we will be paralyzed. I doubt that many churches put this experience on the agenda of the official board meeting, let alone see the sharing of such feelings as an opportunity to advance the kingdom of God.

Yet it is often the sharing of such feelings that can be the beginning of growth. While no church finds this easy, no church avoids the times when all feels like vanity. The perfect pastor turns out to have feet of clay, on close examination the popular pastor turns out not to have met the needs of everyone, or there is the sudden discovery that things have gone smoothly because people have been guilted and bullied into keeping in line with the congregational program. Ecclesiastes would understand. There is, "a time to weep, and a time to laugh; a time to mourn, and a time to dance." No, we are not responsible for avoiding such moments in congregational life. Can people get as close as they do in congregations without having to go through such moments? Can a marriage go without times to weep and laugh, mourn and dance, times to speak and times to keep silence, even a time to love and a time to hate, and time for war and a time for peace? Can we grow in wisdom and stature as Jesus did, according to Luke, without times in our lives to break down as well as build up?

So what is your plan for the new year? Like the preacher of Ecclesiastes, "I have seen the business that God has given to everyone to be busy with." The year ahead will probably include the pleasant as well as the preposterous, the promising as well as the pernicious. It would be nice if we could discern the when and the where of such moments in our lives before they happened. The author of Ecclesiastes knows better, "He has made everything suitable for its time; moreover he has put a sense of past and future into their minds, yet they cannot find out what God has done from the beginning to the end."

God has placed human beings in quite a predicament — able to experience all the ups and downs of life but unable to have enough knowledge to steer a course around some of the most serious downs. It is not our responsibility that we find ourselves in the midst of such a dynamic. Yet while we cannot discern the big picture we can create healthy responses to our context — create a community of faith that can fellowship and pray its way through all aspects of life, develop relationships that affirm that the ebb and flow of life is part of us all, and seek to understand how God is speaking through the best and the worst of times. We are not responsible to avoid all the seasons of life but we can respond ably to what life might throw at us.

I am told that it is hospital emergency room lore that in the midst of crisis the first pulse rate you take is your own. Perhaps the first thing we need to do in the year before we take on more responsibilities is take our own pulse to see how we are responding to the pulse that comes in the season and times of the world.

Revelation 21:1-6a

There is going to be a new heaven and a new earth and there is nothing that you can do about it. This is quite a claim and has always been greeted with a good dose of skepticism. Such things should not be treated lightly. Yet more often than not, history has come down on the side of those who saw a new heaven and earth. No one on the day of the famous Brown vs. Board of Education decision could have envisioned a south that would be sending multiracial delegations to congress and electing black governors. No one looking at the great Mahatma Gandhi would have suspected that one of his legacies would be that India would bring into the middle class a number equaling the entire population of the United Kingdom. A child of the cold war, I still rub my eyes in disbelief at the fall of the Berlin wall and the rise of the Beijing stock market. If anything, history has come down on the side of wiping away many tears, eliminating the death of hope, and making things new in ways people never imagined.

Much death, sorrow, pain, and mourning has been released by those who claimed that it was they, not God, who make all things new. The world is littered with the tragic results that come from those who found themselves getting nowhere by backing the arrival of some utopia (literally nowhere). If history is filled with the possibility of a new heaven and earth breaking in, it also has an uncanny way of stymieing the efforts of those who claim they are responsible for the new heaven and earth. The peculiar institution of slavery and segregation comes toppling down, a thousand-year Reich lasts only twelve years, and scientific socialism proved to have been so flawed in its hypothesis that its walls came tumbling down in less than 75 years.

The theological lesson to be learned here is that we are called to be open to the new heaven and earth that is in store but we are not responsible for creating them. This does not come easily for many church folk. They often behave as if their primary task is to be responsible rather than to be open and responsive.

This past summer, I had the opportunity to undertake interim ministry training for clergy interested in serving in the role of pastors seeking to lead a congregation through the opportunities that develop when a pastor leaves a congregation. Some of the training I received confirmed what I have long observed. Many congregations in such a time feel the keen responsibility to get through that time as quickly as possible: Choose a pastor just like the last one, choose one that is exactly the opposite of the last one, choose a mature one, choose a young one, and in general solve this problem as quickly as possible with a minimum of disruption.

If I understood my training correctly such "quick-fix" approaches are usually a disaster. Feeling responsible, the congregation rushes past being responsive to what God might do in an interim time to help the congregation assess its strength, weaknesses, history, relationship, and future. Seeking answers, congregations rush past being responsive to the questions that might open them to what God is doing.

Often I find couples in the midst of counseling feeling terribly responsible for the mess they may have made of their lives — responsible to be on top of things so they already figured out what to do before they come for help — reaching for the quick fix that will bring about a new heaven and earth in their lives. Few and far between are the couples who seek to be responsive to what wisdom and stature God might bring out of their lives in the journey, together or apart.

What is ahead in the new year? On the one hand who knows? On the other hand the good news is I see a new heaven and a new earth. The good news is that we are not responsible for it but it can wipe away many tears and the death of hope will be no more. The good news is that though we will not be responsible for the new heaven and the new earth we can be responsive to its coming. It is a done deal. "Then he said to me, 'It is done! I am the Alpha and the Omega, the beginning and the end.'"

Matthew 25:31-46

As I write this, I have finished placing a book order for Naomi Klein's *Shock Capitalism*. I understand that this will expose me to 560 pages of text that was two-and-a-half years in the making. However, reviewers and blurbs reassure me that as a result of my labors I will be wiser, more thoughtful, and better able to hold my own at dinner conversations. All this comes on the heels of reading Thomas Friedman and Jeffery Sachs as well as others who promise visions of economic justice and wisdom.

This is not to say that each of these works don't deliver on their promises in some way. Certainly, the new year will bring plenty of opportunity to delve into the latest analysis of where we have gone wrong and how we might go right. Sometimes I ask myself why I do such things as trying to keep up with this kind of stuff. In all frankness, I think it is because of the voices that I heard growing up and still hear, "Craig, you are responsible for understanding your world and you have been blessed with the capacity to understand some of this stuff. You are responsible!" The most devilish voice is the one that says the bigger the book the more understanding will come my way.

I naturally bring a great deal of skepticism to the idea that getting the kingdom into our midst comes down to getting these sixteen verses right. No, it couldn't come down to just these. That would be irresponsible; we all know that the world is far more complicated than just these few verses. How can you get away with assembling the nations without sufficient political theory, appropriate social analysis, and adequate historical awareness? Yet the claim is that what we have here is the final judgment and that to pass muster we must come to terms with these verses.

It is all too irresponsible for my taste. Actually, the nations in the story do not come across as terribly responsible. We know nothing of their economic systems or their political ideology or their military status. Believe me, when the nations assemble on this planet it is highly irresponsible not to know these things. I cannot fault those who make their living knowing these things.

Despite the clear judgment that there is much merit in knowing such things, the final judgment is not that we met our responsibility in knowing such things but how well we related to the hungry, the thirsty, the stranger, the naked, and the prisoner. Did they give you the willies? Did the sick make you so anxious that you were reduced to pleasant conversations about the weather across the hospital bed — anything to take your mind off of the fact that you could not fix them? Did the naked remind you that you are clothed in arrogance and ignorance? Did the prisoner draw attention to how you are bound to lifestyles that impoverish the planet? Did these things so upset you that you took your fears out on them, absented yourself from relating to them as human beings, so that you set your sights on making the most of what you have rather than relate to the least that do not have?

To paraphrase the text — when was it that we did not take care of business? It was when we did not take care to relate to these as full human beings, did not allow their lives to touch ours, and did not take care to visit even if all we could offer was a presence that could only share their misery. My hunch is that we do not pass muster no matter how responsible we behave if we cannot relate to the least among us as a basis of our actions.

Application

One of the great dangers of religion is compulsive moralism that either leads the moralizer to feel hopelessly inferior or endlessly superior. Jesus certainly saw that in the religion of his day as it whipsawed people between a sense of cleanliness and an unwholesome feeling of impurity and impure thoughts. Martin Luther spent nearly a lifetime hung up between these two. As a child, this aspect of religion so reared its head in my life that I could not imagine religion as anything other than meeting your responsibilities and making sure that others met their responsibilities. Such convictions had a way of delivering on the middle class goods of high SAT scores and good incomes. Yet there was still a hole in one's soul.

I suspect that our way of relating to the new year is rooted in asking what responsibilities we have failed to meet in the old year and resolving to meet them in the upcoming days, as well as taking on new responsibilities. All have probably contributed to the impoverishment of our faith. This might be the day to consider what we are not responsible for and how we can create positive responses and be responsive to what God is doing in our lives in the year to come.

An Alternative Application
Matthew 25:31-46. One of the most chilling moments in ministry comes when the seminary professor blows away years of thoughtful reflection on a text by pointing out how you have fundamentally misread the text. This is particularly chilling when done in public in front of your colleagues. The gospel text is particularly vulnerable to such a moment.

There are those who assert that poor, naked, hungry, sick, thirsty, stranger, and imprisoned represents the church. Oh, no! You can feel the air running out of the balloon of social action. While I don't think that the air entirely runs out of the social-action ministry based on any interpretation of this text, I do believe that the more restrictive interpretation does have something to offer.

We do spend a great deal of time confessing the sins that the world commits as opposed to the sins that come as part of the package of being church. Perhaps this day is the one to begin acknowledging and addressing those sins. Indeed, what we might have to offer to the world is less our accounting of its sins than the confessing of our sins as a model of healing.

Judging by what happens to many in our churches who are strangers, the mentally challenged, those whose weaknesses are nakedly exposed, those who thirst and hunger for a deeper religious experience, or those who are imprisoned by their reputations, the more restrictive understanding of this text may help us become the kind of community that can be a blessing to the world.

Christmas 2
Jeremiah 31:7-14
Ephesians 1:3-14
John 1:(1-9) 10-18
by David Kalas

Who's your daddy?

How do you tell your child that he or she is adopted? And when exactly should you tell them?

For some families, this represents a tremendously difficult decision and conversation. And I expect that most of us have known a person or two along the way who has struggled with their identity as an adopted child.

In other cases, of course, the challenge is somewhat smaller. When it is a case of international adoption, for example, the superficial differences between the child and his or her adoptive family are often so apparent that the conversation is likely to occur early and naturally. Or, in the case of an older child (rather than a baby) being adopted, the exact nature of the relationship is known and understood from the start.

In any case, the question is an appropriate one for us as preachers to consider this week, for this is the nature of our task. As we sit down at our desks to compose this Sunday's sermon, we may picture ourselves having this very conversation. For we are the ones who will sit God's children down this week to inform them of the news: They are adopted.

The image of God as a father and his people as his children is woven through all three of this week's selected passages. Through the Old Testament prophet Jeremiah, God declares that he has become a father to Israel (31:9). Paul writes to the Ephesians that God has "destined us for adoption as his children" (1:5). And John, in the famous prologue to his gospel, says, "to all who received him [Jesus], who believed in his name, he gave power to become children of God" (1:12).

So we explore and explain two truths with our people this week. First, there is the very familiar, yet never exhausted, good news that God is our Father. And, second, there is the less familiar, yet equally good, news that he is our Father because he has adopted us.

Jeremiah 31:7-14

If our people are familiar with the reputation of Jeremiah — or even if they have enough of a vocabulary to recognize the word "jeremiad" — they will be surprised by the beginning of the Old Testament lection. "Thus says the Lord," declares Jeremiah, who is widely known as the weeping prophet: "Sing aloud with gladness."

In a word association game, "singing" and "gladness" would not be anyone's response to the cue word "Jeremiah." Yet as incongruous as the opening line seems with the larger reputation of this prophet, that very incongruity is itself a gospel message. After all, it reminds us that even in the midst of a chaotic time, a chronically sinful nation, and a judgment message, still there is a word of hope from God. It's quite remarkable, really. Yet it is absolutely consistent with the larger pattern we see in scripture: namely, that judgment is never the last word with God. He always has a fresh start, a remnant, or something new (new covenant, new creation, new Jerusalem) in view.

Hebrew poetry is famous for its balanced imagery. Sometimes the balance comes in the repetition of a motif and sometimes it comes in the form of contrasting images. That symmetry is typically found within single lines or small clusters of lines. In this passage, however, there is a somewhat larger-scale symmetry to be discovered.

In the earlier verses (8-9), we are introduced to images of need. The people referenced are clearly a scattered lot. Among them are the disabled and those with child, which in some respects may have been understood as a (temporarily) debilitating condition (see, for example, Mark 13:17). We observe, too, that the people are weeping even though they are entering a setting of hope and time of promise, they are clearly emerging from a context of difficulty and sorrow.

The later verses (12-13), meanwhile, offer contrasting images of plenty. Now we're met with a cornucopia of oil, wine, and grain. The flocks and herds will be prolific and life will become a veritable bed of roses. And while the people were weeping before, now they will "come and sing aloud." The will be merry and radiant, rejoicing and dancing along the way.

Then we discover two poetic techniques at work within the passage. First, we see the familiar repetition of ideas and images within the smaller sections. And, second, we observe the contrasting images across the larger passage.

Finally, we may find that the very best devotional material in this passage comes in the form of a medley: a series of statements in which God says what he will do. Along the way he promises to "bring them from the land of the north," "gather them from the farthest parts of the earth," "with consolations… lead them back," "let them walk by brooks of water," "turn their mourning into joy," "comfort them," "give them gladness for sorrow," and satisfy them with his bounty. The trajectory of those successive promises bring to mind not just the Jews' return from exile in the sixth century BC, but also the New Testament's teachings about the end of time. Taken together, these promises from Jeremiah 31 form a grand collage portraying the thoroughly good and generous will of God.

Ephesians 1:3-14

The complexity of such a thick passage from a Pauline epistle invites an expository approach. For those congregations unaccustomed to a verse-by-verse explication, however, another way into the text may be desired. I envision three different thematic emphases.

The first, and most significant, is all that Paul says here about Jesus. Read through these verses with pen in hand, and circle all of the references to "in," "through," and "on" Christ. By my count, there are eleven such references within just twelve verses. It is a compact Christological treatise and many of our congregations would be well served to explore it. So much of contemporary American Christology is thin and uninformed. One prominent strain within the church has effectively declawed the doctrine of Christ by relegating Jesus to the class of history's role models. The pluralism of our culture has made us timid about the unique claims of Christ. And the prevailing relativism in contemporary society has subjected all doctrine to the flexible reality of a focus group world. By the time we have unpacked these prepositional phrases about Jesus, however, we discover that he stands uniquely at the center of God's work and God's plan, and all of God's sovereign will, provident care, and gracious salvation are mediated through him.

The second grand theme is that sovereign will of God. Those of us from an Arminian tradition may have to chew longer on this passage in order to swallow it, for it speaks in terms less commonly emphasized in our churches. That said, however, the will of God is a strong and lovely theme within this passage, featured in recurring terms like "destined," God's "good pleasure," and "his will." And even those who are naturally uneasy with the language and look of God "destining" things will find gospel truth within this theme: For the sovereign will of God as it is revealed here is a thoroughly good and gracious will.

We struggle with a certain sequence of logic. We think that "fair" means "equal," and we reason that "equal" must mean "same." But since the sovereign will of God, with its particular choices, does not appear to treat every soul and situation the same, we regard his actions as unequal and hence unfair. At some level, we are encouraged in the belief that God is unfair — see, for example, the laments of the older son (Luke 15:29-30) and the workers hired first (Matthew 20:11-12) — but we observe that he is never less than fair. Rather, in his sovereign will, he is frequently more than fair with us.

Finally, the third prominent theme may be better understood as a motif. Paul is not writing specifically about bounty, and yet in writing about Jesus and about the will of God, the passage is replete with images of bounty. Phrases like "every spiritual blessing," "glorious grace," "good pleasure," and "inheritance" all speak of the bounty that God has to share, while the phrases "freely bestowed" and "lavished on us" bear witness to the generosity of his sharing.

John 1:(1-9) 10-18

Our gospel lection, excerpted from the famous and powerful prologue to John's gospel, begins with a statement about Jesus' relationship to the world: "He was in the world, and the world came into being through him; yet the world did not know him."

That sentence serves as a kind of thesis statement for the whole gospel of John, for "the world" is a central concern of the fourth gospel. In just 21 chapters, the "world" is referenced nearly eighty times. The world is a prominent theme especially as it relates to God.

Consider this quick and incomplete survey of how the world is portrayed in John. On the one hand, we read that "God so loved the world that he gave his only Son" (3:16), and yet the world hated that Son and will also hate his followers (15:18-19). We understand that the world is enemy territory (14:30) and that Jesus' kingdom is not of this world (18:36), yet he declares that he has conquered the world (16:33). The world is doomed for judgment (12:31), yet Jesus came to save it (3:17; 12:47).

This ironic relationship of unrequited love is introduced from the very beginning. On the one hand, the Lord made the world and came into the world; on the other hand, the world did not know him, recognize him, or accept him. Like Ray Kroc walking into a particular McDonald's restaurant and not being served, so the Creator himself makes a personal visit to his creation, only to go largely unrecognized and rejected. "We esteemed him not," as the Old Testament prophet predicted (Isaiah 53:3 RSV).

The episode in the Nazareth synagogue, recorded by every gospel writer but John, serves as a kind of microcosm of the larger pattern to which John points. "He came to what was his own," John writes, "and his own people did not accept him." That line could be the caption beneath the synoptics' picture of Jesus' rejection in Nazareth. It captures, too, the later rejection of the gospel by the Jews, which so breaks the heart of the apostle Paul (see, for example, Romans 9-11).

Yet the rejection was not unanimous. There were those "who received him, who believed in his name." They were the ones who became "children of God," which we are considering as part of our larger theme for all three of this week's lectionary passages.

John's statement that "the word became flesh and lived among us" is the quintessential expression of the incarnation. John is more deliberately concerned with the doctrine of the incarnation than the other three evangelists, and it is a doctrinal concern that carries over into his epistles (cf. 1 John 4:2-3; 2 John 7).

Meanwhile, the natural companion to John's emphasis on the incarnation is the doctrine of the preexistence of Christ. This, too, is thematically important to John (cf. 1:1-3; 8:56-58), and it is introduced to us here in the testimony of John the Baptist. "He who comes after me," John declares, "ranks ahead of me because he was before me."

Finally, we also see in this early excerpt from the fourth gospel the significant theme of witnesses. The significance of the incarnation ("the word became flesh") is immediately followed by the significance of witnesses ("and we have seen his glory"). The theme is revisited in the introduction to the ministry of the Baptist ("John testified to him") and recurs as a matter of central importance throughout the Johannine literature (e.g., John 21:24; 1 John 1:1-2, 5:7-10; Revelation 1:8a).

Application

People who have little or no knowledge of scripture are likely to bring to their understanding of Christianity only the vague impressions of the world. And the world, you know, so often underestimates Christianity, thinking of it in purely philosophical or anthropological terms. Beliefs and ethics are given perhaps undue prominence; rituals and dogmas are disproportionately weighted.

Once someone becomes familiar with the testimony of scripture, however, it becomes clear that the primary issue in the Christian life and faith is not the traditional trappings of religion, but rather the animating reality of a relationship — a right and reconciled relationship with God.

Relational terms permeate scripture: shepherd, lord, creator, savior, redeemer, and king are all terms and images frequently employed in the Bible to capture what God is to us. They are relational terms with each one suggesting a counterpart term that applies in turn to us. The oft-neglected question, however, is just how we human beings come into any or all of these relationships with God.

That practical question is our particular concern this week as we consider the relational term that may get closest to the essential identity of God: Father. This is the term that Jesus used for God and the one he taught his followers to employ in prayer. If your church is like mine, we use that model prayer — and therefore that relational term for God — on a weekly basis during our worship services. But just how and when did he become "our Father"?

In the scope of my own ministry, I have witnessed two common errors on this point.

On the one hand, I have known many church folks who rather carelessly assume that the "Father" language is an entirely New Testament phenomenon. They make a Marcionite distinction between the portrayal of an angry, vindictive God in the Old Testament and the loving Father revealed by Jesus in the New. The reference in Jeremiah to God "becom(ing) a father to Israel," however, is just one example of many Old Testament references to this truth about God and his relationship to us (see also, for example, Psalm 103:13; Proverbs 3:12; Isaiah 64:8; Hosea 11:1; Malachi 1:6).

On the other hand, I have just as commonly encountered a carelessness that goes too far in the other direction: namely, a theology that equates "Father" with "Creator." By the logic of such an equation, every human being that God created is, consequently, a child of God. Indeed, this is the unquestioned and unchallenged assumption of a great many Christians, but it does not find much support in scripture.

The fact that God created me does not make me his son any more than the table I created is my son or the tree that God created is also his son. Rather, we affirm that God has an only-begotten Son. For the rest of us, we are creatures: that is, the product of the Creator.

That status got worse before it got better. Because of our sinful rebellion against our Creator, we actually qualified as enemies of God (Romans 5:10). That's quite a different image from the blithe assumption that we are all God's children.

Of course, all of this backpedaling from the image of God as Father is not likely to appeal much to our congregations. Talk of being God's creatures and God's enemies is not particularly warm and affirming. Yet those facts set the stage for the marvelous truth of the gospel: namely, that God has adopted us.

It is only against the reality of our status as creatures that we will recognize the profundity of God's sovereign choice to adopt us. It is only against the reality or our status as mutinous creatures — God's enemies — that we may fully recognize the grace of his calling us his children.

In human relations, it is a difficult conversation to inform a child that he or she is adopted. But in spiritual terms, this adoption is unfathomably good news, for it tells us that the Creator and king of the universe has personally chosen you and me. He has adopted us. Now we, who were worse than orphans, are invited to call him "Father!"

An Alternative Application

"Pictures of plenty." It's hard to emerge from a reading of this week's lections without a nagging sense that God's will is exceedingly generous. From the very beginning, you recall, the enemy has been trying to raise doubts in our minds about God's generosity (see Genesis 3:1), but the testimony of God's word is unambiguous on this point. From the Creator who seems to have over-provided exponentially for one lone couple in a garden (Genesis 1:27-29) to the Father who welcomes back without penalty or probation his inexcusable son (Luke 15:20-32), this God is conspicuously over-indulgent with his people.

Each of the passages we have considered this week echoes this same truth. In the Old Testament lection, we observed the images of abundance that characterize God's promise to his troubled people. Likewise, we noted in Paul's letter to the Ephesians the tone and language of bounty in exploring the sovereign will and grace of God. Finally, in John's introduction to his gospel, he makes this simple, powerful declaration to which both Jeremiah and Paul would say, "Amen": "From his fullness we have all received grace upon grace."

I saw recently an episode of a television sitcom in which a father had excitedly arranged a surprise for his little boy. Unbeknown to the son, his father had purchased for him a brand new bicycle, even though it was not his birthday, Christmas, or any other occasion when one might expect a gift. The father hid the present and then watched eagerly as his son came to the spot where he would happen upon the gift. Because of other things happening in the boy's life, however, he was almost completely emotionless in his response to the bicycle. His expression of gratitude was functional at best and then he went back to his room without even taking the bike for a ride.

The father was visibly disappointed. After all, the purchase of the bike itself was of no benefit to the father. His whole motivation was the pleasure and enjoyment of his son. And so it was saddening for the father that his son had shown no pleasure and gained no enjoyment.

I wonder how often that happens with God and us. He happily envisions us rejoicing, dancing, and being merry (cf. Jeremiah 31:13), and yet we are so blasé that he must wonder if we have even noticed all the gifts that he has provided on our behalf.

Epiphany of Our Lord
Isaiah 60:1-6
Ephesians 3:1-12
Matthew 2:1-12
by Wayne Brouwer

Shine, Jesus, shine!

In their book *Resident Aliens*, Stanley Hauerwas and William Willimon tell the story of a United Methodist congregation whose Education Committee was determined to make Confirmation a meaningful exercise. They held discussions as to the preferred outcomes and then drew up a master plan by which the high school seniors would be partnered with more mature members of the congregation in order to be mentored into adult Christian responsibilities.

Young Max was teamed with 24-year-old Joe, a single fellow who seemed to have his head on straight and worked well with young people. Several weeks into the venture, however, Joe called the pastor in great distress. He wanted someone to put Max in his place and make him behave. Gently the pastor tried to soothe Joe's obviously frayed nerves and calm him to a place where talk could regain its balance.

Slowly the problem emerged. Joe was fine with meeting Max now and again and telling him some stuff about the Christian faith. He had even dropped the remark that Max could come by sometime, if he wanted, and the two of them could hang out together. Well, it seems as if Max thought Joe meant it, for he came by Joe's house unannounced, in what turned out to be a very awkward moment. Joe had been in bed with his girlfriend and there was no easy way to cover it up. Joe was embarrassed and turned it all on Max, blaming him for intruding on Joe's personal life. Max, in turn, delivered a blistering accusation against Joe for being a phony and said that if it was all right for Joe to have sex with his girlfriend, Max could do the same. Now Joe was caught in a host of moral lies and inconsistencies and the shouting match ended with Joe telling Max to get out, Max stomping off and slamming the door, and Joe calling the pastor in irritation over the whole mess.

What had begun as a venture in modeling Christian behavior to those entering adult religious responsibilities had turned into an object lesson in the moral quagmire of general church life. M. Scott Peck wrote that one of the most unlikely places to create true community in modern North American society is in the church, because we have bought into isolation and performance mentalities. Joe and Max only proved the truth of this and they were but a symptom of a much larger problem in most of our congregations. We gather on Sundays to say pious things about God and morality, but we live isolated and hidden lives in which we too often don't practice what we preach. When we get caught at our lies and deceptions, as in the case of Max and Joe, we attack each other or we complain that the system is broken.

Epiphany Sunday reminds us that the secret things will be brought to light. God shines a powerful beam into our world in the person of Jesus Christ. All who come into this radiance begin to glow or hide, depending on their lifestyle preference. Let the light shine today but be aware of the crises it may surface.

Isaiah 60:1-6

A spate of apocalyptic movies has toured the silver screens of our world recently. A jilted planet fights back in *The Happening* and nearly destroys the human race in a bid for ecological survival. *War of the Worlds* has fetid aliens drugging it up on human blood until they catch a nasty virus from our biological systems and die ignobly as their harvesting spacecraft slam into skyscrapers and their crews melt down into sticky ooze. In *Star Trek*, time-traveling Romulans seek to annihilate the worlds (including earth) that produced their enemies before those combatants have a chance to be born. An earlier episode in the series had the *Enterprise* taking *The Voyage Home* in order to prevent earth's destruction by its ancient alien creators, siblings of ocean's whales, who no longer heard the cry of the humpbacks from their outer space listening posts. More recently, on *The Day the Earth Stood Still*, interstellar civilizations have determined that humans are destroying earth, one of the few planets rich enough in resources to serve as home to multiple varieties of organic life, and so a ship of destruction is dispatched, only being thwarted in its endeavors when its robotic captain, while assuming human form in order to communicate, begins to understand the complexities of *homo sapiens* and calls off the destruction. Even shows aimed at children get in on the act, with the *Transformers* vividly portraying the battle between human-hating Decepticons and human-loving Autobots, with our planet nearly sacrificed as a prize.

Dozens more could be named but the point is that when our world is in great stress (as it has been for the last decade with the rise of aggressive international terrorism and enormous financial crises), apocalyptic productions of stage, screen, or sentence proliferate. Doomsday books roll off the presses, television shows like *Fringe* or *Eleventh Hour* or *The 4400* replicate and disaster movies multiply.

Apocalyptic visioning is nothing new. Every civilization, and especially those that were dying, has had end-times doomsayers. Even the Bible shows evidence of that. When the Assyrians stormed through Israel and devastated it in 722 BC, little Judah to the south was engulfed in a cloud of moody and frightening prophecies, including dozens collected in Isaiah's volume. The book of Revelation would serve much the same purpose in the early Christian church as the early days of power and glory gave way to the darkening killing fields of persecution.

But the biblical apocalyptic visions never end in total annihilation. These nasty times are always the gateway to salvation, restoration, and renewal. This is seen powerfully in today's Isaiah reading. Note the "darkness" that covers the earth, so powerful that it must be repeated as "thick darkness" in verse 2. In this tragedy-engulfed world, however, shines a light. It is a light of grace, a light of hope, a light of salvation, a light of transformation. It is, of course, a divine light, whose source is none other than Yahweh, the God of Israel and the Lord of the nations. But this marvelous light of hope and restoration, on the apocalyptic battlefields of our world, is prismed through the faith community of God's peculiar people, the Israelites, now reduced to only the hill country remnant of Judah.

The message is clear. Earth will not end with either a bang or a whimper, as T.S. Eliot presumed, but with the blazing light of divine love, which will restore, renew, and resuscitate all things until God's good intentions are finally experienced by all. Whatever apocalyptic doom holds sway in any society is only the prelude to God's next great act of re-creation, which will produce a great dance of recreation among all of humanity.

The symbolic language of the Old Testament gains specificity in its New Testament realizations, of course. First of all, the prophetic "Day of the Lord" was split in two, so that the blessings of realized eschatology could begin with the Messiah's first coming as a baby in Bethlehem, while the catastrophic divine cleansing would wait until a later date. Second, through Jesus and the church that lived in the power of his Spirit, some of the shades and shadows of humanity's self-destructive trammeling are pushed back and pockets of glory shine around every congregation that throbs with the radiance of heaven.

Ephesians 3:1-12

Paul stutters at the beginning of Ephesians 3. What he intends to say about God's good plans and his own awestruck response to them is picked up again in 3:14. But as Paul begins to write about his unique mission to the Gentiles in 3:1, he realizes that he has to explain how this special commissioning transpired. But his call to ministry is only one little piece of a vast divine conspiracy (to use Dallas Willard's term) that has hovered over humanity like a mysterious cloud for centuries. In today's reading, Paul tries to summarize that great tale.

We breeze through our days and experiences believing that we can make it on our own, Paul would say. At the same time we wrestle with resources and responsibilities, knowing that there are some moral values and cosmic principles that affirm certain directions and activities in life while denying and negating or punishing others. Caught somewhere in between is our mixed hope and dread that a higher power out there will fill in the gaps and accommodate our weaknesses and make things right when we mess up.

The religion of the Bible is predicated on the assumption that all of experiential reality had a beginning and was brought into being by a creator, and this deity desires an on-going relationship with the worlds that exist. More particularly, this God nurtures a special longing to engage the human race as the unique and crowning species within the grand complexity of molecules and moons, fish and fowl, galaxies and granite, emotions and electrons.

But in its understanding of this on-going arm-wrestling of creator and creature, biblical religion is deeply rooted in human history. This expression of values and ideas is not merely a moral construct that makes life easier. Nor is it a set of centering exercises that will keep the imminent more fully tuned to the transcendent. Instead, the story put forward in biblical literature is that the creatures of earth have lost their ability to apprehend or understand their creator and that the deity must necessarily take not only the first, but many recurring steps in an effort to reconnect with them. So revelation is a concept involving both action and content. The deity must somehow interrupt the normal course of affairs in human existence in a way that will catch our attention. And when we have stopped to notice or ponder or even step back in fright, there must be some information that becomes accessible to us in a way that allows and encourages us to rethink the meaning of all things.

It is in this sense that Paul explains the literature of the Bible. It is rooted in two major divine interruptions into human history — first, the events of the exodus and Sinai covenant that first created Israel as a missional nation and then later the unusual and unrepeatable incarnation of deity in the person of Jesus Christ. All of the literature of the Bible is gathered around these two redemptive events and their implications. For this reason the Pentateuch and the gospels are the critical elements shaping the biblical religion. They are not codes of law or wise ethical teachings from a distinguished school of thought; they are the documents articulating an unusual intrusion of divine will into the human arena for the threefold purpose of actively transforming lives by redemptive transactions, teaching the creator's original worldview, and establishing a missional community that will live out and disseminate those perspectives.

If the Bible is to have any on-going religious value, its two historical nodes of divine redemptive activity must be taken seriously. Stripped of the exodus/Sinai covenant or of the redemptive divinity of Jesus, the Bible makes little sense. Suddenly its moral codes are no better than others that have been formed and articulated at various points throughout history. Its pilgrimage images are little different from other quests for significance and the sacred, and its personalities become only another bunch of interesting heroes and drifters who give moral lessons through their flawed frolicking.

But if there is a God, and if that God wished to reclaim by creatorial right a relationship with those brought into being as an extension of the divine fellowship and heavenly energy, the Bible makes a good deal of sense. It is a collection of covenant documents that trace the divine redemptive mission through two stages: its early history in locating a transformed community at the crossroads of human society in order to be seen and desired, and its later expression through an expanding and transforming presence in every culture that tells the story of God along with the other tales of life. Paul finds himself helping the faith community of the Old Testament transition into this new age of mission. This is his special calling and it is directly related to the great "mystery" of God's intentions that have been hovering over us from the beginning.

Like the rest of literature, the Bible can be ignored, misread, or improperly used. But like the best of literature, when allowed to speak from its own frame of reference and respected as a collection of documents that are inherently seeking to enhance human life rather than deviously attempting to exploit it, the Bible is truly, in a very powerful and exciting way, the Word of God.

Matthew 2:1-12

The theme of Jesus' royal identity is consistently emphasized throughout Matthew's gospel and rooted directly in the covenant Yahweh made with David in 2 Samuel 7. There the themes of God's house and David's house came together in powerful symmetry. Now that Israel was settled in the promised land, David wished to build a house for God. While God appreciated the appropriate desire on David's part, through the prophet Nathan God communicated that it would be David's son, a man of peace, who would take up that honor and responsibility. But because David's heart and desires were in the right place, God made a return commitment to him. God would build a royal "house" out of David's descendents and there would always be one of his sons ruling as king over God's people.

Although the intervening years since the Babylonian exile had not allowed Jewish self-determination until very recently, and even though this new small freedom of the Jews failed to follow the Davidic dynasty in restoring the throne in Jerusalem, Matthew makes it clear that Jesus is indeed the one who will fulfill, both now and forever, God's commitment to David. This he communicates powerfully in the opening chapters of the gospel.

First, Matthew makes sure his readers connect Jesus' birth to David's lineage in 1:1-17, including a special division of the years to indicate that God was about to act once again in salvation, and Jesus showed up at precisely the right time.

Second, Jesus' birth is as marvelous, mysterious, and miraculous as were the births of Isaac, Samson, and Samuel — great patriarchs and deliverers for ancient Israel. Jesus is another in the line of God's special ambassadors to bring about the salvation of the people.

Third, when Jesus is born, nations far beyond these tiny borders recognize that an international ruler of transcendent significance has come to earth. Matthew alone records this story of the Magi, not to make us speculate about who they were or how many came or even what their names might have been. The essential point is clear: while in Jesus' own homeland there remain bloody contests for local rule, within the international community the quest to finally find a king of consequence has been divinely channeled toward baby Jesus. The signs have been posted in the heavens.

The message of Epiphany Sunday is not about the mystery of the Magi but about the divine revelation. God makes it abundantly clear that God is interrupting human affairs to bring a salvation that we cannot devise on our own. Jesus is not merely one among the many good religious leaders that have happened along through time; he is the Creator's last and greatest attempt to bring us home. Christianity is not just one dimension of the multifaceted religious landscape that surrounds us in a pluralistic world; it holds the core doctrines that bring about the salvation of all.

Epiphany is not about the marvel of seeing potential in a tiny baby. It is a reminder that the religion of the Bible is exclusive in its origins and in its message of salvation. This does not make Christianity petty or prideful; it simply means that once you know the larger story of God's redemptive purposes toward our world, it is a privilege to share the good news about Jesus!

Application

Light has to be a key theme today and the revelation it cast into dark places. Perhaps the lighting in the building could be subdued and increased gradually or dramatically as the message ends and a hymn or chorus about light is sung. Isaiah announces the coming of the divine light while experiencing the apocalyptic night. Paul unfolds the historical mystery of God's lighting plans and shows how Jesus is the beam that pierces the mystery of darkness. And Matthew's specially selected story of the coming of the Magi is a reminder that the Creator has not done all of this in some secret corner, but in the very religions of our world that have left vestiges of human groping through blindness for a divine redemption. Let the light shine! Shine, Jesus, Shine!

An Alternative Application
Matthew 2:1-12. Epiphany Sunday is traditionally the time to explore either the story of the Magi or Jesus' baptism, both of which are public "epiphanies" or manifestations of the glory of God among us. So today, the gospel passage can be exploited homiletically with great benefit. But care must be taken, as noted above, not to reduce the meaning of Matthew's clearly outlined declaration of Jesus' royal divinity and purpose into some trite tales of heroic Magi.

Baptism of Our Lord
Epiphany 1
Ordinary Time 1
Isaiah 42:1-9
Acts 10:34-43
Matthew 3:13-17
by David Kalas

Divine debut

The people had been waiting for a very long time. Our Isaiah passage reflects a centuries-old promise from God about his chosen servant and that was not even the first of God's promises. So the people had been waiting for a very long time for a certain kind of savior and leader, for deliverance and restoration, for a new covenant and a new age of God's reign. They had waited through the Assyrian threat and the Babylonian captivity. They had waited through the tug-of-war among Alexander's generals, and now they were waiting in the midst of the stranglehold of Rome.

To their credit, the people were waiting expectantly. That cannot always be said of God's people, for we sometimes give up hope. Perhaps we stop expecting because we are so discouraged. Or perhaps we stop expecting because we are so preoccupied. The latter may be truer of the American church. But the Jews in the days of Jesus and John were, to their credit, waiting expectantly.

One sure sign of expectation, of course, is prematurely seeing the thing for which you're looking. When we watch carefully for something, we usually perk up and say, "Is that it?" several times before "it" finally arrives. Mirages come with thirst.

So it was in first-century Palestine. The people had perked up and taken notice of several folks along the way, including John the Baptist. Is he the one? No. John's not the one. John, it turns out, is not even worthy to untie the sandals of the one.

Finally one day he appeared. He had already come, of course, some thirty years before in Bethlehem. But he had not really appeared yet. Then came that day at the Jordan River when he finally appeared: the divine debut.

Isaiah 42:1-9

Throughout scripture, Christ is proclaimed by many different folks: prophets, angels, John the Baptist, the apostles. First and foremost, however, it seems that Christ is proclaimed by God himself.

At Jesus' baptism in our Matthew lection, God the Father speaks his word of affirmation about Jesus, and here in this Isaiah passage, centuries before Jesus' earthly ministry, God announces what that special, chosen servant will be and will do.

The image of God putting his Spirit on that servant is an important theme in this week's lections. It is promised here in Isaiah, embodied in the Matthew passage, and declared by Peter in the Acts passage.

The mission of this chosen servant is described in terms of both style and content. The content is, first of all, justice. "He will bring forth justice" (vv. 1, 3) is promised twice, and then he will not give up until "he has established justice in the earth" (v. 4). Justice may be, for us, like certain parts of our bodies — we pay no attention to them until something goes wrong with them. For as long as we ourselves are not the victims of injustice, we are not much troubled by it or perhaps even aware of it. But widespread and deep-rooted injustice is one of the great blights of a fallen world and so that is first on the agenda of God's chosen servant.

Next, there follows a series of deliverance images — light to the nations, opening blind eyes, setting free prisoners. This is very much the mood of another Isaiah passage, with which Jesus chooses to identify himself in the synagogue in Nazareth (see Luke 4:16-21; Isaiah 61:1-2). Deliverance was a prominent feature of the promised servant, and it was a part of Jesus' self-understanding in his work.

Finally, the other key element of the content of the servant's mission is found in verse 6: "I have given you as a covenant to the people." Here the promised servant parts company from any ordinary ruler or hero. Other leaders before and after Isaiah 42 were agents of justice and deliverance. But tucked within those other promises comes this unique role of this unique servant: namely, he himself will be given as a covenant (see also 49:8). Time and again throughout the Old Testament, God had initiated covenants, established covenants, promised new covenants, and given certain signs of the covenants. But this is different: He gives a person as a covenant. Our covenant-relationship with God is in Christ and is Christ.

Meanwhile, the promises about this chosen servant offer a glimpse into the style, as well as the content, of his mission.

Bruised reeds and dimly burning wicks are compelling images. They are wounded and vulnerable. Ordinary events that stronger versions might survive would spell the end of these. A sturdy reed or a thriving flame would take a deliberate effort to break or extinguish. The bruised reed or flickering wick, however, can be finished off by accident or by mere carelessness.

The chosen one, however, does not finish off these vulnerable items. That bespeaks a carefulness, a gentleness, and perhaps even a deliberate attentiveness to those that are wounded. Moreover, in a discarding culture, we are surprised by the manifest patience with stuff that is not full-strength and fully functioning. And in a culture where standard operating procedure is the survival of the fittest, we are challenged by the one who guarantees the survival of the frailest.

The Isaiah passage concludes with the Lord's own majestic statement about himself. He declares his name, and he does not share his glory or his praise. That is an important corrective for his people to hear, for we are always endeavoring to share around that which belongs rightly and exclusively to him.

Finally, the Lord offers a time line. Look to the past and you will see there that "former things have come to pass" (v. 9). In the events of the past comes verification of God's word and God's providence. Then God promises "new things" in the future and he "(tells) you of them" (v. 9) in the present. The occasional pool player sinks a combination shot, quite by accident, and then jests, "I meant to do that," but the great player calls his shots and tells all those around what he intends to do. So does God. The Lord God calls his shots so that there will be hope in the present and no mistaking or misattribution in the future.

Acts 10:34-43

Peter's speech in Cornelius' house comes at the climax of a remarkable series of events. God has orchestrated this meeting between the apostle and the Gentile, and it represents a landmark event in the life of the church.

In order for us to appreciate Peter's remarkable opening statement, we have to remove ourselves from our contemporary mindset. Pluralism and tolerance are so ingrained in our present culture that we are not struck by Peter's words, but they would have seemed scandalous to any devout Jew of Peter's time. The thought that God shows no partiality was not without precedent in the Old Testament scriptures, particularly the prophets, but still the total blurring of the lines between God's chosen people and other nations would have bordered on heresy.

Such a dramatic, all-inclusive statement just a few days before would probably have stunned Peter himself. In between, however, other things had surprised him: his vision on the rooftop in Joppa, and God's orchestration in bringing him and Cornelius together. And then, most stunning — and most telling — of all was the manifestation of the Holy Spirit among the Gentiles there in Cornelius' house while Peter was still speaking.

While Peter recognizes now the universality of the gospel and of God's grace, a few distinctions between people do remain. Israel, for example, may not be the exclusive beneficiaries of God's plan and covenant, but they were the chosen recipients of God's word (e.g., v. 36 "the message he sent to the people of Israel"). Likewise, after Jesus was raised, his appearing was "not to all the people but to us who were chosen by God as witnesses" (v. 41).

Here is where Peter has latched onto a concept that is evident throughout scripture and yet not consistently evident in either the theology of ancient Israel or of the early church. The reality is that God has, in fact, chosen some people throughout history but that choice has not been an exercise of exclusiveness. Rather, it has been a choice made for a broader and more inclusive purpose.

Abram was plainly chosen by God — and it was from that early choice that Israel traced its self-understanding as a chosen people — but God's expressed purpose for Abram was far broader than just his own descendants: "... in you all the families of the earth shall be blessed" (Genesis 12:3).

The disciples of Jesus were clearly chosen by him. Again, though, the choice was not for the purpose of forming a separate and exclusive group. Rather, Jesus told them, "You did not choose me but I chose you. And I appointed you to go and bear fruit, fruit that will last" (John 15:16). Of course, the final instruction Jesus gave to those chosen disciples was to go and make more disciples, and of all nations at that (Matthew 28:19).

Interestingly, the Greek words used in Jesus' Great Commission in Matthew are the same as Peter used in Cornelius' house. In the Matthew passage, Jesus says "of all nations" (*panta ta ethnay*), while in the Acts passage, Peter uses the same words but in the singular form, "in every nation" (*en panti ethnei*).

Paul, too, was manifestly chosen by God, but the Lord said that Paul was "an instrument whom I have chosen to bring my name before Gentiles and kings and before the people of Israel" (Acts 9:15).

Here in Peter's remarks to those gathered at Cornelius' house, the paradigm consists of select, chosen instruments with a broader, all-encompassing mission. God sent his message "to the people of Israel" (v. 36), but people "in every nation" (v. 35) can be acceptable to him. Jesus did not appear "to all people" (v. 41), but rather only to the ones "chosen by God" (v. 41), and those for the specific purpose of being "witnesses."

The content of Peter's speech, meanwhile, makes an interesting outline. His preaching of the gospel provides an embryonic version of a gospel. Click on each of these phrases from Peter's preaching: "the baptism that John announced" (v. 37); Jesus "went about doing good" (v. 38); "they put him to death" (v. 39); "God raised him on the third day" (v. 40); "God... allowed him to appear... to us who were chosen by God as witnesses" (vv. 40-41); and "he commanded us to preach" (v. 42) — let them become drop-down menus and expand on each. In the end, you'll have something very much like Matthew, Mark, Luke, and John.

Finally, Peter affirms the gospel content of the Old Testament scriptures: "all the prophets testify about him..." (v. 43). This is a neglected truth in some of our churches where the Old Testament has been set aside as outdated, irrelevant, or replaced. Peter does here without specifics the kind of thing he does more explicitly on the Day of Pentecost (such as Acts 2:16-21, 25-28, 34-35). The accounts in Acts suggest that it was common fare for the early church to preach Christ with Old Testament passages as their text (see, for example, 17:2-3; 18:27-28).

The most striking example of this comes from Jesus himself, though we don't have the details. On Easter Sunday afternoon on the road to Emmaus, Jesus "beginning with Moses and all the prophets, he interpreted to them the things about himself in all the scriptures" (Luke 24:27).

Our people know that the New Testament is about Jesus. Peter's words in Cornelius' house resonate with other New Testament references to remind us that the Old Testament is about Jesus too.

Matthew 3:13-17

The ministry of John the Baptist is a mystery and a marvel. All four gospel writers include it — which is more than can be said of Christmas, the Transfiguration, or any single thing that Jesus said on the cross — and yet none of the gospels give us many details about it. Between the four accounts, we get a sense for John's rough look and lifestyle. We also put together the accounts of his words to discover a man bold enough to confront the crowds and condemn the king, on the one hand; yet humble enough to defer completely to just the prospect of Christ, on the other.

At this point in Matthew's story, we have been only briefly introduced to John when Jesus arrives and takes the spotlight. John's mission — according to both Old Testament prophecy (3:3) and John's own understanding (3:2, 11) — is purely preparatory. He is not on stage to be the star but to be supporting cast. He is not the main event but he introduces the main event.

We don't know how long John had been baptizing people in the Jordan River, but Jesus evidently knew where to find him. Matthew indicates a sense of deliberate purpose on Jesus' part because he traveled from Galilee down to the Jordan "to be baptized by [John]" (v. 13).

John resists the proposal, for John has a profound sense of his place relative to Christ. He has no delusions about himself. The whole world could come to John to be baptized. All the descendants of Abraham and the most religious people of the land could come to be baptized by him. But in this one, solitary person there was an exception: He did not need to be baptized at all and certainly John was not worthy to do it.

Jesus, however, sought "to fulfill all righteousness" (v. 15). That emphasis on righteousness seems ironic, given the later complaints by scribes and Pharisees that Jesus was careless and casual about matters of righteousness (such as hand-washing and Sabbath-keeping). Meanwhile, Jesus himself later declared that "unless your righteousness exceeds that of the scribes and Pharisees, you will never enter the kingdom of heaven" (Matthew 5:20). Clearly he and the religious leaders of the day had different understandings of righteousness.

John's willingness to cooperate with Jesus even though it didn't make sense to him is, of course, exemplary. This is precisely where we so often fall short: that the plan of God needs to pass the test of our understanding in order for us to participate in it. Not so for John, however. He "would have prevented" (v. 14), but "then he consented" (v. 15).

Jesus' baptism is followed by the heavens opening, the Spirit descending as a dove, and the voice of the Father speaking. While we are given no graphic detail about the actual look of the heavens opening, the image appears several places in scripture (see also Isaiah 64:1; Ezekiel 1:1; Acts 7:56). The image suggests that there is a kind of cosmic barrier between us and God — between our location and his — and for the heavens to be opened affords us a glimpse into his place and somehow especially allows his word and his work in our place.

Application

God's anointed servant, promised and anticipated for centuries, had come into the world. But his entrance was backstage and barely noticed. Only the smallest handful of folks — some flea-bitten shepherds, a few foreign astrologers, an old man and an old woman in the temple, and a bewildered couple from Nazareth — were even aware of his arrival. He was scarcely detected when he arrived and lived below the radar of public attention and recognition for some thirty years.

The mood of the people was ripe, meanwhile. There was a rampant hunger in first-century Israel for God's special leader: the promised one who would come to set them free, to defeat their enemies, and to reign on David's throne in peace, strength, and security. The appetite was so great, in fact, that the people had gone rushing after others, whether curiously or enthusiastically (see, for example, Luke 3:15; John 1:19-22; Acts 5:36-37).

Then came the day — a day that was like no other, except for the fact that it probably seemed just like every other. The sun was hot. Roman soldiers traipsed the roads and streets. The Judean wilderness was inhospitable. It was a day just like any other. But the people who had gathered at the Jordan River to see and hear John the Baptist that day ended up seeing and hearing a great deal more.

Jesus presented himself to John to be baptized. John's reflex was to resist. Like Peter who knew better than to let Jesus wash his feet, John knew that he should be baptized by Jesus rather than the other way around. But Jesus insisted, and John consented. And when Jesus had been baptized and came up out of the water, there was "the Spirit of God descending like a dove (Matthew 3:16) ... and a voice from heaven said, 'This is my Son' " (Matthew 3:17).

Take a snapshot of that moment, for it is unique in all of human history. On this one occasion, the whole Trinity is manifested on earth: the voice of the Father is heard, the Son is incarnate, and the Spirit descends in the form of a dove. Centuries before, Isaiah recorded God's promise that he would put his Spirit on his servant. Some years later, Peter would affirm that God anointed Jesus with the Holy Spirit. Here, on an ordinary day by the Jordan River, it happened. The promised one appeared. The divine debut.

An Alternative Application

Matthew 3:13-17. It's a standard children's game. Show a child a picture that contains a surprise or two — a bird flying upside down, a cow climbing a tree, a starry sky in the middle of the day — and ask, "What's wrong with this picture?"

When Jesus came to the Jordan to be baptized, John knew something was wrong with the picture. "I need to be baptized by you, and do you come to me?" (v. 14). This is every kind of backward and upside down. This can't be right.

Jesus responded, however, "Let it be so now; for it is proper for us in this way to fulfill all righteousness" (v. 15).

It's a backward picture we see again and again in the gospel of Jesus Christ. It's the picture of humility, obedience, and matchless grace. God becomes a baby. The master washes feet. The judge of all the earth stands trial in a human court. The immortal dies. We look at the gospel story, and we wonder again and again at all that's wrong with the picture.

Charles Wesley knew what to make of it all: " 'Tis mystery all: th' Immortal dies: Who can explore His strange design? In vain the firstborn seraph tries to sound the depths of love divine. 'Tis mercy all! Let earth adore, let angel minds inquire no more."

Epiphany 2
Ordinary Time 2
Isaiah 49:1-7
1 Corinthians 1:1-9
John 1:29-42
by William Shepherd

Called before born

"Who's your family?" Southerners know this greeting well, but it is not unheard of above, beside, and around the Mason-Dixon line. Many people value roots — where you come from, who your people are, what constitutes "home." We speak of those who are "rootless" as unfortunate; those who "wander" are aimless and unfocused. Adopted children search for their birth parents because they want to understand their identity and to them that means more than how they were raised and what they have accomplished — heritage counts. Clearly, we place a high value on origins, birth, and descent. We long for a place to call home.

The Bible, however, often counts birthright as secondary, not primary. "God is able from these stones to raise up children to Abraham" (Luke 3:8), said John the Baptist. Moses and the prophets warned the people of Israel against trusting in their lineage rather than their obedience to God's law, and Jesus himself warned that many would come from north, south, east, and west to sit with Abraham at the final banquet, while those who were content to rely on their hereditary connection to Abraham would be outside weeping and gnashing their teeth.

Today's lections give us reason to value God's call over human birth. Isaiah's servant speaks of being called *before* he was born. Paul told the Corinthians that just as he was a "called apostle," they were all "called saints." In the gospel of John, we find a story about the call of the first disciples, which will prove to be a foreshadowing of the call of every disciple.

Isaiah 49:1-7

Our lection from Second Isaiah is one of the well-known "Servant Songs," four poems spoken by the servant (42:1-4; 42:5-7; 49:1-6; 50:4-9), and two about the servant (50:10-11; 52:13—53:12). All the poems have a common theme: God's servant suffers and is rejected but nevertheless will bring justice at some future date. The third servant song, in 49:1-6, combines thanksgiving with a commissioning form: The focus is on the call of the servant, not just to bring justice to Israel, but to extend it to all people.

The third servant song is intimately connected with the first two and reflects what has happened in Isaiah's story since then. There are a number of thematic and verbal parallels between our lection and 42:1-7 (cf. 42:4 and 49:1, "the coastlands"; 42:1 and 49:6, "to the nations"; 42:3 and 49:4, "justice/cause [*mishpat*]"; 42:6 and 49:6, "light to the nations"). Since chapter 42, however, things have changed: Cyrus has, as promised, come to liberate Israel from Babylonian captivity (chs. 44-45), the deities of Babylon have been exposed as false and impotent gods (chs. 46-47), and Israel has once again proven to be unfaithful to its responsibilities (ch. 48). Now the voice of the messenger in 48:16 picks up a new song.

One other thing has changed since chapter 42: The servant has taken on an individual identity. There are several clues that the collective designation of all Israel as the servant has taken on an individual, representative cast. That the servant was known and called before birth fits an individual better than a group (v. 1). The commission to the servant to go to Jacob and Israel (v. 5) makes more sense if addressed to an individual (Jacob and Israel would hardly be sent to themselves!). Most importantly, the identification

"Israel" in verse 3 should not be taken as a vocative (as in NRSV) but as a predicate: "You are my servant, you are Israel" (author's translation). The individual is made the faithful embodiment of the entire people and given the role of the entire nation, similar to the way we might speak of a "king" or "president" when talking about the entire nation. The servant sums up all there is to know about the entire community.

The mission of the servant is the mission of that community, to bring justice (*mishpat*) to the nations. This reflects the original commission to the servant (42:1). So far the mission has not seen much success (ch. 48). Israel has complained that God has disregarded justice (40:27, where NRSV translates *mishpat* as "right"), but God has promised not to grow weary until *mishpat* is established in the earth (42:2). In 49:4, the servant is indeed tempted to grow weary and despair, but he rallies, knowing that "my cause (*mishpat*) is with the Lord."

The servant's mission is not just to Israel; this has been clear from the beginning. It would be trifling of God to restrict the mission of the servant to Jacob and Israel (v. 6). Therefore, the servant is given as "a light to the nations, that my salvation may reach to the end of the earth." Even kings and princes will find themselves prostrate before God's servant, despite the servant's continuing status as "one deeply despised, abhorred by the nations, the slave of rulers" (v. 7).

1 Corinthians 1:1-9

"Why do we have to read the beginning of Paul's letters?" Many churchgoers wish we could get past the preliminaries and on to the good stuff. However, a closer look at the openings of Paul's letters show that the good stuff is already there in compressed form. This is certainly the case with the address and thanksgiving of the "First Letter to the Corinthians."

Paul christianized the conventional address of the Greco-Roman letter, "A to B, Greetings." First of all, he adds his own self-description as a "called apostle of Jesus Christ by the will of God" (1:1, author's translation). Paul does not speak in his own voice, but in that of the one who called and sent him. Further, Paul adds the name of a co-author, Sosthenes, described as "our brother." Sosthenes is otherwise known only from Acts 18:17 as "the official of the synagogue" who took a beating from the mob before the Corinthian tribunal. Clearly his presence (and presumably, assistance in writing the letter) lends Paul a personal connection to his audience.

His address also includes a characterization of the community he writes to in Corinth. Like Paul, they are "called" — in this case, "called saints," who are "sanctified" (or set apart) as those "in Christ Jesus." As such, they are part of a community that is larger than themselves, "together with all those who in every place call on the name of our Lord Jesus Christ, both their Lord and ours" (v. 2). Paul uses a variant of the traditional Greek greeting, combined with a Jewish greeting, to stress that the source of their community lies outside of themselves: "Grace to you and peace from God our Father and the Lord Jesus Christ" (v. 3).

The thanksgiving is a common opening element in Paul's letters (cf. Romans 1:8-15; Philippians 1:3-11), and it often foreshadows the main themes of the letter. Here it covers three things that will prove to be issues of contention in Corinth: the gift of God, the call to community, and the nature of the end times. We'll take these themes one by one.

One of the main issues before the Corinthians was the nature of the gift of God. Paul affirms that they do indeed have "the grace of God that has been given you in Christ Jesus" (v. 4). The word "grace" (*charis*) simply means God's attitude of favor, which is made known in particular "gifts" (*charismata*) given to human beings. These gifts will provoke contention between Paul and the Corinthians (cf. chs. 8-11, 12-14). Paul establishes common ground with the Corinthians by acknowledging that they "are not lacking in any spiritual gift" (v. 7). In fact, "in every way" they "have been enriched in him, in speech and knowledge of every kind" (v. 5). Paul establishes this common ground only to undermine it, for he will later make clear that their gifts of speech and knowledge are imperfect. It is precisely the use and abuse of these gifts that is in question.

The problem is not with the gifts *per se*, but with the Corinthians' appropriation of them as matters of individual pride rather than communal edification. As we have seen, the theme of community was struck already in the greeting and continues into the thanksgiving. Paul stresses that they are "called" to community in the same way that he was "called" to be an apostle, "set apart" as part of a universal community (v. 2). They are the church *of* God *in* Corinth — they did not call themselves. As such, they are enriched in Christ, not of their own doing (v. 5). They are called into a fellowship *of* the Son; it is not their own fellowship (v. 9). What they have, they have received as a gift, and this includes each other. This is not a voluntary community of the like-minded, but an assembly called together by God. As such, the Corinthian Christians must treat each other with a degree of maturity, a measure of sanctification (v. 2). This issue will come up again and again (cf. chs. 8-11, 12-14).

Paul puts these concerns in the context of the imminent return of Christ. The time is to be spent wisely, in preparation and anticipation. The spiritual gifts are to be used "as you wait for the revealing of our Lord Jesus Christ" (v. 7). God's gifts are given to "strengthen you to the end, so that you may be blameless on the day of our Lord Jesus Christ" (v. 8). Some scholars believe that the core problem at the root of all the Corinthian church's issues was the belief that they had already arrived at a measure of perfection, because Christ had already returned in the Spirit to them (this is known as a "realized eschatology"). Paul will spend an entire chapter correcting the mistaken notion that Christians will not rise from the dead at some future point (ch. 15). Already in his thanksgiving, he has signaled the importance of the last days for Christians. We must not mistake our present religious experience, no matter how exciting it may be for those who have received a measure of the refreshment of the Spirit, for God's final plan for us, which will take place only at "the day of our Lord Jesus Christ" (v. 8). There is more to the Christian life than ecstatic experience; it involves the mature and sober assessment of our long-term situation in Christ.

Note that all of this foreshadowing of Paul's teaching takes place *within* a thanksgiving. These are the things that Paul is thankful to see in the lives of the Corinthian disciples. It is all the more noteworthy that Paul gives thanks, in light of the rest of the Corinthian correspondence. Clearly, Paul had a rotten relationship with the Corinthians. Nevertheless, he was able to give thanks for them. They, in turn, must have seen something in his instruction worthy of preservation and transmission to the next generation; otherwise, we wouldn't be reading it today.

John 1:29-42

The call of the first disciples in John is "similar to" yet "different from" the more familiar stories found in the synoptic gospels. For one thing, the role of John the Baptist is greatly enhanced in John's gospel. The first disciples do not leave their boats and nets, but they leave the Baptist himself; they become Jesus' disciples rather than John's (John 1:35-37). John explains that this was the entire focus of his ministry, for his purpose was not (as in the synoptics) to baptize for the repentance of sins, but to help reveal the one who was to come (vv. 30-31). The familiar story of Jesus' baptism becomes a story about how Jesus was revealed to John (vv. 32-33). The action here focuses on Jesus, God, and the Spirit. John is just a bystander in this spectacle. John and the others become responsible for bringing new converts to Jesus, and in doing so, they use descriptive tags that seem to relate to John's prologue (1:1-18), as they call Jesus, "The Lamb of God," "Rabbi," "Messiah," "Son of God," and "King of Israel." Note that the story is mostly direct discourse. John lets his characters speak for themselves, as they witness to who Jesus is and what he does. John's method is not to talk about Jesus so much as to let others talk about him.

The story traces the steps of becoming a disciple, according to John. Discipleship follows a discernible process (he repeats this narrative pattern again in 1:35-51 and 4:39-42). First, the potential disciple is pointed to Jesus. The disciple comes to Jesus. S/he is recognized and named by Jesus. The disciple remains with Jesus over time, until at last s/he comes to "know" Jesus. Finally, the disciple seeks out and brings new prospects to Jesus and recedes from the narrative.

John's account of discipleship is filled with wordplay. The disciples are said to "follow" Jesus (v. 37). "Whom do you seek?" Jesus asks them, looking ahead to what will become a central theme in John (1:38, author's translation; cf. 4:27; 7:18-19; 18:4; 20:15). The disciples ask a related question, "Where are you remaining?" (1:38, author's translation). Their question splits between two cruxes, because on one hand the issue of "where" Jesus is and comes from is a crucial question for John (cf. 7:34, 36; 8:14, 21-22; 9:4; 14:3, 4, 15; 17:24; 20:2), and on the other, the word "remain" (*meno*) describes for John a crucial aspect of the relationship among Jesus, God, the Spirit, and believers (1:32-33; 8:31, 35; 14:10, 17; ch. 15). Jesus indulges in further double-entendre when he asks them to "come" (3:21; 5:40; 6:35, 37, 45; 7:37) and "see" (5:40; 6:40, 47; 14:9; 20:29), both words used by John to describe faith. The disciples' initial encounter with Jesus becomes a metaphorical feast, dancing around the themes that John will develop throughout his gospel.

The two new disciples follow the example of their former leader, John the Baptist, and bring new converts to Jesus (and like John, recede in importance to the narrative as the new character comes to the fore). They are not fully disciples until they have brought others into the fold. Andrew brings his brother Simon for renaming. Unlike the story in the synoptics, which makes the naming of Cephas a turning point in the middle of the story, John pictures Jesus handing out nicknames from the very beginning. John's stress is on Jesus, not Peter; his prescient naming indicates his knowledge of both the future and the human heart. Simon does not so much *become* "The Rock" as *finds* the rockiness that was always embedded within him.

Application

"But I don't want to be a priest or a monk, I want to be a pharmacist." My college friend Brian was objecting to the notion that becoming a Christian meant giving over your entire life to God. "If I were to give all my being to God," he said, "then it seems to me that I would have to give away all my possessions and devote myself to God. I'd have to become a monk, or a priest, or a preacher. I don't want to do that."

Fortunately for Brian, becoming a disciple doesn't necessarily mean becoming a monk, priest, or preacher. Nor does the disciple need to leave all possessions behind in order to follow Jesus (a prescription that made perfect sense during his lifetime, since he did not travel to Jerusalem in a moving van — but now we can be with him anywhere, in the power of the Spirit). Brian had confused call with vocation. The monk, priest, and preacher all have a vocation. So did Brian — to be a good pharmacist. But he shared with the monk, priest, and preacher the call to become a disciple.

Many people seem to think that following Jesus involves doing something differently, whereas perhaps all that is required is going about doing the things you already do in a different way. The Bible teacher Verna Dozier is fond of saying that lay people have a much harder job than the clergy; all the clergy have to do is be Christians for a living, while lay people have to be Christians *on top* of working for a living! When told that she knows so much about the Bible and theology that she ought to get herself ordained, she says, "I refuse to accept the demotion."

Our highest calling is indeed the call to be saints, sanctified in Jesus Christ. If we scrape the stained glass off that language, we will learn that a "saint" who is "sanctified" is simply someone who is "set apart" for God's work — not some otherworldly paragon of piety, but any normal red-blooded Christian who has a sense that God has touched him or her personally. That word "saint" is used in the Bible of each and every Christian, not the elite few; it may well be best translated as "Christian." We are not saints because we have worked hard to be holy. We are saints because God has called us and made us disciples.

An Alternative Application
Isaiah 49:1-7; 1 Corinthians 1:1-9; John 1:29-41. Real disciples have disciples. Perhaps the true test of your discipleship is whether you yourself have disciples. That is, are there people who look to you for spiritual leadership, who credit you with helping them understand what it means to be one of the saints

of God? Second Isaiah's servant was sent to influence not just the people of Israel but to be a light to all the nations. Paul made an explicit connection between his "call" as an apostle and the Corinthian's "call" as saints. But the most emphatic portrayal of serial discipleship is found in the gospel of John. John the Baptist's entire existence boiled down to the revelation of Jesus to two of his own disciples; after that, he practically disappeared from the narrative, because "he must increase, but I must decrease" (3:30). So too, his disciples went and found others to join them as disciples. Later in John's story, Philip will bring Nathanael to Jesus (1:43-51) and the woman of Samaria will bring her whole town to him (4:28-30, 39-42). Following Jesus is infectious. Remember, you are contagious.

Epiphany 3
Ordinary Time 3
Isaiah 9:1-4
1 Corinthians 1:10-18
Matthew 4:12-23
by Wayne Brouwer

The day boy and the night girl

In 1882 George MacDonald wrote a fascinating story that powerfully illumines the thought behind today's lectionary passages. MacDonald called his tale "The Day Boy and the Night Girl: the Romance of Photogen and Nycteris" (it is available online at http://www.ccel.org/m/macdonald/daynight/daynight.html). In MacDonald's fable a witch steals a newborn girl and raises her in the total darkness of a cave. The witch experiences both light and darkness, but not the girl. She is completely immersed in the black world. Even as she grows, the witch will only allow her to step outside during the nighttime hours. Long before dawn's graying blush, Nycteris would be back inside her dark cave home. Although she may have been meant for light by birth, the witch's training kept her now in the dark. In fact, one night when she strayed unusually far, her running steps were driven by fear of pursuing light as she fled home near daybreak.

There was another young person in the same world. His name was Photogen, and he had been raised to experience only the bright light of day. His guardians ensured that he was never in the dark, not even to sleep. By the time the sun set, bright lights burned in the castle where he was raised.

Yet there came a day when Photogen hunted too far and was caught beyond the point of no return when dusk filtered the skies and darkness crept on. In terror Photogen stumbled into a garden and hugged himself in distress. Fortunately this happened to be on a night and in the vicinity where Nycteris' nocturnal roaming brought them together. Nycteris comforted Photogen and helped him understand the world of the night. Intrigued, Photogen began to plan forays that prevented his daylight return home, and Nycteris became his nighttime guide and friend.

Friendship grew into love and eventually Photogen helped Nycteris endure the blazing sun of a day. In the end they were married, each appreciating the world of the other, yet both gravitating toward the day and the light. MacDonald's tale ends with Nycteris expressing confidence that ever-greater lights will lead them forward.

The parable is powerful. We are like Nycteris, stolen away from our original life in the glory and care of God by a witch we might call the devil. We are raised in the dark night of sin and evil on planet earth. But into this world comes Jesus, our Photogen. He grows to understand our nighttime existence and loves us in it. Yet never does he become part of its darkness. Finally we are able to wed him and share a brighter way of life, partly because of his love, and partly because of our originally created character that knows the world of light is truly our home.

Themes of darkness and light pervade today's passages. If the passion of MacDonald's love story can energize our preaching, our people will long for the light and understand what it means to escape the night.

Isaiah 9:1-4

Isaiah's metaphor of people wandering in darkness is haunting. It begins in 8:19-22 with a divine lament expressing consternation that God's people choose to look for meaning in all the wrong places. They seek wisdom from mediums. They assess direction from sorcerers. They look among the dead for answers to the questions of life. In this they have become zombies, animated corpses without souls. Where once the glory of God shone and gave illumination through Israel to the nations beyond, the light in the tower is now extinguished. The land of promise has become a graveyard where Eden's fruitfulness is replaced by vampire-like blood sucking. In their failure to live in covenant harmony with their God (8:11-18), Israel morphed into a nest of moral cannibals.

But hope nudges in with the turn of the chapter. Although divine displeasure caused the mist of darkness that seeped down through the hills of Galilee (9:1), it is also by divine decree that honor and hope will come. The reference to Zebulun and Naphtali backpedals history to the time of Joshua and the initial distribution of Canaan among the tribes of Israel (Joshua 19:10-16, 32-39). This seems intended to evoke for the original readers/hearers of Isaiah's prophecy a reminder of the Sinai covenant, with its blessings and curses (see Exodus 23:20-33; Deuteronomy 27-28). Obviously, if the people have left the worship of the God of the covenant to seek direction elsewhere, the covenant stands in judgment against them, and the distress that closes chapter 8 is to be expected.

Yet at the same time that Isaiah looks backward to Israel's early history and meaning, he also peers into its future. The term "Galilee of the Gentiles" anticipates a broader coming interaction between Israel and the nations, which will result in the spread of the glory of God. When this happens, the promises made to Abraham (Genesis 12:1-3) will be fulfilled. In fact, the reason why God placed Israel in Canaan, rather than on many seemingly better real estate choices, appears to be that tiny Palestine was at the crossroads of international commerce in its day. The "way of the sea" in verse 1 is actually the technical term *Via Maris*. This was an international highway running from the nations of the Fertile Crescent (Assyria, Babylonia, Persia) and beyond (India, China) through Canaan and on to Egypt. In other words, God positioned Israel right on the major highway of the time in order to provide through it a witness to the other nations as to who God was and how life with God might unfold. In turning away from God, the light went out in Israel, and it also killed the streetlights for the nations traveling through.

Soon, however, light will return. Israel, currently losing its sense of self, will return to its place of honor (vv. 3-4). And when the nation is restored in its splendor, the glory of God will shine over it and through it (v. 2). Light will begin to dawn in the very near future, pushing back the night of evil, pagan worship, and missed opportunities for witness.

1 Corinthians 1:10-18

Paul was on his third mission journey (Acts 18:23—20:38) when he wrote this letter. It was part of a correspondence that included at least three more documents sent by Paul to the Corinthian congregation from Ephesus. He was involved in a long-term church development mission in Ephesus from 51-53 AD. Earlier Paul had written a letter chastising some members of the Corinthian church for their immoral behavior (1 Corinthians 5:9-13). Because of his harsh tone in that letter, some in Corinth appear to have challenged Paul's authority and then resisted any attempt on his part to speak into their lives (1 Corinthians 4). After all, he was no longer living among them.

The divisions of the Corinthian congregation may have emerged at least in part out of this desire by some in Corinth to pick and choose among spiritual authorities. In the mission age of the early church it was easy to assert that certain leaders taught different ideas, since there was little written material to back up such claims and no immediate access to these teachers through instant communication. Even though Paul was the key figure in establishing the Corinthian church (see Acts 18), some were now claiming that other teachers (Apollos, Cephas/Peter, or Jesus himself) were their guiding lights (v. 12). The result was a splintered ministry that no longer housed the glory of God (3:16-17) and reduced the "power" of the gospel in its further reach (1:17). A few verses later (2:7-8) Paul uses the theme of God's glory and the mission of the church together, building upon the light and darkness motif of the Old Testament.

Paul undermines the fragmentation in the Corinthian congregation by reasserting the central teaching of Christ crucified (1:13, 17). This is not a minor message among the many teachings available from Christian leaders, but rather the key theme that all put forward (see ch. 3). Furthermore, he undermines his own prestige by pointing out that few in Corinth can even call him their spiritual father or claim some special esteem in the community by virtue of who might have officiated at their Christian initiation (v. 14). Paul does seem to have a special personal bond with Gaius, since in late 53 Paul would stay for three months in Gaius' home (Acts 20:2-3; Romans 16:23). But this does not allow Gaius to claim spiritual superiority. Similarly, Stephanas is recognized as a leader in the Corinthian congregation (16:17) but that does not arise from Paul's initial connection with the family (1:16).

Verse 18 is a transition verse and belongs more to the explanations that Paul gives in verses 19-25. Nevertheless, it helps to set the tone for how Paul's words should be interpreted in these prior verses. In Paul's view, the world is "perishing" (v. 18). The term is not only linked to death, but to the darkness that envelops humans without access to the glory of God. Similarly, the idea of "the power of God" evident in salvation through Jesus, is always freighted with connotations of God's glory. For further development of this see 2 Corinthians 3:7—4:17 and Ephesians 4:17—5:14.

Matthew 4:12-23

Matthew deliberately picks up Isaiah 9:1-2 in order to explain the ministry of Jesus (vv. 13-17). We are reminded by this that Matthew's audience is largely Jewish and sees in Jesus the fulfillment of Old Testament prophecy. Furthermore, Matthew connects Jesus directly to the "Day of the Lord" that was predicted by the prophets during the tense eras of Israel's demise under Assyria (2 Kings 17) and Judah's capture by Babylon (2 Kings 25). This "Day of the Lord" was initially a coming time of judgment on both Israel and the nations around (see Amos 5:18-27). Later it also gained elements of divine deliverance for a remnant of the faithful (see Isaiah 40) and the onset of the messianic age (see Joel 2). All of these converge for Matthew as Jesus appears on the scene.

For one thing, Jesus begins his ministry only after John has been removed from his public witness. Since Matthew clearly understands John's role as that of the final Old Testament prophet (see Matthew 3), his end and Jesus' coming signal the transition from the old age into the new, messianic age.

Furthermore, Matthew sees in Jesus the fulfillment of Isaiah's promise of a light to dawn in Israel that will become a daybreak of God's glory for the nations around. Matthew even traces the movement of Jesus from his hometown of Nazareth to the Galilean fishing village of Capernaum (v. 13) as initiating this process. After all, Nazareth lies on the edge of what was once the territory of Zebulun among the tribes of Israel, and Capernaum was found within Naphtali's former district. Also, Capernaum was a rest stop on the *Via Maris*, the highway to the sea, mentioned in verse 15. Because of Jesus' location and travels, Matthew identifies his movements as fulfillment of Isaiah's direct geographical map-painting. Similarly, Jesus' reiteration of Israel's role as light to the nations is now coming alive in the beginning of Jesus' public ministry.

This is the way that Matthew also interprets Jesus' initial teaching. "Repent, for the kingdom of heaven is near" (v. 17) is exactly the same message as that of John the Baptist (3:2). It is a message that carries with it all the imperatives that earlier prophets had included in their anticipation of the "Day of the Lord." Now, however, the urgency is heightened; John had said that the event so long anticipated (both with longing and with dread) would happen within his lifetime (3:11-15). Therefore, when Jesus picks up John's muted message, the "Day of the Lord" has arrived.

This is confirmed in the call of Jesus' first disciples (4:18-22). A mere command from Jesus ("Come, follow me!") is all that is necessary to get these four young men (possibly in their late teens or somewhere in their twenties) to leave the family businesses and join the glory march. Since this is the dawn of the New Age, there is no need to worry about daily toil or supplies (see Isaiah 35); God will provide. Furthermore, in these initial days of the divine invasion, it is important to gather as many people as possible into the spared remnant. Too soon, the blaze of judgment will annihilate the rest, so the most important work is that of international ingathering.

Verses 23-25 affirm this. Jesus walks along the *Via Maris* as it runs through Galilee, declaring the good news of the kingdom of God and healing the sick. Later Matthew will directly identify Jesus with the messianic servant foretold by Isaiah (Matthew 12:15-21); here he shapes the ministry of Jesus so that it exactly coincides with the announcement of messianic ministry found in Isaiah 61. Jesus is the "day boy" of George MacDonald who is entering the "night girl" world of first-century Palestine and bringing the dawn of the kingdom of God in great power.

Application

The power of dawn is astounding. A world that is segmented and individualized by its reliance on senses other than sight, a world that is robbed of depth perception and color, a world that is threatening because of its hidden weapons is suddenly overthrown. Those with eyes to see it coming are forewarned by the graying eastern sky. But soon all are entranced by its pervasive presence. Daylight creates space, distributes color, organizes area, and allows for community. While night robs us of the use of some of our senses and buries us in the land of sleep, day calls us to rise in glory and return to life.

Isaiah's portrait of day dawning was a metaphor for the coming kingdom of God. One day, he predicted, the world that had grown dark and cold because the light of God's glory had been dimmed in Israel, would glow again with divine power. Interestingly, during the exact period of time that ancient Israel was losing its sense of self and its place of witness in Palestine, seven of the major religions of the world were beginning to emerge. In other words, exactly as the peoples of the ancient world set out in their wanderings to find a religious light that would penetrate the darkness of their perspectives and understandings, the light of God's glory went out in Israel. Only with the coming of Jesus would the light return (as Matthew says).

Furthermore, whenever the light of Jesus is dimmed in the church, its members fragment over secondary issues (as Paul declares) and its witness is diminished. The light goes out. The darkness overtakes things again.

Today is a great day to remind our people what it means to see the light of the world (Jesus) and to live in the light. MacDonald's story carries with it the power of moving from the world of darkness into the kingdom of light, hand in hand with the one who belongs to the day and the light.

Alternative Applications

1) Isaiah 9:1-4; 1 Corinthians 1:10-18; Matthew 4:12-23. The Isaiah and Matthew passages are easy to tie together. Matthew has already joined them in his direct quotation of Isaiah's prophecy.

What is more difficult is fitting the Corinthians passage into the same theme. It does fit, but only if the larger context of Paul's use of dark and light metaphors is taken into account.

It is certainly possible to focus on Paul's teachings to the Corinthian church on their own. A good approach would be to focus on one or more of the dimensions of fragmentation in our current politically charged ecclesiastical environment, and compare these to the splintering of the Corinthian congregation. Some possibilities include:

• Denominational divisions that mute the church's witness (such as "Catholic" and "Protestant" at odds in Northern Ireland; theological judgments made by some groups over against different communions);
• Tensions between churches dominated by different racial or ethnic groups;
• Divisions within denominations over theological emphases that become labeled as "liberal," "progressive," "moderate," "conservative," "fundamentalist," or "reactionary";

- Failure to work together for a community's good by neighboring congregations of different denominations; and
- The tragedy of "worship wars" that rip through congregations and cause bitterness to replace common joy and witness.

The Isaiah and Matthew passages could be used to show the effects of such divisions by comparing them to what happened in ancient Israel — the lights went out in God's great temple and the nations were left to wander in the darkness.

2) Matthew 4:12-23. The Matthew passage has the powerful story of Jesus' call of his first four disciples. Since we are still very early in this new year, it might be possible to use Jesus' call and the response of the disciples to challenge people about their "New Year's resolutions." In a sense, the best of our New Year's resolutions are intended to help us follow Jesus more closely. How are we doing? Where do we hear the call of Jesus? Have we decided to follow Jesus and are we keeping at it? How long do the new dawn's resolutions last, and how will we ensure that they keep current in our lives? Where is Jesus saying today, "Repent, for the kingdom of heaven is near!"?

Epiphany 4
Ordinary Time 4
Micah 6:1-8
1 Corinthians 1:18-31
Matthew 5:1-12
by David Kalas

Of simplicity and simpletons

We have a prejudice in favor of things complex. Not that we necessarily desire complexity, but somehow we trust it more. We figure that complexity is the prevailing reality in our world, and so we feel obliged to be in touch with it. We would love to hear that this thing or that is really quite simple, but doctors, politicians, futurists, ethicists, economists — and even some preachers — keep discouraging us. It's actually quite complicated, we are told, and there is no simple answer.

In our world, complexity is exalted over simplicity. The person who offers a simple solution is the person who has not grasped the complexity of the problem. Complex organisms are more highly evolved than simple ones. "Go Fish" is simple; chess is complex.

In response, we continually fall into the trap — as individuals and as institutions — of making things too complicated. No one wants to be the simpleton who falls for the simple solution.

Much of the teaching of scripture, however, is really quite simple. As such, it meets with disdain in the world. But that simplicity, we discover, is the wisdom of God.

Micah 6:1-8

As a rule, prophets appear in the land like white blood cells; their presence is not the problem, but it indicates a problem. This particular prophet, Micah, appeared on the scene in the ninth century, which was the age of the great judgment prophets (Isaiah and Micah in the south, Amos and Hosea in the north). Their presence indicates a problem, and the problem exists in the relationship between God and his people (both Israel and Judah).

From time to time, we take our relationship troubles to some outside arbiter. The husband and wife see a marriage counselor, or perhaps, they end up before a judge in family court. The dissatisfied player and his team enter binding arbitration. Two countries engaged in peace talks or negotiations invite an impartial third-party into the process to help. And so, here in the message of Micah, God takes his issues with his people to an outside observer. Who is available for such a post? The mountains and the foundations of the earth are invited to hear the case between God and his people.

The people had abandoned God and so he begins making his case by asking what he had done wrong, how he had in any way mistreated them. In his own defense, God reminds the people what he had done for them in the past, and specifically rehearses for them some of the details from their salvation history — events recorded particularly in Exodus and Numbers.

It's an interesting tactic for God to take. It is surely his prerogative to insist on his will and to recite his people's guilt. Instead, he condescends to reason with the people, even to beg them. Rather than firing a barrage of what the people have done wrong, God asks instead what he has done wrong. The answer, of course, is nothing, which makes it an effective device. But God's approach is more than a strategy; it is a symbol. It represents to his people the nature of his love for them and his primary desire to restore a right relationship with them.

As the text reads, God's case elicits a human response. It is not attributed to any particular human being, it is written in the first-person singular, and as such does not seem to represent the response of the nation as a whole. Perhaps Micah is suggesting what our right and reasonable response to God's word ought to be in this case. Micah proposes what the people should say much like the mother who coaches a "Thank you" out of her child by asking, "What do you say?"

The proposed human response is a poetic and heartfelt series of questions expressing the bewilderment of a penitent human being wondering what to do next. It is Isaiah's "woe is me" (6:5) in the presence of God's glory and holiness. It is the prodigal son in the moments before he formulates his plan to return home.

Then Micah adds a third voice — presumably his own — to the passage. If the first verses are God speaking, and the middle verses are spoken by some imagined representative of the people, then the final verses are the prophet's words. He refers to God in the third person and to human beings in the second person. He is the priest on the other side of the confessional booth, encouraging the lost soul in the way.

The final verse of this passage, of course, is arguably the most familiar part of the prophet Micah's book. Indeed, I expect we have folks in our churches who couldn't tell you or me a thing about Micah, but who could fill in the blanks if we said, "What does the Lord require of you but to...."

Micah's response about simple, godly living stands in deliberate contrast to an emphasis on ritual. It is reminiscent of passages from some of Micah's contemporaries (see Isaiah 1:10-17; 58:1-7; Amos 5:21-25), Samuel's terse correction of Saul (1 Samuel 15:22), and numerous teachings and sayings of Jesus that elevate living with integrity above superficial religiosity and acts of piety that are unaccompanied by real charity, compassion, and justice.

1 Corinthians 1:18-31

In *The Poseidon Adventure*, the 1972 disaster movie about a group of passengers trying to survive and escape a capsized luxury ocean liner, there is an eerie scene where two groups of would-be survivors cross paths. The one group — the one that the audience follows through the movie and the one that ultimately survives — is traveling a corridor going one way. The other, equally determined group, however, is pursuing a different route down a perpendicular corridor. In the end, we realize that this other group's chosen course was doomed.

The two groups briefly see one another in passing, and they make their appeals to each another. But no one from either group changes course. In each case, the one group's plan of escape seems like nonsense to the other group. It appears that the course chosen by the people who ultimately survived was "foolishness to those who are perishing." To those who took the right course, however, it was their salvation.

So it is that Paul, like us, encounters the world around him and discovers a strange antagonism to the gospel. It is good news and it is salvation, yet it is treated so often as irrelevant nonsense. "To us who are being saved," it is precious and life-changing, and so we are surprised and confused by the world's indifference or opposition to it, but Paul explains the disconnect here.

The apostle Paul summarizes what different folks look for. The "Jews demand signs and Greeks desire wisdom."

We surely see the Jews' demand for signs in the gospel accounts of Jesus' life and ministry. The crowds follow — indeed, pursue — Jesus the miracle-worker all over Galilee because of his signs (such as John 6:2). He often discourages those who have benefited from his miracles from telling about them, though no one seems to cooperate. The crowds are especially drawn to the possibilities they see when Jesus fed the 5,000 (John 6:14-15). Herod was spectator-curious to see some sign from Jesus (Luke 23:8). Jesus repeatedly chided the people of his day for demanding or needing a sign (such as Mark 8:11-12; John 6:2). And signs were important enough to the people that it became a problem for Jesus' opponents (John 11:47-48).

Since the spotlight of scripture is on the Jews rather than the Greeks, we do not see so much biblical evidence of their characteristic quest for wisdom (although Acts does make an almost scornful reference to their fondness for new ideas in 17:21). Even without the testimony of scripture, however, the ancient Greeks' love of wisdom — our word "philosophy" comes from a compound Greek word meaning "lover of wisdom" — is legendary.

Paul's world was divided into those two camps — Jews and Greeks — and each had its own thing for which it was looking. I wonder if our world is so easily and neatly divided. I wonder if we have people whose desires correspond to those cited by Paul when considering the Jews and the Greeks. I wonder if how we, in American Christianity, do evangelism and worship reflects our efforts to meet those different desires.

Is our Christian apologetics for the "Greeks"? Is our experiential worship for the "Jews"? Are we still, like Paul, taking the gospel to folks who either want to be persuaded or shown? Either folks who need to grasp it with their minds or folks who need to see it with their eyes?

Paul has sized up his audiences: He knows what each one is looking for. What does God provide in response to those audiences? God supplies the message of Christ crucified, which Paul admits is "foolishness to the Greeks" and "a stumbling block to the Jews."

In other places and many settings, Paul endeavors to prove Christ to both Jews and Gentiles. For the present, however, he is willing to concede that the message of the cross is an unwelcome misfit in both groups. Yet still, he insists, there is a higher order.

The cross may be foolishness, but it is God's foolishness, and that trumps even the best human wisdom. The cross may seem like weakness, but it is God's weakness and that dwarfs all human strength. Perhaps, by way of analogy, Paul is saying "that star in the night sky may look small and faint to you here on earth, but in reality it is bigger and brighter than anything you've ever seen!" So, too, with Christ and the cross. At a distance, from the perspective of this world, it seems foolish and weak. Once we come to know it up close and personal, however, it outshines all else.

Matthew 5:1-12

My recollection is that I saw the "Beatitudes" in churches a lot when I was a child. They were displayed in hallways, parlors, and Sunday school rooms. Perhaps the Ten Commandments were somewhat more common in the classrooms, but the "Beatitudes" appeared more frequently in the other, social parts of the church. I remember them being a favorite subject of needlepoint, and I recall them often being accompanied by some very peaceful portrait of Jesus teaching on a green hillside, perhaps with children near at hand.

Now that I read the "Beatitudes" as an adult, however, I think that they should be accompanied by a portrait that is upside down.

The music of a song ought to fit the lyrics. I wonder, therefore, what sort of tune we would choose to accompany the lyrics of the "Beatitudes." The pictures that I associate with the passage from my childhood suggest almost a lullaby, but I think the music ought to be much more disturbing. The recurring motif of "blessed" is surely a tranquil start to each movement, but it is so often followed by a kind of harsh discord: poor in spirit, hunger and thirst, persecution, reviling, and all kinds of evil. As the inharmonious elements crescendo, they are matched by a swell of bold and joyful chords, climaxing with a great "rejoice and be glad."

The "Beatitudes" have a deliberately upside-down quality to them, for Jesus is inviting a kind of kingdom re-think. From the categories of people who are commendable (the merciful, the pure in heart, the peacemakers) to experiences that are downright undesirable (mourning, persecution, having evil spoken falsely against one), Jesus is encouraging a reevaluation of just who in this world is truly blessed, who is happy, who is fortunate, and so on.

That is a recurring challenge in Jesus' teaching, of course. The "first will be last" theme (such as Matthew 19:30; 20:16; Mark 9:35), the story of the rich man and Lazarus (Luke 16:19-31), and the repeated invitation to humility and servitude (Matthew 18:4; Mark 10:43; John 13:12-16) all encourage Jesus' followers to turn the world's paradigm upside down. The broader context for that paradigm shift is the kingdom of God.

The theme of God's kingdom is central to Jesus' teachings, and that kingdom exists both in the midst of, and in contrast to, this world. So much of what follows the "Beatitudes" in Jesus' ethical teachings contained in the "Sermon on the Mount" reflect the dramatic contrast between how this world works and how kingdom-living works. The "Beatitudes" serve as an introduction to that contrast, for they turn the assumptions of the present world upside down.

The passage we call the "Beatitudes" consists of nine "blessed are" statements. Six of the nine (poor in spirit, meek, hunger and thirst for righteousness, merciful, pure in heart, and peacemakers) relate to what qualities should characterize kingdom people. The other three (mourn, persecuted, and reviled plus) relate to the experiences of kingdom people in this world.

"Blessed" — or, as some translations have it, "happy" — seems like nonsense in several contexts. Happy are the poor in spirit? Happy are those who mourn? Happy are those who are persecuted? It seems strange that such twaddle should be widely displayed in church hallways, parlors, and classrooms. But what seems like nonsense to the world is the experience and testimony of the kingdom.

In his 1990 album, *For the Sake of the Call*, Christian singer and songwriter Steven Curtis Chapman marveled at the improbable and inexplicable joy of a Christian: "What kind of joy is this / That counts it a blessing to suffer / What kind of joy is this / That gives the prisoner his song / What kind of joy could stare death in the face / And see it as sweet victory / This is the joy of a soul that's forgiven and free."

So it is that there is a promised reward and an abiding joy for kingdom people. Some of the characteristics — meek, pure in heart, peacemaker — may not be the keys to getting ahead in this world, but they have a sure reward in the kingdom. And blessing is guaranteed in such unexpected places as mourning, persecution, and unfair, undeserved mistreatment.

Most of the statements — the first eight — are third-person references. When Jesus arrives at the final statement, however, he makes it personal: "Blessed are you...." It is both more personal and more elaborate. While all of the other statements are simple and brief, this final, personalized statement is much longer and more detailed. The trebled layering of images — "revile you," "persecute you," "utter all kinds of evil against you" — is reminiscent of the Hebrew poetry found in the Psalms. It also has the effect of making the statement emphatic.

The other personalization of the final beatitude is that Jesus introduces himself into the picture too. Just as it is the first occurrence of "you," it is also the first occurrence of "my" in the "Beatitudes." The prior statement (v. 10) about being persecuted was "for righteousness' sake," but here (v. 11) it is persecution "on my account." So it is that our kingdom living is, ultimately, very personal business. It is not theoretical and detached. Rather, it is us for him and us with him.

Application

The final verse of the Micah passage is a monument to simplicity. In our despair over our own sinfulness, in the midst of being overwhelmed by all the requirements of the law, Micah distills godly living down to three simple statements: "to do justice, and to love kindness, and to walk humbly with your God."

Six-hundred-and-some commandments I cannot remember. Layers and centuries of interpretation and application is more than I can digest. But these three, simple keys I can remember, I can understand, and I can repeat.

When it is all boiled down, we discover that it is really quite simple. Not easy, but simple. Not simplistic, but simple. And, it is the wisdom of God.

But the world does not understand and recognize the wisdom of God.

In our discussion of the "Beatitudes," we noted that perhaps they should be accompanied by a picture that is upside down, for that is how the "Beatitudes" — and, for that matter, the kingdom — seem in this world. In the end, however, we will discover that it was God's way that was right-side-up all along. It is this world that has lost its compass and doesn't know which way is up.

Paul, too, recognizes that this confused world scoffs at the wisdom of God. But that scoffing does not deny or refute it.

It has been said that when it comes to great masterpieces, we do not judge the art; the art judges us. If I raise an eyebrow at Mozart or question the talent of Michelangelo, they are not diminished; rather, my taste and judgment are shown to be poor.

Likewise, the world's failure to grasp and embrace the wisdom and word of God is not a reflection on God. It is a reflection on the world.

"He has told you, O mortal, what is good" (Micah 6:8). It may seem simple. It may seem upside down. It may seem foolish and weak. But when we get it up close and personal, it is the biggest and brightest thing we've ever seen.

An Alternative Application
Micah 6:1-8. The Micah lection cuts to the heart of how we, as the people of God, ought to live. What is our motivation for doing what we do? What animates us? What are our guidelines, our governing principles?

In our fallen condition, we are motivated by selfish things — the appetites of our bodies and the cravings of our egos. Remnant traces of the image in which we were originally created urge us higher, and we find that we are sometimes motivated by love, compassion, or justice. We are motivated to do some things for others even when there is no benefit to ourselves.

The passage from Micah, meanwhile, calls us to a still higher pair of motivations. Motivations that originate with God rather than with self. At the end of the passage, there is the issue of what God demands — "What does the Lord require of you...?" (v. 8). And perhaps somewhat obscured at the beginning of the passage, there is the lovely issue of what God deserves — "What have I done to you? In what have I wearied you?" (v. 3).

Let me make these my sweet and simple guidelines. Let me be animated and motivated by these: What my holy God demands, and what my loving, saving God deserves.

Epiphany 5
Ordinary Time 5
Isaiah 58:1-9a (9b-12)
1 Corinthians 2:1-12 (13-16)
Matthew 5:13-20
by Wayne Brouwer

Internal medicine

Some years ago *Europa Times* carried a story in which Mussa Zoabi of Israel claimed to be the oldest person alive at 160. *Guinness Book of World Records* would not print his name, however, simply because his age could not be verified. Mr. Zoabi was older than most records-keeping systems. Whatever his true age, Mussa Zoabi believed he knew the secret of longevity. He said, "Every day I drink a cup of melted butter or olive oil."

Doesn't that sound like a great diet? Diets are quite the rage. Everybody has a special diet. One says his diet can cure cancer. Another promises to reduce your weight and then to keep those extra pounds off.

Already in ancient times there were diets that supposedly turned on the sex hormones and made a person incredibly irresistible. Most of us know the truth and the lies about dieting and for that reason, perhaps, think we know all about the issue of fasting that scripture raises. Fasting sounds a lot like dieting. You stop eating for a while, or at least you slow down, and you do it for a noble cause (even if it is just to fit into those slacks again!).

But fasting is not dieting. Neither is fasting like the hunger strikes we read about now and again. Comedian Dick Gregory, for instance, used to stage hunger strikes in protest of the Vietnam War. The mayor of Cork, Ireland, died of a hunger strike against English rule in the 1920s, giving rise to much larger protests. History repeated itself in the 1980s, when Irish political prisoners in Maze Prison, near Belfast, carried on widely publicized hunger strikes. Several died in their protests against England. Again during the days of the Cold War when tension tightened in the old Soviet Union, some of the Jewish people who weren't able to get exit visas went on hunger strikes. The media turned on the spotlights, and the Soviet government was forced to comply.

While it is true that hunger strikes can be powerful tools for peaceful resistance in our societies, especially where they have "religious" motives, biblical fasting is actually something else. This is particularly true in our passage today from Isaiah's prophecy. But the New Testament and gospel readings as well focus on the spirituality of hunger and poverty in which denial is great gain. It is, indeed, a very good "internal medicine."

Isaiah 58:1-9a (9b-12)

In the biblical world there were three specific reasons why people fasted. The first was repentance. You fasted because you sinned. You fasted because you did something wrong. You fasted to say to God: "I'm really sorry!"

When my older sister first got her driver's license, she suddenly knew how to drive! That summer we were going to go on a long trip together as a family. The day before we were leaving, Jean asked if she could wash the car and get it ready for the travels. It was a nice thought, of course, but what she really wanted was a chance to drive the car.

We lived on a farm out in the Minnesota countryside and the garage was really an ancient horse buggy barn with very small doors. The car could barely squeeze in. Mom and Dad had told her so often, "Make sure you check behind you when you back up! Be careful for anyone else who might be there!"

So Jean got in the car and started it. She stepped on the brake and slipped the gear shift into reverse. Then she turned around and looked back to make sure there was no one behind. She let off the brake and revved the engine. And, as she looked back she turned the wheel!

SCREEEEEEEECH! She proved the law of physics: Two bodies of matter cannot occupy the same place at the same time! The left front fender is wrapped around the doorjamb on the garage.

I'll never forget what Jean did then: She jumped out of the car crying and shouting at the top of her voice, "I'm so sorry! I'm so sorry! I'll stay home! I won't go on vacation!"

She was saying what we all need to say sometimes: If you do something wrong you need to make amends and that might include giving up something significant to you. So it is with fasting. Great King David fasted after he did his thing with Bathsheba. When God checked in with David through Nathan the prophet, David collapsed in grief. "What have I done?" he wept. "How did I get myself into this? Where did I sell my soul to turn this corner?" That's when David fasted. He fell on the floor of his room in prayer and repentance, and he would eat no food until God resolved the matter with him. That's why people fast! They know just how deep sin sinks into their lives, and they know that without the struggles of pain in the body there is sometimes no struggle of agony in the spirit.

The Bible tells us of other fasts like that. King Ahab fasted in repentance before God after he and Jezebel stole Naboth's reputation, life, and property. The people of Nineveh fasted in repentance to God after Jonah shouted his warning through the city streets. Fasting was even built into the regular rhythm of Israel's life as a nation. There was the annual Day of Atonement when the whole nation fasted and prayed. They had a sense that it was possible to flit through life too carelessly without taking stock of the grit of sin that sticks to the soles of our feet, as the writer of Hebrews described it, and the tether of evil that snags our hearts at inopportune moments.

The second reason people fasted in Bible times was to remember. When King Saul and Prince Jonathan died in battle with the Philistines, David, who took up the reins of power, called the nation of Israel to a day of fasting because something tragic had happened. When tragedy strikes, only the careless and the cowardly and the callous are unmoved. "No man is an island," said John Donne. "Any man's death diminishes me, because I am involved in humankind!"

Daniel fasted when he remembered the destruction of Jerusalem and the loss of his people's homeland. In Jesus' day there was an annual fast to remember the holocaust that nearly wiped out the Hebrew race when the hordes of Babylon swept down from the hills of Ephraim.

Fasting showed solidarity. Fasting declared shared involvement. Fasting said: "What happened was tragic, and I will not forget the pain of it!"

The third reason people fasted during biblical times was to rivet attention on God. When Queen Esther had to go to her husband, Persian King Xerxes, to plead for the life of her people, she asked her friends to fast with her. She couldn't do something like that without getting in tune with the spiritual dimensions of her soul.

In a similar incident, when Ezra was about to lead a contingent of Jews across the desert wastes to Jerusalem, they prepared well by gathering food for the journey, obtaining letters of legal documentation, and organizing the travel groups. But when they had finished their other preparations they fasted together for several days, riveting their attention on God, whose leading they hoped to follow.

Jesus fasted for forty days before he started his public ministry! Can you imagine that? The very Son of God fasted in order to get in touch with his own father!

In Acts 13 we find Paul and Barnabas fasting and praying, and the whole congregation at Antioch with them, in order to find the future directions of the ministry God was calling them to. Fasting helps people get in touch with God.

That is precisely what the word of God is about here in Isaiah 58. The people may have been practicing ritual fasts, but their hearts were not in it. Only when they got back to the real reasons for fasting would they find God once again. And only then would they begin to live out the justice and righteousness of God in society.

1 Corinthians 2:1-12 (13-16)

There is an ancient legend first told by Christians living in the catacombs under the streets of Rome picturing the day when Jesus went back to glory after finishing all his work on earth. The angel Gabriel meets Jesus in heaven and welcomes him home. "Lord," he says, "who have you left behind to carry on your work?"

Jesus tells him about the disciples, the little band of fishermen and farmers and housewives.

"But Lord," says Gabriel, "what if they fail you? What if they lose heart or drop out? What if things get too rough for them, and they let you down?"

"Well," says Jesus, "then all I've done will come to nothing!"

"But don't you have a backup plan?" Gabriel asks. "Isn't there something else to keep it going, to finish your work?"

"No," says Jesus, "there's no backup plan. The church is it. There's nothing else."

"Nothing else?" says Gabriel. "But what if they fail?"

And the early Christians knew Jesus' answer. "They won't fail, Gabriel," he said. "They won't fail!"

Isn't that a marvelous thing? Here are the Christians of Rome, dug into the earth like gophers, tunneling out of sight because of the terrors of Nero up above. They're nothing in that world! They're poor, despised, and insignificant! Yet they know the promise of Jesus: "You won't fail! You're my people, and you won't fail!"

That's what Paul tells us in these verses, doesn't he? "When I came to you, I did not come with eloquence or superior wisdom," he says. "I came to you in weakness and fear, with much trembling." Why? So that the true power of God might be revealed.

Tony Campolo once told of a friend of his who was walking through the midway at a county fair when he met a tiny girl. She was carrying a great big fluff of cotton candy on a stick, almost as larger as herself! He said to her, "How can a little girl like you eat all that cotton candy?"

"Well," she said to him, "I'm really much bigger on the inside than I am on the outside!"

That's essentially what Paul is saying here. On the outside we seem to be nothing, but on the inside we are as big as the kingdom and the power and the glory of our God. Says Paul, "This is what we speak, not in words taught us by human wisdom but in words taught by the Spirit, expressing spiritual words." Indeed.

Matthew 5:13-20

Can salt lose its saltiness? Is it possible for salt to become unsalty? Not really. Any chemistry teacher will tell you that. Sodium chloride is one of the most stable compounds in the whole of the universe. It doesn't change. It doesn't lose its character.

Still there is truth to what Jesus is saying. Much of the salt used in Palestine came from the area around the Dead Sea, which at more than a mile-and-a-half *below* sea-level, is the lowest land area in the world. The waters of the Sea of Galilee flow into the Jordan River and run down there to the bottom of the earth. Once they get there, it's the end of the line. There's no place to go. The hot desert sun evaporates the water and leaves behind a chunky white powder made up of a combination of salts and minerals.

That powder contains enough salt to season meat or to add a little flavor to soup. For that reason the people of Palestine have always scooped it up to use in trade and in cooking. But the salt is mixed with minerals. It's not pure sodium chloride. Indeed, it is possible, under certain circumstances, with a little dampness in the air, for the salts to be dissolved first and leached away.

You may not notice it. What you have left looks the same, yet the taste is gone, and people throw it out. There may be a little salt left, but it isn't enough to make a difference, so the whole batch is chucked out into the street.

The comparison point Jesus makes, in essence, is that strength is found in community. A single grain of salt may make a slight difference, but it takes the concentration of a cluster of them to make a real impact. Similarly, one disciple with a sense of purpose may make a statement in the world, but it's the community of Christians that turns the world upside down.

Besides the power of flavor there was an even greater strength of salt in the world of Jesus' day. Salt was used to confirm agreements, seal treaties, and establish covenants. If you ate salt with someone, you became blood relatives. You had a stake in each other's lives. You were part of the same family.

King Abijah, in the Old Testament, reminds the people that they made a "treaty of salt" with David, and therefore they can't break it. The enemies of the Jews, in the book of Ezra, write a letter to King Artaxerxes of Persia, telling him that they will be his servants forever because they have eaten salt from his treasuries. They are his servants, confirmed by eating his salt.

In Arabic, the word for "salt" is the same word as the word for "treaty." Similarly, in Persian, the word for traitor means "someone who is faithless to salt." Such an idea resonates with what Jesus gives us here. "You are the salt of the earth!" he says. You are the essence of God's relationship with the world around you. The church isn't just a little community off by itself somewhere. It is the confirmation that God still has an interest in our world!

The apostle Peter picks up that same theme in 2 Peter 3. He says there is enough evil in society and enough wickedness in our world for God to let loose the fires of his judgment. But he's not going to do that yet, says Peter, because he has people living throughout the whole wide world, and they make a difference. They confirm his relationship with his world. They are the salt of the earth!

What would our neighborhood be without us? What would our area be like without the church of Jesus Christ? Where would our nation be without the conscience of the people of God? "You are the salt of the earth!" says Jesus. "You are the light of the world!" It's not enough to be anti-abortion; you must be pro-life and remind your community what real life, God's life, is all about! It's not enough to be against immorality; you have to be the conscience of society, turning its thoughts toward love and laughter and life! It's not enough to protect your own interests; you have to speak out for the welfare of the poor and the disabled and the oppressed!

It's not enough to be socially active, socially responsible, socially concerned. "Let your light shine before men," says Jesus here, "that they may see your good deeds and praise your Father in heaven!" Turn people's thoughts toward God, says Jesus. No mind is truly enlightened until it is flooded with the glory of heaven. No body is truly healed until it is touched by the power of the Creator. No person is truly set free until there is freedom of the Spirit of Christ. And this is how it happens: "… that they may see your good deeds, and glorify your Father in heaven!" That's great internal medicine!

Application

There's a marvelous little story tucked away in the pages of Edward Gibbon's seven-volume work, *The Decline and Fall of the Roman Empire*. It tells of a humble little monk named Telemachus living out in the farming regions of Asia.

Telemachus had no great ambitions in life. He loved his little garden and tilled it through the changing seasons. But one day in the year 391, he felt a sense of urgency, a call of God's direction in his life. Although he didn't know why, he felt that God wanted him to go to Rome, the heart and soul of the empire. In fact, the feelings of such a call frightened him, but he went anyway, praying along the way for God's direction.

When he finally got to the city, it was in an uproar! The armies of Rome had just come home from the battlefield in victory and the crowds were turning out for a great celebration. They flowed through the streets like a tidal wave, and Telemachus was caught in their frenzy and carried into the Coliseum.

He had never seen a gladiator contest before but now his heart sickened. Down in the arena men hacked at each other with swords and clubs. The crowds roared at the sight of blood and urged their favorites on to the death.

Telemachus couldn't stand it. He knew it was wrong; this wasn't the way God wanted people to live or to die. So little Telemachus worked his way through the crowds to the wall down by the arena. "In the name of Christ, forbear!" he shouted.

Nobody heard him, so he crawled up onto the wall and shouted again: "In the name of Christ, forbear!" This time the few who heard him only laughed. But Telemachus was not to be ignored. He jumped into the arena and ran through the sands toward the gladiators. "In the name of Christ, forbear!"

The crowds laughed at the silly little man and threw stones at him. Telemachus, however, was on a mission. He threw himself between two gladiators to stop their fighting. "In the name of Christ, forbear!" he cried.

They hacked him apart! They cut his body from shoulder to stomach, and he fell onto the sand with the blood running out of his life.

The gladiators were stunned and stopped to watch him die. Then the crowds fell back in silence, for a moment, no one in the Coliseum moved. Telemachus' final words rang in their memories: "In the name of Christ, forbear!" At last they moved, slowly at first, but growing in numbers. The masses of Rome filed out of the Coliseum that day, and the historian Theodoret reports that *never again* was a gladiator contest held there! All because of the witness and the testimony of a single Christian who had the power of the internal medicine of grace and God's goodness.

An Alternative Application
Matthew 5:13-20. During the time of the Reformation John Foxe of England was impressed by the testimony of the early Christians. He gleaned the pages of early historical writings and wrote a book that has become a classic in the church, *Foxe's Book of Martyrs*.

One story he tells is about an early church leader named Lawrence. Lawrence acted as a pastor for a church community. He also collected the offerings for the poor each week.

A band of thieves found out that Lawrence received the offerings of the people from Sunday to Sunday, so one night as he was taking a stroll, they grabbed him and demanded the money. He told them that he didn't have it and that he had already given it all to the poor. They didn't believe him and told him they would give him a chance to find it. In three days they would come to his house and take from him the treasures of the church.

Three days later they did come. But Lawrence wasn't alone. The house was filled with the people of his congregation. When the thieves demanded the treasures of the church, Lawrence smiled. He opened wide his arms and gestured to those who sat around him. "Here's the treasure of the church!" he said. "Here's the treasure of God that shines in the world!"

Indeed. You are the salt of the earth. You are the light of the world. You can make a difference together in the world for God!

Epiphany 6
Ordinary Time 6
Deuteronomy 30:15-20
1 Corinthians 3:1-9
Matthew 5:21-37
by David Kalas

Heart condition

As a middle-aged man, I am forced to be conscious of my heart health. And if I try to overlook the subject, I discover that both my doctor and my wife restore my focus.

A person cannot neglect the condition of his or her heart, for it is a matter of life and death. If I am careless with my eyes, my teeth, or my skin, I will pay a price, but it won't likely cost me my life. If, on the other hand, I am careless about my heart health, then all the rest will no longer matter.

Just as the heart is central to our physical health, so it is also the key to our spiritual well-being. We're not speaking any more, of course, about the muscular organ that pumps our blood. Instead, we have in view that mysterious inner part of a human being, which is the seat of our loves and allegiances, our personality and our nature.

Because the heart is so important, it behooves the Christian to be attentive to it. And the passages of scripture we will consider together this week may prove diagnostic as we contemplate the condition of our hearts.

Deuteronomy 30:15-20

It is a testimony to the mercy of God that we are presented with a choice.

In the beginning, in the Garden of Eden, the Lord presented Adam and Eve with a choice between life and death. He had given them life, and he surrounded them with all that they needed to nourish and enjoy that life. At the same time, there was in their midst a cause of death and the Lord warned them about it. They had a choice between life and death, and God urged them to choose life.

Having made the choice that they did — the choice that we human beings chronically seem to make — you would think that the Creator might leave his errant creatures to face the consequences of their choices. "They made their own bed," he might reasonably say, abandoning them to their own waywardness.

Yet that is not the case. He is unwilling to leave us lost, as exemplified by the story of the good shepherd (Luke 15:4-6) and articulated by the one who claimed to be the good shepherd (Luke 19:10). And so he does not relegate us to our fatal foolishness. Mercifully, he keeps presenting us with a choice.

We see the pattern throughout the scriptures. Joshua gave the people a choice in his farewell address (24:14-15). Elijah gave the people a choice in his famous showdown with the priests and prophets of Baal (1 Kings 18:21). And wisdom offers us a choice at every fork in life's road (Proverbs 8:1-11).

Likewise here, in our Old Testament reading, Moses gave the people a choice. In a sense, of course, it is always the same choice in every instance.

On the one hand, there is God's way. Moses characterizes that way in three imperatives: love God, obey his commands, and walk in his ways. In the spirit of Hebrew poetry, these are not necessarily three separate and distinct ideas, but rather a kind of elaboration. To love him is to obey him, and to obey him is to walk in his ways. If the people will choose that path, then Moses guarantees the goodness of the destination to which it leads. "Life and prosperity" wait at the end of this road. The nation will grow and the people will enjoy God's blessings.

On the other hand, there is a way of living that is not God's way and that is always an option as well. Interestingly, Moses also characterizes that way in terms of three images: the people's hearts turning away, the people not hearing, and the people being led astray to worship other gods. Sin always begins in the heart, and so that's where Moses points first. The next image — "you do not hear" — suggests a people who are unresponsive to correction. God sought to intercede with Cain when darkness filled his heart (Genesis 4:5b-7), but Cain did not heed God's words, so it might be that the people will fail (or refuse) to hear what God says to them. Then those wayward hearts and closed ears combine to issue forth in a people who are easily led into the bondage of serving other gods. And that path, according to Moses, will result in God's own people perishing.

The stakes are life and death. This is not merely the relative earning power of having or not having a college degree. This choice marks the dramatic difference between the sort of abundant life that characterizes God's will for his people from beginning to end, on the one hand, and the comprehensive misery that comes from moving outside the boundaries of his blessing, on the other.

The life-or-death issue is not for Moses' immediate generation alone. Rather, what his contemporaries choose will impact generations to come, whether for better or for worse. So Moses exhorts them, saying, "Choose life so that you and your descendants may live." Just as John Donne famously declared that no man is an island, neither is any generation a self-contained unit. Each one is heir to its ancestors and each one leaves some sort of legacy to its descendants. So Moses encourages the people to leave a legacy of life.

Finally, one more recurring theme within the passage — a part of what is at stake — is "the land." We will give that separate attention below.

1 Corinthians 3:1-9

We have a 29-chapter peek into Paul's relationship to the church at Corinth. Other than Ephesus, the apostle spent more time in Corinth, it seems, than any other single missionary outpost. He knew them well and his correspondence with them suggests to us that they were something of a high-maintenance congregation. The Corinthian church presented Paul with a great many questions, issues, and problems to address, and we are richer so many centuries later that they evoked such a volume of counsel, instruction, and correction from the apostle.

No one welcomes the label of "immature" and least of all people who fancy themselves rather advanced. We surmise from Paul's later discussion about the gifts of the Spirit (1 Corinthians 12-14) that the Christians in Corinth may have suffered a bit from spiritual self-importance. Because they were so accomplished in what they (perhaps wrongly) assumed were the truly important and impressive gifts, they credited themselves with a great spiritual maturity. So Paul's words here must have been a real comeuppance, calling them "infants" and "people of the flesh."

For us or for our congregations, tongues and miracles may not be the source of spiritual pride but that doesn't mean it's not a problem. Perhaps for us the issue is education or money. Perhaps it is reputation or influence within the community. Perhaps it's our building, our staff, our programming, or our budget. Whatever the blessing, it can become for us a portal for pride, and so Paul's word to the Corinthians becomes a proper word for us, as well. "For as long as there is jealousy and quarreling among you, are you not of the flesh, and behaving according to human inclinations?" (v. 3).

We observe again and again in Proverbs how noxious to God — and how contrary to wisdom — is quarrelsomeness. It finds its source so often in ego and self, which work contrary to love, and therefore contrary to the will of God. We know that Jesus desired for his followers to be marked by unity (John 17:20-21) and characterized above all by love (John 13:35). For as long as we are bickering with one another, therefore, Paul says we're still spiritual babies and operating out of the flesh — that is, the sinful nature.

In the case of the Corinthians, the disputes came in the form of factions. Specifically, factions that had identified themselves with different significant leaders and influences within that church's experience.

The unwilling players in this rift are Paul and Apollos — and, we discover somewhat earlier, so are Peter and Christ (1 Corinthians 1:12)! Ironically, the people of Corinth have assigned to Paul and Apollos an importance they did not seek for themselves. They did not desire to be leaders of competitive movements or captains within a divided church. No, Paul recognizes that their true role is as "servants," and their only real importance is as those "through whom you came to believe."

This is no small importance, of course, for it is an eternal importance. How often, however, are we tempted to trade in eternal significance for a temporal one? Making an impact for eternity is all well and good, but we are so flattered when we find people rallying around us and according us an importance in the here-and-now. Paul is to be commended for keeping his eye on the ball in the midst of this particular Corinthian controversy. For rather than taking the opportunity of the letter to assert his own importance and bolster those who are on his "side," he focuses his attention and theirs on the bigger picture.

Finally the apostle moves to a metaphor, as he so often does, in order to illustrate his point. We are accustomed to agricultural imagery in Jesus' parables, while Paul generally looks elsewhere for his analogies. In this case, however, he sees that "bigger picture" as being like a field, very reminiscent of several of Jesus' kingdom teachings. And in that field, he and Apollos have a job to do, to be sure. Yet each task is essential, neither could succeed without the other, and neither is the final source of success, for that is God.

So while the Corinthians have — immaturely — used God's servants to form intramural squabbles, Paul insists that he and Apollos are actually teammates, "working together." And the bigger picture is that all of them — Paul, Apollos, and the Corinthian Christians — are all a part of what God himself is endeavoring to do.

Matthew 5:21-37

In my twenty years of pastoral ministry, I have met a lot of church folks who are carrying around in their minds some caricatures of the Old Testament and the New. The Old, they believe, is stern and harsh, while the New Testament is all love, grace, and forgiveness. The Old Testament is the rugged and fiery Mount Sinai, while the New is the gentle, green hills of Galilee. This perspective is nothing new, of course. All the way back in the second century, a guy named Marcion had already developed a whole system around this general impression.

The argument has so many facets. For our narrower purposes just now, though, we observe this: Can the Old Testament law possibly feature any requirements so demanding, so challenging as this excerpt from Jesus' Sermon on the Mount?

Jesus clearly has in mind the Old Testament law, along with the subsequent layers of tradition grown up on top of it, as he offers these teachings. "You have heard that it was said to those of ancient times," he begins, recalling a familiar excerpt from the Ten Commandments. He makes explicit reference to what they have heard said four more times in the passage. And, in every instance, he follows it with his word on the subject: "But I say to you...."

At first blush, it seems almost blasphemous. How does a person quote God's law, followed by "but"? How does a person recall what God has said, only to add, "But I say"?

If what Jesus went on to teach had contradicted the spirit of the law, or had even diminished the letter of it, we might raise an eyebrow. Instead, however, we discover that he has only intensified the law magnifying its spirit and faithfully cutting through to the very heart of the matter. When it comes to sin, of course, the heart of the matter is always the heart. This is our primary theme for the week.

Meanwhile, one of Jesus' primary themes in this selected lection is our relationship with other people. He begins with the subject of murder but moves quickly to the internal and driving concerns of anger and hate. And his solution is not mere repression. No teeth-gritting saints here. He does not just want his followers to keep their anger on a short leash, he wants reconciliation.

His instruction to "leave your gift there before the altar" must be translated for a twenty-first-century audience. The people of Jesus' day did not have a church on every corner. To take a gift to the altar was, for his listeners in Galilee, a several-day journey by foot. The prospect of making that trip, only to interrupt the act of worship in order to hustle home and make things right with some friend or relative, only then to return to Jerusalem and its altar was a dramatic one. It is marked by the same sort of hyperbole for effect as his later teaching about plucking out eyes and cutting off hands. Yet in each case, the extreme language serves to illustrate what is truly important to God. And, in this case, we sense that reconciliation between people is so important to him that our worship is unacceptable without it.

Jesus' emphasis on coming to terms with one's opponent (as opposed to our natural emphasis on defeating an opponent) resonates with Paul's against-the-grain counsel to the believers in Corinth (1 Corinthians 6:7). Furthermore, Jesus' counsel to settle "quickly" also reminds us of Paul's sense of urgency regarding interpersonal strife (Ephesians 4:26-27). We certainly see in our epistle passage how eager Paul is for the believers in Corinth to be marked by unity and peace, rather than division and strife.

Our listeners may be either amused or horrified by Jesus' instruction about how to handle the eye or hand that causes sin. At the same time, who can refute his logic? Would it not be better to enter the kingdom without a hand than to enter whole into the fires of hell? We don't believe that is actually the choice we face; yet it does put in perspective the no-nonsense way we are to deal with those things in our lives that undermine our faithfulness.

And no-nonsense is the tone that characterizes all of these teachings. While we may generalize about the sternness of the Old Testament, therefore, let us not overlook the still higher standards of holiness that Jesus sets for his followers in the New.

Application

We have noted above how Jesus' ethical teachings cut to the heart. The laws and traditions he cites were all designed to address sinful behavior. Yet for all the laws that endeavor to regulate behaviors, those behaviors are only what grow visibly above the surface. The root of every behavior, good or bad, is planted and nourished in the heart. So Jesus' teachings point to matters of the heart: anger, lust, reverence, integrity, and such.

Likewise, more than a millennium before Jesus' earthly ministry, Moses addressed the heart of the matter with the people under his care, as well. He cautioned them about their hearts turning away from the Lord, which reads like the first step toward every manner of trouble.

In our own individual Christian journeys, we may discover that real change happens from the inside out. We struggle to curb and control certain outward actions and habits, but they just keep recurring until our hearts are changed. You have to get a weed by the roots.

But how shall we effect such a change?

Fortunately, Moses gives us the answer and it turns out to be a simple one. In our day, we use the symbol for a heart to signify love. Indeed, on some T-shirts and bumper stickers, the heart symbol is used as a substitute for the word "love." And so it will be easy for us to remember the heart condition that is both our goal and our key: "loving the Lord your God."

An Alternative Application

Deuteronomy 30:15-20. "What comes after conquering." Perhaps you remember from your childhood this little rhyme: "Finders, keepers; losers, weepers." The saying is almost exclusively employed by the "finder," and it is usually recited rather uncharitably. We want to give a moment's consideration to that standard playground rule, however, because it includes a bit of wisdom that sheds some light on the words of Moses.

"Finders, keepers; losers, weepers." The saying assumes a certain paradigm: namely, that something of value originally belonged to Person A, but he misplaced it. When Person B finds it, then, it is rightfully his, and Person A is out of luck. The natural (albeit selfish) assumption is that Person B will keep for himself the valuable thing that he finds.

Finding a thing of worth, you see, is not the only part of having that thing. Once you have found it, you must also keep it. If you do not, then suddenly Person B turns into Person A. The finder becomes the loser. Because he failed to keep, he will weep.

That is the principle that was at stake for the children of Israel as Moses addressed them in the plains of Moab. They were about to find — or, in their case, to take — a thing of great value. Before them was the land flowing with milk and honey, promised to them and to their ancestors. The Israelites would be, at once, the agents of God's judgment on the wickedness of the inhabitants of the land (see Genesis 15:16; Leviticus 18:24-25) and the heirs of the promises made to Abraham, Isaac, and Jacob.

The land, however — this valuable find — needed to be kept. It was not sufficient simply to conquer the land or even to settle it. They had to keep it. And Moses knew that the Israelites, if they were not careful, might end up as the "losers, weepers."

As the people prepared to cross the Jordan and take the good land that God had in store for them, Moses gave them instructions about how to keep it. If the people will love and obey God, Moses promises, then he "will bless you in the land that you are entering to possess" (v. 16). Conversely, if they turn away from him and refuse correction, then "you shall not live long in the land that you are crossing the Jordan to enter and possess" (v. 18).

The land, you see, was not only God's promise and the people's destination; it was also part of what was at stake. For as formidable as the inhabitants of that land were, the Lord, Moses, and Joshua express complete certainty about the people's successful conquest of the land. What was more in question, it seems, was whether or not they would manage to keep what they conquered.

We recognize this theme from the beginning to the end of scripture. In the Garden of Eden, we see a desirable place that God had prepared for people, but they lost that place on account of their sin. Meanwhile, at the other end of scripture, we catch glimpses of the heavenly place that God has in mind for people, but we recognize that that good destination, too, is potentially lost to us by sin. In between, we have the story of the Israelites and the promised land. It is a most desirable land (see, for example, Numbers 13:27) and yet Moses puts them on notice here that the land could be lost by their sin.

The place that God has for his people is always at stake. And so we are urged to choose wisely: to choose life. Otherwise, "losers, weepers."

Epiphany 7
Ordinary Time 7
Leviticus 19:1-2, 9-18
1 Corinthians 3:10-11, 16-23
Matthew 5:38-48
by David Kalas

Tall order

Basketball fans who are thirty years old or older will remember watching Michael Jordan at his prime. And, in all likelihood, they will also recall the Gatorade advertising campaign built around him in 1992. The theme of the campaign, and the recurring motif of its catchy theme song, was "Be like Mike." The television commercial featured video of Jordan's fabulous feats on the basketball court, interspersed with winsome footage of him being playful, as well as children and youth on playgrounds and basketball courts striving to do what he does.

The prospect of being like Mike was most appealing. He was charismatic, successful, and a winner. I am sure that a whole generation of kids grew up wanting and hoping, indeed, to be like Mike. Even the professional basketball players in today's NBA, with all of their own individual accomplishments, are compared to him and occasionally asked to compare themselves to him. He remains the gold standard: to be like Mike.

For the average kid on a playground in the 1990s, however, Jordan was an improbable role model. For starters, most kids don't begin by being six-feet-six-inches tall and incredibly athletic. What chance do I have of being like Mike if I'm five-feet-eight-inches tall and a bit of a klutz? Add to his natural giftedness the coaching he enjoyed and the opportunities he received, and the fact is that a minute percentage of aspirants have any chance at all of ever being like Mike. Indeed, even the majority of professional basketball players cannot live up to the comparison.

Imagine, therefore, a typical high school basketball team. It has several passable players, a handful of good ones, and perhaps one or two very good ones. Yet the coach bears down hard on all of them. He shows them footage of Jordan in his prime. He immerses them in Jordan's statistics and achievements. And he challenges them — no, he requires them — to be like Mike. Every one of them.

That, we would say, is an unreasonably tall order.

Which brings us to this week's scripture readings. As we read and unpack these passages together, we will discover the theme that you and I, along with all the benchwarmers in our churches, are commanded to be, not like Mike, but like God.

Leviticus 19:1-2, 9-18

Most Christians have their favorite places to turn. We have those books, chapters, and verses we depend upon especially for guidance or comfort, for meaning or inspiration. I suspect that the psalms and the gospels are turned to most often; perhaps then certain parts of the epistles. It would be an interesting exercise to guess at your congregation's "top ten" list of Bible books or passages. And unless your people are very different from mine and from most, the book of Leviticus would not make that group of ten. Or twenty. Or perhaps even thirty.

This week's Old Testament lection comes from one of the least appreciated books in scripture. Many a soul's effort to read through the Bible cover-to-cover has foundered on the seemingly tedious and irrelevant rocks of Leviticus. When we announce that our Old Testament reading comes from that book, therefore, the news will likely be met with ignorance at best and resistance at worst.

Yet a closer look at this passage reveals profound meaning, remarkable beauty, and significant personal relevance.

The first observation to be made is the passage's recurring refrain: "I am the Lord." To the average reader, the repeated phrase seems like an awkward intrusion into the text. It appears, after all, to be a collection of instructions and the insertion of that statement does not seem to fit in its context. In truth, however, it fits in a very important way, and we will give more detailed attention to this phrase below.

The second observation we make as we read our passage is the variety of people who are guarded and relationships that are guided by these instructions. A mere listing includes "the poor and the alien," "your neighbor," "a laborer," "the deaf," "the blind," "the poor," "the great," "your kin," and "your people." Such is the breadth and depth of the law's concern. While it is sometimes unfairly criticized as primitive and chauvinistic, the truth is that the Old Testament law is remarkably sophisticated and balanced.

Included in that commendable balance is the instruction not to "be partial to the poor or defer to the great." Justice must not be contaminated by either special interest or by misplaced compassion. It is a standard we still struggle to define and to meet today; yet it was already established in Israel 3,000 years ago.

Justice is, naturally, a central concern of the law and this brief excerpt from that law prompts a discussion of justice at three important levels. As suggested above, there is the question of the relationship between justice and compassion (i.e., the instructions concerning the poor and the alien, the deaf and the blind, and even such matters of the heart as hating and bearing a grudge). There is also the issue of the relationship between justice and vengeance (e.g., v. 18), which we will consider in more detail in the gospel lection. Finally, there is the connection between justice and correction (see v. 17). This is an underdeveloped theme in most conversations about justice, but it is an important, recurring principle in scripture (Ezekiel 3:17-21; Matthew 18:15-17; James 5:19-20). Let punishment be justice's "Plan B," for our first effort should be to correct.

In the end, this Old Testament book, which suffers both scorn and neglect in the average American church, provides a great treasure for us this week. We see in it the profound themes of integrity and compassion, a concern for justice and righteousness, and a sense for the holiness and reverence that are meant to characterize the people who belong to a holy God.

1 Corinthians 3:10-11, 16-23

Every text has a context, though not every context is equally relevant. In the case of these excerpts from Paul's first letter to the Christians in Corinth, the context is extremely important, for the threads that make up this pericope are woven throughout the larger letter. Specifically, three recurring themes are involved.

First, there is the issue of sects within the Corinthian congregation. Paul deals with this problem early in the letter (1:10-17), as the believers there were apparently aligning themselves with different human leaders (Paul, Apollos, Peter). We have no indication that those three men were competing with one another or vying for distinctive allegiance. Paul addresses those unfortunate divisions in chapter 1, and he returns to the issue here in chapter 3. The three central characters are referenced by name at the end of our passage, and the issue is implicit at the beginning, as well, when Paul refers both to his own initial work in their midst ("like a skilled builder I laid a foundation") and to his successors in Corinth ("someone else is building on it").

We should note that Paul's final word on this whole issue is always the same. In his chapter 1 discussion, Paul asks, "Has Christ been divided? Was Paul crucified for you? Or were you baptized in the name of Paul?" (1:13). The issue, you see, is neither Paul, nor Apollos, nor Cephas; the issue is Christ.

Likewise, in our selected verses. The foundation that Paul laid — and on which his successors build — "that foundation is Jesus Christ." At the end, Paul dismisses the individual significance of the human servants, declaring, "All belong to you, and you belong to Christ, and Christ belongs to God."

The second prominent issue is the theme of "God's temple." Paul's reference to the believers as God's temple in verse 16 follows on the heels of his building imagery in verses 10-11. The sense, then, is of an extended metaphor in which Paul and his successors in Corinth have been constructing God's temple, and the foundation of that temple is Jesus himself. The Spirit dwells there and the Christians in Corinth are that under-construction dwelling place of God. Paul's language is highly reminiscent of imagery used by Peter later (1 Peter 2:4-5).

Meanwhile, Paul returns to the theme of the believers as God's temple later in this epistle to the Corinthians, when he asks, "Do you not know that your body is a temple of the Holy Spirit within you, which you have from God, and that you are not your own?" (6:19). And he echoes the motif again in his second letter to that congregation, saying, "What agreement has the temple of God with idols? For we are the temple of the living God" (2 Corinthians 6:16).

In my years of pastoring, I have heard numbers of people along the way correct some behavior — usually some child's behavior — by saying, "No, no. We don't do that in church!" Perhaps we should broaden our sensibilities to recognize that we ourselves — not just the building in which we worship — are holy, dedicated to God, and therefore there are certain things that shouldn't go on with or in us. That was Paul's point to the Christians in Corinth.

Finally, the third significant strand of our passage, which is woven throughout the larger letter, is the theme of wisdom and foolishness. At the very beginning of the letter, the Corinthians read a long discourse by Paul on wisdom and foolishness. He embarks on the theme in 1:17 and he continues to develop it through the rest of chapter 1 as well as all of chapter 2. He makes a sharp distinction between the world's wisdom and God's, noting along the way that he is not called to mimic worldly wisdom, and that God's own preference seems to be to use the foolish things of this world.

Note that Paul is not dismissive of wisdom. He is only eager for his congregation to distinguish between what passes for wisdom in this world and the true wisdom of God — even though that may be disdained and discounted by this world. The challenge to them remains a challenge for us. We, too, are natural heirs to the perspective of the world in which we live. Yet that world is contrary to God, and so we must recognize that everything is turned upside down. I imagine, therefore, that he would urge us to jettison the world's so-called wisdom and "become fools so that you may become wise."

Matthew 5:38-48

"You have heard that it was said." Five times in Matthew 5 Jesus begins a teaching with that introductory phrase. Prior to the beginning of our selected passage, he referenced "you shall not murder" (v. 21), "you shall not commit adultery" (v. 27), and "you shall not swear falsely" (v. 33). Then, in our excerpt, he adds two more: "an eye for an eye and a tooth for a tooth" (v. 38) and "you shall love your neighbor and hate your enemy" (v. 43).

This recurring "you have heard that it was said" phrase introduces Jesus' commentary on the Mosaic Law and the traditions that had grown up around it. Many contemporary Christians casually assume that Jesus nullified the law. Some base their conclusion on theological grounds: that is, Christ's atoning death fulfills the righteous requirements of the law. Others derive their vague impression from Jesus' responses to the Pharisees. But Jesus' argument with the Pharisees is not that the law is less important than they make it; rather, it is more important than they make it. For they had turned the law into a mere collection of superficial, legalistic observances. Jesus, however, as illustrated in our selected passage, always made obedience to God a matter of the heart.

The "an eye for an eye" principle, found in the Old Testament law (Exodus 21:22-25) and referenced here by Jesus, epitomizes for some people what they think is wrong with the Old Testament. They see it as angry, bloody, and vindictive and they contrast it with the prevailing forgiveness that they associate with the New Testament. In truth, however, the "eye for an eye" rule was precisely the opposite of what so many folks assume. It was designed to restrain vengeance; not institutionalize it. The harsh reality is that revenge is naturally disproportionate. The desire to "get even" is seldom actually about making things "even." Rather, revenge is blinded by its own rage, and so it tries to get more than even. Revenge double-counts the offense, calculating in not only the wrong that was done but also its own hurt and anger. And so the wise but ridiculed Old Testament law put a leash on human vengeance, setting a fair and reasonable limit on punishment: "an eye for an eye."

For society still today that ancient standard remains a quite reasonable one in the administration of justice. Yet for the individual follower of Christ, there is a higher standard to be sought. In this teaching, Jesus encourages us not only not to steer clear of revenge, but also to let go of our quest for justice (justice for ourselves, that is; we must remain vigilant about seeking justice for others). Instead of revenge and justice, the aspiration of the followers of Christ is mercy: a generosity of spirit and magnanimity of love and action.

For some of us, the first challenge of these teachings is to remove them from the sentiment that comes from familiarity and from the lovely embroidered hangings in our church parlors. We need to insert personal situations and specific names into these teachings in order to see how outrageous they are.

Since I don't have anyone striking me on the cheek, for example, I must think instead of that woman whose words were a slap to my ego. Since I don't have anyone suing me for my coat, perhaps I should think of that man who is so demanding of my time. And since no Roman soldier is compelling me to carry his pack, I should turn to the interruptions that are part of my day and the people who seem to have no regard for my schedule and itinerary. Once I have translated Christ's teachings to my daily experience, then I will see them for what they are: astonishing.

The second half of the passage continues the astonishing expectations. Loving enemies requires a polar shift in our fallen natures. And praying for those who persecute us is equally unnatural. What comes naturally is to pray for my loved ones — my wife and children, my parents, and dearest friends. But the people who are antagonistic to me and give me grief do not appear on my heart's default prayer list. If they appear in my prayers, it is that the trouble they cause me prompt me to pray for myself!

Then comes the logic behind the absurdity, "So that you may be children of your Father in heaven." And that is the logic we shall consider below.

Application

"So that you may be children of your Father in heaven," Jesus says.

The phrase should not be misunderstood. Jesus is not making our relationship with God as Father a function of our performance or our merit. It is not when I love my enemies that I become his child. Rather, it is when I love my enemies that I prove that I am his child.

"He makes his sun to rise on the evil and the good," Jesus famously observes and then makes the same point about the blessing of rain. In other words, God is indiscriminate in his generosity, and therefore we should be too.

We noted above that these teachings from Jesus should astonish us. If we have managed, however, to make it all the way through the gospel passage without being astonished, then Jesus guarantees our shock with his conclusion. "Be perfect," he commands, "as your heavenly Father is perfect."

As though telling me to turn my cheek, give away my cloak, and love my enemies was not enough, now Jesus commands me to be perfect. Perfect like God, no less. Hang that in the church parlor!

While Jesus' statement may seem like an absurdity, it is not an anomaly. On the contrary, it stands right at the heart of scripture. Our other two lections bear witness to the larger theme. In the Old Testament law, God unblushingly commands his people, "You shall be holy, for I the Lord your God am holy." In short, they are to be like him. Paul's word to the Corinthians echoes that truth, for "you are God's temple" and "God's temple is holy."

If even most professional basketball players cannot reasonably hope to "be like Mike," what chance do you and I have to be like God? How outrageous an ambition, how tall an order is that?

Yet from the beginning, that has been God's will for us. For his stated purpose was to "make humankind in our image, according to our likeness" (Genesis 1:26). And that continues to be his will and his purpose, for what seems way beyond you in your own power is enabled by the truth that Paul declares: "God's Spirit dwells in you."

An Alternative Application
Leviticus 19:1-2, 9-18. "Non sequitur." The dictionary says that the phrase "non sequitur" comes from the Latin, and it originally meant, "It does not follow."

As we noted above in our consideration of the Old Testament lection, this chapter from Leviticus seems to contain a non sequitur. For woven throughout the instructions and prohibitions we find this recurring phrase: "I am the Lord." To the modern reader, it appears as an awkward interruption of the text. It does not seem to follow. In truth, however, it suggests a critically important theological principle.

The scope of God's laws for his people is as broad and as deep as life itself — from worship to commerce, from Israel's relationships with foreign nations to their most intimate personal relationships, from annual holidays to daily hygiene.

Meanwhile, we recognize that the centerpiece of God's law for and covenant with his people was the Ten Commandments. We observe that, at the very beginning of that famous passage of scripture, the Lord introduced his commandments with this statement: "I am the LORD your God, who brought you out of the land of Egypt, out of the house of slavery; you shall have no other gods before me" (Exodus 20:2-3).

Israel's entire law was given and understood, you see, within the larger context of their God and their relationship to him. The recurring insertion — "I am the Lord" — therefore, is not an intrusion. On the contrary, it is the central support beam to which everything else is attached.

That pattern in the Old Testament law serves as a helpful reminder for you and me as Christians. The Lord is not segregated off in some religious corner, separate from the rest of daily life. Rather, his presence with us and his claim on us is woven through every aspect of our lives: all of our living and choosing, all of our commerce and relationships, the occasional and the daily, the special and the routine. Perhaps we would do well to scatter that phrase — "I am the Lord" — throughout our checkbooks, our calendars, and our address books. Let me pin it to my clock, my bathroom mirror, and my refrigerator.

The constant reminder of who he is — and whose I am — is not a non sequitur. On the contrary, everything in my life follows from that.

**Transfiguration of Our Lord
(Last Sunday after Epiphany)
Exodus 24:12-18
2 Peter 1:16-21
Matthew 17:1-9**
by William Shepherd

Mountaintop experience

It was the most boring sermon I ever heard, until it became the most interesting.

At first, I did not understand what had come over my student. Up to this point in the class, I thought she had been getting it. She laughed when I quoted Kierkegaard, "Boredom is the root of all evils." She nodded her head when I said that the dullest presentation would not be redeemed by the soundest content. Her critiques of the other students' sermons were right on target.

So why was she droning on about the literary sources of 2 Peter? What a mishmash of scholastic irrelevancies! On and on about pseudepigraphy and source criticism and whether Peter was friends with Paul. I could feel the other students snoring on the inside. It was ten minutes of total exasperation.

But then, with a short transitional sentence, everything changed. She started talking about her grandfather, who was a Greek fisherman. Suddenly, we were on the banks of the Mediterranean. We could smell the salt air, feel the weather-beaten hands, see the wooden barks that had hardly changed since the days of Homer. As she talked about the faith of her grandfather, we were utterly changed. We could see Jesus in his very person.

After the sermon, we took a moment or two to collect ourselves, then proceeded to the discussion. By the rules of the preaching seminar, the preacher was allowed only to listen in on the discussion as a silent partner, to overhear but not participate — she had had her opportunity to communicate, now it was our time to say what we had heard (after all, they don't give us a chance to butt in when they discuss our sermons in the parking lot!). We all agreed that we had heard a two-part sermon. We all agreed that the first part was utterly boring. We further agreed that the second half was equally strong in the opposite direction — utterly fascinating. We just could not understand how the two parts fit together (we laughed and joked that we wished the preacher were there to explain it!).

But then it hit me: 2 Peter 1:16, "For we did not follow cleverly devised myths when we made known to you the power and coming of our Lord Jesus Christ, but we had been eyewitnesses of his majesty." Her sermon had followed the form of the text exactly (see, she had been paying attention!). The first part was the "cleverly devised myths" endlessly argued by scholars to no conclusion. The second part was the "eyewitness of his majesty," embodied in the faith of her grandfather. It was a clever, clever sermon. Too clever, I think!

Today's lessons stress the experience of the revelation of God. While there are a good number of theories out there about these lessons, and it won't hurt anyone to become a little better educated about them, the sermon is never mere lecture. These texts call out to be experienced and re-experienced. They are about meeting God on the mountain. Scholars call these stories "theophanies" (the "appearance" of God), but through the ages believers have been content to let the experience speak for itself. The preacher's job today may be nothing more than to step out of the way and allow the congregation to see the theophany themselves.

Exodus 24:12-18

This brief passage of Exodus is about one thing: direction. Moses "went up the mountain," it says, not once, but four times! The movement is from the human to the divine, from the everyday concerns of politics, community, religion, economics, family, and work to one overriding and overwhelming concern: God. Moses leaves the human community behind and goes up the mountain to spend forty days and forty nights in the sole presence of God.

Our lection picks up the story from Exodus 24:1-2, where the seventy elders of Israel begin to come up the mountain. The numbers thin until Moses and Joshua alone ascend, leaving Aaron and Hur behind to take care of business (thus setting up the story of the golden calf in ch. 32). Finally, Moses alone goes up into the cloud of the glory of the Lord.

Moses has figured as the center point of a larger narrative (in Exodus) that is arranged in a chiastic or cross pattern (a form common in ancient narrative):

    A The theophany at Mount Sinai, 19:1-25
        B The giving of the Ten Commandments, 20:1-17
            C Moses the mediator between God and Israel, 20:18-21
            C' The giving of the covenant code to Moses, 20:22—23:19
        B' The law concerning the conquest of Canaan, 23:20-33
    A' The theophany concerning the covenant ceremony, 24:1-18

This narrative of the giving of the law at Sinai is at the center of the entire book of Exodus. At its peak is Moses, who receives both the law and the vision of God. The combination of law and theophany show that this is no human legislation, and Israel no voluntary organization. The people and the rules that hold them together are the direct doing of a God who is beyond human imagining. This is a priestly kingdom, set apart to reveal God's glory to the world, and Moses is assigned as point man in this theophanic purpose.

Moses' place in this scheme is symbolized by the language of the story: he seems to keep going up, up (Exodus 24:1, 9, 12-13, 15, 18). On his way he encounters that cloud which has been with Israel throughout their journey (13:21-22; 14:19-20, 24; 16:10; 19:9, 16; 24:15-16, 18; 33:9-10; 34:5; 40:34-38); it is the *Shechinah*, the presence of the glory of the Lord (so-called because the glory of the Lord "settled" or "dwelt" [*shachan*]) on Mount Sinai (v. 16). Coupled with the cloud is the burning fire, as before (cf. 13:21; 14:4, 7; 16:10). Where the imagery of the cloud characterizes God as mysterious, that of the fire makes God unpredictable and even dangerous. In the story that follows, Moses will be given the instructions for the building of the tabernacle, which will serve as the new home for God's glorious presence. Such is the magnitude of entering into God's glory that Moses is made to wait six days (the same number of days it took to prepare the earth for human habitation). Moses is completely dependent on God to act; nothing he can do will move up the timetable or shorten the preparation period. The initiation in appearing to Israel is entirely that of the Lord.

Moses finally leaves the human zone to enter into God's presence (v. 18). It is not clear that he will ever return. He leaves behind on the mountain Joshua, Aaron, Hur, and the seventy elders. None of them know what is going to happen, though Joshua and Aaron symbolize two future possibilities. Joshua, who went up the mountain partway with Moses, will prove to be his true successor. Aaron, on the other hand, despite being Moses' brother, represents those who would easily abandon the true presence of God for an idol made by human hands. The unexplained disappearance of the human mediator into the mystery and danger of God will prove to be more than many in the community can handle; it is simply easier to believe in a dead and idle deity.

2 Peter 1:16-21

Many scholars believe that the document known as the Second Letter of Peter is itself a cleverly devised myth, an anonymous composition written long after the death of Peter but claiming the authority of his name. Rather than bore you with the details, I will refer you to the various commentaries and handbooks that discuss this issue in depth. Whatever the provenance of the letter, clearly it is a species of the ancient form known as "paraenetic," a kind of exhortation, cast as a reminder. It is a string tied around a finger, a "Post-It" note in familiar handwriting. The author (we'll follow traditional usage and call him "Peter") writes to Gentiles (1:1) to exhort them on certain matters of apostolic tradition. Some see the opening of the letter (1:3-11) as a kind of mini-sermon on the basic themes of apostolic preaching. These themes are taken up one by one in the body of the letter. Peter characterizes his teaching not as new information (it is a defense of traditional teaching, after all), but merely a gentle reminder of what they have always known (1:12-15).

First and foremost, Peter must refute the false teachers. Here the letter follows traditional polemical rhetoric, painting the enemies of traditional teaching not only as intellectually, but morally, false. Our passage lays down the grounds for Peter's authority on these matters: his teachings are no mere myths but based on eyewitness testimony (1:16). In particular, the letter alludes to the scene recorded in the synoptic gospels of Jesus' transformation on a mountain before Peter, James, and John. The recounting of the episode is remarkably like the version from Matthew's gospel in today's lection. The focus is on the words of the heavenly voice: "This is my Son, my Beloved, with whom I am well pleased" (v. 17). This is taken as God conferring "honor and glory" on Jesus. It also certifies Peter's credentials as a teacher, because "we ourselves heard this voice come from heaven, while we were with him on the holy mountain" (v. 18).

Thus, Peter is given his bona fides as an interpreter of "the prophetic message," that is, the Hebrew Bible (v. 19). The message is characterized as belonging to God's final acts, symbolized by the dawning of the day (cf. 2:9; 3:7-8, 10, 12; Romans 13:12) and the rising of the morning star (cf. Numbers 24:17; Revelation 2:28, 22:16). The light at the end of the tunnel is certain, because the teaching is not just human speculation: "No prophecy of scripture is a matter of one's own interpretation" (v. 20). This does not mean that individuals cannot interpret the prophecies by themselves, but they must take into account the divine origin of those prophecies. The prophets spoke not by human will, but because they were moved by God's Spirit (v. 21). They not only received God's message, but they reported it accurately in the Spirit. Since the Spirit continues to be active in the community's own teaching, Christians can be assured that what they have received from eyewitnesses like Peter is in fact rooted in the true experience of God.

Matthew 17:1-9

Matthew's account of the transfiguration of Jesus sits neatly inside yet another chiastic form that helps interpret this extremely odd story. It sits surrounded by its exact opposite: stories not of glory, but of suffering and death. It is part of a larger story that puts Jesus on the road toward Jerusalem and the passion. The passion hangs over the section (of Matthew) that has the transfiguration at its center:

    A Passion prediction, 16:21
        B Rebuke of Peter, 16:22-23
            C Saying on suffering, 16:24-28
                D Transfiguration, 17:1-8
            C' Saying on suffering, 17:9-13
        B' Rebuke of disciples, 17:14-21
    A' Passion prediction, 17:22-23

The effect is to place the vision of the disciples firmly within the context of suffering, both that of the Son of Man and that of the disciples themselves. The disciples can "tell no one about the vision until after the Son of Man has been raised from the dead" (v. 9), because the vision of glory does not function except in the context of sacrifice. They need to "listen to him" (v. 5), because what he has to say is about suffering. To pay attention to his teaching about suffering is to understand his glory; it reveals the true meaning of Peter's confession, "You are the Messiah, the Son of the living God" (16:16).

The section furthers a major theme in Matthew: Jesus is the new Moses. The parallels with the Moses story are striking: the mountain as the place of theophany (Exodus 24:18), the timing of six days (Exodus 24:16), the prophet going up the mountain with only trusted companions (Exodus 24:13-14), the reference to the Mosaic Law (Matthew 17:4), the exhortation to listen (Deuteronomy 18:15). Sealing the deal is the appearance of Moses himself (v. 5), who along with Elijah represents the entirety of the prophetic tradition, embodying both law and prophets (both figures were said to have been taken to heaven rather than having died in the conventional manner, Deuteronomy 34:6; 2 Kings 2:11, and both were expected to play roles in a future kingdom, Deuteronomy 18:15, 18; Malachi 3:23-24). Jesus is the new prophet like Moses, and yet something greater than Moses is here.

The dreamlike vision leaves the disciples dazed and confused, their faces in the dust (v. 6). Jesus treats them with a gentle touch (v. 7). What they have seen will not be easily digested. Yet one day, after Easter, these three will become the authoritative bearers of Jesus' message about suffering and glory. They will proclaim things that have not been understood: The Messiah's glory is to be found in his suffering and his leadership will take his disciples toward self-sacrifice. They, too, will be raised from the dead, as gently as Jesus raised them from the ground (v. 7). They, too, will see the light of the glory of the Lord (vv. 2, 5). But when they look carefully into the light, they will see that it consists only of Jesus alone (v. 8).

Application

Just as a beginning preaching student can follow instructions too literally and make sermon form and content coincide in ways that are painful to listen to, so liturgical preachers should beware of stressing the liturgical context at the expense of scriptural message. The church year provides the context in which we read scripture, but it does not have the substance of scripture itself. When I hear sermons taking their content from the liturgy rather than its foundation, I suspect we are being served the sauce rather than the meat.

That being said, rarely do context and content meet so vividly than on the final Sunday of Epiphany. Epiphany is the season of light, while Lent leads to three hours of darkness. The Transfiguration emits a final, blinding bit of epiphanic light, before the ashes descend to our foreheads. The journey toward the cross is not all gloom; it is glory itself, because of Jesus. Yet this glory, as Matthew tells the story, is wrapped in suffering. There is no Epiphany (nor Easter) without Lent.

Some people believe that the Transfiguration story in Matthew serves as a brief foreshadowing of the resurrection. It seems to be the answer to Jesus' enigmatic prediction, "There are some standing here who will not taste death before they see the Son of Man coming in his kingdom" (16:28). If the Transfiguration looks ahead to the end of Matthew's story, the last Sunday of Epiphany looks ahead to the end of Lent. Suffering is never lauded in and of itself, in the biblical tradition. It is presented as part of the earthly journey of discipleship, an imitation of Jesus' self-sacrificial love, but it is not the end-all, be-all. God does not let the suffering stand. Like Jesus, the disciples will be raised to new life. Like our master, we will all walk up into the light.

Alternative Applications

1) Exodus 24:12-18. Some people speak of their "mountaintop experience" as a fairly friendly experience. They had a sense of peace, felt a warming of the heart, or came to a great and important realization.

It does not diminish these experiences to point out that they are nothing like the experience of Moses on the mountain of God. For one thing, it is quite clear that the presence of the Lord in fire and cloud evoked terror among the people, not warmth. More importantly, Moses was there for a quite specific purpose: to receive the law of God. It was not just a once-in-a-lifetime experience, it was a once-in-all-history experience, given to one man and one man alone. He left the frightened masses at the foot of the mountain, the appointed leaders somewhere in the foothills, and his most trusted companions on the side of the mountain. Moses went alone into the cloud to meet the Lord who would instruct him in the way the people of God must live.

2) Matthew 17:1-9. Matthew adds a line to the story of the Transfiguration: "Jesus came and touched them, saying 'Get up and do not be afraid' " (v. 7; "get up" translates *egeiro*, the same word used for resurrection in v. 9). One might argue that being "overcome with fear" (v. 6) was a perfectly rational response on the part of the disciples (cf. 8:25-26; 14:26; 28:8-10). For that matter, it was a perfectly traditional response on the part of those who received a vision of God (cf. Exodus 34:30; Judges 6:22; Daniel 8:17-18, 10:7-9). It wasn't enough that Jesus turned white before them, Moses and Elijah appeared out of nowhere, and a bright cloud overshadowed them. Worst of all was the voice that thundered, "Listen to him!" (v. 5). Anyone who had been paying the slightest bit of attention to what Jesus was saying would in fact be afraid — especially in light of what he had just been saying. He has been talking about things that are very hard to hear. The vision is too hard to see; the words are too hard to hear, and yet, we disciples manage to see and hear, despite our fear. This, only because he has touched us and raised us up.

Ash Wednesday
Joel 2:1-2, 12-17
2 Corinthians 5:20b—6:10
Matthew 6:1-6, 16-21
by Mark Molldrem

Called to a different life

The summer of 2000 was a devastating one for the western United States. Wildfires broke out in almost every state. Montana was declared a disaster area. The landscape was changed and will be different now and for generations to come. Grey smoke covered the horizon and ashes covered the earth.

We enter the season of Lent on Ash Wednesday, when ashes symbolically cover our lives with the sign of a sooty cross made upon our forehead. Lent, a forty-day preparation for Easter, helps us reflect upon our need for repentance and discipline in our lives. Any one day of the year we live our lives will give us grist to chew on for forty days, as we consider our relationship with God and with other human beings. Any one of us has enough sin in us to go around for everyone, amplifying the need for all of us to take seriously this opportunity to examine ourselves in light of the Law and the Gospel. Whatever we personally discover can be carried sorrowfully, yet expectantly, to the cross of Christ and offered for burial with him so that a new self can rise with him and live before him daily in a manner worthy of the gospel.

Joel 2:1-2, 12-17

Whose son are you? Joel was son of Pethuel. As such he could have been spokesperson of the family heritage or the family vision of itself for the future. Instead, Joel, gifted with words, surrendered his mouthpiece to Yahweh. Joel's name means "Yahweh is God." Joel became the spokesperson for God. He reminded the people of their heritage with Yahweh and of Yahweh's vision for his people. The people of Judah were his audience. The context was a locust plague described as God's army (2:11) bringing judgment upon the people for their sins. This plague was also a presage of other armies to come, notably the Assyrian hordes that would wreak their own blackness upon the mountains of both northern and southern kingdoms. Then would come the invasion of the Babylonian army, like waves of devastation one after another, like locusts — the cutting, swarming, hopping, destroying locusts (1:4).

At the heart of Joel's message of judgment, however, is the invitation to repent. Turn from sin and turn toward God, who, though capable of judging his people, "is gracious and merciful, slow to anger, and abounding in steadfast love" (2:13). *The Lutheran Book of Worship* (ELCA) uses these very words in its liturgy during Lent as a musical response of the people to the reading of scripture. The call to repentance is expressed with such exhortations as "awake... lament... be confounded... call... gather... cry" (1:5-14). Whereas some prophets use the expression, "Thus says the Lord," to garner attention, Joel scripts the blowing of the trumpet (2:1, 15). The people are to give heed to what is happening. The first blasting of the trumpet makes the people mindful that the day of judgment is coming. As much as one would like any day of reckoning to be far off, God's day "is near" (2:1). The second blasting of the trumpet draws the people's regard to the discipline of fasting. This can be an outward sign of an inner transformation of heart, as one comes before the heavenly judge with the paltriness of one's earthly efforts.

When Joel speaks of the coming day of the Lord as near, the question can be asked if there is time to repent. In one sense, the answer is no. The judgment is coming. It has been unleashed. That cannot be changed at this level of engagement. In another sense, the answer is yes! There is always time for repentance because this is the purpose for the judgment. The judgment is, in this regard, open-ended. It is not final. With the appropriate response of repentance — which is the purpose of the judgment in the first place — there are opened up all sorts of possibilities for God to work out the divine plan of salvation.

The image of rending the heart and not garments (2:13) defines the experience of repentance as necessarily an inner transformation, not necessarily an occasion for outward show. True change of behavior originates in a change of attitude, which comes from the heart. It is like when Jesus said that the good tree produces the good fruit, not the other way around (Matthew 7:17-20).

It is with the prophets' sense of judgment and their uncanny way of reaffirming the goodness of God in the midst of all evil that we enter into the Lenten season once again. We can accept the ashes on our heads as a temporal sign of our sorrow for sin and the acceptance of the judgment that must fall upon us as outcasts from Eden.

2 Corinthians 5:20b—6:10

The Corinthian church was a divided church. There were severe differences within the Christian community regarding worship practices (e.g., tongues), personal behavior (e.g., sexuality), public witness (e.g., lawsuits), and leadership (e.g., jealous sectarianism). That's a lot of conflict happening in just one place! Paul attempts to address these problems in his correspondence. It is doubtful that he was very successful in improving the situation in Corinth. He ends his first letter with a plea for the Lord to come (1 Corinthians 16:22)! That's like saying, "Let's get the boss down here on the line to square this mess!" His second letter ends with a straightforward plea/command, "Mend your ways, heed my appeal..." (2 Corinthians 13:11). If Paul could have written a later letter in the spirit of Philippians, we may be able to see Corinth in a better light. But no such letter seems to be forthcoming. Perhaps it is the stark contrast between Corinth and Philippi that enables Paul to express his heart so tenderly to his Christian friends to the north.

Arguably, the two key words in this text are *kataggassw* (reconcile) and *diakonoz* (servant, as in waiting on tables). The plea for reconciliation is his main thrust and part of his plea is based upon the personal example of his servanthood. (The portion of the letter prior to this lectionary text bases his plea for reconciliation on theological ground: the Corinthians are to be newly shaped by Christ in them and they are to recognize Paul's reconciling mediation as modeled after Christ's reconciling work between God and humanity.)

Paul demonstrates great patience and perseverance in his attempts to bring the Corinthian congregation to a state of reconciliation. He could have considered them as a whole as *anathema* (*anaqema*, accursed, 1 Corinthians 16:22), for which he opens the door at the end of his first letter. But he draws up short on that and continues to appeal to them so that they may yet have opportunity to "clean up their act."

The theological motivation for this to happen is what Christ did for us. In verse 21, Paul describes what Martin Luther would call "The Happy Exchange." Christ Jesus, the one who was sinless, takes our sin (rebellion against God manifested through contention with one another) upon himself and imputes to us his righteousness with which we can stand before God forgiven and accepted. This experience and the remembrance of it should provide a kind of template on which we can perceive our human relationships and model them in like manner. Paul uses the image of imitation in his correspondence with Corinth (1 Corinthians 4:16; 11:1) and also with other congregations (Ephesians 5:1; Philippians 3:17). The imitation is ultimately of God's love as demonstrated through Jesus. Much later, *The Imitation of Christ* (associated with Thomas à Kempis, 1380-1471, and the Brethren of the Common Life) would be written, describing how the Christian life is an imitation of Christ, helping Christians of many other congregations for centuries thereafter to come to terms with this noble calling of walking in the steps of Jesus.

When juxtaposed to Joel, one might say that the Day of the Lord is the Day of Jesus, thereby defining the coming judgment and the present mercy experienced in the work of Christ upon the cross. The locust plague has become the Lord's pain, whereby humanity's sin is placed on him, so that salvation can be given to us. We would accept the grace of God in vain were we not to let it shape our lives and pervade every pore of our being and direct us in all our relationships.

Paul adds another weight to his appeal, hoping to tip the balance in favor of more appropriate behavior from the Corinthians. He lifts up his own servanthood. It is important to note that he does not use the word *douloz* (slave), which has sometimes been translated "servant" (e.g., Romans 1:1; Galatians 1:10 RSV). When Paul describes his relationship with Christ, he uses that term to describe his abject submission to Jesus' ownership of his heart and soul. In describing his relationship with fellow Christians, specifically the Corinthians, he uses the image of waiting on tables. He is offering all that he has gone through as evidence that his ministry is authentic and he is worthy of being listened to when it comes to the practical matters of getting along and of witnessing faithfully to the gospel. He does not hold anything back. Amazingly, this does not come across as pompous boasting, but as a humble ledger, crediting Paul the *walk* to back up his *talk*.

Matthew 6:1-6, 16-21

Jesus is on a roll! Unfortunately for his hearers, he is rolling right over them. He is striking right to the misshapen heart of piety that misses the mark of purity. Centuries later, Saint Augustine would correctly observe that sin is basically turning in upon oneself. Here, Jesus applies the practical consequences of this when it comes to alms, prayer, and fasting.

In three tightly packed paragraphs, Jesus treats three primary examples of the spiritually disciplined life. In keeping with the prophetic tradition, as well as being consistent with other religious traditions at their best, Jesus identifies alms-giving, prayer, and fasting as worthy practices of piety. There is a delightful rhythm to these passages, which any preacher or public speaker should note well.

What is interesting to note about the content of Jesus' words is that he does not describe the *what* of piety, but the *how* of it. That is to say, Jesus does not prescribe how much alms one is to give, what exact words one should pray (Matthew's redaction in 6:7-15 needs to be taken into account here), or even what constitutes a fast. Jesus focuses on the heart of the pious one. What is motivating the righteous activity? Is it truly and purely an action offered for God and as an expression of one's devotion? Or is it performed for the public so that others may see just how religious and virtuous one is? For these acts to have spiritual impact, they are to be directed toward God.

With a twist of sarcasm, Jesus says that those who perform their religious activities so that others may see them and laud the doer have already received their reward. What is that reward? Human acclaim! We all know what that is worth. Hollywood speaks of everyone's desire to have fifteen minutes of fame. The world is willing to give that but then moves on quickly to other, more novel entertainments. Shakespeare described fame well when he wrote of every person being an actor "that struts and frets his hour upon the stage and then is heard no more" (*Macbeth*, Act V, scene v). In light of this, is it any wonder that Hamlet asks the existential question — "to be or not to be" (*Hamlet*, Act III, scene i)?

How much more satisfying to have the heavenly Father's eternal acclaim, his everlasting valuation! The pure in heart will seek only the joy of their maker as they give alms, pray, and fast. This can best be assured "in secret," where there is not the distraction of a public parade.

This is not to discredit totally temporal acknowledgment. As earthbound creatures, living in community, we need notable, public examples to emulate. This comes by hearing and seeing in the community square. What Jesus is driving at is the motivating factor and the reward sought. He wants his followers to realize that the true reward of pious activity is the deep, inner growth that develops in the relationship between the earthly believing child and the heavenly rewarding Father.

Application

We may have lost the trumpet as the public herald of tidings, but we still have our church bells. Would that they could be like Edgar Allen Poe describes them in "The Bells": "Brazen bells! What a tale of terror now their turbulency tells! ... How they clang, and clash, and roar!" But, alas, they are used only for chiming the hour or playing melodious hymns. The siren perched over city hall has replaced the church bells in sounding an alarm to the community — and, then, only with secular concern for safety of life and limb, not of soul. It remains for the trumpet voice of the preacher to ring with the truth of God's judgment and mercy for the world's soul in need of repentance.

With all the extensive bad publicity the church has received over sex scandals and money mismanagement, one has to wonder if the church has lost its moral authority to be heard by the world. The church itself needs to repent and return to righteous ground on which to stand. That ground is the scripture, on the one hand, and not the accumulated wisdom of the ages (secular humanism at its best), which is often passed off as gospel; on the other hand, that ground is also a public life worthy of the gospel. Christians need to understand clearly that our life together is not defined by a sense of good-feeling social fellowship nor good-doing social action. Our life together finds its source and center in God, who wields the weal and woe for all creation. Our life together stands, not on our work or lack thereof, but on the work of Christ for us. This is what we have to communicate clearly to the world, or we will be seen simply as but one element in a very complex social network of the human community hurdling through space on this particular speck of dust called earth, instead of the Body of Christ, the community of the covenant, that is to mentor the world to the living God.

This work can be taken up by individual congregations as they take a close look at themselves to identify where work needs to be done in order to mature in Christ-likeness. Neighboring congregations are at odds with one another. There is dissension within a congregation over worship practices, theology, or the acceptance of a new pastor. Misconduct suits are filed by parishioners against clergy or other staff. Unbecoming behavior is accepted too easily for the sake of retaining members. Corinth is alive in our own hearts and has come to roost in our pews. Congregations who dare to take an honest look at themselves will come to the conclusion that there are many things for which they need to repent as a group. The Christian witness to the community is at stake.

Just as the longest journey begins with the first step, so too the road to recovery for the church will begin with the actions individual Christians take in response to the gospel. Personal repentance can be likened to that first step. Although repentance itself is a complex movement of the spirit (involving conviction, contrition, confession, and correction), it can manifest itself by the simple acts of alms-giving, prayer, and fasting. Christians need to be encouraged in these ways so that they do not become lost arts of the religious life. There are already many reports documenting the poor giving habits of people, as we use most, if not all, of our money for "paying the bills" and "playing." Prayer becomes an exercise "at church" and "at mealtime" ("We even do it at McDonald's, Pastor!") but not the regular breath of the soul throughout every day, because we are so busy or distracted with other matters. Fasting becomes a foreign language in corpulent America, even while fitness fads of workouts and diets flash across the screen unendingly.

We can affirm the dignity of such spiritual disciplines, pointing out specifically the rewards that endure. The practitioner should not engage in these activities for public display or acclaim, but for the deeper, abiding rewards of peace and contentment and a growing relationship with the heavenly Father. Giving alms, praying, and fasting will also direct one into better choices in other various aspects of one's life, providing increased courage and wisdom to live righteously. There will also be increased humility, as one realizes there is so much more one could do for the Lord in these disciplines and in all areas of one's life. From humility comes a more gracious posturing in life, as one lives in relationship with others and the whole created order as a reflection of God's loving and merciful relationship with us all.

Perhaps then we will hear together "the rhyming and the chiming of the bells," replacing "the moaning and the groaning of the bells!"

Lent 1
Genesis 2:15-17; 3:1-7
Romans 5:12-19
Matthew 4:1-11
by Wayne Brouwer

The day God got lonely

Today is the first Sunday *during* Lent. This is an important fact to note. In Advent, Christmas, Easter, and Pentecost, the Sundays belong to the season. They are Sunday *of*... But during Lent, the Sundays are not part of Lent. The forty days of the season flow around the Sundays, calling us to share the journey of suffering with Jesus. The Sundays themselves, however, are islands of mercy, reminding us that Jesus is alive and forever victorious.

Still, the Sundays and the days of Lent cannot be separated, as the scripture passages for today remind us. Lent is about suffering, sadness, pain, and heartache. Mostly we focus on these things in the general life of humanity since the fall, and then concentrate them in the life of Jesus, particularly in the tough final weeks as he moved toward the cross. Yet the scripture passages for today remind us of another side of the suffering, sadness, pain, and heartache. It is the heart of God that aches and breaks, too, when we move away from our creational goodness.

Imagine the conversations among the Father, Son, and Spirit from all eternity. There are terms of endearment, songs of praise, and words of encouragement. Next imagine the creative energies that gave rise to this universe — the expression of the desires in the heart of God to spill out and spread lavishly the care and commitments and kindness that flow through the Trinity. This world, according to the Bible, is the grand outpouring of God's generous desire to multiply love and to enjoy creatures made in God's own image, having in themselves the ability to ever expand the joy of divine blessing.

The early days of creation must have been a marvelous time, both here on earth and in heaven above. The book of Job hints at the wonder when these words are found on the lips of God: "Where were you when I laid the earth's foundation... while the morning stars sang together and all the angels shouted for joy?" (Job 38:4-7 NIV). Imagine the amazement of creatures, mineral and animal, terrestrial and celestial, and physical and spiritual springing into being at the winsome song of God. Imagine all of these as the preparation for God's final creative work — shaping human life to be the reflection of the community of the Trinity! Suddenly the universe was alive with prayer, conversation, drama, and love. Suddenly there was music of oratory and tenderness of intimacy. Suddenly the house of divine manufacturing became a home of divine Spirit interconnected with human spirit.

Then we read of the disobedience in the Garden, and we feel the shuddering horror of humanities lost in sin. Later we encounter Jesus less than alone in the wilderness — "comforted" only by the devil. Out of these stories the impact of Lent takes a different turn; it is not only we humans who suffer and cry, who wander in death lands and cemeteries, who struggle to find meaning in an alien world. It is God, too, who is lonely. The loneliness of God is found in the Garden of Eden after Adam and Eve have left. No more daily walks and talks. No more teas or nectars. No more playful observations of the bounding impalas or the sneaky geckos. God is lonely.

When we walk with Paul down the family tree of humanity, we find the feud of the ages: Adam the First's kin on one side; Adam the Second's kin on the other. God is lonely again and Matthew reminds us that the loneliness of God takes on very human shape and pain when Jesus' own preparation for ministry was a forty-day tour of duty with only himself and the devil as companions. Feel the loneliness as these passages come alive today.

Genesis 2:15-17; 3:1-7

There are many ways to enter the book of Genesis and most of them are not easy. It seems that the world of Genesis is too far removed from our own. The creation stories do not answer many of the questions we want to ask of them. The people of the early chapters are almost cardboard cutouts with only one or two notable features each. The genealogies leave us wondering about their correlation with archaeological records.

One helpful way to listen to Genesis is through the ears of those at Mount Sinai in Exodus 20-24. While we may quibble about how the text of these early books of the Hebrew Bible came into being, there is no question that the story within the text indicates that the Bible began at Mount Sinai. Prior to the Exodus there was no written scripture. Abraham did not read a Bible. Jacob did not memorize Psalms. Joseph had no prophetic meditations to reflect upon while imprisoned in Egypt. Moreover, the Israelites forget who the God of their ancestors was during their multiple centuries of slave labor. Even Moses, who was specially saved and prepared by God for a work of leadership, did not know who this God was until Moses himself was about eighty years old! Only after the rushed exit from Egypt and the arduous trek through the wilderness did a number of things fall into place at Mount Sinai.

The covenant struck (or "cut," to be more accurate to the Hebrew) at Mount Sinai was shaped in the typical contract arrangements of the day. The Hittite nation had fashioned a standardized form of international treaty in something we today call the Suzerain-Vassal covenant. It usually had six parts: a *preamble* declaring the right of the sovereign to initiate the covenant relationship, a *historical prologue* explaining the background that produced this moment of covenant-making, the *stipulations* of the covenant relationship, *curses and blessings* that expressed outcomes to the covenant or its failure, a list of *witnesses* who would confirm the making of this covenant, and a *document clause* that told where the copies of the covenant would be kept and when they would be read. Interestingly, all six parts of this Suzerain-Vassal covenant structure are found in Exodus 20-24.

With that in mind, it appears that Genesis forms an extended historical prologue to the Sinai covenant, explaining in greater detail why this covenant has become necessary. Reading Genesis from that perspective begins to pull things into meaningful and preachable form. From the backward glance of the Sinai covenant-making event, Genesis falls into four story-cycles roughly encompassed by these chapters: 1-11, 12-25, 26-36, and 37-50. While every major story-cycle is composed of a number of shorter tales, there seems to be either a dominant character or an over-arching theme in each. Genesis 1-11 explain to the Israelites at Mount Sinai who God was (Creator) and the character of this God's creation (endowed with freedom, intended good, but now in a state of war with its Creator). Chapters 12-25 give Israel a sense of her special identity and how a covenant with God had shaped her from the very beginning. Chapters 26-36 answer the question of what kind of character Israel had based upon the stories of Jacob (the conniver) who became Israel (the one who wrestles with God). And chapters 37-50 tell how Israel came to live in Egypt.

In this light, the story of Adam and Eve in the Garden of Eden teaches Israel the nature of life (stewardship of the natural order), the desire of God (intimacy with humankind), and the limits of human conduct (freedom within the definable boundaries of God's commands). This is explained through the poetry of creation's birth (Genesis 1-2) and summarized in the first half of the Genesis text for today (Genesis 2:15-17).

The second half of today's text unfolds the beginnings of human rebellion. The origin of the serpent is not explained, nor is the serpent's unusual understanding of the human situation. Later, after the curse of Genesis 3:14-15, the serpent will effectively disappear from the narrative. In other words, the serpent functions here merely as a foil by which to process initial human transgression. Questions about the serpent cannot be answered from the text. The text is not about the serpent; it is about how humans became enemies of God. The text goes on to tell of the first sins — deliberate disobedience to a direct command of the Creator God — and then explains the outcome: alienation, separation, isolation, shame.

While the text for today cuts off the rest of the story, the outcome between Adam and Eve is the same as that between the humans and their God (3:8-24). Whatever intimacy there had been between God and these honored creatures is now gone. Adam and Eve lose communion with each other, and the human race begins its murderous slide. More importantly, God loses communion with Adam and Eve and both grow very lonely.

Romans 5:12-19

Paul was concluding his third mission journey (Acts 18:23—20:38) when he wrote this letter. He was wintering in Corinth at the time (Romans 16:23), staying with his good friend Gaius. Paul was on his way to Jerusalem to bring a financial offering for the poor in the Jerusalem church (Romans 15:26); he hoped soon afterward to make a personal visit to Rome (Romans 15:24-25). This letter anticipated Paul's coming and included a summary of his teachings.

In large outline, the first three chapters of Romans focus on the desperate plight of humankind, chapters 4-8 announce God's remedy through the work of Jesus, chapters 9-11 wrestle with the matter of Jewish election and Gentile participation in the plans of God, and the rest of the letter expresses ways in which Christian faith can be lived out in society. Here in chapter 5, Paul is summarizing the significance of Jesus' work. In the previous chapter Paul had pointed out that God must do what we cannot do; this was true even for Abraham. Although we cannot earn God's good pleasure, we are connected to it through faith and since the recent full revelation of God's plan in Jesus, the object of our faith is Jesus himself.

In the text for today, Paul sets next to one another two family trees. The first is the blighted and wilting horror growing from the misshapen stump of Adam (vv. 12-14). The second is the marvelous and vital sturdy living thing emerging from the trunk of Jesus Christ (vv. 15-17). All of us participate in the first by the accident of birth. As one wit put it, "Life is a sickness for which the only cure is death."

Theologians continue to debate whether this passage promotes ideas of universal salvation. The minimalist approach says no; we only transfer from one tree (Adam's) to the other (Christ's) when we actively believe in the sacrificial work of Jesus. The moderate version says maybe; we are all automatically transferred from Adam's family tree to Jesus' family tree, but those who choose again to challenge God and intentionally disobey will be sent back and perish when Adam's tree is burned. The maximalist understanding is that the grace and gift of God (see v. 15) exceed our ability to cling to any tree, and automatically places us in the family of Jesus. The call now is for us to live as if we honor that gift.

Whatever approach you take, the larger theme is clear: God was lonely when Adam's tree began to die outside the Garden of Eden, so God replanted a tree of human grace and glory and brought those whom God chose (some, many, or all of us) back into the family.

Matthew 4:1-11

Matthew's original audience was largely composed of Jewish Christians. Matthew's method of tying Jesus to the Old Testament heritage of Jewish faith involved demonstrating how Jesus relived the history of Israel in miniature, replaying the major events and eras of its formative period. Here Jesus mirrors the forty-year wilderness wandering of Israel in the Sinai desert by way of his own forty-day wilderness sojourn.

The three temptations that Jesus endures echo specific challenges Israel faced early in its national existence. Each of these incidents is reviewed by Moses in the early chapters of Deuteronomy. First, while traveling through the deserted wastelands of the wilderness, Israel had complained to God about lacking food and facing starvation (Exodus 16). Jesus encounters similar famishment and uses Moses' teaching in Deuteronomy 8 to resist a quick fix that would remove him from following Israel's path.

Second, Israel quarreled with Moses in Exodus 17:1-7, declaring to him that God's power was insufficient to care for their needs. Moses recalls this incident in Deuteronomy 6:16 and reminds the people that God has never failed them in the past. Because of this they ought not doubt or question God's ability to care for them in the future. When Jesus is placed by the tempter in a situation where God's care might be tested, Jesus quotes Moses' words (Deuteronomy 6:16) to resist such unnecessary exercises and stands his ground.

Third, immediately after these two incidents in Exodus 16-17, Israel faced the prospect of becoming lost among the other nations and reduced to being merely like them. The battle between Israel and Amalek in Exodus 17:8-16 was resolved only when Moses went up to "the top of the hill" (v. 9) and kept the national focus upward (Moses' hands needed to be lifted toward heaven) to Israel's true leader. The strength of Israel that day was not found in its military might but in its devotion to the God who transcended all national affairs. Similarly for Jesus, from a "high mountain" he is enabled to see the power and wealth of the nations, but only when he quotes Moses' reminder from Deuteronomy 6:13 can he resist the prospect of becoming merely a world leader. As with Israel, his mission is much greater.

Matthew clearly wants his readers to understand Jesus' forty days in the wilderness as parallel to Israel's forty years in the wilderness. In each case the messenger of God is tempted to give up or deny God's power or settle for a typically human resolution to a problem. Yet, as Matthew shows, Jesus mimics Israel's reliance on God and emerges from the wilderness experience with integrity intact and facing the next state of his mission with renewed confidence in God.

Two themes surface from this story of Jesus' wilderness temptations. First, there is the loneliness of God. It was the loneliness of God, following the expulsion of Adam and Eve from the Garden of Eden, which led God to seek other traveling companions. In Old Testament times, Abraham and his descendents were called to be God's tour partner. The wilderness experiences they went through together strengthened their dependence on one another, especially Israel's on God. In New Testament times Jesus replays Israel's existence and becomes the visible divine partner on earth. Jesus makes evident to those around him what it means to walk with God, even through wilderness times. In Jesus' steadfast commitments is found the example that others who wish to travel with God can follow.

Second, since Jesus is himself fully divine, his wilderness struggles allow God to experience life as an exile. Just as Adam and Eve were forced out of the Garden and into the "wilderness" apart from intimacy with God, so in Jesus God experiences the wilderness loneliness that humans have had to face these many centuries. It will be through this wilderness experience, leading right up to the loneliness of the cross, that Jesus endures the painful loneliness of humanity in its quest to return to the Garden and intimacy with God. Only when the words, "My God! My God! Why have you forsaken me?!" (Matthew 27:46; Mark 15:34) have been wrung from Jesus' heart on Golgotha will a solution to God's loneliness be found. That day God would rip apart the temple veil and emerge from God's isolation to return to human interaction once again. From that time forward the Spirit of God would come on the church and its people would again be the dwelling place of God.

Through the loneliness of Jesus is the remedy to the loneliness of both God and humanity finally found. So on this first Sunday during Lent we spend time on the island of grace that lifts us above the lonely forty-day walk of suffering and pain.

Application

Some years ago a woman wrote the following poem that she called "A Lonesome Middleager":

Do you know what it means to be lonely?
Do you know how it feels to be blue?

*Do you know what it's like to feel
No one really cares just how things are with you?*

*Yes, it's nice to be friendly at church time;
You are thankful when they tell you they pray.
But what about long, lonely night hours,
Not to mention the following day?*

*You can call up your friends, and I do that;
You can ask them how they're doing, too.
But you wish that they'd say, "Come on over
And help us eat up the leftover stew."*

*Most everyone has a son or a daughter,
A husband, a mother, or sis.
But when you're alone with no loved ones,
To me, I just merely exist.*

This woman has captured the painful power of loneliness. Charles Williams, when asked about the meaning of the Old Testament, said that it could be summarized as depicting "the loneliness of God." Dorothy Day gave this title to the story of her lifelong search for meaning and God, *The Long Loneliness*. In all of these we are reminded of the agonizing alienation that settles into our world when God and humanity are separated by sin (Genesis 3). Two family trees develop side by side (Romans 5), and Jesus walks through the wilderness experiencing both God's loneliness and also that of humanity (Matthew 4).

On this first Sunday during Lent, dig into the pain of alienation and let your people feel the angst of a world come undone by the separations of racism, social stratification, spiritual isolation, philosophic skepticism, and sinful inability to be ourselves or with others who matter. Then point to God's long quest to rejoin us, and God's desire to have us rejoin God in fellowship and show how each is powerfully portrayed in the wilderness walk of Jesus at the outset of this Lenten season.

Lent 2
Genesis 12:1-4a
Romans 4:1-5, 13-17
John 3:1-17
by David Kalas

Far from the tree

Two thousand years earlier, Abram sat alone one night, when the Lord came to speak to him. He had no children, but the Lord promised to make him into a great nation. His roots had grown deep into the Mesopotamian soil, but the Lord wanted to transplant him to Canaan. He had more years behind him than ahead of him, but the Lord's greatest plans for him were still yet to come.

Abram believed God, and Abram obeyed God. He trusted God's promises to him, though they were the height of improbability. And he went where God sent, though the apprehension and sacrifice involved are nearly inconceivable to most of us. The old hymn "Trust and Obey" could have been written by that ancient patriarch.

After 2,000 years, his descendants had numbered in the millions. His family tree was immense and his descendants were firmly established in and identified with the land where Abram himself was only and always an alien.

One of the descendants on Abram's family tree was Nicodemus. He was the sort of great-great-grandchild that a man of faith prays for. He was pious, knowledgeable, and a leader of his people. He was precisely the sort of descendant that should make Abram proud.

Two thousand years after Abram, Nicodemus came by night to speak to the Lord. He was full of questions and uncertainty. He had knowledge, to be sure, but little understanding. He had a manifested spiritual hunger, but he seems to have gone away unsatisfied. He reappears at the end, aiding in Jesus' burial, but it looks as if that he did not have the courage to do more than follow Jesus from a safe distance.

This particular apple, it seems, fell far from the tree.

Genesis 12:1-4a

The biblical author's style is terse. We are given no background information about Abram's relationship or contact with the Lord, we are offered no glimpse into the previous 75 years of Abram's life in his homeland, and we are provided with no details about Abram's decision-making process, his conversations with Sarah at this juncture, or the impetus for Lot accompanying him. All of these matters, where we would be glad for some elaboration, remain mysterious.

The Lord is not vague about the nature of the sacrifice he asks Abram to make. He itemizes what he asks Abram to leave behind: "your country and your kindred and your father's house" (v. 1). But the Lord is not equally clear about where Abram will go: "to the land that I will show you" (v. 1).

Could it be that this was Abram's first contact with the Lord? Poet Killian McDonnell imagines that it might have been: "Talk about imperious. / Without a 'may I presume?' / No previous contact, / no letter of introduction, / this unknown God / issues edicts. / This is not a conversation. / Am I a nobody / to receive decrees / from one whose name / I do not know?"

Of course, while we lament God's lack of specificity about Abram's destination, we face a different problem where God is specific. The Lord lays out for Abram his plans — big plans. The old man who has precisely no children will, in that new, strange land, become "a great nation" (v. 2). And though this anonymous Aramean is on the back nine of his life, God will make his name great. Even though he has, at present, no heir, he will have a heritage in which "all the families of the earth shall be blessed" (v. 3).

Perhaps it takes less faith to launch out into an unknown future than an improbable future. That was surely the sticking point in the majority report of Israel's search committee at the border of the promised land (Numbers 13:25-33), and so it is right that Paul should praise Abram for simply believing God.

Could it be that Abram's obedience was as quick a reflex as the text suggests? The Lord spoke to him and without fanfare or fuss Genesis simply reports, "So Abram went, as the Lord had told him" (v. 3). As we follow the story of Abram, we discover soon enough that he is not perfect. But here in this episode, he is surely a model of faithful obedience.

Again, McDonnell lends insight into Abram's mind: "In ten generations since the Flood / you have spoken to no one. / Now, like thunder on a clear day, / you give commands: / pull up my tent, / desert the graves of my ancestors, / leave Haran / for a country you do not name, / there to be a stranger.... / You come late, Lord, very late, / but my camels leave in the morning."

Romans 4:1-5, 13-17

Family lines and genealogies have always been big deals. They have been the source of bitter conflicts and dynastic wars in countries where it is essential to trace the royal line. They are the common-knowledge database in small towns and rural areas where everyone knows who was married to your grandpa's second-cousin. They are a source of pride for individuals who like to track their lineage back to a certain group of immigrants, to the American Revolution, or to the Pilgrims. They were important records in ancient Israel (much to the consternation of modern readers who get bogged down in the lists of who begat whom), and today we find that there are many emerging new resources for folks who are eager to trace their own family line as far as they can go.

Family lines were important to the Jews of New Testament times too. That's why the half-breed Samaritans were so despised. That's why Paul includes his lineage in his list of things he could boast about (Philippians 3:4-6). That's why John the Baptist and Jesus had to challenge the self-satisfied "children of Abraham" (Luke 3:7-8; John 8:31-41).

Paul presents to the Romans a new perspective on Abraham's family tree.

The distinction between the Jews and the Gentiles was an important one for the Jews. It may have been more or less of an issue for the Gentiles in different places, but faithful Jews everywhere made it an issue. Their law — or at least their prevailing understanding of it — required them to make it an issue.

That distinction naturally carried over into the early church, which was entirely Jewish at the beginning. As growing numbers of Gentiles came to Christ in the years following Pentecost, a genuine disagreement and debate rose up within the church. By what way can a Gentile come to Christ? To what extent does a Christian have to be a Jew?

The question sounds strange in our day. Most of our churches are probably 100% Gentile, and some of the people in our pews may never even have known a Jewish Christian. The controversy that was so heated within the early church, therefore, does not resonate much today.

We do understand at least this much, however, in most of our churches: when something has always been done a certain way, it's hard to change.

All of the early Christians had come to Christ by basically the same route and from the same point of departure. One can hardly blame them, therefore, for assuming that everyone needed to follow the same directions in order to arrive at the same destination. And those directions included the path of circumcision, with a right turn at the law, and regular stops at the Sabbath.

Paul looked at the Old Testament people of God, their covenants and their patriarchs, however, and he saw something else at work: faith.

Paul's argument takes several forms along the way, especially in his letters to the Romans and the Galatians. In this particular passage, the argument focuses on the example of Abraham, which is a powerful one. Abraham predates the law, and his "reckoned to him as righteousness" (v. 3) moment also predates his circumcision. That righteousness, Paul contends, was a function of Abraham's faith.

In the end, therefore, Paul is not trying to defend an additional way to salvation and to Christ; he's making a claim about the only way. The unquestioned assumptions about the law are false assumptions, for it is actually faith that puts us right with God and that is not a new thing, but rather that is the way it has always been. The real family line that traces a person back to Abraham, therefore, is not flesh and blood, but faith.

John 3:1-17

The chapter opens and we are introduced to a man named Nicodemus with three pieces of information: He was a Pharisee, a leader of the Jews, and he came to Jesus by night. None of those statements constitutes outright criticism of Nicodemus, but each one has an unfavorable connotation.

The word "Pharisee," of course, has acquired an entirely negative meaning for the people in our pews. That was probably not the prevailing connotation in Jesus' day, but the Pharisees are surely depicted in an unflattering way in the four gospels. We surmise that they are hypocrites in their living, superficial in their religiosity, blind to God's work in John the Baptist and in Jesus, and petty in both their legalism and their opposition to Jesus and his followers.

That Nicodemus was "a leader of the Jews" (v. 1) is also an uncomplimentary observation by John. The phrase "the Jews" appears sixty times in the gospel of John, and often they are characterized by either ignorance or antagonism toward Christ. To be one of their leaders, therefore, was not a favorable association.

Finally, that Nicodemus came to Jesus "by night" (v. 2) is not a small detail. Even if it seems insignificant to us as we read, the gospel writer insists on its significance sixteen chapters later when Nicodemus reappears and is identified as the one "who had at first come to Jesus by night" (John 19:39).

The significance of Nicodemus coming "by night" may be understood in the larger context of what "darkness" means in the fourth gospel. Darkness suggests confusion and uncertainty (12:35), the comfy refuge for evil (3:19), and the enemy of the light (1:5). In contrast to the darkness, Jesus identifies himself as the light (8:12), and thereby the antidote for both the darkness of the world and the darkness in which any individual soul lives. Finally, elsewhere, Jesus says to his arrestors that the night "is your hour, and the power of darkness" (Luke 22:53). The fact that Nicodemus came to Jesus "by night," therefore, is not a flattering detail. At best, it connotes confusion and bewilderment, and, at worst, it suggests something sinful and sinister.

The initial point of friction in Nicodemus' conversation with Jesus, of course, is over the matter of being "born from above" (v. 3). The original Greek phrase can be translated in several ways: hence the traditional "born again" in the KJV and "born anew" in the RSV. Jesus almost certainly spoke in Aramaic, and so the Greek adverb (*anothen*) in the text cannot be attributed directly to him. Nevertheless, the variety of possible meanings probably reveals the breadth of the truth involved.

That Nicodemus heard born "again" is evident in his response ("Can one enter a second time into the mother's womb and be born?" v. 4). That the birth is "anew," meanwhile, is consistent with other New Testament affirmations (such as 2 Corinthians 5:17; Colossians 3:9-10; 1 Peter 1:23). And that the new birth is "from above" is implicit in Jesus' later explanation that it means being "born of the Spirit."

From the start, Nicodemus is in over his head. He doesn't comprehend what Jesus is saying to him, and he's not on the same page with the spiritual truths Jesus is conveying. Illustrative of Nicodemus' confusion is the parallel use of the word "enter" in this passage. Nicodemus doubts that a person can enter a second time into the mother's womb, while Jesus declares that "no one can enter the kingdom of God without being born of water and Spirit" (v. 5). So Nicodemus' misunderstanding of this new birth has him looking back to the womb, while Jesus is pointing forward to the kingdom.

Jesus' reference to "being born of water" (v. 5) can be taken two ways.

On the one hand, the passage has often been cited as a reference to water baptism. There is nothing in the immediate context of the verse to suggest a baptism allusion, but other passages certainly juxtapose water and Spirit baptisms (such as Matthew 3:11; Mark 1:8; Luke 3:16; John 1:33; Acts 1:5, 11:16).

On the other hand, the "being born of water" phrase may be a reference to physical birth. We have observed that a woman's water breaks at the time of a baby's birth, and it may be that this is what Jesus had in mind. That interpretation would certainly fit as a response by Jesus to Nicodemus' reference to the womb in verse 4. Also, the distinction between physical birth and spiritual birth is clearly the theme of verse 6.

We see Nicodemus' arrival in this episode, but we never see his departure. For the first few lengths of the conversation, Nicodemus is hanging in there with Jesus, albeit struggling to understand. By verse 9, however, Nicodemus is stymied and far behind, and by the time the chapter ends he is no longer visible.

By the time our particular passage ends, Jesus has presented Nicodemus and us with three great truths to digest. The first is the aforementioned theme of being born again, anew and from above. The second is the nature and work of the Spirit, which Jesus uses a play on words with "wind" (v. 8 — both are *pneuma* in the Greek) to illustrate. And the third is the gospel truth of Jesus' own purpose and mission.

The final four verses of the lection offer three different insights into Jesus' mission. Verses 14-15 borrow from Israel's wilderness experience with the serpent on a pole (Numbers 21:1-9) to offer a picture of Christ on the cross. Verse 16, the classic gospel-in-a-verse, reveals God's motivation behind Christ's mission. This is of particular importance because it shows God's attitude toward "the world," which is another prevailing theme in John's gospel. The fourth gospel refers to "the world" or "this world" 71 times and it appears another twenty times in the five chapters of 1 John. Finally, verse 17 articulates God's saving purpose and merciful will. Ever since guilty Adam and Eve heard God coming in the Garden, human beings have expected that God was coming to condemn. We are profoundly surprised and relieved each time we realize that, no, he comes "in order that the world might be saved."

Application

The three lections for this week present us with two main characters: Abram and Nicodemus. They are a study in contrasts, and perhaps a side-by-side examination of the two men could instruct and challenge our congregations.

Abram appears in the Genesis and Romans passages, while Nicodemus is the key character in John 3. In the Genesis lection, Abram is notable for his quick and quiet obedience. In Paul's consideration of Abram's example in Romans, he focuses on Abram's faith. In John 3, meanwhile, Nicodemus appears in the shadows, uncertain and confused, and disappears again with hardly a trace.

Different people have come to different conclusions about Nicodemus. Some see his effort to speak up on behalf of Jesus (John 7:50-52) and his presence at Jesus' burial (John 19:39-40) as signs of his discipleship. Others regard these as weak efforts, half swings without follow-through, suggesting a man who remained basically timid and confused in his relationship to Jesus. John's gospel surely gives us a clearer endorsement of the Samaritan woman in chapter 4, and a more apparent redemption of Thomas (20:26-28) and of Peter (21:15-19).

Nicodemus reads a little like the third servant in the parable of the talents (Matthew 25:14-30). He certainly does not seem like a bad guy, an antagonist, or a villain, and yet, in the end, he seems to come up tragically short.

The irony is that he seems so promising at the beginning. He is pious, knowledgeable, and a leader among his people. He has the spiritual appetite to come to Jesus, the sense to initiate a meeting with him, and yet, in the end, we are left to wonder whatever became of him.

Abraham, by contrast, seems not at all promising. Sports fans like to debate, "If you could choose any player to build your franchise around, who would it be?" Well, if you were going to build a new nation, you wouldn't naturally choose a childless 75-year-old man. And you wouldn't plant him as a wanderer in a land already occupied by other peoples.

But the same God, who used a boy to defeat a giant and an undersized army to defeat the much larger Midianite force, also made a great nation out of Abraham. More than one, actually. We are not left to wonder whatever became of Abraham.

And so it seems that, in the providence of God, the real issue is not how promising a person is. God is the promising one in this relationship. The real issue is not how promising a person is, but how believing a person is.

An Alternative Application
Genesis 12:1-4a. We observed above that God was very clear with Abram about the details of where, what, and whom he would leave, but not nearly so clear about where he would go. Could it be that this is something of a pattern with God? Is it always the nature of his call on our lives that what we leave is explicit and what we gain is unknown?

This runs somewhat contrary to our nature, of course. When we make our plans, the destination is usually the first thing we determine. Which airport I fly out of, which airline I take, and where I have my layover — these are particulars about which I am flexible. But my destination — that is the given, the known.

God's itinerary for Abram, by contrast, was very detailed about his point of departure but the rest was rather vague.

Perhaps something of that uncertainty is captured in Jesus' words to Nicodemus when he compares the movement of the wind to "everyone who is born of the Spirit." If we are willing to allow the Spirit to fill our sails and guide our ship, we cannot predict where that wind will take us.

Perhaps Abram's own experience is embodied, too, in the calls to discipleship of Peter and Andrew (Matthew 4:18-20), James and John (Mark 1:19-20), Levi (Luke 5:27-28), and the several would-be disciples (Luke 9:59-62; 18:18-24). In every case, what they have to leave behind is rather obvious, while their future is unclear and unspecific.

Except that their future is with the Lord.

That was the key for Abram. That was the key for the disciples. And that is the key for us, too, in whatever call God has for us.

Lent 3
Exodus 17:1-7
Romans 5:1-11
John 4:5-42
by William Shepherd

The jar left behind

I was reading the work of a well-known biblical critic who said, "Adequate water sources were crucial to migrant desert dwellers." Like it isn't for the rest of us?

Most of us do not have to search for oases, draw water by hand, or carry jugs back and forth. I still remember the television theme song of my hometown water company (although why a public monopoly needed commercials is beyond me):

Turn it on, and we'll come running.
Turn it on, and we'll be there.
Clean and bright, day and night,
Indianapolis water comes running!

Perhaps there were Hoosiers in the 1960s who could remember hauling their own water and would be grateful for indoor plumbing. Nowadays, city water companies sell their product in grocery stores. Not only do we take drinking water for granted, we are willing to pay extra to get it in designer bottles.

Not everyone is so lucky. As I write this, Florida residents are lining up for water in the wake of four (so far) hurricane strikes. They will not soon forget how much a jug of water weighs, something many in this world are quite familiar with. Our friends in Romania, Elena and Marjana, load up their plastic water jugs and drive into town to draw from the common well. It's a lot of work, even if you have a borrowed Volvo to bear the burden. But there is no running water at their house.

The biblical imagery of water is best understood once we get a grasp on the physics involved. Though the Romans had indoor plumbing, the Bible is largely shaped by a nomadic and rural culture in which water was both precious and a burden. You couldn't live without it, but you either had to live next to it or carry it. Weightlifting thus required no special equipment, only the basic necessities of life. And unless you lived next to it, the hike would get your aerobic training in as well.

The provision of water in the desert is the sign of God's presence according to the book of Exodus. The gospel of John takes the theme and pushes it further, casting Jesus himself in the role of the substance of life. Meanwhile, Paul's letter to the Romans states in plain language the function of Jesus in providing life to all.

Exodus 17:1-7

God sent Israel on a camping trip. It was outward bound, except the campers learned to trust not in themselves, but in the one who sent them on their way. As part of their training, Israel was taught to look to God for the most basic of needs, food (Exodus 16:1-36) and water (Exodus 15:22-27; 17:1-7). Their response would be a paradigm for their future life.

The wilderness stories (Exodus 15:22—18:27) trace the transition of Israel from Egypt to Sinai, from slaves to people whom God has instructed. Israel is on a journey somewhere between promise and fulfillment; the wilderness becomes symbolic of their progress in faith, which is slow at best. The standard pattern in these stories (as in today's lection) is the complaint: The people are needy and they make an accusation against Moses, who prays and receives instructions that resolve the issue, at least temporarily. Here the names of the stops along the wilderness route are said to reflect the "complaining" and "testing" of the people. The issue in the wilderness is that Israel continues to confuse God with Santa Claus; a deity who does not produce on demand must be an absent deity or a non-entity. This attempt to manipulate God, to treat the Lord as a manifestation of their own will, is a precursor to the idolatry of the golden calf.

The Lord is leading the people, though Moses gets the blame when the water runs dry (vv. 1-2). This is ironic, since their salvation came via the sea — yet in the wilderness, they think that God has no command of the water. "Why did you bring us out of Egypt, to kill us and our children and livestock with thirst?" (v. 3). At least slavery had its benefits! Moses' cry in response, "They are almost ready to stone me" (v. 4) is also ironic in light of the subsequent command to strike a stone. The action itself is somewhat ludicrous — how could simply striking a rock produce water? However, the point is not the magic of the rod but the faithfulness of God. God has promised to provide for this people; despite their lack of faith and ingratitude, God will give them all they need.

Exodus points to the future when it describes "the rock at Horeb" (v. 6). Israel has not yet reached the mountain of God, but it looms over the story. God's provision will prove to be part of a covenant established with Israel, which is itself God's provision of life. Just as water flowed from the rock, life for Israel will flow from God's law. As we shall see in the gospel of John, the symbolism was not lost on subsequent generations of readers.

Romans 5:1-11

Romans 5 sits at the center of Paul's argument about how God is at work making human beings righteous through faith. The chapter is connected by theme and vocabulary to the four chapters that precede it, as it continues the discussion of what it means that "we are justified by faith" (v. 1). But it shares material as well as a basic format with the three following chapters: a basic statement concerning the meaning of justification, followed by further clarification of that statement. In chapter 5, Paul affirms that justification by faith produces a state of peace with God and reconciliation naturally follows from justification.

Paul uses all the rhetoric in his toolbox to make his point. Prominent in this section is the rhetorical "climax," a chain of phrases in which the last word of one phrase is picked up as the first word of the next. Paul's chain leads from suffering through endurance to character and hope (vv. 3-5); he thus affirms that "the sufferings of this present time are not worth comparing with the glory about to be revealed to us" (8:18). In verse 7 he uses the rhetorical device of "amplification" to demonstrate the extraordinary character of God's action in Christ, while in verses 9-11 he makes use of a lesser-to-greater argument to underline the implications of that action for our future.

Paul's argument so far has been that human beings are "justified" (or "made right") with God through the faithful action of Jesus, which we in turn share by faith (cf. 1:16-17; 3:21-26). This justification produces "peace with God," not a subjective feeling of peacefulness but an objective state of reconciliation, the cessation of hostilities between enemies (v. 1). Paul describes this state as "this grace" or "this gift" (*charis*, v. 2) in which we stand. It is "access" to a God who was literally our enemy (v. 10), because we were too weak to overcome our alienation from God (v. 6). We were in fact "sinners," those who had chosen not-God over God (cf. 1:18-32; 3:19-20, 23). Despite our alienated state, Christ died for us, resulting in justification, reconciliation, and salvation (vv. 6-10). This is our only basis for boasting, since none of this is dependent on our own actions, but everything on the initiation of God (vv. 2-3, 11).

Christ's faithful act has concrete results for those who share that faith. We have the "love of God... poured into our hearts" (v. 5). This does not refer to human affection for the deity, but to God's undiscriminating goodwill that becomes integrated into our lives through the power of the Holy Spirit (cf. ch. 8). God's love is transformative, in that it replicates specific characteristics in those who receive it: hope in the future, endurance through suffering, and a tested character (vv. 2-3). Paul's concern is for the future as well as the past, as he links reconciliation with "salvation," in the same way that Christ's death is linked to his resurrection (v. 10). Thus he sets up his argument in chapter 6 that participation in the death of Christ is also participation in his resurrection, meaning that Christians have died to sin and thus are able to live transformed lives.

John 4:5-42

John's narrative begs to be experienced rather than summarized, and nowhere is this more evident than in the story of the woman at the well in chapter 4. The story twists and turns as Jesus and the woman banter back and forth, and the "point" is to ride along with them, not to jump to a premature conclusion. The story reveals Jesus' identity as it goes along.

John's story has left the heart of the religious and social world of first-century Palestinian Judaism to head for its boondocks. Chapter 3 saw Jesus in Jerusalem, with John the Baptist testifying to his importance. Chapter 4, however, puts Jesus on the road to Galilee. Strikingly, he goes through rather than around Samaria — unheard of for the pious Jew, since Samaria was filled with foreigners and syncretists sent to colonize the area by Sargon of Assyria (cf. 2 Kings 17:24-34). The Samaritans had opposed the Jewish restoration of Jerusalem and had assisted in the persecutions of the Jews by the Syrians. At best, Samaritans were considered to be religious renegades. Yet Jesus' path takes him straight through this questionable region.

Even more questionable is Jesus' congress with a woman at Jacob's well. Not only do Jews "not share things in common with Samaritans" (v. 9), but men in general and rabbis in particular did not speak to strange women. In merely asking for water, Jesus has violated a number of social conventions! The woman is taken aback, but this momentary disorientation allows Jesus to focus the woman's attention on who he is (v. 10). The promise of "living water" not only reflects an ongoing biblical theme, highlighted in John (cf. Jeremiah 2:13, 17:13; Zechariah 14:8; John 7:37; Revelation 21:6), but is a pun of sorts, for "living water" was a common expression for running water, as opposed to a stagnant cistern. This sets the stage for a typical Johannine misunderstanding: the woman will think that Jesus is offering plumbing, where Jesus has something more symbolic in mind (vv. 11-12). Her question, "Are you greater than our ancestor Jacob?" (v. 12) shows that she does not understand the first thing about who Jesus is. But note that we the readers aren't much further ahead of her — we know that Jesus is in fact greater than Jacob, but we are not exactly clear what the symbolism of the water refers to (grace? revelation? the Spirit?). Jesus never fills in the blank for us — the imagery is left for us to ponder over, never flattened into a pat answer.

Jesus certainly puts Jacob in his place when he notes that "everyone who drinks of this water will be thirsty again" (v. 13). But that is not the case with the water Jesus carries: "The water that I will give will become in them a spring of water gushing up to eternal life" (v. 14). He has sold the goods — the woman definitely wants some of this stuff (after all, who wants to lug water jars back and forth?). The problem is that she has not fully understood what Jesus is offering — she asks for what she cannot fully comprehend, because she is still thinking in literal terms. Where Jesus is offering a life of grace, she sees only the freedom from household drudgery.

Jesus' reference to her husband is not a change of subject but a change of tactics. The woman still has not addressed the fundamental question of Jesus' identity. The question about her personal life will allow her to see correctly that he is a prophet (v. 19). The mention of five husbands — excessive even in that day — is not an attempt to highlight the woman's past life (sinful or not), but simply reinforces Jesus' stunning ability to see inside the heart. The woman's response is to engage Jesus on the level he has presented himself, as a prophet. Far from changing the subject, her question about the proper place of worship (v. 20) moves her back toward the crucial issue of Jesus' identity (in vv. 25-26). While John notes the superiority of the Jewish religion over that of the Samaritans (v. 22), the idea of worship has been transformed by God's new work in Jesus. The issue is now not a place, but "spirit and truth," both of which are to be found in Jesus (vv. 23-24).

The woman correctly perceives that this is a subject for the Messiah. The Samaritans expected the Messiah to be a teacher, so it is natural for the woman to affirm that "when he comes, he will proclaim all things to us" (v. 25). Her mention of the Messiah allows Jesus to bring the discussion full circle, as he reveals, "I am he (*ego eimi*), the one who is speaking to you" (v. 26). The woman did not need any more convincing — her previous conceptions of religion had been overturned: "Then the woman left her water jar and went back to the city" (v. 28).

Her report to the townsfolk, however, contains both a seed of exaggeration and a seed of doubt: "Come and see a man who told me everything I have ever done! He cannot be the Messiah, can he?" (v. 29). Her enthusiasm causes hyperbole, while her doubt is ever so subtly expressed in her question. Her faith is tentative, and yet sufficient for her to witness to others. As often in John, the focus shifts away once the witness has done her job: "Many Samaritans from that city believed in him because of the woman's testimony" (v. 39). Once again Jesus "stays" or "remains" (*meno*) with potential disciples, just as God "stays" with him (v. 40, cf. John 1:38-39; 2:12; 11:54; 14:10, 17, 25; 15:4-7, 9-10, 16; 21:22-23). This results in multiple conversions (v. 41), which the new believers attribute not to the woman's testimony, but to their own experience of Jesus (v. 42).

The woman's story illustrates the lesson that Jesus gives the disciples after her departure. She has become the (unlikely) sower who makes possible the later work of the reapers (vv. 35-38). Unfortunately, the disciples have the same problem of misunderstanding as the woman. They do not understand why he has broken social convention to speak to this woman (v. 27). Nor do they understand what he means when he says, "I have food to eat that you do not know about" (v. 32, note how the symbolic weight has shifted from water to its related necessity, food — the reverse of the movement in the Exodus story). Their lack of understanding is highlighted in their response, "Surely no one has brought him something to eat?" (v. 33). Jesus speaks in a more direct fashion to the disciples than he did to the woman, eliminating any misunderstanding at once: "My food is to do the will of him who sent me and to complete his work" (v. 34).

Application

I have always been intrigued by the woman's water jug. She came to the well to draw water but became so involved in her conversation with Jesus that she left the jug behind and ran away to tell everyone. She never does come back for it — it just sits there, all during Jesus' lecture to the disciples (and for all we know, during the whole two days he stayed in Samaria).

The jug, of course, plays a literary function by uniting the successive scenes in the story, even as the imagery shifts from drinking water to food. But the jug also serves a symbolic purpose. After all, Jesus did promise the woman "living water" that would lead to "eternal life." And she did leave her jug with him. I imagine him keeping his promise and filling the jug to the brim (cf. John 2:7).

As we have seen, even as the woman runs away, she hasn't quite made up her mind. The jug stands for the unfinished business between Jesus and the woman. The woman's jar remains by the well, because the story isn't through with her yet. It will never be through with her. She will keep coming back to Jesus for the living water that leads to eternal life, because it is not a one-shot inoculation. It involves "remaining" with Jesus. She has to leave her jar with him. He isn't done with her yet.

As the woman's story is open-ended, so is ours as readers. We must now decide how to respond to Jesus' self-revelation. And if we want the water he offers, we must leave our jars by the well for Jesus to refill. He's not done with us yet either.

An Alternative Application
Exodus 17:1-7; Romans 5:1-11; John 4:5-42. "Is the Lord among us or not?" The question posed by the people of Israel did not have an obvious answer. The Israelites considered the lack of water to be a sign that God was not with them. Moses, on the contrary, considered their doubt a test of the Lord, which the Lord had no need to pass. God was with them, whether they realized it or not. The water was merely the sign that God had been there all along.

Paul echoes the sentiment when he includes suffering in a chain that leads to hope. For Paul, suffering is actually a matter for boasting, because it is a sign that God is indeed present. Why does Paul come to the exact opposite conclusion that the people of Israel did? Paul was influenced by Hellenistic philosophical traditions that saw suffering as educational; it produced endurance, which produced character, which produced hope. Far from bringing him to doubt, he took his suffering as proof of God's favor.

Jesus, too, understood that adverse outward conditions play no part in the assessment of one's spiritual health. He never did get that drink of water. Nor did he show any interest in the food his disciples brought from town. His sustenance was solely based on his obedient faith to God.

Lent 4
1 Samuel 16:1-13
Ephesians 5:8-14
John 9:1-41
by Wayne Brouwer

Believing is seeing

Sometimes we see people who are wide-eyed with wonder. Children especially can appear this way, in part because of the size of their eyeballs. Our eyeballs grow very little during the course of our lives and certainly not at the same rate as the rest of our bodies' organs. For that reason children stare at life with eyes bigger in proportion to their faces than those of adults. Compared with big people, children's eyes dominate their facial features and can thus appear more piercing and inquisitive.

While all five of our senses help us connect with our environment, we tend to rely more dependently on our sight than on smell, taste, hearing, or touch. We are people who trust our eyes before we will accept input from our other senses. Missouri claims that it is the "Show me!" state, and most of us take up residence there intellectually, whether we ever physically resettle into those borders. In fact, one of our favorite proverbs is "Seeing is believing!" Like Thomas among Jesus' disciples, we won't believe until the proof of something stares us in the face.

But sometimes sight blinds us. Rather than helping us understand life, our vision can distract us from reality. We find that in each of our passages for today. Samuel assesses each of the sons of Jesse in one way but does not find the next king of Israel until he begins to see with the unique eyes of God and believes in God's promises. The apostle Paul reminds us that physical sight and spiritual insight are not exactly the same thing and on the day that Jesus brought healing to a man who had been born blind, there was a great confusion about how people were to "see" this event.

While in much of our lives "seeing is believing," there are truly times when "believing is seeing." Today, you, as a pastor, must be in part a spiritual ophthalmologist who gives to your congregation an eye exam that improves the sight of every heart.

1 Samuel 16:1-13

Samuel's Israel is in chaos and the conflict has emerged from within the royal house itself. After Saul began his reign with great promise (1 Samuel 9-11), a number of events led both Samuel and Israel to question Saul's ability to rule well. First, Saul deliberately attacked a Philistine outpost to provoke war with Israel's much more powerful neighbor (1 Samuel 13:1-5). Then when Samuel was delayed in coming to the troops to confirm God's blessing on their fight, Saul jeopardized the religious pep rally by assuming a spiritual leadership for which he was not called or qualified (1 Samuel 13:8-13).

Next, Saul left the battlefield as if he were uncertain about the wisdom of the commotion he had set in motion (1 Samuel 13:14-15). When Saul's son Jonathan carried out a bold maneuver to resolve the tense standoff, Saul is caught indecisive and unprepared (1 Samuel 14:1-23). Furthermore, Saul shames himself before his troops, first by stupidly denying them any nourishment to carry on with the demands of battle (1 Samuel 14:24), and then later condemning his own son Jonathan to death when Jonathan disobeys this restriction that he had never heard in the first place (1 Samuel 14:25-44). Fortunately, Saul's armies had more sense than Saul and stopped this senseless abuse of power. But the tide had turned and both the nation and God fell out of alliance with Saul (1 Samuel 15).

Several people make judgments about David and his suitability for royal office in this short passage. First, Samuel meets Jesse's oldest and strongest sons and assumes that they are the stuff of kings. God needs to remind Samuel that royalty is not determined merely by size and bearing. After all, Saul was handsome and stood head and shoulders above the rest of his community when Samuel had anointed him as king (1 Samuel 9:2). Samuel found out the fickleness of mere physical assessment, as Saul had become a burden to both him and Israel. Yet here Samuel was, again playing the beauty pageant game rather than waiting for the whisper that would help him to truly see the qualities of leadership that may be hidden inside the ugly or the unlikely. Only when he believes in the inner anointing of God on the true candidate will he be able to see David as king.

Then Jesse and the rest of his family also make a judgment about David. Evidently they think that David is a rascally runt who lacks the physique and maturity of his older brothers. Verse 11 is actually rather comical, if its implications are drawn out: first, the family doesn't think enough of David to allow him to be part of the great party that has come to town with Samuel's arrival. Next, they refuse to believe that Samuel's direct command to Jesse to assemble all his sons includes David (Can you imagine what an inferiority complex David could have gotten from being treated in such a way by his own parents?). Then when they finally remember that David is also part of the family, Jesse dismisses him offhandedly as merely "tending the sheep," as if his place is more with the hired servants than with the family. Jesse and his family believe David is not the stuff of leadership quality, and they sideline him from the selection process without a second thought. They do not believe in what David is truly made of, and therefore they cannot see him as king.

Thankfully, however, there is actually another onlooker. He does not make a cameo appearance in the story, but Samuel alludes to his presence. This other observer is God. While Samuel is uncertain as to what assessment God gives to each of the older sons of Jesse, he eventually becomes certain about God's measuring tools in the process and confident about God's ultimate choice: "The Lord does not look at the things man looks at. Man looks at the outward appearance, but the Lord looks at the heart" (v. 7). God understands the heart and qualities of David's life, and therefore God authorizes David's right to rule Israel. God believes in David and sees a king.

During this season of Lent, several themes from this passage may serve as helpful hooks on which to carry the sentiment of suffering. First, there is a deep-seated evil in our world that cannot be simply explained or excised. Saul's loss of his throne, the distresses in his family, his varied popular opinion polls, and his future are all complexly shifting around a variety of evils resident in the system. Saul's story at least requires us to think about the wiles of sin that confound all our daily lives. During Lent, we must take sin and evil seriously, and not minimize their contortions of God's good world.

Second, as David put it in Psalm 23, all of us will walk at one time or another through the "valley of the shadow of death" and be forced to eat at a table "in the presence of [our] enemies." This story in David's life echoes the misunderstandings and sufferings that we all share on the pilgrimage of life. Furthermore, it reminds us that the hardest thing we can do is walk the journey alone. Thus, to know that others have walked this way, including David and Jesus, we find some camaraderie, even in difficult times.

Third, there is the hopeful promise in Samuel's awareness of God's presence and constant direction. We may be surrounded by those who view us with scandalized eyes and torment us with inappropriate judgments, but one sees and knows and feels and has a heart disposed toward "good." It is precisely during Lent that we need to know that God believes in us as God's children, and therefore sees us with eyes of grace, mercy, and care.

Ephesians 5:8-14

Paul's letter to the Ephesians appears to have been a circular message of encouragement sent along with Tychicus (6:21-22) and the slave Onesimus (Colossians 4:7-9) whom Paul is returning to his master

Philemon (Philemon 8-12). It was written while Paul was imprisoned (see 4:1), probably in Rome in the early '60s, and was likely meant to be circulated among the Christian congregations of the Lycus River Valley near Philemon's home (note that earliest manuscripts do not identify the recipients in 1:1, indicating that it may have gone to several churches before ending up in Ephesus; also see Colossians 4:16).

The letter is usually divided into two major parts, with chapters 1-3 explaining the supremacy of Christ in all things, and chapters 4-6 giving implications of Christ's rule for Christian living. In these verses, Paul deals with perceptions that change actions. There is no physical movement of Christ-believers from an arena lost in darkness (v. 8) into a realm constantly flooded with light. Instead, Paul wishes for his readers to understand the transformation of their mindsets and outlooks from one corrupted by sin into an intellectual and volitional perspective that is ruled again by God's original designs. Darkness is a spiritual condition that all of us are born into; light is the gift of God's grace in Jesus Christ and allows us to be reborn into a new moral and ethical posture toward ourselves and those around us.

Once we *believe*, we begin to *see* in new ways. Believing is seeing. During the season of Lent this takes tangible shape in the islands of grace that Sundays form in the dark morass of Lenten pain and suffering. The Sundays during Lent do not belong to the season of Lent, but are, in fact, early echoes of Easter victory. So on this fourth Sunday during Lent, it is important to remind our people that they may be surrounded by darkness, but they live as children of the light. The darkness presses in and causes turmoil, but the light of Christ is the guiding norm of our existence. We must, as one author has put it, "set our sights by the true North Star, Jesus."

John 9:1-41

While the synoptic gospels tell of many miracles that Jesus did, John enumerates only seven. He calls these "miraculous signs" (2:11) and tracks them moving the disciples and others from doubt to faith in Jesus as the Christ, as the Son of God, and as the Savior (John 20:30-31). Some Johannine scholars see a correlation between the seven signs and a rehearsal of Old Testament events. If that is so, the healing recorded in this passage is miraculous sign number six, and parallels the blindness of ancient Israel that could only be undone with God's interruptive coming on the "Day of the Lord" (see Isaiah 6:8-13; 9:2; 60:1-3; 61:1).

It is obvious from the start of this story that something unusual is happening, even for Jesus. While most miracles are done with a word or a touch, here Jesus goes through a strange process of several steps in order to bring sight to the blind man. First, he interprets the man's blindness not in causal terms as the disciples wanted to read it (9:1), but as a divinely ordained preparation for Jesus' own revelation (9:2). Second, Jesus places this healing in the context of the cosmological wrestling of darkness and light that are used to describe his coming in the prologue (1:1-18). Third, Jesus makes a mud pie of his spit and the clay of the earth in an act that seems reminiscent of the divine creative activity in Genesis 2:7, even to the point of dependency on divinely appointed moisture giving life to all things (Genesis 2:6). Fourth, the man's eyes are not opened immediately, but only after he goes to the pool of Siloam and washes off the mud packs. Of course, the only way he could get to the pool is by having family or friends guide him there, since he is still blind. This means that the act of healing would involve the presence, witness, and shared faith of others, placing the man into a believing community in order to receive his sight.

But the healing is met with confusion rather than faith. Many who had known the man in his blinded condition could not believe that the sighted man was the same person (9:8-9). Already this gives an indication as to how "believing" will be "seeing" for all in this story and not the other way around. Furthermore, it seems that John is giving a second message through the disbelief of the neighbors, namely that all who believe in Jesus as Savior have a new disposition about them that former acquaintances find confusing.

The incident becomes a matter for public debate. At stake is not the man's sight, but the character of Jesus. Is he a breaker of the Sabbath (9:14, 16)? Is he a common sinner like everyone else (9:16)? Is he a prophet (9:17)? Is he the Christ (9:22)? While the sign itself is undisputed, the message of the sign is debated. Jesus stands as a signpost, but all who gather around him argue as to what his signboard is declaring. Those who recognize his power believe in him as divinely sent (9:31-38); those who refuse to acknowledge their need for him deny Jesus' divine character and the healing he brings. In the end, the choice between blindness and sightedness is not physical but spiritual (9:39-41). Believing is seeing.

In order to tie this to our journey through Lent it might be appropriate to make a connection with those things in our lives that confuse, confound, and torment us: a threatening disease, a sudden death, a broken marriage, a moral failure of someone we trusted, a lack of work, a terrifying terrorist attack. Why these? Why me? Why us? Why now? Just as with the man's blindness in John's story, we can get caught up in micro-assessments and lose sight of the big picture. Jesus came to share our walk with us, as marked by our Lenten remembrances, but he came as a sign of the big picture of healing that God was providing for our darkened world. Each incident of evil is of concern to God, but no single happenstance of cruelty or disease ought to detract us from the important goal of God — the total restoration of God's creation. During Lent we can get caught up in our shared sufferings with Jesus. What we need to remember is their redemptive purpose.

A second theme from this story is that of the community of faith. While the formerly blind man has great trust in Jesus, his original healing came only through a communal effort to get him to the waters of Siloam. Furthermore, there is a communal ownership of the outcomes of faith — the man's parents fear being expelled from the synagogue as a result of their connection with their son. To John's first readers this message likely resonated in their current situation and called them to communities of faithfulness over against the communities of persecution that threatened them. We in North America tend to view faith and belief as personal, individual matters. The truth is that we cannot walk either through Lenten suffering or Easter hope alone. We need community.

Application
Believing is seeing. It was so for the characters that surrounded the boy David when even his family did not recognize his true worth. It was true for Paul's readers who attempted to live according to divine ethics in a world contorted by devilish designs. It was also this way for the many people who saw the miraculous sign of Jesus in John 9, and who chose to respond with different faith perspectives.

So, too, it is with us. Every year we take this torturous pilgrimage through Lent, bent with the burdens of sin and evil clinging to us. Sometimes it feels good to wallow in misery. There is a psychological desire in each of us to want to play the martyr, to cry for others to pity us, and to lament the uniqueness of our particular load of injustice and hurt. These passages remind us that what we see is not necessarily what we get, and what we experience will not be the last chapter written about our condition. When we believe, we see things anew. When we understand God's perspectives and designs, we move from slugging it out in the shadows to life in the light, and the turning point is not merely some pious wish or some psychological self-babble or some political promising, but rather the person of Jesus. Who is Jesus? Is Jesus the Son of God, the divine messenger, the physician of the soul? Or is Jesus merely another "sinner" among us who taunts us with false pledges? Those who trust Jesus may not be able to explain it, but neither do they stumble in darkness any longer.

Lent 5
Ezekiel 37:1-14
Romans 8:6-11
John 11:1-45
by David Kalas

No spring chicken

Each year about this time, we in the church are fond of making a misplaced analogy. Tennyson wrote, "In the spring a young man's fancy lightly turns to thoughts of love." Perhaps if he had observed the contemporary American church, he would have written, "In the spring a preacher's fancy turns to thoughts of nature and Easter." Again and again each March or April, we see trotted out the symbolic connection between the event we celebrate on Easter — Christ's resurrection — and the season in which we celebrate it — springtime. Spring, we are told, is the season of new life, and so the resurrection of Christ is tied to nature's annual display of spring flowers and buds on trees.

The association between Easter and spring is a lovely one and quite sentimental. Unfortunately, it is also quite misleading. Christ's resurrection is not at all paralleled by nature. Christ's resurrection was, in fact, entirely unnatural and to make the association between the two is to apply the wrong analogy, and therefore to perpetuate a misunderstanding.

Our three lections for this week invite us to ponder the issue of dead things being brought back to life. Ezekiel witnesses a startling demonstration of that event in the valley of dry bones. Jesus brings dead Lazarus back to life, and Paul bears witness to the Spirit "who raised Christ from the dead" and who will do the same for us. We have the opportunity this week to set aside the beauty of what nature does each spring and see, in contrast, the beauty of what God does, what Christ did, and what the Spirit will do in us.

Ezekiel 37:1-14

A marvelous matrix of relationships is contained here in this familiar passage, and any of the relationships could be explored by the preacher to great effect.

There is, first, the relationship between Ezekiel and God. We could be endlessly fascinated by the biblical accounts of how God deals with his servants, for it gives us fresh insight into our own relationship with him. In this instance, we have the fascinating appellation consistently used by God for Ezekiel, *ben adam*. The NRSV translates the Hebrew phrase as "mortal," while the KJV, RSV, NIV, and NKJV all opt for "son of man." The Septuagint's translation (*huie anthropou*) seems to favor a "son of man" or "son of mankind" reading. Meanwhile, the Living Bible's paraphrase is perhaps more picturesque: "son of dust." Whatever the best translation, the title offers deliberate perspective and constant reminders to Ezekiel of who and what he is. It is not belittling; it is merely a reminder of fact, and a reminder that we and our native egocentricity need God.

The irresistibly appealing hallmark of Ezekiel's relationship with God, meanwhile, is its personal and dialogical quality. Most of the book is written in the first-person, which gives the account a very personal flavor. The personal testimony offered there is of a God who almost continuously speaks with Ezekiel. Nearly thirty times, the prophet recalls that the Lord "said to me," and it is not a one-way lecture, but more of a guided tour. Again and again throughout the book, as in our selected passage, the Lord shows Ezekiel things (e.g., 44:5), invites him to go and see (e.g., 8:5; 8:9), or asks him if he has seen (e.g., 8:17).

Even if the *ben adam* term is "off-putting" to us at first, the actual playing out of the relationship that we see between God and Ezekiel has a terrifically personal quality to it. The Lord is walking the prophet through a series of lessons, like a tutor, and it is experiential and conversational, at that. Our particular passage certainly has that quality. God does not merely say to Ezekiel what he wants Ezekiel to know — or, a step further removed, what he wants his people to know. Rather, Ezekiel and the Lord experience the event together.

Next, we have the relationship between Ezekiel and the bones. That is an impersonal relationship, to be sure, but it is one that may resonate with our experience. We, and the people in our pews, will from time to time, look out over a hopeless landscape, and what shall be our relationship to that inanimate despair? Will we wave the white flag at what is an obviously lost cause? Will we shrug our shoulders in dismay? Or will we open our minds to the possibilities of what God can do, following his instructions all the way to new life in the midst of dried up and dismembered death?

Then there is the relationship between Ezekiel and the people of Israel. It turns out that they are the ones represented by that hopeless valley of dry and detached bones. The experience in the valley was meant by God to be a kind of training exercise for Ezekiel. Like the astronaut who goes through all sorts of simulation experiences on earth before being launched into outer space, so God walked Ezekiel through a simulation of what his ministry must be: prophesying in the midst of hopelessness and despair; believing upstream; and participating in the miraculous work, word, and will of God.

Finally there is the relationship between God and his people Israel. That is the central issue, of course. The entire ministry and message of the prophet are subsets of this larger matter: God's relationship to his people. That relationship is, we discover, an uneven two-way street. Love and loyalty flow in both directions, but the volume is so very much greater going one way than the other.

God's people had been scandalously disloyal to him, and their unfaithfulness is chronicled and condemned in earlier chapters of Ezekiel. So, too, are the details of God's judgment on his people for their infidelity. In the end, however, the Lord does not abandon his people. They deserve to be divorced, to be sure, but that is not God's choice. They deserve to be utterly crushed, but instead he preserves a remnant. So here, in this episode, the people are represented by the brokenness and hopelessness of the valley of dry bones, but God will not leave his people in that condition. Rather, as only he can do, we read that the Lord will "open your graves, and bring you up from your graves... and you shall live."

Romans 8:6-11

The operative word in verses 6 and 7 is not immediately apparent in most translations. The King James and New King James Versions render the first part of verse 6: "For to be carnally minded is death." Meanwhile, the Revised Standard and New Revised Standard Versions take a slightly different approach: "To set the mind on the flesh is death." The New English Bible, by contrast, reads: "Those who live on the level of our lower nature have their outlook formed by it, and that spells death."

If a person in your congregation sat down and read several such English translations side-by-side, he or she might be confused. The various translations lead one to think that there must be a very complex verb in the original Greek. It seems to be a verb that can be variously translated as "to be," "to set the mind," or "to live on the level of."

In fact, however, what lies behind the different translations is not a very complex Greek verb, but rather no Greek verb at all.

The New International Version, in this case, may come nearest to giving the sense of it: "The mind of sinful man is death." Even the English word "is" represents an insertion, for the Greek has no verb at all. Rather, the construction of verse 6 simply juxtaposes two subjects and in the absence of a verb it almost suggests the mathematical sign for "equals" in between.

Read literally, verse 6 would run like this: "For the mind of the flesh death, and the mind of the Spirit life and peace."

The original Greek word that Paul uses, which I have translated above as "mind," is not the standard New Testament Greek word for "mind." Rather, it is a word that appears only three times in the entire New Testament, and all three occurrences are right here in Romans 8 (vv. 6, 7, and 27). It is perhaps more satisfactory to translate it as "mindset" or "way of thinking."

It is really just two equations that Paul presents: The way of thinking of the flesh equals death; the way of thinking of the Spirit equals life and peace. "You do the math," Paul says in effect. If our mindset is of the flesh, it follows naturally that we will not submit to God's law and cannot please God, so we are invited to have the mindset of the Spirit.

The other fascinating intersection of grammar and theology in this passage is found in the use of the preposition "in." On the one hand, Paul says that the Christians to whom he is writing are not "in the flesh" but rather "in the Spirit." On the other hand, he also notes that "the Spirit of God dwells in you." Moreover, "if the Spirit... dwells in you," becomes the key to the resurrection of the body.

There are no special things to be said about the Greek preposition involved here. It is not uncommon or profound. Our English "in" is an adequate translation of it, but its recurring usage here does invite the preacher to ponder these three realities: our being in the flesh, our being in the Spirit, and the Spirit being in us.

The reference to the resurrection within this context suggests another kind of mathematical equation. The church has, for years, struggled with the relationship of our works and our salvation. Even apart from the in-depth theological debates throughout church history, there are the over-the-back-fence theologians who also weigh in on the subject. They, the folks in our culture who believe that there is a heaven, find it almost irresistible to assume that it's "good people" who go there.

The components of this passage, however, suggest another factor that can help the equation to make sense. That factor is the Spirit. Rather than limping along with the happy but somewhat shallow assumption that folks who live good lives will go to heaven, we see in Paul's understanding that the Spirit is actually the key. Namely, it is the Spirit that engenders righteous living, and it is the Spirit that raises us from the dead. We might conclude, therefore, that our salvation is not the by-product of our good lives, but rather our good lives and our salvation are both products of the Spirit's work within us.

John 11:1-45

The preaching potential of John 11 is staggering. I'm a believer that the whole Bible is worth preaching — every book, every chapter — but I will quickly concede that the sermon material is a bit more obvious in some passages than in others. In John 11, there are more sermons than one Sunday can accommodate. So many larger themes come into play in this passage.

First, there is the relationship between Jesus and this particular family — Mary, Martha, and Lazarus. In addition to this episode, we have at least two other glimpses into this group of friends (Luke 10:38-42; John 12:1-11).

Second, we are met, again, here with this matter of purpose. Jesus does not merely chalk up Lazarus' sickness and death to the natural order but rather claims that "it is for God's glory, so that the Son of God may be glorified through it." The teaching is reminiscent of the healing of the blind man earlier in John's gospel, when Jesus explains, "He was born blind so that God's works might be revealed in him" (John 9:3).

Third, this occasion is part of the larger plot of Jesus' opponents who seek to kill him. The disciples were conscious of this issue (John 11:8), though it is interesting that danger, fear, and opposition, which can be primary factors in most human decision-making, do not play a part in where Jesus goes or what Jesus does. Also, just beyond the boundaries of our selected passage, Lazarus' return to life becomes another point of controversy and consternation for Jesus' opponents.

Fourth, there is the faith-crisis issue of God's timing. This is not limited to some theoretical theme in scripture, of course; this is a daily faith issue for the people in our pews. Early in the episode, we see Jesus deliberately delaying his trip to Bethany. Later, observers at Lazarus' tomb asked, "Could not he who opened the eyes of the blind man have kept this man from dying?" (v. 37). And, in the most poignant, human moment of all, both Martha and Mary individually lament to Jesus, "Lord, if you had been here, my brother would not have died" (vv. 21, 32).

Finally, this passage features one of the "I am" statements of Jesus. These statements are a significant theme in John's gospel, accumulating and cooperating to reveal who Jesus is, which is the real issue of the gospel. What Jesus said and did are reported, it seems, as a means to that larger end: recognizing who Jesus is and the occasion of Lazarus' death yields one of the most famous of those statements: "I am the resurrection and the life" (v. 25).

Application

We have often used the surrounding context of springtime as a metaphor for the resurrection we celebrate at Easter. As we consider the three death-to-life passages we have before us today, we should consider a revamping of the analogy. Use nature's springtime not in comparison with but in contrast to Christ's resurrection.

At springtime, we say, nature shows signs of new life. The flowers begin to poke through the ground and the branches on the trees show the buds of new leaves. That's all very lovely, of course, but it is not resurrection. It is not even resuscitation.

Ezekiel was confronted with what must have been a horrid sight: a valley full of dry bones. Every syllable of the phrase connotes death, doesn't it? We already figuratively associate death with a valley. The bones are surely a symbol of death, and the fact that they are just scattered bones — not assembled skeletons — makes them seem still further removed from life. Finally, they are dry. Whenever they were alive, it was a long time ago.

Lazarus had not been dead so long, of course, but it was long enough. Long enough that he had been wrapped up and buried. Long enough that the tomb was sealed off with a stone. Long enough that the ever-fastidious Martha was concerned about the stench.

How shall we set nature side-by-side with Ezekiel's valley? How shall we take springtime and contrast it with Lazarus?

Ezekiel's valley would not be full of trees that are bare in the winter — for those trees are still alive. No, Ezekiel's valley would be full of leaves that have turned brown, fallen off, and been mulched. For those leaves to come together, turn green, and reattach themselves to trees — that would not be nature and springtime but would be Ezekiel's dry bones coming to life again.

Lazarus' tomb would not have an empty garden within it waiting for spring to bring dormant bulbs to bloom. No, Lazarus' tomb would have within it the bagged clippings from last month's lawn mowing. It would be dead, yellowed, stale, and smelly. Jesus calls in and the bag bounces out. "Tear it open," he commands, and we find the clippings alive, verdant, and growing.

What God did at the valley of dry bones was not natural. What Jesus did at Lazarus' tomb was not natural. What the Spirit did at the empty tomb was not natural. It is not mimicked by spring.

What Christ can do in our lives — and in our deaths — is not bound by the limitations of nature or dictated by the natural order. Because real resurrection and life are not found in nature: they are found in him.

An Alternative Application
Ezekiel 37:1-14. Typically a question raises doubts. A question challenges our certainty. Are you sure? Can you prove it? But what if...?

We see the phenomenon at work right from the beginning. The serpent asked a question in an effort to raise doubts in Eve's mind. "Did God say, 'You shall not eat from any tree in the garden'?" (Genesis 3:1). Well, no. No, that's not at all what God said. But the question raised that bit of doubt in Eve's mind: a doubt about God, on which the serpent later expanded and capitalized.

The writer of Proverbs observes, "The first man to speak in court always seems right until his opponent begins to question him" (Proverbs 18:17 TEV). So it is that a question typically raises doubts.

When Ezekiel stands before his own Death Valley, however, God asks a question that points in a different direction. "Can these bones live?"

If the question came from anyone else, it would be an insult, an offense, salt in the wound. Walk into the lawyer's office where the divorce papers are being signed and ask, "Can this marriage be saved?" Stand in the hospital room beside what remains of a disease-riddled body, struggling through its final breaths, and ask, "Can this person be healed?" Preposterous questions.

But God's question is meant to raise a wholesome doubt in Ezekiel's mind. Or perhaps it was something else. Surely doubt already prevailed in the face of that panorama of death. Can you raise a doubt about doubt? God asked a question to raise faith in Ezekiel's mind!

As we noted above, both we and the people in our pews might — today, tomorrow, or one day soon — look out over a seemingly hopeless landscape. The hymn writer encourages us to "ponder anew what the almighty can do, if with his love he befriend thee" ("Praise to the Lord, the Almighty" by Joachim Neander, translated by Catherine Winkworth). We might help ourselves ponder anew what the Lord can do by asking questions — preposterous questions, outlandish questions, questions that raise faith.

Can this marriage be saved? Can this body be healed? Can this addiction be broken? Can this person ever change?

Can these bones live?

Passion / Palm Sunday (Lent 6)
Isaiah 50:4-9a
Philippians 2:5-11
Matthew 26:14—27:66
by William Shepherd

The wrong anthem

The choir director was aghast. "I just didn't realize," she said. "It was totally inappropriate. I chose the wrong anthem."

Her mistake was understandable. The service schedule said, "Palm Sunday," and the usual Palm Sunday choir anthem includes shouts of "Hosanna." The problem was the placement. In the *Book of Common Prayer*, the "Hosanna" part comes at the beginning of the service. Following a procession with singing and palm-waving, the congregation settles down to a much more grave matter: a participatory reading of one of the passion narratives from the synoptic gospels. The choir director's anthem, coming after this solemn reading, did seem a bit inappropriate.

Yet Palm Sunday and Passion Sunday are one and the same, and today's readings all describe the same Messiah, and the same God who is defined by that Messiah: One who is self-giving to a fault. The difference between the triumphal entry into Jerusalem and the crucifixion is simply that the definition of messiahship has been clarified; it is not to be manifested in the royal palace, but among the poor, the weak, and the neglected. Whatever historical reality may underlie these stories, on this day we read about a humble king who is humbled further, and we enact our own participation in these stories by taking the part of "the crowd" in both stories. The same crowd that shouts "Hosanna to the Son of David!" will soon shout, "Crucify him!"

Isaiah 50:4-9a

The Third Servant Song in Second Isaiah is a monologue, with the Servant as the speaker. The monologue reflects the broader genre of a trust psalm; the Servant expresses his trust in God. Here in Isaiah, the Servant should be thought of as the embodiment of Israel (or the faithful remnant in Israel) and not as an individual (cf. 48:16; 49:3).

The passage in which our lection occurs is divided into three sections. The introduction (vv. 1-3) shares with the previous chapter the invocation of Zion but now it is specifically the "children of Zion" who are called (v. 1). The speaker poses questions that will be answered in the Song proper (vv. 4-9). The final verses (vv. 10-11) are a commentary in response to the Song (here the Servant is no longer the speaker): The community is divided in their response to the Servant, and those who do not believe are warned of dire consequences.

The Servant is empowered by God "to sustain the weary with a word" (v. 4). Specifically, the Servant is given an ear for the gift of God's word: "The Lord God has given me the tongue of those who are taught" (the NRSV translation, "tongue of a teacher," is possible, but not likely). What the Servant is learning here is not information as much as lifestyle; the community is taught to accept suffering and shame on God's behalf (v. 5). "I gave my back to those who struck me, and my cheeks to those who pulled out the beard; I did not hide my face from insult and spitting" (v. 6). Despite this trial, the community asserts its faith: "The Lord God helps me; therefore I have not been disgraced; therefore I have set my face like flint, and I know that I shall not be put to shame" (v. 7). The Servant uses legal language to picture his exoneration, with God sitting in the defense attorney's chair: "He who vindicates me is near" (v. 8). The prosecution's witnesses are faulty ("Who are my adversaries?"), and the judge will find no guilt (v. 9).

With this vivid picture of personal suffering, Second Isaiah embodies both the grief and hope of a community that had suffered badly in exile. No wonder Christians understood this passage to reflect and interpret the life and death of their Messiah!

Philippians 2:5-11

The Song continues in Paul's letter to the Philippians. Most scholars see this passage as a literal song, an early Christian hymn inserted by Paul into his letter as support for his exhortation. This is certainly possible. The unusual and poetic vocabulary may not be Paul's own, and the structure is reminiscent of Hebrew poetry in its stress and parallelism (it is usually thought to be influenced by Isaiah's Servant Songs, though some scholars see its primary background in the story of Adam's fall in Genesis). However, the themes and even the language are well within Paul's rhetorical repertoire, so he may have written this ode to Christ himself.

Clearly the hymn moves in two directions: first downward in humility, then upward to glory. It is not so clear what this movement actually represents. Traditional interpretation has seen here a reference to the pre-existence and incarnation of Christ, who came down from heaven to take human form, and then returned from whence he came. But an equally good case could be made that the poetic language imagines no pre-existence, and that the entire tale is told of the incarnate Christ, who humbled himself in service to others. Both interpretations fit the hymn (though I incline to the traditional one).

Neither is there a consensus on how the main focus of the hymn is to be understood. The crux here is the elliptical opening sentence, which reads literally "This think in you (pl.) which also in Christ Jesus" (v. 5). The verb must be supplied in the second half of the sentence. Traditionally, the simplest translation has been preferred, with the verb "to be" (so NRSV, "Let the same mind be in you that was in Christ Jesus"). This implies that the point is simply ethical imitation, and the life of the community should parallel the life of Christ ("in you" is best understood as "among yourselves," specifying not individual inner disposition but group character). However, this translation does not quite capture all the nuances of Paul's expression "in Christ," which indicates a state of union and power that goes beyond mere aping of actions. We might translate the phrase, "which is yours as those who are in Christ," or "which you think as those who are in Christ" (supplying the verb from the first half of the sentence). The sentence could be taken in a number of ways, as paradigmatic (Christ providing the model mind), mystical (the mind shared in union with Christ), ecclesiastical (the mind of those who are the Body of Christ), or soteriological (the mind that comes from being "in Christ"). These different ways of understanding the introductory sentence are not necessarily contradictory, however — in fact, they are quite complementary. Following Jesus is not merely imitating his example but participating in his life and being energized by his power. It is not just that we follow Christ but that we are in some sense sharers in Christ's nature and power, which the hymn specifies.

However we understand the introduction, we must understand how the hymn functions as part of Paul's argument. Philippians is a letter about friendship and possessions and how one expresses the other. Paul writes to his friends to thank them for their monetary gift (1:7; 4:10, 15-18); it is not going too far to say that Philippians is one long thank-you note! In Greco-Roman society, it was a common notion that "friends share all things," and Paul rightly takes their gift as a sign of that kind of friendship. His exhortation to them is to live out the implications of their gift of friendship by sharing their hearts and minds. Paul then evokes several examples of the kind of mindset he is commending: Jesus (2:5-11), Timothy and Epaphroditus (2:19—3:1), and Paul himself (3:20—4:1). In this case, he starts his examples with the climax, pulling out all the rhetorical guns to exhort them to "make my joy complete: be of the same mind, having the same love, being in full accord and of one mind" (2:2).

The "one mind" they are to share is the mind of Christ, which is described in the hymn. He was, first of all, in "the form of God." Traditionally, this has been understood as a reference to the divine Christ's pre-existence, but it could refer to his human form, as Adam was created in "the image of God." In either case, he did not regard that form as *harpagmos*, "something to be seized, grasped, robbed," such as booty or plunder (v. 6). The poetic idea here is that Christ chose not to use his gifts to his own advantage; he did not take the opportunity that they presented for self-promotion. Note that this is "possessions" language, and that the "possessions" symbolize a spiritual state, a notion that probably would not be lost on a congregation that had so recently sacrificed their own goods for Paul's mission.

Rather than looking out for himself, Christ "emptied himself" or stripped himself of the privileges that came with his status (like a reverse Adam). He took on the identity of a slave, much like Isaiah's Servant (the hymn uses several synonyms for "form" and "likeness," all of which are poetic variants of the same idea). He did not thereby cease to be in the form of God but by doing so defined that form — it is that of a slave (v. 7). The slave is humble and obedient (here the stark contrast to Adam), and Paul takes the logic of his argument to its obvious conclusion: the ultimate emptying and humbling is found in a death on the cross (v. 8).

Having reached the bottom, the movement is reversed (v. 9). The humble Christ is exalted and given "the name that is above every name," either the name "Jesus" (v. 10) or more likely "Lord" (v. 11). This leads to a cosmic proclamation, in which "every knee should bend, in heaven and on earth and under the earth, and every tongue should confess that Jesus Christ is Lord, to the glory of God the Father" (vv. 10-11). The entire universe is thus brought under the lordship of Christ. On the basis of this declaration, Paul will launch further into his exhortation, which includes not only the request for good works but also the promise of God's assistance (vv. 12-13).

Matthew 26:14—27:66

The long passion narrative in Matthew is dependent on the tradition passed along by Mark (which in turn is similar to the Johannine framework; no doubt a common oral tradition stands behind both). It is set during the Jewish Passover, with its symbolism of the sacrificial lamb. The Passover was a pilgrimage feast, during which a great many visitors would come to Jerusalem; this sets the scene for the explosive political machinations that lead to the cross. Like many other Passover pilgrims, Jesus and his disciples have to find a place to eat the feast, but their feast will soon turn to sorrow. The synoptics picture Jesus being tried and executed on the night of the Passover meal (John's alternate chronology is considered by many to be more historically likely).

Matthew manages to add his own unique touches to the traditional framework. He makes a number of editorial changes to his source; for example, he makes the order of the mockery before the cross more logical (27:27-44). He tends to simplify Mark but is not averse to adding adjectives (27:57, 59-60) and even whole scenes (27:1-10, 62-66). He rearranges things in light of the current practice of his Jewish-Christian community; for example, in his account of the Last Supper, the words of institution reflect later liturgical practice and the actions have been condensed and merged into one ceremony of bread and cup in the middle of the meal. His major changes, however, have to do with broad theological concerns.

Foremost of these Matthean themes is the fulfillment of prophecy. In Matthew, Jesus is presented as a teacher of Torah, but also as himself the fulfillment of Torah. Jesus is himself a prophet whose words prove true again and again (26:17-18, 21-29, 31-35, 45-46). This is because God has planned and is in control of all these events. The episode of the severed ear illustrates God's control: When one of the disciples draws a sword and strikes the slave of the high priest, Jesus immediately orders the cessation of all violence in his defense. "Do you think that I cannot appeal to my Father, and he will at once send me more than twelve legions of angels? But how then would the scriptures be fulfilled, which say it must happen this way?" (26:53-54). Less important than what particular scriptures Matthew had in mind here (he probably refers to Zechariah 13:7) is simply *that* all these events are the fulfillment of scripture. God has planned it this way all along, and the scriptures show the way. Thus they are cited often (26:15, 24, 31, 54, 56; 27:9-10, 46) and even when they are not cited explicitly, they are alluded to (note especially the broad allusions to Psalms 22 and 69 in the crucifixion and death scenes).

That God is in control is part and parcel with Matthew's concern with eschatology, the coming of the last days. Though on a human level, it is Judas who has "handed over" (*paradidomi*, usually translated "betrayed") Jesus, actually it is God who is doing the handing (the same verb, *paradidomi*, is used in the "divine passive" in 26:2). God is handing over the Son on behalf of the whole world. This is happening in eschatological time, *kairos*, as Jesus himself admits when he says, "My time is near" (26:18). As foretold in the prophets, there will be a heavenly banquet in these last days (26:29). What Jesus is doing here, as Matthew sees it, is ushering in the end of the age. Other instances of eschatological imagery include the legion of angels (26:53), the portents attending the crucifixion and resurrection (27:51-53; cf. Ezekiel 37:1-4), and the appearance of Elijah to "save" Jesus (27:49).

Matthew is unique in his concentration on the role of Judas in God's plan. Only Matthew includes the tradition that pictures Judas' interaction with the Jewish leaders (27:1-10). In contrast with the woman who lavishes expensive ointment on Jesus (26:14), Judas "hands over" Jesus for a paltry sum. His "kiss" proves hollow, used only as an identifying mark in the Passover hubbub. His words show his true nature, as he identifies Jesus with a term used only by Jesus' enemies in Matthew, never by his disciples: "Rabbi" (26:25, 48-49). Jesus in response gives him a sarcastic "Friend" (probably the equivalent of "Bub") and asserts God's control over the whole process: "Do what you are here to do" (26:50).

Judas may be culpable, but Matthew leaves no doubt which human agency is ultimately responsible. Pilate is let off easily, although historically crucifixion was a punishment used only by the Romans. Matthew even brings in a scene with Pilate's wife to lessen his culpability (27:19). The scene of Pilate washing his hands (27:24) is almost laughable; no one got to that level of power in the Roman Empire with clean hands, and we know Pilate's ruthlessness from other contemporary sources. But Matthew, whose community was deeply in conflict with the synagogue, placed the blame squarely on Jewish shoulders, to the point of having the people as a whole cry, "His blood be upon us and on our children" (27:25).

All along, though, Jesus is presented as a sacrificial innocent. He is declared "innocent" again and again (cf. 26:58-59, 66; 27:18-19, 23-24). In Passover imagery, he speaks of his death as a sacrifice for sins (26:28). Throughout the process, he remains in total control (26:18-19, 21-29, 45; 27:14). He lives — and dies — only according to God's plan.

Application

People are surprised when I tell them that I don't believe in preaching on Palm Sunday. They think I'm kidding but I'm not. The passion narrative is long and intense. If read in parts and with congregational participation, it can be emotionally draining. The last thing I want to see at the end of it is some preacher belaboring the point (or worse yet, telling a joke).

Which is not to say that there should be no explication of the text on Palm Sunday. I propose replacing the sermon with a short introduction to the passion narrative that precedes rather than follows the reading. The introduction could point the congregation to what they should be listening for (particularly the unique emphases of Matthew's version). It would set them up to properly hear the reading. Following the reading there should be extended silence to let it soak in.

The usual objection to my "No Sermon Palm Sunday" is that "the people might need help applying the text to their lives." But that is really the point, isn't it? The congregation must work out their own salvation with fear and trembling (Philippians 2:12). The passion narrative provides the model for all of Christian life; it is not "applied" so much as it *is* that life. Jesus' death provides the model for the life of faith, as his resurrection assures the power to be faithful. The passion narrative is the gospel in a nutshell: He gave himself for us so that we could give ourselves for him.

An Alternative Application
Matthew 26:14—27:66. The great Jewish scholar Samuel Sandmel used to tell this story: A Jew is walking down the street on Palm Sunday. All of a sudden, a Christian comes out of church and starts beating the Jew on the head.

"Why are you hitting me?" the Jew asks. "What have I done to you?"

"You Jews killed Jesus," says the Christian.

"That was 2,000 years ago!" says the Jew.

"Well," says the Christian, "I just found out today."

Sandmel and others, both Jews and Christians, would conclude that reading the New Testament is a very dangerous thing, and as we know, the Bible is a dangerous book to read. But it's supposed to be dangerous to us, not to others.

One problem with preaching today is that the church doesn't do enough to challenge outlandish interpretations of the gospels. We should protest the notion that God blames the Jewish people for Jesus' death. Matthew wrote as part of a broader interreligious fight, in which the Gentile church was asserting itself in contrast to its Jewish roots. As with all such internecine conflicts, the rhetorical juices flowed. We should not take the depictions of the Pharisees, Sadducees, and Jewish people in the gospels as gospel truth. It is polemic, slanted, and a bit unfair.

At the very least, we should tell our congregations this: Do not, repeat, do not march out of church looking to beat up a Jew. Do not blame the Jews. Do not let prejudice, stupidity, and violence rule your hearts. Christ died for all of us, so that we might walk in new life.

Maundy Thursday
Exodus 12:1-4 (5-10) 11-14
1 Corinthians 11:23-26
John 13:1-17, 31b-35
by David Kalas

Long table

Perhaps you've been part of a large group going out to eat together. You arrive at the restaurant and they don't have a single table that can accommodate the whole group. The hostess asks you to wait for a moment, and she combines efforts with several of the servers to rearrange some of the vacant tables and chairs, pushing tables together to create one long table for your oversized party.

I recall several occasions when I have been part of such a group. I've even seen restaurants assign more than one server to our "table" because it was so populated.

Such occasions are usually very jovial — lots of conversation and laughter. If, by chance, you have a moment when you aren't part of a conversation, then you have the leisure to look down the long table and see the all the faces of these cherished friends and family members, gathered together in fellowship.

Of course, a very long table is somewhat impractical for conversation. You can't easily converse with someone who is clear at the other end. Still, there is something satisfying about sitting all together — a feeling of connectedness that is missing when your group is scattered over several different tables and booths.

Conjure up the images of such a long and loving table for your congregation this night, for that is where we sit. We gather this evening at a very long table, indeed — and getting longer every day. For this is a table that does not merely stretch across part of a room: it spans generations and centuries. We cannot even calculate the number of people seated there.

Yet our scripture passages for this holy day will help us to pause our conversation, to look up and down the table, and to see the faces of the cherished family and friends who are gathered for fellowship with our host.

Exodus 12:1-4 (5-10) 11-14

The far end of our very long table stretches back over 3,000 years. Our first task is to squint our eyes to try to see the folks all the way at that other end. There they are: Moses and the Hebrew slaves in Egypt.

People who pay some attention to the liturgical or church calendar will appreciate the Lord's instruction in verse 2. Speaking of the current month — that is, the month that the Israelites celebrated the Passover and left Egypt — the Lord said, "It shall be the first month of the year for you." One senses that, perhaps prior to this time, that particular month was not regarded as the first month on the Hebrew calendar. So the Israelites made an adjustment that is reminiscent of what we do in the church: namely, while the calendar says that the new year begins in January, and while the schools say that the new year begins in late August or early September, in the church we affirm that the new year begins with Advent. For the Hebrews, the new year began in the month of the Passover.

Next, God gave the people instructions for preparing and eating the Passover meal. We are accustomed to instructions for preparing food: We call them recipes. When it comes to eating the food, however, the only sort of instructions we get in most cases is the training in manners that our parents provided. "Elbows off the table." "Napkin in your lap." "Feet on the floor." "Chew with your mouth closed." And such.

Against such standard fare, God's instructions seem quite strange. For, if anything, the instructions from God seem to us rather unmannerly. We picture people wolfing down their food while wearing their overcoats and holding their car keys. It seems to us both an impolite and an unhealthy way to eat.

Over the millennia, the Jewish celebration of the Passover meal has become so rich with symbolic acts and liturgical elements that it is anything but "fast food." In that original context in Egypt, however, the key element was speed. "You shall eat it hurriedly," God told the people, for after centuries of waiting, now their deliverance was going to come quickly.

God's statement that "on all the gods of Egypt I will execute judgments" is a fascinating insight into the Passover event, if not the meal itself. At a purely human level, of course, we don't see the gods of Egypt in the picture at all. It is the human element we see: the massive, national grief, as nearly every household suffers some sudden death by supernatural cause. Yet the Lord does not cast it as a punishment on the people of Egypt but rather on the gods of Egypt. It suggests a larger principle: that to align oneself with the enemy of God is to be defeated along with that enemy.

Finally, we observe God's intention that "this day shall be a day of remembrance for you" and his instruction that "throughout your generations you shall observe it as a perpetual ordinance." These Old Testament themes of "remembrance" and future observances of the meal are surely recalled by Jesus' Last Supper words: "Do this, as often as you drink it, in remembrance of me" (1 Corinthians 11:25).

1 Corinthians 11:23-26

The long table began back in Egypt in the days of Moses. As we fast forward through the generations — past Joshua (Joshua 5:10), past Hezekiah (2 Chronicles 30:1-26), past Josiah (2 Kings 23:21-23; 2 Chronicles 35:1-19), and past Jerusalem of the Persian era (Ezra 6:19-22) — we come eventually to Jesus and his disciples. That spot on our table is the focus of our next lection.

Move your eyes just a little further down the table, however, and you come to the Corinthians of Paul's day.

Those first-century Greeks may seem far removed from us in terms of time and space, but the fact is that we may think of ourselves sitting right next to them at this table. In broad strokes, you see, their context is identical to ours.

Paul was writing to a congregation of Christians about their celebration of the Lord's Supper. That's what this table had become, even just a few decades after Jesus' Last Supper with his disciples on that Thursday night of Holy Week. Paul wanted to help that Christian congregation understand what they were doing.

As we read the larger context, we discover that not everything is copasetic in the Corinthian church. They are struggling with a variety of issues — divisions, infighting, immorality, to name a few — and unsurprisingly their worship and fellowship had been compromised. An unhappy family is not likely to have a cheerful dinner table just because they all agreed to sit down to eat together. Likewise, a troubled church will bring its troubles, one way or another, to this table of the Lord, as well. Accordingly, Paul wrote to help correct the problems in Corinth, including their mishandling of this meal.

In the course of his instructions, he includes these verses, which read to us more like a gospel than an epistle. And, indeed, he is functioning very much like a gospel writer, as he reports and records a piece of the narrative from Jesus' life.

The detail about Jesus giving thanks gives rise to the traditional term "Eucharist" for this meal. Meanwhile, for all of the elements that were likely a part of the disciples' Passover meal, it is just these two elements — the bread and the cup — that Jesus singled out as representative of him. The reference to a "new covenant" echoes Luke's account (22:20) and forms part of an important thread throughout scripture (Jeremiah 31:31; 2 Corinthians 3:5-6; Hebrews 8:8-13, 9:15, 12:22-24).

Jesus' instructions to "do this in remembrance of me" anticipate a continuing practice on the part of his followers. It is that practice in which Paul's congregation was participating. And it is at that table we sit next to them tonight.

John 13:1-17, 31b-35

This is the part of the table to which our eyes naturally turn on this holy day. Indeed, some of our people may not even know how much further back in time this particular table extends. But the narrator alludes to that history as he sets the stage with the reference to "the festival of the Passover." Still, Maundy Thursday is primarily about this moment in time, this part of the table, Jesus' Last Supper with his disciples.

John's gospel gives us a different view of this scene than Matthew, Mark, and Luke. That's not surprising, of course, because John gives us a very different view of most everything about Jesus' life and ministry than the synoptic gospels do. For starters, John's account of the Last Supper is several times longer than any of the other gospel records. We observe that two of the elements that are unique to John's Last Supper scene are found here in our selected verses: the foot washing and the new commandment.

Most of our congregations are unaccustomed to the practice of foot washing. While many folks who have tried it in various church settings have found it deeply meaningful, the fact is that the whole experience is a new and self-conscious one for most Americans. Consequently, we do not begin at the same starting place as Peter and the other disciples.

For those men around that table, foot washing was not a novel experience. Rather, in that world of dusty roads and sandaled feet, it was common practice. The mere experience of having another person wash one's feet, therefore, was not as awkward and uncomfortable for them as it is for us.

The experience of having Jesus wash their feet, however, was quite a different matter. That culture had a strong sense of hierarchy, and washing feet was servant's work. Jesus, however, was one whom they identified with titles like "master" and "lord." For them, he was at the other end of the spectrum from "servant." This is like having your boss come over for dinner only to roll up his sleeves and start cleaning your bathroom. This is the governor shining your shoes. This is the president washing and folding your laundry.

It was understandable, therefore, as well as personally typical that Peter would object. First, it seemed to him too backward that his lord should wash his feet. Then it seemed too little that only his feet should be washed. But Jesus walked his most mercurial follower through the logic and significance of the act. Then, when it was completed, he told his followers that the very inappropriateness of what he had done was precisely the point: "If I, your Lord and Teacher, have washed your feet, you also ought to wash one another's feet. For I have set you an example."

This symbolic act resonates with other teachings of Jesus (such as Matthew 20:20-28; 23:1-11; Mark 9:33-37). And whether or not our particular congregations are comfortable with the practice of washing one another's feet, the larger principle remains and must be applied: namely, that we are to live with the humble attitude of a servant. This is a high calling in the kingdom of God, and it is the posture we adopt before him and before one another.

Meanwhile, the "new commandment," which is another feature unique to John's Last Supper account, follows a similar trajectory. He commands his disciples to "love one another," which at first blush does not seem like a new commandment at all (cf. Matthew 22:37-40; Leviticus 19:18). But we discover that it is the standard for love that is new. No longer are we called to love "as you love yourself," but rather "just as I have loved you."

So the love commandment matches the message of the foot washing. That is to say, in both our serving and our loving, we are following Jesus' lead. As he has set an example for us, so we adopt an attitude of servitude with one another. And as he has loved us, so we love one another.

Imagine the church where these simple principles prevailed and became reality! Imagine the congregation where each one sought to serve the other and to selflessly love one another! By this, indeed, everyone surely would recognize that we really are his disciples!

Application

We come to a table on Maundy Thursday. Your table might look quite different from mine, of course. Most of us will not literally have tables at all. As we kneel at the altar rail, file up and down the aisles, or even just remain in our seats with the elements of bread and cup brought to us, there's a table. And it's a very long table.

In order for our people to understand what we are doing together this evening, they need to see the whole table. So we begin with our ancestors who sat at the far end: Moses and his generation, hurriedly celebrating the first Passover meal together in Egypt. The meal marked God's saving act. Central to that saving act was the blood of a lamb. The meal was to be reenacted as a remembrance on that date throughout their generations.

After a good many generations had passed, Jesus and his companions sat down at that same table to eat, celebrate, and remember. Only now, suddenly, there was talk of different blood, and the anticipation of a different saving act. Again, there was the expectation that the meal would be reenacted as a remembrance throughout the generations.

So it was that, a few years later, the Christians in Corinth gathered at that table to eat, celebrate, and remember. And tonight we sidle up next to them, hearing again the story of "the night when he was betrayed."

There's something sweet about the faces we see as we look up and down this table. From the weathered skin of those Hebrew slaves in Egypt to that beloved collection of fishermen and more that gathered in that upper room; plus every imaginable look, size, complexion, and language that has appeared at this table in the generations since.

Then there is the sweetest face of all. He sits at the center of the table, and he is the host. As Charles Wesley sang, "Let every soul be Jesus' guest." He is the one who really brings us together, for it is because of his love and by his saving act that we are gathered here. He is the one we remember tonight. He is the greatest common factor among that widely disparate group represented across the generations and continents at this table. This meal is all about him.

Our host is the Paschal Lamb anticipated by Moses, the rabbi followed by Peter, the Savior proclaimed by Paul, and the Lord worshiped by us. We gather in his name, and we partake of his body and blood. We remember his saving act, we celebrate our salvation, and we proclaim his death until he comes.

An Alternative Application
Exodus 12:1-4 (5-10) 11-14; 1 Corinthians 11:23-26. "The act of remembering." Some of the remembering we do is deliberate. Some of it is inspired. Some of it is accidental. Of course, sometimes we don't remember, at all: we just plain forget.

Accidental remembering is that sort of experience in which some experience has the unintended effect of triggering a memory. I drive by a car with a Connecticut license plate, and I suddenly remember that my brother-in-law who lives in Connecticut has a birthday coming up. There is no design involved — except for the occasions when the design may be God's providence. It is just how the human brain works.

Inspired remembering is more like nostalgia. It is prompted by some smell, song, picture, group of friends, or what have you. You are inspired to indulge your memory in the fond exercise of reminiscing. It is like a floral centerpiece on the kitchen table: it has no real practical purpose, it's just a bit of loveliness.

Deliberate remembering is what we do most often. Specifically, it is what we do with the things we cannot afford to forget. With our alarms and alerts, our lists and notes to ourselves, our calendars and address books, we take deliberate steps to remind ourselves about those things we must not forget.

Deliberate remembering is what God had in mind for his people. There are certain things — big things — that we must not forget. So he built into his people's calendar the holy days and festivals that would prompt them to remember the truly important stuff.

We may think of "remembering" as a passive thing, and the phrase "in remembrance," which graces so many of our altars and Communion tables, sounds almost funereal to us. Yet biblical remembering is alive and active.

Whenever the scripture tells us that God remembered someone or something, it is followed immediately by action (Genesis 8:1, 19:29, 30:22; Exodus 2:24; 1 Samuel 1:19; Revelation 16:19). Naturally, therefore, when God commands his people to remember something (e.g., Exodus 20:8), appropriate corresponding action is expected.

Even the remembering itself is an action in God's design. The Old Testament Israelites were not merely instructed to pause once a year and recall God's saving action for their ancestors. No, they were to eat a meal and observe a festival, for participating in those actions would be full of remembering for them.

As we gather this evening to share the Lord's Supper together, we do so "in remembrance." It is to be "a day of remembrance for you," just as the Passover was for Israel. Our remembering will be active, not passive. And once we have remembered his atoning sacrifice, some corresponding action on our part would be appropriate.

T.O. Chisholm had a sense for what our corresponding action ought to be. "O Jesus, Lord and Savior," he sang, "I give myself to thee; for thou, in thy atonement, didst give thyself for me."

Good Friday
Isaiah 52:13—53:12
Hebrews 10:16-25
John 18:1—19:42
by Wayne Brouwer

Why did Jesus have to die?

While Don Richardson was a student at Prairie Bible Institute in the 1950s his heart burned in anticipation of bringing the good news about Jesus to an unreached tribe. He and Carol found their prayers answered in 1962 as they sailed out of Vancouver harbor toward Netherlands New Guinea. Before long they were deposited by missionary plane among the Sawi people, a group of tribes living in the trees of the interior rain forest.

The jungle floor was too damp for permanent dwellings, so the Sawi helped Don and Carol, and their infant son, Stephen, build a tree house in their neighborhood. Carol learned the ways of the Sawi women while Don spent time with the men, attempting to understand their language and reduce it to writing. Afternoons would find the Sawi males in one of their treetop workrooms, buzzing in conversation while they mended nets and hunting equipment, and swapped stories of fish and boars.

It was in this setting that Don took his first furtive steps toward speaking the Sawi language and reciting stories from the gospels. Most of the time the others ignored him, caught up in their own manly concerns. So the months progressed, with little Stephen becoming a Sawi child, Carol adapting meals to local produce, and Don attempting to get the message of the Bible into a form the Sawi could understand.

One day everything changed. Don was moving along in the gospel story to the last weeks of Jesus' life. As he related the tales about Jesus heading toward Jerusalem and the conspiracies that were swirling about him, the Sawi men began to listen. At first it was only that their conversations with one another died down, while their hands continued in busywork with their hunting and fishing tools. But then even this work ceased, and every eye was fixed on Don. He happened to be talking about Judas' secret meetings with the religious leaders and the betrayal that ensued.

Suddenly there was a murmur of approval and the delighted smiles of those who seemed to know this story. Don asked his translating helper what was going on. The reply chilled him to the bone, even in the heat of the tropics.

The Sawi, he was told, prided themselves for their hunting and fishing prowess. There was an even greater expression of manhood. They called it "Fattening the Pig for the Slaughter." It happened when one young man chose to target another young man in this or a neighboring clan and built a strong web of friendship. The two would hunt together and fish together and roam the forests together and eat together and laugh and talk together. They became best buddies. Then, when the relationship was secure, the initiator of the friendship would invite his comrade over to his mother's home for a grand meal. During the middle of the feast, when laughter was the language of the hour, and back-slapping good humor seasoned the supper, the first young man would suddenly pull out a long knife, brandish it with delight before the other's face, and when looks of dawning horror increasingly webbed out from the betrayed's eyes, plunge it through his "friend's" chest, piercing his heart.

The mother would come quickly with freshly baked bread that the traitor touched to his dead comrade's genitals before eating it. Then mother and son would open the skull of the victim, scoop out his brains, and consume these as well.

The deadly project was complete: one brave young Sawi warrior had displayed his cunning prowess and then had ingested all the power of his target. He became a greater man by taking into himself the strength and energy of his betrayed friend.

Don was dumbstruck! How could he communicate the story of Jesus and the love of God to these people if they viewed Judas, the betrayer, as the hero of the tale? Just as important, what was on the tribal menu for supper tonight? Were the Richardsons the next victims of "Fattening the Pig for the Slaughter"? Don slipped out of the men's lodge a wary and troubled man.

The story has a wonderful ending that will come at the conclusion of this article. But the central issue for Don and Carol Richardson is one that is key to all that Christians talk about and "celebrate" this week and this day: Why did Jesus have to die? Is his demise at a young age a symbol of weakness rather than strength? Is Christianity a religion of wimps who pride themselves in following the loser rather than the winner? How do you preach Christ on another Good Friday in a world that thrives on war, one-up-manship, devious politics, profits at all costs, and survival of the fittest in a cosmic game where the rules are heralded every Thursday evening: "Outwit, Outlast, Outplay!"?

Isaiah 52:13—53:12

Three major families of atonement theory have been proposed over the centuries to answer such questions. The first is linked to Isaiah's prophetic impressions in today's passage. God has been wronged. God's people have gone the way of wickedness and wastrels. The world is imbalanced and the Creator isolated from the people who are to him like loved but wayward children.

How will things be made right? Who will bring restoration and renewal and reconciliation? According to the word of the Lord through Isaiah, it will happen when "my servant" enters the picture and rewrites history. It is not clear exactly what the Suffering Servant will do, but the outcome is certain. After what appears to be a lackluster residential sojourn, those around the servant will attack him and cause him pain and kill him cruelly. But when all of that has happened, there will be a new peace between God and humanity and the former times of alienation will be gone.

Anselm interpreted this as Jesus' mission into our world to defend the honor of the Father. Because of the arrogance of spreading sin and the hubris of human communities that took the image of God, which they possessed for rebellious license, the Creator had been shuttered away from the creation, and Yahweh was forgotten except as a curse word.

But along came Jesus. Like one who still remembers the true nature of reality and appearing in the guise of a humble but faithful servant, Jesus takes up the thankless chivalric duty to restore the honor of the king of the castle, the lord of the estate. The Father might have been ready to wipe out the whole of humanity, just as Yahweh had threatened to Moses in Exodus 33, but then he saw the face of the Suffering Servant and realized that one still held him in honor. The faithful obedience of the one mitigated the divine wrath of God for the many and life on planet earth was restored and balanced.

Calvin took Anselm's ideas a step further, paying close attention to the forensic language of Paul in Romans and Galatians. It was not merely God's honor that had been violated, he said, but the righteousness of God's justice. We humans were not just rebellious clods, we had become downright guilty lawbreakers. Before the court of heaven none could stand with either pride or dignity. The eternal codes of propriety accused every person of failure, transgression, and fault.

Enter Jesus. Jesus comes as the lawyer for the accused. He does not pretend we are innocent but openly marks our guilt. Yet when the holy sentence is passed and capital punishment is ascribed against us, Jesus shows the extent to which he will advocate on our behalf. He himself steps into the penalty box, he himself climbs up to the gallows, he himself is strapped into the electric chair, he himself receives our toxic chemical cocktail and dies our death for us. There is good news about resurrection to come on Easter morning, of course, just as Isaiah hints at in the closing notes of his lament. But on Good Friday, the good news is that of escape and substitution.

Hebrews 10:16-25

A second family of atonement theories connects well with the book of Hebrews. It is not the Creator/Father who needs to take note of Jesus in his sufferings, but we humans. We have forgotten who we are. It may well be that we have offended God, but God is big enough to be able to handle it. What is more important is that we have offended ourselves. We have lost touch with our place in the house of God. We need a high priest who can help us find our way back home.

Jesus does this in a variety of ways. Irenaeus thought that Jesus had to be at least fifty years old when he died, because the point of Jesus' coming to earth was to go through all the stages of human life (fifty was certainly old age at the time!) in order to show us how to live and die correctly. We had lost our way. Only when we saw Jesus living our lives out of grace and love and courage, and even dying well, would we be able to do the same. He called Jesus' work "recapitulation," a replaying of human identity done right. What we observe most of Jesus on this Good Friday is his ability to die with courage and dignity, just as he had lived. When we see Jesus we buck up, get our acts together, and recover the best of our humanity.

Later theologians would further emphasize that exemplary character of Jesus' life and death. Abelard saw in Jesus' death the power of moral influence. We have grown complacent in our degradation, according to Abelard. Jesus comes among us and all we can see is his goody-goody character, and we despise him for it. We taunt him, trying to make him become a normal sinner like the rest of us. We tease him as if he were sub-human. When he refuses to play our dirty games we get angry with him and plot to get rid of him and ultimately throw him up on a cross in despicable shame. Only when the dastardly deed is done, it is not he but we who are suddenly cut to the heart. We hear his words from the cross, "Father, forgive them, for they know not what they do!" and we are embarrassed beyond loss of face. We see in his reflection what we have become and come to know the ugliness of ourselves for the first time. His morality pierces our immorality and we must turn away. Like the dirty, old man in one of O. Henry's stories, the one who sees by lamplight the beautiful woman he once called friend, but lost because of the blackness of his own rotten character and suddenly remembers what he could have been if he had stayed with her instead of becoming his awful self, we turn with him down a dark alley and bang our heads against a wall and cry out, "Oh God, what have I become?" Still in Jesus' love we find ourselves anew for the first time.

Schleiermacher and Ritchl would take up the same sermon generations later, preaching a morality in Jesus that becomes an example for us. Jesus' death was not a failure, but the ultimate testimony of love. Did not Jesus himself declare it? "Greater love has no one than this, that a man lay down his life for his friends!" Here is Jesus on the cross, condemned by the political powers of the day for combating power with love. While all of his troupe could have been sentenced and killed, Jesus was willing to stand alone, allowing the others to scurry off to save their skins. When they later realized what Jesus had done, they gained new courage to be like Jesus as well and formed a socially transforming movement that has since spanned the globe. "Be like Jesus!" they declare.

This is the kind of courage that comes in the final paragraph of our New Testament passage today. See what Jesus did and then live and die in similar fashion, for the good of the world.

John 18:1—19:42

There is also a third approach to atonement theory, and our gospel reading connects with it. For John, God's good world has been plunged into darkness by the viral effects of sin. Creation's brightness has been swallowed up by the shades of evil. Those who were made in the image of God have become ruined, warped, and distorted. It is the scene of Mordred in Tolkien's Middle Earth, where everything once righteous and holy has become twisted, perverted, distressed, and rotten.

All power appears to be in the hands of the Evil One, the "Father of Lies" as Jesus terms him in John 8:42-47. No relief from the shadows seems possible (note the place from which Nicodemus emerges in chapter 3 and the arena to which Judas exits in chapter 13) until Jesus calmly steps into the chasm manufactured by iniquity and it closes around him.

Origen called it a ransom to the devil. Satan, he said, was the greatest fisherman of all times, snagging every flippin' creature from the waters of this world. When his boat was filled to the limit, he headed for shore and a ravenous meal of consumption that would send us to his infernal bowels forever. Like any good fisherman, the devil snaked a troll line into the boat's wake on the journey back to harbor. Suddenly the reel whizzed out in a furious tug. A giant fish had gone for the devil's spinning lure!

Satan stopped rowing and fought the line. The fish at the other end was huge beyond belief. After playing it with practiced dexterity, the devil finally saw the fish near the gunwales. It was enormous! More than that, it was the Creator's own first creation! It was the Son of God!

Now the devil was in a dilemma. He did not have room for the big fish in his boat. He could keep either his current catch or toss it aside and claim the prize of the day, but he couldn't do both. Like any great fisherman, he chose the record breaker. Shoveling the little fish out of the boat, he managed to tease, taunt, and gaff the big one over the edge and get it to flop heavily onto the deck. His catch would be the news of heaven and earth!

As he wrestled his over-committed craft toward the docks, the trophy fish he prized gave a sudden wallop of its mighty tail, capsizing the boat and escaping into the water. In an instant the devil was left with nothing.

So, said Origen, is the story of Good Friday, when Satan, the prince of the powers of this age, played his biggest hand, trading all of wicked humankind for the big prize of God's own Son, and lost everything in the bargain. Why did Jesus have to die? Because it was the only way to get the rest of us free.

There is much of this in John's telling of Jesus' death. Everyone evil wants a piece of the action. Still Jesus himself is in charge of his own existence. On Easter morning, as we shall soon see, the big fish gets away, as do all of us who swim after him in the waters of baptism.

Application

The story of Jesus' horrible death is as familiar as it is enigmatic. We know that Jesus died and did so in a cruelly painful way but the why of it still remains fuzzy. Did Jesus have to satisfy God's honor or justice? Yes, that is indeed a message of the New Testament. Was his death an example to us and an act of moral persuasion? Certainly, for Jesus' own words testified to that. Were the evil powers that have locked their claws into this good creation of God weakened and perhaps ultimately destroyed in Jesus' infamous demise? That, too, is an element of the tale. But all are mixed together in ways that refute easy dissection or quick categorization.

Don and Carol Richardson survived their Sawi sojourn and even succeeded in bringing the gospel to these people. The story begun above took a later strange turn. Due to increasing scarcity, the Sawi people needed to range further in hunting and fishing. This, in turn, caused them to run into conflict with other area tribes and peoples. Soon there were skirmishes and fights and all-out wars. People returned to Sawi homes bloodied, battered, or missing limbs. Sometimes they failed to return at all, claimed by assassins' wounds and swallowed up by the putrefying womb of the jungle.

It was then that the men began to talk openly about the possible need for a "Peace Child." Intrigued, Don asked what they meant by that term.

Sometimes, they said, when war got too pronounced and murderous, when tribes were in danger of killing one another off, when brutality bested their will to live, one of the chiefs might grab the youngest newborn male baby from its mother's arms, and run swiftly, despite the woman's wailing, across the no-man's-land between the tribes. Reaching the first enemy village, he would thrust the baby into the arms of a young woman.

All knew what this meant. A son from one child was now the possession of the other tribe. Both tribes had a stake in the child's future and all warfare would cease for as long as that child lives. The "Peace Child" reconciled the foes.

Interest mounting, Don asked a further question. What would happen, he queried, if someone should kill the "Peace Child"? Horrified, the group shook their heads aghast. No one would ever think to do such a dastardly deed. It was beyond belief!

Hmmmm… thought Don. Then he proceeded. "Let me tell you a story…" he said. He related a tale of a time when the tribes of heaven and earth were at war with one another. He told of the chief of heaven bringing his own Son across the no-man's-land into our tribe as a "Peace Child." He explained how one day someone had instigated the murder of that "Peace Child." When the horrified Sawi warriors begged him about what could be done to erase this monumental human blunder, Don preached Christ and grace and the forgiving love of God.

An Alternative Application
John 18:1—19:42. The gospel story needs to be read today even if it is not preached. But if it is preached, and the approach above is taken, one of the greatest endings to the message would be a powerful recital of the dark night in C.S. Lewis' *The Lion, the Witch and the Wardrobe* in which Aslan is slain in the place of Edmund, but the magic from before time prevents the White Witch and her evil brood from winning the day. Declare the victory of Aslan with all the splendor of great drama.

Easter Sunday
Acts 10:34-43
Colossians 3:1-4
John 20:1-18
by Wayne Brouwer

Breaking boxes

The central message of Christian faith is that Jesus was raised from the dead. It is what sets apart Christianity from all other religions. As a teacher, Jesus was very good, but there were others who were also keen. As a prophet, Jesus was a tremendous cultural critic, but others also blasted the powers that ruled. As a miracle worker, Jesus was captivating, but so, too, have been many who pulled novel tricks. Yet when it comes to Easter, Jesus is unparalleled. No one else died and came back to life. In his resurrection Jesus proclaimed the dawn of a new age. The ultimate threat to human existence had been overcome. Jesus is alive and lives forevermore!

Today is a good day for some religious swaggering. We boast so easily about the little things of life: a winning sports team, a new car, and a birthday celebration. But the really big thing of life is our main focus today: Jesus came back from the dead and changed our thinking about life forever! We need to make this known and not hide it in tedium or ordinariness. Today is a good day for shouting and dancing a little! (See Paul's encouragement to boast in 1 Corinthians 1:31 — "Let him who boasts, boast in the Lord!")

For many years our family lived in Canada, and while there we adopted an expanded calendar of social holidays. Along with the usual Christmas and Easter, the shifted Thanksgiving and National Days, came the extra Canadian public festivities of "Civic Day" in August and "Boxing Day" on December 26. "Boxing Day" moved to Canada from England, where it began its career hundreds of years ago as the day on which the excesses of Christmas food were boxed up and distributed to the poor. More recently it has taken on the connotations of a time when the boxes and Christmas wrappings are smashed and trashed and discarded as unwanted leftovers from Christmas gift giving. After the thing of value has emerged from the box, the box is no longer needed. Such boxes need to be broken and made irrelevant. That idea fits with today's Easter preaching.

The three passages of today's lectionary all focus on breaking boxes, not literally, but metaphorically and theologically. When Peter preaches the good news of Jesus to Cornelius, he is breaking the box of ethnic separation that previously bound him, and also the box of religious understandings that had trapped both him and Cornelius prior to this. Paul's commands in his letter to the Colossians call for us to break the boxes of human perception and perspective by stepping into the vantage point of another person — the resurrected and ascended Christ. In John's gospel, all of the time-honored boxes of funeral regimen are obliterated as Jesus emerges from the shattered box of his tomb.

A good setup for today might be to create some boxes that are labeled with various falsely held myths of our human past (such as the earth is flat, no one can run the mile in under four minutes, heavier-than-air ships will never fly, communication is limited to earshot or eyesight distance, and the like) and then to break these boxes as a visible illustration.

Acts 10:34-43

The book of Acts is shaped according to Jesus' command in 1:8. In successive ripples we see the expansion of the church in and beyond "Jerusalem," through "Judea and Samaria," and then reaching past Asia Minor and Europe to the "ends of the earth." Luke makes this movement obvious to us through five similar "progress reports" (6:7; 9:31; 12:24; 16:5; 19:20). Each brings to a conclusion a mission movement that is broader than the last: Jerusalem (2:1—6:7), Judea, and Samaria (6:8—9:31), bridging the way to Gentiles (9:32—12:24), Asia Minor (12:25—16:5), and Europe (16:6—19:20).

It is helpful to understand the above plan for the book of Acts in order to appreciate the significance of Peter's words to Cornelius. Prior to this time Peter, along with virtually all of the early Jewish Christians, understood Jesus' coming, power, and meaning, primarily in terms of Jewish messianic terms. Nearly all of the first preaching of the good news of Jesus' resurrection was brought to Jews in Palestine. Suddenly, however, Peter is divinely led (Acts 10:9-23) to tell the same message of current divine favor and future hope to a prominent Gentile leader. This is a moment of historic significance, for it returns global significance (see Genesis 12:1-3) to the Israelite religion that has been marginalized and localized since the Babylonian conquest. Peter's perspectives are broadened to see God's eternal plan for the recovery of all God's children, not merely the Jews.

In bringing this hope to Cornelius, Peter declares that the confirmation of God's good favor is the Easter message. Jesus' resurrection, according to Peter, has several implications. First, it is God's affirmation of Jesus' ministry (10:40). While there have been many great religious teachers, none have had this kind of divine commendation. One can ignore Jesus' teachings and healings only until one confronts the empty tomb and the post-resurrection appearances of Jesus among his friends. After Easter, no one can write Jesus out of the picture because God did not.

Second, the resurrection of Jesus confirmed the power of Jesus' perspectives and theology for his followers (10:41). Suddenly they had a new understanding of what God's kingdom was about. Suddenly they became aware of the lengths God would go to bring reconciliation between heaven and earth. Suddenly they were emboldened to speak with strangers everywhere about a message of absolute significance for everyone. No one can remain the same after attending the funeral of a dear friend, spending time in the cemetery where his body is buried, and then seeing the exploded tomb and talking with him alive again. Jesus' resurrection confirmed the validity of his life, his teachings, and his view of God's history.

Third, Jesus' resurrection confirmed the urgency of the gospel message (10:42). People may hear a great orator and walk away with little or no permanent response. They may see mighty acts of healing and be religiously entertained for a time. But Jesus' open grave announced a new era in human history, according to Peter, one in which the future broke into the present and stared us in the face. These are suddenly the last days and they demand a response from all people.

In bringing this message of Easter's good news to Cornelius, Peter was breaking boxes. He was breaking out of the box of Jewish ethnocentricity. While Jewish monotheism required full devotion of members of its race, it was benignly pluralistic when it came to other races and other religions. Jewish monotheism was neither evangelistic nor "exclusivistic." Those from other nations might come to and adopt the God of Judaism, but it was a choice they would freely make. If they did not, there was no clear Jewish theology of divine judgment against them. But Peter's new understanding of God's broadened concerns changed all that. The box of Jewish ethnocentricity no longer made sense. The God of Israelite past was still the God of all nations. Jesus' resurrection was not a Jewish matter but a human issue — all people will die, all must face their maker, all are in need of the divine favor expressed through Jesus.

Peter was also breaking the box of Old Testament centripetal missiology. In the days of ancient Israel, Canaan was the land of covenant promise. Israel was to be a blessing to all the nations of the earth but was to transmit that blessing from its location on the crossroads of society. Israel's unique geographical location — squeezed between the Mediterranean Sea and the great desert, with Africa, Europe, and Asia on its southern and northern contact points — meant that all trade routes, all communication lines, and all conquest strategies would eventually bring the nations of its world into its borders. This would allow its religiously defined culture to be observed by other nations with the hopes that they would be attracted and become proselytes to its covenant identity (see Psalm 87). In this new stage of missiology, ushered in by Jesus' resurrection and the divine vision that had driven him to connect with Cornelius, the centripetal attraction to Israel's place was being transformed into a centrifugal thrust into the world at large. The box that limited the good news of God's work in human history to Israel's borders was being blasted from within.

Finally, Peter was acknowledging that the box of the grave was no longer absolute. If Jesus broke out of the tomb, no grave is any longer "safe." We can no longer assume that making it through life is enough. We must also become concerned about life beyond life, or life of eternal consequence. This places more of a moral imperative on the choice we make during our lives. The boxes are broken and, like Humpty Dumpty's shell, cannot be repaired. We have entered a new world order because of Easter.

Colossians 3:1-4

Paul wrote this letter from prison in Rome around AD 60. He was waiting for his case to be heard by the emperor (see Acts 21-28). A former slave acquaintance named Onesimus found his way to Rome and ended up as a constant and "useful" companion to Paul (see Philemon). Now Paul was sending Onesimus back to his master Philemon, who lived near Colossae. Tychicus would be Onesimus' traveling companion (see Colossians 4:7-9), and with such mail-deliverers available, Paul decided to send a letter to the Colossian church as well.

The focus of Paul's letter to the Colossians was his address of the "heresy" hinted at in chapter 2. That aberrant teaching appears to have been an early form of Ebionism, which was prevalent among Jewish Christians and Gentile proselytes to Judaism who later became Christians. This view held that Jesus was certainly a prophet divinely affirmed by God, but that the strength of Jesus' teachings was his ability to keep the commands of the Torah. Christians ought to follow Jesus' lead and observe the cultic rituals of Jewish faith, including the accretions that had been added over the years.

Paul resoundingly denies the validity of this approach. Furthermore, he espouses a Christology that is not adoptionistic (like that of the Ebionites), but rather incarnationist. Jesus was not merely a good man who was "adopted" by God because of his faithful observance of laws and commands but is actually the fullness of deity itself (2:9).

Because of that, the "normal" understanding of life is not from earthbound human perspective but from the divine, creator view. Since Christians are to identify with Jesus, they ought not limit their understanding of him to the times of his earthly sojourn, but also travel with him post-Easter as he returned to his heavenly frame of reference. This is the instruction Paul gives in 3:1-4.

A wonderful image that can be used effectively with this passage takes its title from E.M. Forester's great novel, *A Room with a View*. Forrester described the Italian travels of Lucy Honeychurch (note the name!) with her chaperone, and their disappointment in a fashionable Florence hotel where their explicit reservations of rooms with "views" (such as the sculpted gardens and open countryside) cannot be honored. Lucy is given a room overlooking the courtyard where the drama of human life is played out. In the end, it is she, not her chaperone, who has the true room with a view. This is what Paul is describing in godly terms. Our limited perspectives on human life are really boxes in which we have isolated ourselves. Jesus' resurrection and heavenly perspective allows us to break out of the boxes in which we have trapped ourselves, and see things from God's broader and more realistic view.

John 20:1-18

John begins his gospel with a philosophic perspective that ties the meaning of Jesus to the creation of the world (John 1:1-13) and the unique revelation of God to Israel through the Shekinah glory light (John 1:14-18). Chapters 2-12 are rightly called "The Book of Signs" because, through seven "miraculous signs," the glory of Jesus as the incarnate deity is gradually revealed. Chapters 13-20 are often called "The Book of Glory" because Jesus completes his revelation of divine glory first in his on-going relationship with the church through the witness of his disciples (13-17), and then through his sacrificial death as the true Passover Lamb (18-19). Here, in chapter 20, Jesus' resurrection is told in both its historical and cosmological significance. First comes the historical eyewitness report of the tomb being opened and emptied (20:1-13). Then, in verses 14-18, a cosmological dimension is added. John has told us that the tomb was located in a "garden" (19:41); here Mary supposes that she sees the "gardener" (20:15). While this is an explanation of real-time events, it is also an interesting return to John's original "creation/re-creation" themes of chapter 1. God created a garden in which humankind would dwell. Humans fell out of touch with their creator/gardener who used to come and talk with them in the garden. Now Jesus (the true gardener) is found again by his own in the garden. John is certainly making a play on this theme. Even the idea that Mary is not to cling to Jesus in the garden (v. 17) is part of the play; Jesus' resurrection is only the first stage in the process of "re-creation," and Mary must not halt it at this point.

Once again, boxes are broken on Easter. First, there is the box of the tomb. What ought to have held Jesus secure in death is demolished by *life*. Second, the human perspective of Jesus merely as a human companion is broken from the inside out when Jesus' full resurrection glory is displayed. Here Jesus cannot be held by limited earthly contacts. A few verses later he cannot be boxed into mere prophetic identity but must be declared "Lord" and "God" by Thomas (20:28).

John wants us to know that Jesus' resurrection on Easter Sunday is a message that has both personal and cosmological significance. Those of us who have been trapped into lifelessness because of the death of friends and relatives, know the personal release that Jesus' return to life brings. And all of us who have felt the limiting boxes of a cause-and-effect world begin to see outside the box when Jesus brings us back into fellowship with our Creator who wants to walk with us in the garden once again.

Application

We are in the habit of making boxes and God is in the habit of breaking boxes. Adam and Eve got trapped in the shame of their sinful nakedness; God restored their dignity with clothing and promises (Genesis 3). Lot got caught in the demonic box of Sodom's sin; God smashed the box and brought them back to life (Genesis 18-19). Pharaoh thought he could stash Israel in a confined corner of his empire; God exploded the myth of Egyptian supremacy and released the people of promise to find their way to a land of their own (Exodus 1-24). When Sennacherib and his Assyrian armies had Hezekiah and God's people locked up in the box of Jerusalem; God erased the limits of siege, sending the entrappers home and releasing the captives (2 Kings 18-19). Even when Israel played the same game and thought it had God locked in the box of the temple (see Ezekiel 1-10), God refused to stay in the box.

Easter is a box-breaking event. Nothing seems more secure to us than the metal-clad coffins in which we place the bodies of our dead, and the cement secure vaults in which they are buried. But God is in the habit of breaking boxes, even those that seem incredibly secure, and Easter proves it once and for all. No box could hold Jesus. No trap of death could snare him. Easter is "Boxing Day," when the last great boxes that confine, outline, refine, define, and malign us are broken. So boast about it!

An Alternative Application
John 20:1-18. If you would like to focus only on the resurrection story in John, several themes emerge. First, John tells us that the events take place early in the morning, "while it was still dark." Light and darkness are very meaningful in John's gospel — in chapter 1, God creates the world full of light, but it becomes dark; Jesus is the light of God entering this dark world, and only those who see his glory become bearers of the light of God. In chapter 3, Nicodemus comes to Jesus at night, but is given a sendoff that surrounds him with light; in chapter 13, Judas enters the room of Jesus' farewell discourse surrounded by the light of Jesus' glory, but when challenged about his motives, leaves the room "and it is night." Here

darkness is both the condition of the morning and the figurative blindness or uncertainty of those who do not yet fully comprehend the significance of Jesus' resurrection.

Second, in John's description of the tomb there is evidence of resurrection that resoundingly speaks against grave robbery. Grave robbers would not unwrap a body at the grave; they would make sure they were in a safe place before doing so, but here the strips of linen that were used to wrap the body of Jesus appear to have fallen in place. This would not be so if Jesus' body were unwrapped from the outside; nor could it happen if the one wrapped had only fainted and then come back to life (remember how Jesus commanded others to unwrap Lazarus in John 11). At the same time, the headpiece was folded and placed off to the side by itself. John's testimony speaks of a body that miraculously passed through its death wraps, dropping them in place, and of a living human who took off his death skullcap, folded it and put it away because it was no longer needed.

Easter 2
Acts 2:14a, 22-32
1 Peter 1:3-9
John 20:19-31
by David Kalas

Now it's time to preach

The Sunday after Easter is an unenviable time for preachers in many churches. The mood and events of Holy Week have both a depth and an excitement that can make the Sunday after Easter something of a letdown. The palm branches are gone. The lilies are gone, and it will seem that a great many people are gone too. Surely the attendance in so many of our American churches is a letdown on the Sunday after Easter.

So what shall we do on the Sunday after Easter? Take a vacation? Follow the lead of our people who stay home in great numbers this day? Bring in someone off the bench to fill the pulpit?

Throughout the gospels, Jesus repeatedly told people not to spread the word about him. After they were healed (Luke 5:14), after they witnessed miracles (Matthew 17:9; Mark 7:36; Luke 8:56), after they had discovered something of his identity (Matthew 16:20), he consistently admonished people not to tell anyone.

That gag order was not permanent, however. Jesus indicated as much when he was coming down from the mountain where he had been transfigured before Peter, James, and John. "Tell no one about the vision," he said, "until after the Son of Man has been raised from the dead" (Matthew 17:9). And therein lies the key for us. What are we to do after Easter? After he has been raised from the dead? Tell!

The gospel does not consist of his miracles, healings, teachings, or even identity. Only after he had been crucified and raised was there something to tell. So now, especially on the Sunday after Easter, it's time to preach.

Acts 2:14a, 22-32

We preachers feel considerable pressure to be relevant. The world in which we live does not widely cherish preaching. Indeed, in everyday idiomatic English, "preach" is a rather negative word. For example, "Don't preach at me!" and "I didn't mean to sound preachy." When you and I stand up to preach, we feel the need to say something that will be perceived and received as relevant to the folks in our congregation. "What does this have to do with me and my life?" is the relevancy litmus test.

In light of the contemporary demand for personal relevancy and immediate application, we may rightly be startled by Peter's sermon on Pentecost. In our excerpted passage, for example, the only real point of personal connection Peter makes with his audience is to refer to them as the ones to whom Jesus was handed over and by whom he was crucified.

I'm trying to imagine Peter distributing to the crowd at the beginning a little photocopied sermon guide with blanks to be filled in. "You see the line," Peter says, "that reads, 'God sent Jesus. God used Jesus. And we _____ Jesus'? Go ahead and write 'killed' in that blank."

That's more personal relevancy than we bargained for.

Peter does not suffer from any confusion, however, about the subject of his preaching. He preaches Christ. He preaches what Christ did, what the scriptures say about Christ, the people's culpability in not recognizing but rejecting Christ, God's act of raising Christ from the dead, and the witness of those who had known and seen Christ. He preaches Christ.

Sometimes the demand for relevancy tempts us to preach about current events but that may reflect a fallacious paradigm: one that we ought to help our people out of, rather than climbing into it ourselves. The paradigm assumes that "current" and "relevant" naturally go together. Our proclamation of the gospel, however, asserts two other things. First, that some very ancient events are relevant — indeed, more personally life-impacting than many or all current events. And, second, that these ancient events are, in fact, current, for the resurrection makes them so. Our gospel is not dead and buried in the past. Rather, we proclaim one who is risen and alive. He is, therefore, always current and his saving death and resurrection are always relevant.

In the end, Peter called upon the Pentecost congregation to repent, to be baptized in Jesus' name, and to receive the Holy Spirit. The gospel calls for personal response. It seems, therefore, that the preacher of the gospel does not need to seek some relevant message for the people. Rather, the preacher of the gospel implores the people to make the message personally relevant in their own lives.

1 Peter 1:3-9

Call it, "Theology on a Time Line." That's the style of this intricate opening paragraph from Peter's first epistle. Tightly woven together in just these few verses, Peter has expressed his understanding of the Christian's past, present, and future.

The past is the part least elaborated here, although he returns to that theme repeatedly in later portions of this epistle (see, for example, 1:14, 18; 2:9b-10; 4:3). Within the present passage, the past is summarized by the reference to the new birth that God has given us (v. 3).

The present, meanwhile, is a manifestly mixed bag. On the one hand, it is a time of testing and suffering. This is one of the recurring themes of Peter's letter — the problem of suffering was clearly a major issue for the Christians to whom Peter wrote. At the same time, however, the present is also a time of hope and rejoicing. It is a time lived under God's protection, and it is the time of "receiving the outcome of your faith, the salvation of your souls."

Finally, the future. The future is not at all a mixed bag. The future is all good. Paul piles up unalloyed adjectives to describe the inheritance that awaits us in God's good future. It is also anticipated as a time of "praise and glory and honor when Jesus Christ is revealed," and the implication is that the suffering will be past and we will finally and fully see the one in whom we have believed and whom we have loved.

Two broad points can be derived from these observations. First, there is the central role of God in past, present, and future. In our past, God gave us something — and that gift, of course, was predicated upon a great many things he did in the past! In the present, he protects, saves, and proves us. In the future, he marvelously fulfills all that he has in store for us and for the world.

We do not see any period of our lives clearly if we do not see God in the midst of it. We all ought to devise a kind of "time line theology" — and help our congregations do the same — by which we affirm the presence and providence of God in our past, present, and future.

Second, there is the relative influence of the past and the future on the present. We are more naturally conscious, of course, of how the past influences the present. We see the past more clearly, which makes its influence easier to trace. Also, our deeply ingrained sense of cause-and-effect gives perhaps disproportionate credit to the past for the present.

What comes after is the heir of what comes before, right? It cannot work the other way, can it? Can it be that what will come after gives birth to something in the present?

Precisely that phenomenon is very much a part of our common experience, and it is a part of Peter's testimony and teaching here. While organic cause-and-effect flows always from past to present, and from present to future, the tide of influence can flow the other direction in other areas of life.

It is the future prospect of college, not the past experience of middle school, that makes the high school student work hard in the present. It is the upcoming summer's swimsuits, not the past winter's sweaters and coats, that prompt us to diet in the present. "Effect" may be the past's heir. "Preparation," however, is the progeny of the future.

And so, as Peter lays out his theology on a time line, we are struck by this unavoidable conclusion: The Christian's life in the present is meant to be more a response to the future than to the past. Our joy, our hope, our confidence, our faithfulness, our peace — these are not traced back to what has gone before, and they are often very much in spite of what goes on now. We live toward a final destination rather than a point of origin. God's future is the greatest influence on our present.

John 20:19-31

Some biblical characters rightly deserve the negative reputations that they have: Jezebel, Nebuchadnezzar, Judas, and Pontius Pilate. Thomas, however, does not. He has an undeserved reputation.

We know a fair amount about a few of the disciples, for they play significant roles in the gospels and Acts, and perhaps wrote some of the New Testament epistles. Meanwhile, we know practically nothing about others among the twelve. They are just names on the list, but we don't have a record of anything that they individually said or wrote or did.

Then there is Thomas. We don't know much about him, for he does not figure prominently in the gospel stories or in Acts. Rather, what we know about him comes mostly from this passage from the gospel of John, and this episode has so fashioned our impression of him that his reputation has become an expression, his name has become a nickname — "doubting Thomas."

I suggest that Thomas has been wrongfully singled out from among the disciples, for they were no paragons of belief on Easter or even afterward.

When Mary and the other women first returned from the empty tomb with the good news, what was the response of the disciples? Did they begin singing alleluias? No, but rather the women's "words seemed to them an idle tale, and they did not believe them" (Luke 24:11). That's a remarkable statement, isn't it? Here we have no less than the apostles hearing nothing less than the gospel word that Jesus is risen, and they reject it as nonsense. We, as preachers, need never be discouraged by the slow, halfhearted, or incredulous response of a congregation. Our congregations are in good company, for the apostles themselves did not make much of an audience for the gospel on Easter Sunday.

Mark reports, meanwhile, that Jesus appeared to two disciples, but when they returned to tell the rest of the group, the others would not believe (Mark 16:13). Accordingly, after that event, when Jesus did appear to the disciples all together, Mark writes that "he upbraided them for their lack of faith and stubbornness, because they had not believed those who saw him after he had risen" (Mark 16:14).

Even at the penultimate moment in Matthew's gospel, just before Jesus ascends into heaven, the author reports of those gathered around Jesus: "When they saw him, they worshiped him; but some doubted" (Matthew 28:17). Well after Easter, after many experiences and exposures, still "some doubted."

Upon further review, therefore, we discover that Thomas does not deserve to be singled out. He is singled out in history only because he happened to be the one not there when all the others were. Let's not call him "doubting Thomas," therefore, just "absent Thomas," or "bad-timing Thomas," or some such. But his doubt is no more remarkable than any of the other disciples.

Honestly, we don't even need to travel beyond the confines of this pericope from John's gospel to vindicate Thomas. On the first occasion when the risen Christ appeared to his disciples — the time when Thomas was not present — see the order of events. Jesus appeared and greeted them. Did they respond with recognition and rejoicing right away? Not according to the story. Rather, "after he said this, [Jesus] showed them his hands and his side. Then the disciples rejoiced when they saw the Lord."

There's no evidence that Thomas was not more incredulous than the others, just perhaps more outspoken in his incredulity. And, of course, his outspokenness cuts the other way, for while the other disciples may rejoice in the risen Christ, none matches Thomas' testimony and Christology in the end: "My Lord and my God!"

Application

I was sitting in a meeting recently in one of our denominational offices. Within view, I could see an assortment of resources on the bookshelves: resources for pastors, churches, Sunday school classes, and so on. There were packages of curriculum, church-growth resources, assorted programs for different ages and stages of life, church advertising tools and kits — a whole range of products, some designed for folks within the church and others targeting people outside the church.

As I sat there, examining the materials from a distance, I was struck by a theme in the packaging. People's faces. On so many of the products: collages of faces, with a healthy diversity of age, gender, and ethnicity represented.

I know that packaging is about marketing, and I don't pretend to be an expert in that very sophisticated field, but the packaging I saw made me wonder just what it is that we are selling — or, more appropriately, what it is that we are offering.

I have a recollection from my childhood that there used to be within the church a real preponderance of pictures of Jesus. He was pictured on the covers of our children's Sunday school booklets. His picture was on mission bulletin boards, on classroom walls, on bulletin covers, and on adult curriculum materials.

Admittedly, our old pictures of Jesus had their problems. He was Caucasian, and he seemed to come from either North America or Western Europe. Nonetheless, he was pictured everywhere and on everything we did, and while that is not an achievement by itself, it perhaps offered a certain clarity of purpose and message.

The marketing was not nearly so slick back then, to be sure, with all of our mimeographed bulletins and newsletters, but the message of our packaging was clear. What we had to offer was Christ.

That's what you and I have to offer this week. As we continue to celebrate and affirm his resurrection, we preach Christ. Just as Peter preached Christ to the curious crowds in Jerusalem on Pentecost, Christ is our message to the congregations we serve. All three of this week's lections give us ample material to explore and declare, not just his resurrection, but his person and work.

The pictures on so much of our present packaging neglect the product. Let that not be said of our preaching. We ought not begin with the ones to whom we are preaching, but rather with the one about whom we are preaching. He is current and relevant all by himself. He suffers only — now, as with the doubting disciples, as with the crowds whom Peter addressed — from being unrecognized. Our preaching sets out to change that.

An Alternative Application

John 20:19-31. This passage is so full that its possibilities for preaching are nearly endless. We devoted most of our attention above to Thomas, and, in preaching the main suggested theme for the week, we might devote ourselves especially to Thomas' exclamation, "My Lord and my God!"

Verse 23 stands out even within this brimming passage, however, for it is a verse that gives pause to many Protestant Christians. If you have an appetite for preaching the hard sayings of Jesus, this Sunday's gospel lection offers you an opportunity.

If I were going to preach Jesus' word to his disciples in John 20:23, I would not begin there. I would begin, instead, with a story. Two stories, really, from the Old Testament and I would set them side by side.

The first story would be the tragic story of King Saul. Few characters in scripture are as sad as Saul. He has no particular ambition at the outset, yet greatness is thrust upon him. Then he mismanages it in such a disastrous way that, in the end, we see him disguising himself to visit a witch, falling on his own sword in battle, and having his weary corpse paraded and abused by the Philistines.

The second story would be the grand story of King David. Not only is his reign strong and majestic, the groundwork for Israel's golden age under Solomon, but his legacy is like no one else's in scripture.

His life becomes the standard by which subsequent kings in Jerusalem are measured. His reign becomes the symbol for the messianic reign and God's ultimate kingdom. From Jesus' birth in Bethlehem to his triumphant entry into Jerusalem, David is recognized as the key ancestor in Jesus' lineage, and David's star still flies on the flag over the modern state of Israel.

A side-by-side comparison of Saul and David, however, reveals two kings with significant failures. Indeed, upon further review, David's terrible episode with Bathsheba and Uriah seems much more marked by calculated wickedness than any of Saul's misdeeds, which smack more of weakness than willfulness. Yet Saul is tragic, while David is triumphant. Why?

I suggest that the difference between these two men is not so much in their performance as something else. I wonder if the difference between these two men — an immense difference, in the end — is partly attributable to the prophets who worked with them.

From the very suggestion that Israel was to have a human king, the prophet Samuel is offended by and opposed to the idea. His introduction of Saul seems to hamstring him from the start. And his in-person response to Saul's failures is harsh and unforgiving.

Nathan, by contrast, becomes an agent of grace in David's awful hour. He tells the famous story that touches the former shepherd's heart, he enables David's repentance, and he assures David of God's forgiveness.

I would juxtapose the stories of Saul and David, with special attention to the comparison of Samuel and Nathan. Then I would introduce Jesus' words: "If you forgive the sins of any, they are forgiven them; if you retain the sins of any, they are retained." It is not authority for the apostles; it is responsibility for Christ's followers. We may be instruments of condemnation or we may be agents of grace.

Easter 3
Acts 2:14a, 36-41
1 Peter 1:17-23
Luke 24:13-35
by William Shepherd

Read the manual

My friend was overwhelmed by his first church convention. "It's all so big," he wrote in his report. "There is so much going on. I wish I had a manual to instruct me on what to do, where to go, and how to vote."

Someone responded to his report with a letter to an editor. "How sad," said the letter, "that a leader of our church would not know that we Christians already have a manual on how to live the Christian life. It's called the Bible."

The letter writer was vastly unfair to my friend, who was asking for a manual to the convention, not to the faith. But the letter writer was also unfair to the Bible itself, which is far from a manual. It is not a set of instructions. It contains history, poetry, and fiction as well as instruction. It must be read in a complex dialogue with tradition and common sense. Much of it makes sense only in an ancient context and cannot easily be translated into a modern setting. (I defy anyone to come up with an adequate modern analogy to Paul's prohibition of eating meat offered to idols in 1 Corinthians 8-10.)

However, there are passages in the Bible where the "manual" analogy works on a small scale. We read three such passages today. Peter's sermon in Acts is a manual on how to live the resurrected life. The letter that goes under Peter's name addresses the same subject, and Luke, who is telling a story rather than writing a manual, still subtly manages to instruct us in how to live under a risen Lord.

Acts 2:14a, 36-41

Peter's long Pentecost speech is divided into several sections in the lectionary. Today we read his closer — this is where he asks for the signatures that would close the sale. To review the story: the twelve (and perhaps 120 disciples with them) have been filled with the Spirit and inspired to preach the risen Lord (2:1-4). This has drawn a crowd of Pentecost pilgrims to listen (2:5-13). Peter, as the leader of this group, stood to proclaim that these events proved that the last days predicted by the prophets were upon them; God was at work here (2:14-21). This gave Peter the opportunity to preach the gospel (2:22-36, the first of several summaries of early Christian preaching in Acts, which Luke notes is merely a *précis*, v. 40). The interaction with the crowd (2:37-42) will lead to an idealized portrait of the early community (2:43-47).

The heart of Peter's speech is the affirmation that the resurrection proves Jesus' true identity: "Therefore let the entire house of Israel know with certainty that God has made him both Lord and Messiah, this Jesus whom you crucified" (2:36). The issue of "certainty" is crucial to Luke's work; he has already told us that "certainty" is the purpose of his writing (Luke 1:4). Peter's listeners (and Luke's readers) can be certain that God is fulfilling the promises made to Abraham — because it's happening before their eyes! Luke reinforces the connection to the tradition by using the archaic-sounding "House of Israel," and by giving Jesus two traditional titles, "Lord" and "Messiah."

Peter's last words were pointed directly at the crowd ("this Jesus whom you crucified"), and as so often in Luke-Acts, his speech is interrupted at its climax. The emotional response of the hearers, "Brothers, what should we do?" is a sign of the Spirit's work (2:37). Peter's response is twofold: "Repent, and be baptized every one of you in the name of Jesus" (2:38). "Repent" indicates a complete change of life, a turning around to walk in the opposite direction. It is an especially poignant word on the lips of Peter, who knew what it meant to get a second chance — and now all Israel is given that second chance! Peter commends baptism (although there is no record of the twelve or even the 120 being baptized) "in the name of Jesus" (it is not clear whether this was an alternative to the trinitarian baptismal formula, or simply a recognition of the power and authority behind Peter's proclamation). The promised results are also twofold: "Your sins may be forgiven, and you will receive the gift of the Holy Spirit." Peter is using a financial image in the promise that sins will be forgiven, like a debt. His promise of the Spirit extends beyond those listening to his sermon, "For the promise is for you, for your children, and for all who are far away, everyone whom the Lord our God calls to him" (2:39).

Luke tallies the number of those who responded to Peter's challenge at 3,000 (he does not mention the mechanics of getting all those people baptized!). The large number indicates the magnitude of the growth: from a mere seed of 120, the community has grown nearly thirtyfold. This is the restored people of God, God's new work in Israel, the firstfruits of a new Pentecost.

1 Peter 1:17-23

What Luke did for the Jewish people, 1 Peter does for the Gentiles — trace the theological connection between God's act in raising Jesus from the dead to its practical benefit for those who believe. Peter lays out the whole system, step by step. It is truly a manual for the community of the resurrection.

The manual might be titled, "How to Be Holy." The instructions specify that holiness is God's work, not ours. Peter moves to his main theme almost as soon as he begins the body of the letter: "Be holy yourselves in all your conduct; for it is written, 'You shall be holy, for I am holy' " (1:15-16). Peter quotes from Leviticus 19:2, in full acknowledgment of the Hebrew notion of "holiness," which at root is "separation." God is "holy" in the sense of being "set apart" from all created things. The people of God are to be "holy" in that same sense — set apart and different from their pagan neighbors. Thus, Peter employs the metaphor of the "Diaspora" as our lection begins: "If you invoke as Father the one who judges all people impartially according to their deeds, live in reverent fear during the time of your exile" (v. 17). Like the Jewish Diaspora, Gentile Christians are to live as aliens and sojourners in a hostile land. Their lives and actions prove them to be different from others.

Peter grounds his instruction in some theological basics. God is judge; that is, God is the only one who sees human beings impartially, for who they really are and what they really do (v. 17). Further, the God who knows us truly has sacrificed for us; God is the one who has bought our freedom. Peter uses the image of the "ransomer," one who pays to free a slave (it was not unheard of for a philanthropist or temple to redeem and set free a slave; Peter pictures God doing this on a widespread scale, v. 18). Peter invokes Passover imagery when he speaks of "the precious blood of Christ" being "like that of a lamb without defect or blemish" (v. 19; cf. Exodus 12:5; Leviticus 22:21); his contrast of perishable/imperishable will carry over into his discussion of the power of God's word in 1:23.

The redeemer judge God was at work from the beginning in Christ, who was "destined before the foundation of the world" (v. 20). Fortunately for you, Peter says, "he was revealed at the end of the ages for your sake" (the parallel clauses are hymnlike). This is the same language he has already used to describe Christians (v. 2); there is an analogy between God's work in Christ and God's work in Christians. God's work included raising Christ from the dead and to glory, with the corresponding result of faith and hope among believers (v. 21). This is the new birth that comes through the word (v. 23).

The Christian life is the appropriate response to God's work in Christ on our behalf. Peter exhorts his readers to "live in fear" (the NRSV qualifies the "fear" as "reverent," v. 17). They are to turn "from the futile ways inherited from your ancestors" (v. 18). They are to trust in God (v. 21). This trust is variously specified as including faith, hope, obedience, and love (vv. 21-22; the NRSV's "genuine mutual love" is literally "brotherly love" within the community, a necessary commodity if, as many think, Peter was writing to a persecuted church, cf. 4:14, 16). Yet even these virtues are not human work, because they are guaranteed by God's work in Christ (v. 21). Christians are to live as purified souls (v. 22); again, this recalls the Passover lamb who by virtue of baptism has been "born anew" (v. 23).

Luke 24:13-35

Luke continues the textbook approach to the basics of the resurrection, this time in narrative form. In the Emmaus story, the disciples restate some basic Lukan themes. But Jesus himself fills in the blanks, explaining how these events have been a part of God's plan all along. In teaching the disciples the true meaning of his life, death, and resurrection, Jesus shows how they can come to recognize him on a regular basis in the breaking of the bread.

The Emmaus story is a bridge between the empty-tomb narrative and the appearance of the risen Lord to all the disciples. It touches on a number of important Lukan themes: the centrality of Jerusalem as the place of God's work, the revelation of Jesus in teaching and Eucharist, and the fulfillment of prophecy. It is a "recognition story" of a type common in both the Hebrew Bible and in Greco-Roman storytelling, where hospitality to a stranger pays off in unexpected ways. Most importantly, it puts Luke's readers back on the road, echoing Jesus' original trip to Jerusalem (9:51—19:27).

Emmaus was a short trip from Jerusalem (the exact location is uncertain). Luke identifies Cleopas and his unnamed companion as two of those who had heard yet disbelieved the women's story of an empty tomb (v. 13). These two were having an extended discussion on the meaning of the events of these last few days (v. 14). They were joined by Jesus himself, though "their eyes were kept from recognizing him" (Luke often uses the image of sight and vision as a metaphor for faith and salvation, cf. 1:78-79; 2:30; 4:18-19; 6:39-42; 10:23; 11:34; 18:35-42; 19:42). The defect here was not their comprehension of the things that had happened, but the lack of proper perspective, which only Jesus could provide. Their state of affairs is quite poignantly summed up by Luke in their response to Jesus' greeting: "They stood still, looking sad" (v. 17).

Cleopas recounts the story so far in quite Lukan terms. Jesus is described as the "Prophet like Moses," mighty in word and deed before God and the people (v. 19; cf. Deuteronomy 34:10-12). The response to this prophet was divided: the leaders of the people gave him over to condemnation and death (v. 20), but "we had hoped that he was the one to redeem Israel" (v. 21). The empty tomb story is recounted with some astonishment, but inconclusively, as if the simple fact of its emptiness was not enough to evoke faith in them (vv. 22-24).

Jesus' response is that of a prophet: "Oh, how foolish you are, and how slow of heart to believe all that the prophets have declared!" (v. 25). Of course, what they lack is a proper messianic understanding of the scriptures, and who better to provide it than the Messiah himself? Luke shows the church how to read scripture in this passage: the Hebrew Bible must be read through and by Jesus. It points to him as it details the prophetic pattern he followed: rejection, suffering, death, and vindication. "Was it not necessary that the Messiah should suffer these things and then enter into his glory?" (v. 26).

Luke gives us a recognition scene with a bit of playful suspense, as Jesus threatens to walk off anonymously into the sunset (vv. 28-29). Instead, he accepts the hospitality offered by the two disciples and proceeds to recall his actions at both the miraculous feeding and the Last Supper: he took, blessed, broke, and gave bread (v. 30). Like innumerable Christians since then, their eyes were finally opened, and he was "made known to them in the breaking of the bread" (v. 35). Retrospectively, they understood how he was also made known in the messianic teaching from the scriptures: "Were not our hearts burning within us while he was talking to us on the road, while he was opening the scriptures to us?" (v. 32).

The two return immediately to report to the others. Their report is almost pre-empted with the announcement that greets them: "The Lord has risen indeed, and he has appeared to Simon!" Nevertheless, the two disciples fulfill their duty and become types of the faithful Christian, who not only meet Jesus in the scriptures and the breaking of the bread, but also witness their experience to all who will hear.

Application

I once was working with a church that wanted to do evangelism. "Here's an idea," someone said, "let's get the listings of all the new housing purchases in the area, and we'll make up a flyer and send it out to the new people who move in. We'll be like the Welcome Wagon."

It was not a bad idea in and of itself, publicity-wise, but as a sole plan of evangelism, it had a few flaws (a good response on that kind of mailing would be about one percent). I tried to reason with them.

This was a small church, average attendance less than 100. "What's the most important thing about this church?" I asked, "What makes you come back each week?"

"We're like a family," they kept saying, "We treat each other like a family."

"What does it mean to be a family?"

"You live together," they said, "you eat together, you work together, and you have fun together."

"How do you bring new members into a family?"

That one stumped them.

"Well," I said, "you either get born into it or adopted. Now say you're going to adopt a child — how are you going to find a child to adopt?"

That stumped them too. If only there were an adoption agency for potential new church members; we could just drop by on Sunday morning and pick up a few.

"One thing's for sure," I told that group, "you're not going to invite new members into your family by sending out mass mailings. You wouldn't even send out a flyer to get guests for a dinner party. In a family, you want people not only to eat with you, but live with you, work with you, and play with you. How can you expect to invite people to join your family without a personal invitation?"

Jesus has given us a handbook on how to bring our friends and neighbors to him. First, we need to understand the scriptures. Next, we need to understand theology. Then we need to understand how those two things connect to our everyday lives — we need to repent, be baptized, be born anew, learn from Jesus, and see him in the stranger and in the community. In short, we need to live the Christian life ourselves.

Then we can invite people into the family, personally.

Alternative Applications

1) Luke 24:13-35. Preachers need to keep alert to the dark side of scripture, even in its brightest moments. One prominent problem in recounting the passion narratives is the polemic edge of all the gospels, which could easily be twisted into anti-Semitism, in the form of "the Jews killed Jesus." Good teaching is an effective antidote to that sort of nonsense. In Luke's case, clearly it is not "the Jews" but a subset of a divided Jewish people who is held responsible for the betrayal of Jesus. Cleopas' speech in Luke makes the division clear: The leaders of the people handed him over to be condemned to death and crucified him (and even here, Cleopas is stretching it — only Romans had the power to crucify). As for the common people, they tended to respond positively to Jesus, according to Luke. The theme of division is Luke's way of addressing a fundamental theological question for his community: Why, if Jesus is the promised Messiah, did not all the Jewish people believe in him? Luke's answer is that some did, some didn't — the people were divided, with the leaders going against Jesus. He is not writing history so much as an explanation of how the church came to be dominated by Gentiles. He certainly would have been appalled to find anyone using his work to justify hatred against the Jewish people.

2) 1 Peter 1:17-23. In their book, *Resident Aliens: Life in the Christian Colony* (1989), Stanley Hauerwas and William H. Willimon challenged mainline Christians to rethink their role in contemporary society.

Christendom, the American fusion of state and civil religion, according to Hauerwas and Willimon, is dead. And that, they think, is a good thing! The Christian faith cannot be institutionalized into an unofficial state religion without being distorted into something it is not. True Christianity absent Christendom can now live on as if in a Diaspora, an enclave separate from a society that challenges and provokes the values of that society. We are to be "resident aliens," no longer trying to accommodate our beliefs to the norms of society, but speaking out and living out a vision of faith that sees Christ's self-giving as its norm. Gone will be the appeal to selfish and self-serving religious "needs" in favor of a genuine commitment to the God revealed in Jesus Christ. In the terms used by the author of 1 Peter, we will "live in reverent fear during the time of our exile."

Easter 4
Acts 2:42-47
1 Peter 2:19-25
John 10:1-10
by Wayne Brouwer

Finding safety in the call of the wild

There are two themes that run through the passages for today. On the one hand there is the *Call of the Wild* (like Jack London's 1903 novel), in which we are commanded to follow our Shepherd Jesus through what might be trackless wastes and difficult places in responding to the great challenge of faith. On the other hand, there is the "Call of the Safe" (like Larry Crabb's great book on small groups, *The Safest Place on Earth* [Word, 1999]), which places us in the middle of a community of care and grace.

George MacDonald helps us understand both of these homing calls in his children's tale, "Papa's Story." Papa tells of a shepherd who brings his flock home late on a stormy evening. One lamb is missing, however. So, after supper, the shepherd calls for Jumper the dog and the two of them brace for the cold and wind and rain. Out in the hills they roam, calling for the wee lamb.

Young Nellie is snug in her bed at home but every moaning of the breeze echoes with her father's distant voice. She is frightened for him, for Jumper, and for the little lamb they seek. Suddenly, father is home, and Jumper too! They have found the little lamb and have returned it to safety in the fold. The tests of the night have taken their toll on father. How weary he looks, and how torn, cut, dirty, and bleeding is Jumper!

When little Nellie returns to bed, she dreams that *she* is Jumper and that the little lamb is her lost brother Willie. A year earlier, young Willie left home. He wanted to get away. Now Willie lives in Edinburgh and never writes. Nellie and her parents know from the scuttlebutt of traders and friends that Willie has become only a shadow of himself, cruel and greedy, filthy of body and mind, constantly drunk and lost in a mad world of sex.

In Nellie's dream she is Jumper, searching through the storms of Edinburgh's wilder haunts for the little lamb with Willie's face. When she wakes the next morning, Nellie acts on her dream and goes to find her brother. After hours of struggle and pain, Nellie finally reaches him. Surrounded by his jeering and taunting pals, he laughs at his sister's foolish begging. Nellie weeps at his harshness. She tells him of his mother's broken heart. She gives him a letter of love, written in his father's hand. The scenes of home wash young Willie's mind and the disease of wantonness sickens him. Before long, says Papa, Willie is led back home by his little sister.

The children enjoy Papa's nice story, as always. But there are two footnotes we need to know. First, the story Papa tells his children that night is actually the story of his own life. His name is Willie, and it was his own dear sister Nellie who, one day, years before, came looking for him in the shadowed dens of Edinburgh. Second, George MacDonald gives the tale a subtitle. He calls it "A Scot's Christmas Story." So it is, for the story of Jesus is not first of all a bland tale of pious peace or a study in theological ethics. Rather, it is a rescue story always told best in the first person. Jesus, the Good Shepherd, came from home looking through the streets and alleys of earth's slums for *me*! For *you*!

Acts 2:42-47

Margaret Mead said the first sign of civilization was found where archaeologists uncovered human skeletons with broken femur bones that had healed. The law of the jungle is, "If you fall, you die." Anyone who broke a femur had fallen and could not get away. If a skeleton displayed a healed femur it meant that someone stood between this crippled person and the danger that threatened, took this person to a place of safety, and cared for this person during a time of healing, bringing food and water, and providing protection. A healed femur, said Mead, was the telltale sign of a community that had learned to value life, care for others, and build a network of supportive relationships.

That powerful image could well be the visualization of this passage. The first evidence of Jesus' resurrection power shaping a community of the future kingdom of God is seen here at the close of Peter's Pentecost sermon. It is a strong church that breathes with God's redemptive life in Jesus. It honors the diversity of God's family, expresses optimistic faith, draws others with magnetic love, and celebrates the great king and his kingdom.

Seven themes emerge from Luke's terse description. First, this was a community of humility, living under the authority of the apostles and the guidance of their teaching. Second, this was a community of mutual care, building relationships that were deeper than a puddle after an overnight rain. Third, this was a community that rooted itself in the rituals of Jesus, remembering through sacramental rites the essentials of redemptive history. Fourth, this was a community of spiritual passion, wrestling with God in prayer for themselves and their neighbors and world. Fifth, this was a community of generosity, giving and sharing and ensuring that the poor were constantly resourced. Sixth, this was a community of worship, which amounted to a public declaration of loyalty to God and allegiance to a particular interpretation of the divine cause. Seventh, this was a missionary community, seeking constantly to bring neighbors and coworkers into the fellowship through evangelistic outreach.

Whether Luke's description of the early church is merely factual reporting or somewhat idealized in its expression, the qualities he notes are those that Jesus and the apostles constantly hold up as virtuous. Most congregations need to be reminded of these spiritual characteristics over and over again. Sometimes, however, in times of revival or unusual stress, they seem to leap to the surface.

In his book *To End All Wars* (Zondervan, 2002), Ernest Gordon tells of what he and others experienced in the Japanese prisoner-of-war camp made famous by the movie *The Bridge over the River Kwai*. The camp stood at the end of the Bataan death march that brought Allied soldiers deep into the jungles of Asia. Few would survive and everyone knew it. In order to make the best of a terrible situation they teamed up in pairs, each watching out for a buddy. One prisoner was a strapping six-foot-three fellow built like a tower of iron, but his buddy got malaria. The smaller fellow was much weaker and very likely to die. Their captors did not want to deal with sickness, so anyone who was unable to work was confined in a "hot house" until he succumbed to heat exhaustion, dehydration, and the collapse of his bodily systems. The sick man was locked in a hothouse and left to die. Surprisingly he did not die, because every mealtime his strong buddy went out to him, under curses and threats from the guards, and shared his meager rations. Every night his buddy braved the watchful eyes above that held guns of death and brought his own slim blanket to cover the fevered convulsions of the sick man.

At the end of two weeks the sick man astounded the guards by recovering well enough to be able to return to work. He even survived the entire camp experience and lived to tell about it. His buddy, however — the strong man all thought invincible — died very shortly of malaria, exposure, and dysentery. He had given his life to save his friend. The story does not end there. When Allied troops liberated that camp at the close of the war in the Pacific, virtually every prisoner was a Christian. There was a symphony orchestra in camp, with instruments made of the crudest materials. There were worship services every Sunday, and the death toll was far lower than any expected. All this because of the silent testimony made by a strong man toward his buddy facing death, and the realization that apart from Jesus' forgiving grace that develops God's new humanity, we devolve into mere animals. We need a divine shepherd to create community and guide us home.

1 Peter 2:19-25

Peter's letter appears to be a teaching handbook primarily addressed to those recently baptized into the Christian church. Persecution faced these new believers and suffering is a constant theme of the letter (see 1:6-7; 3:14-17; 4:1; 4:12-19; 5:1; 5:8-10). Here Peter calls for moral strength through suffering, patterned after Jesus' own response to his walk of pain toward the cross. The theme verse that jumps out as a badge to be worn by believers is verse 21. It was used effectively by Charles Sheldon to shape his classic Christian novel *In His Steps*, where a town is transformed by people who begin to ask themselves, "What would Jesus do?" (The WWJD bracelets made popular a decade or so ago emerged from a second "revival" of this creed.)

Peter points to Jesus as the shepherd who leads through trial and offers an example for others who struggle with life. One story from our recent history comes to mind. A young woman stared in disbelief as the Queen of England, Elizabeth II, approached her in open sight of thousands of people and hundreds of television cameras, and crowned her tennis champion of the world. It was the culmination of a powerful story of perseverance, since young Althea Gibson was born in poverty and suffered crushing childhood illnesses that left her muscles weak and her limbs twisted. It was the perseverance of Althea's mother that made the difference. Mrs. Gibson one day pointed to a rock across the yard that looked like an overgrown potato. "I want you to go down there and bring it up to the house," said her mother, "so we can use it as a step by the kitchen door."

The girl sobbed and protested. "Mommy!" she lamented, "I'm so weak that I can hardly even walk down there! How can I possibly move a stone that big?"

Her mother persisted and simply said, "You can do it! I have confidence in you! You'll figure something out."

Indeed, inch by inch, rolling and tugging and pushing, the young lass moved that rock to the house. It took her two months to do what a healthy child would have accomplished in fifteen minutes but as she tussled with the stone, Althea's muscles strengthened and her limbs straightened. Surprised by her new energy, she began a rigorous training program that led to tennis and ultimately to Wimbledon. It was there that Althea Gibson was crowned victor by the Queen of England before an awestruck world.

In Althea's view the story revolved not around her own ability to see things through but rather focused on her mother's steadfast presence. Perseverance was, for her, not so much the confidence of winning at Wimbledon or inventing something new or succeeding in business. Rather, it was being able to count on a relationship that would never let her down, even if she did not accomplish great things.

That is what Peter has in mind as well when he writes about developing perseverance in faith. Perhaps we will be fortunate enough to celebrate our dreams come true. Yet whether we win or lose in life, faith's perseverance reminds us that Jesus our shepherd will always be there for us. That is reward enough for both time and eternity.

John 10:1-10

While this passage stops just short of Jesus' multiple declarations, "I am the good shepherd" (vv. 11, 14), it breathes with the essence of that testimony (see vv. 2-4). Coming between stories of spiritual blindness (ch. 9) and antagonistic unbelief (10:22-39), Jesus' words about thieves, robbers, and strangers who lead Jesus' sheep to destruction are very pointed. They may even have caused some of the backlash in 10:22-39 (see vv. 26-27).

Though the sheep pen (v. 1) where the sheep belong may refer to many things (general well-being, the church community, eternal life, and the like), there is good reason to view it primarily as the realm of the dead. Bad shepherds, thieves, and strangers seek to bring the sheep into a twilight world of pain and judgment at death, but Jesus brings his sheep into the eternal kingdom of life (v. 10). Confirmation for this interpretation comes from the story of the raising of Lazarus in chapter 11. Lazarus has been stolen away by death, but Jesus stands in the cemetery and *calls his name* (11:43), and from the sheep pen of the great thief, Lazarus hears his name and comes out to follow his true shepherd!

Among the representations of Jesus found carved above the burial niches in the catacombs of Rome are pictures of Jesus as Orpheus. The legend of Orpheus told of his journey into the underworld to reclaim his loved Eurydice. While early Christians did not believe in the myths of Rome and Greece, they did see in this story a meaningful way to summarize the truths of John 10 — Jesus alone is the Good Shepherd who can go into the underworld where the thief has stolen away Jesus' sheep; Jesus alone has the power to challenge the thief, call his sheep by name, bring them back to life, and lead them into eternal pastures of grace, mercy, and peace.

Application

In Christopher Fry's play, *The Lady's Not for Burning*, Margaret and Nicholas are talking about a woman who seems to be acting strangely. Margaret says, "She must be lost."

Nicholas responds, wistfully, "Who isn't? The best thing we can do is to make whatever we're lost in look as much like home as we can."

That is what we do with our lives, isn't it? We have so many goals and dreams and hopes in life, yet so few of them turn out. We get old before we have done half of what we wanted. Somehow we never become what we thought we might. We make a few mistakes along the way. We disappoint some people, and they disappoint us. Even our best times have an edge of bitterness attached to them — when they end we walk away nursing our nostalgia. We are always a little bit away from home — from the home we remember or the home we desire, from the dream we miss or the dream we are still looking for. That is what Nicholas is saying to Margaret in Christopher Fry's play. We are all a bit lost in life. We are all a bit away from home. The best we can do is make what we have look as much as possible like what we think "home" should be, until we can finally see our true home and like James says, bring our friends along with us.

No matter where we go, no matter what we do, there must live in each of us a touch of that homesickness, or we die a horrible death. Our trips "home" are only a pale imitation of the place we belong and merely a wayside rest stop on a restless journey to the real home of God's love and God's eternity. More than we know, that is where we all truly want to go and only in finding Jesus and the coming of God's kingdom will our desires find fulfillment and our longings be satisfied. Only then will our homesickness end.

This is what Acts 2:42-47 pictures. This is the pilgrimage to which Peter calls us. This is the assurance that Jesus communicates when he stands and speaks as our shepherd. In him alone we find safety, even as we respond to his call into the wilds.

An Alternative Application

The picture of the church in Acts 2:24-27 is such a powerful picture that it makes a great stand-alone text for a message. In addition to the seven characteristics noted above, this passage can be used to reflect on how we can be and become more faithful in the expressions of these qualities.

One of my favorite parables related to this picture of the church is one in which the abbot of a dying monastery and a local Jewish rabbi meet regularly in the woods to commune and commiserate. Both are discouraged with the lack of faith and practice in their worlds. The elderly abbot complains about the crusty feistiness of the remaining four monks under his care — all old, all crotchety, all difficult. On one of these meetings the Jewish rabbi brings a prophetic message that he himself is mystified by. He tells the abbot that he doesn't know why, but he feels compelled to inform his friend that one among those at the monastery is the Messiah. Both feel embarrassed by this obviously inappropriate declaration and soon part to return to their homes.

At supper that evening, the abbot hesitantly tells of the rabbi's strange message. All five men laugh self-consciously and quickly move on to other conversation. But in the days that follow, the atmosphere in the monastery begins to change. Could Brother John be the Messiah? Does Brother Elred speak with divine wisdom? Is the tenacious care that the abbot gives a reflection of his holy office?

Within a month the quality of life in the monastery has changed. Those who live in the neighborhood notice it and begin attending worship services in the monastery chapel. Families enjoy picnics on the lawns of the monastery, just to be near the older men who are wiser and kinder than any seemed to remember. Then several young men asked to take vows to join the monastery, and before long, the monastery became the thriving center of a new city. They no longer call it a monastery. Instead, they have posted signs at every entrance, welcoming all to come and join "Christ's Community." Indeed, Messiah is among them!

Easter 5
Acts 7:55-60
1 Peter 2:2-10
John 14:1-14
by David Kalas

Between acts

What do you do between Act 2 and Act 3 of a performance? That depends upon who you are.

If you are like me, then you have attended a great many more shows, plays, and performances than you have participated in. As members of the audience, the time between acts is an intermission — an opportunity to stretch your legs, to use the restroom, to enjoy some refreshments.

If you have ever been part of the stage crew for some performance, however, then you understand the minutes between acts quite differently. It is not a casual and relaxing time. On the contrary, it is a period marked by hustle and hard work. There's a clear sense of what needs to be done — moved, changed, turned, or whatever else — in order to be prepared for the next act, and the stage crew member who decides that intermission would be a good time to use the restroom and get a drink will not keep his job for long.

As followers of Christ, we are not invited to be mere spectators. We find ourselves living in the meantime — in the minutes between God's great acts — and one of these days, we know that the curtain will suddenly go up, and the star of the show will make his grand entrance for the final act. Our job is not to stretch our legs, get a cold drink, and wait it out. Our job is to make sure that the stage is set and everything is prepared for what and who is to come.

Acts 7:55-60

This scene opens with a reference to the Holy Spirit.

At a human level, that is of course characteristic of the author, Luke. He is more attentive to the Holy Spirit as a theme than any of the other gospel writers (compare, for example, Matthew 7:11 and Luke 11:13), and Luke uses the phrase "filled with the Holy Spirit" ten times in his gospel and in Acts.

Meanwhile, at a spiritual level, the phenomenon doesn't trace back to Luke; he is just the one most deliberately reporting it. Rather, there is this presence and activity of the Holy Spirit and that is especially central to the story of Acts. Indeed, many have suggested that the book might be more appropriately titled "The Acts of the Holy Sprit" than "The Acts of the Apostles."

See the snapshot of this particular scene in your mind's eye. Freeze the picture and zoom in to get a closer look at the faces. Where do you see peace and where do you see agitation? Where do you see hands raised up in a kind of desperate self-defense and where do you see a placid strength?

On the one hand, you have a crowd with fistfuls of stones. On the other hand, you have an innocent victim, harassed, defenseless, and facing a gruesome execution. Yet it is the crowd that is agitated. They are the ones raising their hands to cover their ears. Stephen, by contrast, seems very much at peace. He makes no apparent effort to resist them or to defend himself. His effort is only to bear witness to Christ and to pray for his tormentors' forgiveness. Stephen puts flesh and blood on that magnificent line from Charles Wesley's hymn: "Happy, if with my latest breath I may but gasp his name, preach him to all and cry in death, 'Behold, behold the Lamb!' " (Charles Wesley, "Jesus! The Name High Over All").

We know the look of the child who, in a tantrum, refuses to listen. He covers his ears, stamps his feet, and wails, "I'm not listening to you!" or "I can't hear you!" That is the look of Stephen's persecutors. They find his words intolerable, unbearable, and so they cover their ears, shout loudly, and hurry to shut him up. But the word of God cannot be shut up (see Jeremiah 20:9; 2 Timothy 2:9). It cannot be contained within an individual. Then much to the consternation of its opponents, even after that individual is silenced, the word of God still cannot be contained.

The great dramatic irony of the scene, of course, is the figure of the young man with the coats draped at his feet. Little did that indignant and bloodthirsty mob know that, while they rushed to silence one voice for Christ, perhaps the man who would become his greatest evangelist was standing there in their midst. He observed, approved, and emulated their zealous persecution. Within a few years, however, that same man would be spanning the Mediterranean proclaiming the same Jesus whose name and whose message that crowd found intolerable.

For preaching purposes, this passage can be taken in several directions. First, there is the theme of the Holy Spirit's activity — within history, within the early church, and within an individual's life — that could be explored in light of Stephen's story and example. Second, there is the character Stephen himself: initially designated to do a seemingly less important work (Acts 6:1-5), and yet in the end, a tremendous witness and example, the first Christian martyr, and the person who has the longest recorded sermon in the book of Acts. Third, there is the response of the crowd: Why does the affirmation of Christ at the right hand of God, both then and now, evoke such violent opposition? Fourth, there is the story of Saul, pondering what long-term influence this episode may have had on him (see, for example, 2 Timothy 4:16).

1 Peter 2:2-10

Mother's milk. It is, I suppose, the most natural thing in the world. As my wife and I read and learned about breastfeeding when our children were born, we were continually amazed by the beauty of the whole design. How this brand new baby, who didn't know anything, knew what to do when she was put on her mother's breast. How everything that she needed — and would need for some months — was contained in that simple, natural formula. How nutrition, comfort, and relationship all came together in a single act. Beautiful.

Meanwhile, our ten-year-old daughter was at an extended family event recently and one of her aunts offered her a taste of coffee. The aunt is a real coffee lover — even a bit of a coffee snob — and so she was sharing with our daughter one of her great pleasures in life. When our daughter tasted it, however, she did not see the appeal. Her aunt read her reaction on her face and replied, "It's an acquired taste."

So it is that the newborn is so naturally drawn to its mother's perfect milk. And so it is that, as we age, we acquire so many other tastes — some of them quite unhealthy for us.

One wonders what Peter's congregation had acquired tastes for. What imperfect, impure, ultimately undesirable things they desired and consumed. Whatever they were, Peter wanted to see them return to what's best — a spiritual version of the pure and perfect mother's milk.

We, and our congregations, would be well served to consider the same question. What unhealthy tastes have we acquired? What do we consume that is so far removed from the pure spiritual milk God has for us?

Next, that exhortation to desire spiritual milk leads Peter into an inspired and poetic invitation to the Lord himself. Here is where the passage becomes a theological statement about the person and work of Christ.

The primary imagery of the passage is stones. If you have a teaching or expository style of preaching, then this Sunday's sermon may be found in the development of that one theme. We'll look more carefully at some of the options involved here below.

In the end, Peter references four different Old Testament texts in this brief passage. Verse 6 quotes from Isaiah 28:16. Verse 7 comes from Psalm 118:22. Verse 8 cites Isaiah 8:14 and verse 10 recalls Hosea

1:9-10. All of this is in addition to verse 9, which is full of images that find elaboration and meaning in Old Testament texts about Israel and Levi.

This tapestry of Old Testament references — whether by direct quote or by borrowed imagery — reminds us of several realities within the early church and its preaching.

First, its text, its scripture, was the Old Testament, not the New. In the modern American church, the Old Testament is so often dismissed as outdated, irrelevant, even replaced. We do well to remember that the apostles managed to preach the gospel from the law, the prophets, and the writings.

Second, the early church understood itself and Jesus in light of the Old Testament. Where we get our understanding of "church" has a tremendous influence on where our churches struggle and what our churches become. Do we operate out of a paradigm of what we're used to or what we grew up with? Do we borrow our understanding from the business world or from a marketing and advertising age? The early church understood itself in light of Old Testament paradigms — holy priesthood, spiritual sacrifices, chosen race, royal priesthood, holy nation, and such. Our congregations may need to be reacquainted with those truths.

Third, the early church employed a hermeneutic that was perfectly willing to excerpt a single verse here and there in order to illustrate a point. This should not, I think, be confused with proof-texting. They were under no pressure — particularly in the latter first-century as the church's chief opponent became not the Jews but the pagan Romans — to manipulate scripture to their purposes. Rather, they readily welcomed as being from God any text or phrase from scripture that seemed to be given new and fuller meaning by Christ.

John 14:1-14

Here is a favorite passage of scripture for so many people. Or, perhaps more accurately, here in this one passage are found three different favorite passages — favorites for different people and for different occasions.

First, here is a favorite passage for funeral services. After Psalm 23, I suppose the early verses of John 14 are the ones I have most often had grieving family members request to have read at their loved one's funeral. We cherish the image of Jesus preparing a place for us and the promise that he will "come again and take (us) to (himself)."

Second, here is a favorite passage for evangelism and for discussions of Christology. For starters, there is another of the "I am" statements of Jesus that are so central to the gospel of John: "I am the way, the truth, and the life." Follow several significant claims of Christ about his identity with the Father: no one comes to the Father but through him, whoever has seen him has seen the Father, and he is in the Father and the Father is in him.

Finally, here is a favorite passage for prayer. Jesus boldly promises that "I will do whatever you ask in my name" and "if in my name you ask me for anything, I will do it." To the skeptical observer, it seems like a reckless kind of statement. To the earnest petitioner, however, it is the very fuel of faith.

Charles Spurgeon, the great nineteenth-century preacher, offers helpful insight into this seemingly blank check signed by Jesus. "Does the text mean what it says? I never knew my Lord to say anything he did not mean... mind you, he does not say to all men, 'I will give you whatever you ask.' That would be an unkind kindness. But he speaks to his disciples who have already received great grace at his hands. It is to disciples he commits this marvelous power of prayer" (Charles Spurgeon, *The Power of Prayer in a Believer's Life* [Lynnwood, Washington: Emerald Books, 1993], p. 35).

In the end, of course, there is something very right about this combination of favorite Bible verses. It is right that these things should be all woven together: who Jesus is in relation to the Father, in relation to us, what we can do for him, what he can do through us, and all that he and the Father have in store. While the familiar verses in this passage may be siphoned off individually for their own use and meaning, they are best understood all together, for they are part of a natural whole. We cannot properly separate our Christology from our hope of heaven, on the one hand, nor from our faith on earth, on the other.

Application

Our lections for this week prompt us to think about life in the meantime: life lived in service to Christ between acts.

In John, we see him on the verge of his exit. He tells his followers that he is about to go and that he is going to come back, and thanks to Stephen's vision in the book of Acts, meanwhile, we catch a brief glimpse of where he has gone: "I see the heavens opened and the Son of Man standing at the right hand of God!" Stephen's testimony brings to mind the familiar words of the Apostles' Creed — he "sitteth at the right hand of God the Father Almighty" — and what follows — "from thence he shall come to judge the quick and the dead."

Bob Kauflin sets the two acts side by side in his song, "In The First Light." View the lyrics at www.cybertime.net/~ajgood/firstlight.html.

We live between those acts, preparing and setting the stage for his return. We see that we are empowered and encouraged in that work by Jesus himself: "The one who believes in me will also do the works that I do and, in fact, will do greater works than these, because I am going to the Father."

We also see in Peter's epistle something of our job description. Words like "royal," "priesthood," "holy," and "chosen" signify the purposeful and differentiated existence to which we are called. These are not the terms that belong to spectators in the lobby. These make up the calling of people with serious and urgent work to do.

We see in Stephen the look of that service. Here is where the stage crew metaphor breaks down, for the analogy only speaks to our timing and purpose, not to our experience. For as long as we are in this world, we are opposed. This stage violently resists being set.

Yet, in the face of all that, we also see our reward. Stephen saw it and we sense it in his face and in his words. Jesus promised it to his disciples: the stage that he himself is setting and the preparation that he is making for us! Such a way for the star to spend this intermission!

An Alternative Application

1 Peter 2:2-10. We noted above that this passage from 1 Peter makes much use of the image of stones. In fact, it becomes an extended metaphor, and we might explore the depth of what Peter is saying by identifying the different relationships to "the stone" that Peter suggests here. That stone represents Jesus and that is a relationship worth considering.

First, there is God's relationship to the stone. It is precious to him, established by him, and central to his work and purpose in the world.

Second, there is the relationship to the stone of those who oppose it. They try to reject it, though they find futility in fighting God's own purpose. (The persecutors of Stephen are a good example of that useless opposition.) And more than rejecting it, it becomes "a stone that makes them stumble, and a rock that makes them fall."

In his 1985 album, *Scandalon*, Michael Card provocatively considers this text, as well as our contemporary situation: Check out the lyrics at www.lyricz.net/C/Card+Michael/89098/.

Third, there is the relationship to the stone of those who "come to him." To us, as to God, he is precious. By coming to him, we ourselves are "built into a spiritual house," and so, in direct contrast to those who futilely oppose what God is doing, it is our privilege to be incorporated into what God is doing.

Finally, in addition to the multi-level references to stones and rocks within the confines of this passage, there are several other points that you may want to employ, whether in the sermon, the hymns, or the scripture readings and liturgy.

First, there is the long-standing tradition of identifying God with a rock (see, for example, Psalm 18:2, 46; 31:3; 61:2; 62:2). It is an image that conveys strength, stability, and protection.

Second, there is the irony that, in the Acts passage, stones become the weapon of choice in trying to silence Stephen. Thus, on the one hand, you have the stone chosen by God and made the cornerstone. On the other hand, you have the small and destructive stones chosen by the antagonists. One is established with purpose, while the others are flung in anger. One is built upon, while the others are scattered. One endures, while the others are dust.

Third, there is the personal component involved in all of this imagery for Peter. Here is the one who grew up as "Simon," but who was renamed by his Lord "Peter," which means "rock." One cannot ignore how central and significant the imagery Peter employs here must have been to him personally.

Easter 6
Acts 17:22-31
1 Peter 3:13-22
John 14:15-21
by David Kalas

Our known God

Pulling off the exit ramp on a highway in Pennsylvania, I saw a sign that caught my attention. It was part of a collection of blue informational signs that featured no words, just icons accompanied by directional arrows. For example, here was a little blue sign with images of a fork and spoon on it, along with an arrow pointing to the left. Then there was a sign with a little gas pump icon and another arrow pointing to the left. Next there was a sign with a picture of a tent and an arrow pointing to the right. Finally, there was a sign with a question mark on it, and an arrow pointing to the right.

Now I presume that the question mark was the icon for some sort of an information center or travel center. Still, when I first saw it, it amused me. It was as if these signs were saying, "We know that food is over here, and so is fuel. We know that if you want to camp, you can just turn this way. And then, farther down that road... well, we're not quite sure what it is... but we know it's that way!"

That is exactly the kind of sign that the apostle Paul saw in the ancient city of Athens. The people there had a vague belief in an "unknown god." They had an altar erected in his honor. But he remained a question mark to the ancient Athenians.

That god was not unknown to Paul, however. And he is not unknown to us.

As we consider the apostle's visit to Athens, along with the counsel of Peter and the promises of Christ in this week's lections, we will affirm that our God is, indeed, known — known and knowable. So we go off into our world with the same calling and opportunity as Paul: to make known the Lord among people who do not know him yet.

Acts 17:22-31

We are fortunate to have a record of Paul's visit to Athens and especially his presentation before the Areopagus. In this brief passage, Paul conducts a veritable clinic on evangelism. It is a model of what to do, as well as a concrete reminder of what not to do.

What Paul does not do is take the ever-winsome holier-than-thou approach. He certainly believes that his audience is intellectually misguided and spiritually lost, but that is not the message he gives them or the tone with which he addresses them. He could have told them that they were misguided and lost, and he would have been right. But being right is not the only ingredient in evangelism.

Neither does he take a smarter-than-thou approach. His message was arguably that they did not really know what to believe, and so he was there to tell them what to believe. But that was not the attitude of his presentation. One senses that Paul was side-by-side with them, rather than talking down to them, even as he endeavored to lead them to the truth.

Meanwhile, we should note that Paul also does not take the live-and-let-live approach. This is the posture that is most at home in the pluralism of our own culture, but it was not Paul's *modus operandi*. He did not say to himself, "These people clearly already have their own beliefs, their own religions, and they're very earnest about it all. I should not force my beliefs on them." That mentality would have seemed nonsensical to Paul.

Too often, in some circles, Christians navigate by the stars of purity and orthodoxy, and in the process they judge and condemn people for where they are. In other circles, Christians will too often set their compass toward tolerance, and thus leave people where they are deliberately undisturbed. Paul, by contrast, met the Athenians where they were and he endeavored to lead them where they needed to be.

In Athens, Paul encountered a population that was religious and educated and he worked with that. "I see how extremely religious you are in every way," he remarks to his audience. It is winsome and complimentary. He might have looked at precisely the same evidence and said, "I see how extremely pagan and confused you are in every way," but that would not have earned the gospel much of a hearing. And so he used their religiousness — indeed, even their idolatry — to his advantage.

Paul also demonstrated his meet-them-where-they're-at approach in the material that he did and did not quote. "As even some of your own poets have said," Paul preached, "we too are his offspring." Now Paul would not have regarded ancient Greek poets as highly as he did the canon of Hebrew scripture. But quoting the Hebrew scriptures would not have scored any points — would not even have made a connection — with his audience. And so, even though the one source had infinitely more value for Paul, he chose to cite the source that would have had more value for his audience.

Finally, we see that Paul also encountered in Athens a people who clearly had some uncertainty — or at least some questions and openness. He made that his welcome mat. "What therefore you worship as unknown," Paul said, "this I proclaim to you." He does not march into town, knock over all of their existing beliefs, and try to erect his own in their place. No, he takes what they already believe and he builds on it. "I've come to tell you about the 'unknown god,'" Paul said in effect, "because I know him."

1 Peter 3:13-22

Unjust suffering is no small theme in scripture. We see it almost from the beginning, in the murder of the innocent Abel. Young Joseph, whose story is one of the longest narratives about any individual character in the entire Old Testament, chronicles the unjust treatment of an innocent man — as well as the prevailing providence of God. We think, too, of David — faultlessly loyal to King Saul, yet hunted and hounded by the madman king through the deserts and caves of the Judean wilderness. Job, Jeremiah, and a number of anonymous psalmists are all part of this large contingent of suffering saints, "of whom the world was not worthy" (Hebrews 11:38).

But there is one more, and he is in a class by himself. The ultimate instance of unjust suffering is Jesus Christ. His case is unique, for he was more innocent than all the rest, and his suffering was also at a different level than the rest.

The people in Peter's audience were evidently suffering. In ten verses, he makes five references to "suffer" or "suffering." It was a theme relevant to those Christians, whom he regarded as exiles (1:1) — that is, alien residents; men and women, whose real home is elsewhere and who live for the present in hostile territory. As he wrote to them in the midst of their struggles, Jesus was very much on Peter's mind.

Perhaps Peter had Jesus' teachings in mind as he wrote. "If you do suffer for doing right," Peter said, "you are blessed." It may be that the aging apostle remembered that lovely day by Galilee, hearing his master and teacher say something which, at the time, seemed completely irrational to him: "Blessed are those who are persecuted for righteousness' sake, for theirs is the kingdom of heaven. Blessed are you when people revile you and persecute you and utter all kinds of evil against you falsely on my account. Rejoice and be glad, for your reward is great in heaven, for in the same way they persecuted the prophets who were before you" (Matthew 5:10-12).

I imagine that Peter had Jesus' example in mind, as well. He encouraged his congregations that "those who abuse you for your good conduct in Christ may be put to shame." Peter had seen that at work. He had watched the conspiring mob drop their stones and walk away (see John 8:2-9). And he had seen those who tried to lay traps befuddled and frustrated (see Matthew 22:15-46).

No doubt, Peter also had a certain personal lesson from Jesus in mind. The first he had heard of Christ's sufferings, Peter had objected that it should never happen (Mark 8:31- 33). Now, on the other side of the cross and the empty tomb, Peter had grown out of his natural human instinct about such matters and he writes with understanding, "It is better to suffer for doing good, if suffering should be God's will."

Then, with all of that in mind, Peter begins to think about Jesus' saving work. The concern for his audience's suffering had moved him to consider Christ's suffering. That, in turn, led him to the greatest encouragements of all: about Christ bringing us to God, our salvation, and the ultimate victory, glory, and authority of Jesus Christ.

John 14:15-21

Love is an important theme in the Johannine literature in the New Testament. It is John's gospel that features the great statement of God's motivation and purpose — "for God so loved the world" — that some have called it "the gospel in a nutshell." It is John's gospel that features the new love commandment (13:34), as well as identifying love as the ultimate proof of whom we follow (13:35). In 1 John, we are introduced to the inarguable logic of love (4:19-21), and we are taught that love is the essential attribute of God (4:8). Even in John's Revelation, amidst spectacles of glory and terror, amidst the cataclysms of the eschaton, there is a poignant appeal to lost love (2:4-5).

In light of that larger theme, then, we are interested to note this truth about love: that it leads to obedience.

This is a point of enormous theological importance, for it gives insight into why God did what he did from the beginning. For we recognize that God could have created us in such a way that we would have obeyed by design. That suggests a human creature, however, that is not free, and therefore one that could not genuinely love. So, instead, God preferred to make a creature capable of love, though consequently free, and therefore susceptible to disobedience.

But this was God's wisdom, for the relationship between love and obedience is not a two-way street. Obedience will not necessarily lead to love. All sorts of joyless and judgmental legalists through the ages bear witness to that. But Jesus says that love, on the other hand, will lead to obedience.

Another significant theme of this passage is the Trinity. There may be no passage in scripture more revealing about the Trinity than these Last Supper chapters in John. Here Jesus speaks repeatedly and freely about his relationship to the Father and to the Spirit.

In our brief excerpt from that larger context, Jesus refers to the Spirit as "another Advocate." Interestingly, John uses that same word for Jesus in his own first epistle (1 John 2:1). Perhaps that explains Jesus using the term "another." In any case, the word is used only five times in the entire New Testament. Four of them are here in this section of John's gospel and the other is the reference to Jesus in the epistle.

Outside of the New Testament, the underlying Greek word was often used in a legal context. And it had a natural counterpart, an opposite: accuser. That is noteworthy for us since, in the King James Version, Satan is referred to as "the accuser of our brethren... which accused them before our God day and night" (Revelation 12:10 KJV). We see that it is Satan who points the finger of accusation against us, while the Spirit and Son of God speak on our behalf.

Finally, in addition to Jesus' frequent references to himself, the Father, and the Spirit in relation to one another, this passage — and its larger context — also offers another significant insight into the Trinity. Again and again, the followers of Jesus are brought into the mix. The persons of the Trinity are not a clique, separate and self-contained. Rather, we ourselves are invited into that divine fellowship. So Jesus explains to his disciples that the Spirit "abides in you." Later, he says, "I am in my Father, and you in me, and I in you." The Trinity may be a mystery to us but this much we may understand: It is a unity and fellowship of love and we are invited into it.

Application

When I was traveling down that one highway, I came across a blue informational sign with a question mark and an arrow pointing off to the right.

When the apostle Paul was traveling in ancient Athens, he came across an altar dedicated to an unknown God.

What Paul saw was a theological version of the sign that I had seen along the highway. Here was an altar with a question mark on it and an arrow pointing up. We don't know what it is but we know it's up there. We don't know who he is but we know he's out there. We don't know what he's like but we've got an altar here where we can worship him.

We, too, live in a time and place of spiritual uncertainty. The people around us have question marks all over their altars. That is to say, uncertainty pervades their sense of meaning and purpose, their understanding of the world, and their assumptions about the spiritual and the supernatural. There is no lack of interest but there is a profound lack of personal knowledge and familiarity.

We also live in the midst of a relativism that betrays the prevailing uncertainty. The mere fact that our culture is so ready to accept every belief, practice, and paradigm as equally valid bears witness to our lack of conviction. Our relativism is simply codified uncertainty.

Sports pundits like to say of teams with quarterback controversies, "If you think you have two starting quarterbacks, then you don't really have any starting quarterback." Likewise, if we think we have a hundred truths, we don't really have any truths.

So it may be that contemporary America is not so different from ancient Athens. Our God is unknown here too. Not that he is unheard of, as Jesus mostly was in first-century Greece. But he is unknown. He is vague impressions and misinformation. He is locked back in the mists of history. He is a question mark.

Jesus told his disciples that "the world cannot receive" the Spirit of truth "because it neither sees him nor knows him." He is, indeed, unknown to the world around us. But he is not unknown to us. "You know him," Jesus said, "because he abides with you, and he will be in you."

Like Paul, we travel among people with question marks on their altars. Our calling is to proclaim the one who is unknown to them, for we know him. We affirm that he is knowable. For this is, after all, the God who came to meet us where we are; who put on flesh and dwelt among us; who said, "Whoever has seen me has seen the Father" (John 14:9).

Our altars do not have a question mark with an arrow pointing vaguely upward. Rather, our altars have an exclamation point with an arrow directing the world's attention to Jesus Christ.

An Alternative Application
Acts 17:22-31. "Altar avenue." The apostle Paul was a big-city missionary. By the end of his journeys, he had taken the gospel to all the major cities in the first-century Mediterranean world, from Jerusalem to Rome, Antioch and Ephesus, Philippi, Thessalonica, Corinth, and more.

One of the characteristics of big cities, of course, is that certain types of businesses tend to congregate together along a single road or in a particular location. So, for example, here's a strip where four or five different car dealerships have all set up shop. Here's an intersection where five different motel chains are all located. Here's a shopping mall whose parking lot is rimmed by every imaginable family restaurant. And so on.

The most famous instances of this happens to be in New York City. One particular street, where several major advertising firms located years ago, has become synonymous with that industry: Madison Avenue. Likewise, the concentration of financial institutions on a single street have made the name of that street — Wall Street — mean business and finance. And the strip of theaters along a single road has made the name of that road the embodiment of the theater: Broadway.

Perhaps the ancient, big city of Athens had such a street: a particular part of town where all the shrines, idols, and temples were built. Call it "Altar Avenue." When the apostle Paul comes to town, he walks that wide way and shakes his head at the idolatry and confusion all around him.

We observed, in our discussion of the Acts passage, how exemplary was Paul's presentation of the gospel in Athens. We should learn from him, for we walk down our own "Altar Avenues" in our day. Indeed, I would make the claim that we not only have more people than the ancient city of Athens; we also have more altars.

By "altar" I do not exclusively mean a designated sacred spot where offerings are presented. Ultimately an altar is not defined by its look, design, or dimensions. Rather, an altar is defined by what takes place there.

We might invite our people — and ourselves — to ponder for a few moments what it is that takes place at an altar.

Wherever you see individuals dedicating themselves, where they serve with all their allegiance, where they affirm their top priority, their guiding principles, and their mission, where they find their sense of meaning and purpose in life — those settings serve as altars, and we have scores of people around us who wander from altar to altar, filled with question marks.

If we would learn from the apostle, we would recognize the altars in our world for what they are. We would meet people there and redirect their attention to the one who is truly worthy of that devotion and role in their hearts and lives.

Ascension of Our Lord
Acts 1:1-11
Ephesians 1:15-23
Luke 24:44-53
by R. Craig MacCreary

Ground rules

This past summer I was treated to viewing one of those baseball donnybrooks in which managers and players are freely tossed out of the game. It came on a play that you would not think should be the cause of such consternation: a home run over the centerfield wall. It seems things were a bit complicated in this minor league park. In order for it to be a home run, the ball had to clear a yellow line where the flat level of an outdoor restaurant met the wall of the ballpark. This was all made a lot more difficult by the fact that one umpire called it a home run only to have the head umpire call it all back. It also struck me as interesting that the dispute broke out even though the umpires and managers met at the beginning to go over the ground rules of the game and of the grounds of this particular park. The game only went on after several ejections and it was evident to all concerned that things would not proceed until all sides agreed at least that the head umpire's ruling was final, which is also one of the ground rules of the game.

As I wondered how it was that we were devoting so much time to this hiatus from the game it dawned on me how like the church was this minor league donnybrook. The rules bear repeating, things do not come back into balance until we recognize who really is in charge, and you never know when a knockdown-drag-out will occur. They will occur; they are likely to occur over something that no one has anticipated. There is nothing that can override the above facts of the game. Like life, baseball is so heavily nuanced that no one can anticipate all the possibilities ahead, knowing the rules will not prove sufficient to cover all eventualities and you will be on your own until order is restored.

In a very real sense that is how Jesus leaves his disciples following the resurrection. Even before he departs, the disciples have their questions, "So when they had come together, they asked him, 'Lord, is this the time when you will restore the kingdom to Israel?' " They have their questions but soon they will not have their Jesus to give them direct answers.

The narration of the ascension in the book of Acts focuses on the future mission of the church, while the narration in Luke focuses more on the basis of that mission as found in scripture. In both cases, Jesus is laying the groundwork for when the ground rules come into question.

Paul certainly had his share of disputes, claims, and counterclaims in the churches that he wrote and visited. The early church had its share of hardnosed moments. It is very clear that the apostles must function in the new context of having no final arbiter of their disputes. Jesus will leave them in the context of having to work out much on their own. The passage in the letter to the Ephesians, chosen as part of today's lectionary reading, seeks to identify the Jesus who is above every interpretation of the ground rules. No single interpretation can be identified with him. To do so would be like saying that one side or the other in the dispute over the home run had an exclusive franchise on the meaning of baseball. As absurd as that is, how often do various sides in church disputes go after each other, reading each other out of the Christian community?

The texts invite us to consider the ground rules by which we are playing the "game" in our disputes and conflicts. Whom do we expect to restore order? Or do we believe that we have arrived at a uniformity of understanding that will result in such conformity that it will not be necessary for there to be community guided by the Holy Spirit?

Acts 1:1-11

For Luke, it is essential to wait for the Holy Sprit in the life of the church. While it is the key for Luke, it often seems to be relegated to a quick prayer over meetings that include perfunctory references to the idea that we will not act until we understand that what is to be done is pleasing to both us and the Holy Spirit. While staying with them, he ordered them not to leave Jerusalem, but to wait there for the promise of the Father. "This," he said, "is what you have heard from me...."

How we understand the work of the Holy Sprit determines what we are waiting for. Do we wait for an ecstatic experience; will the sign of the Spirit's presence be the establishment of a consensus, will we understand the Spirit's presence to be manifested when everyone is happy and in their comfort zone, or when no one rests easy with things as they are? I suspect that the answer is, "Yes." Each of these expresses some of what the Spirit brings us. Paul puts it this way in the first letter to the Corinthians, "Now there are varieties of gifts, but the same Spirit; and there are varieties of services, but the same Lord; and there are varieties of activities, but it is the same God who activates all of them in everyone. To each is given the manifestation of the Spirit for the common good. To one is given through the Spirit the utterance of wisdom, and to another the utterance of knowledge according to the same Spirit, to another faith by the same Spirit, to another gifts of healing by the one Spirit, to another the working of miracles, to another prophecy, to another the discernment of spirits, to another various kinds of tongues, to another the interpretation of tongues. All these are activated by one and the same Spirit, who allots to each one individually just as the Spirit chooses" (1 Corinthians 12:4-11).

There are times when the church should be about waiting. Those occasions come in light of the absence of the physical presence as the church waits for him to be present through the gift of the Holy Spirit. How do we know that we should be waiting? I suspect that we should be waiting on the Spirit when it becomes clear in the life of a church that people are neither free nor challenged to exercise their gifts. This is a major block to the flow of the Spirit. The lesson from Acts says that the apostles are to be engaged in mission, "But you will receive power when the Holy Spirit has come upon you; and you will be my witnesses in Jerusalem, in all Judea and Samaria, and to the ends of the earth" (v. 8). It is time to wait in the Spirit if we have become disengaged from the world and our role in it. A church that is floundering in mission or is frustrating the gifts of its members has blocked the Spirit.

In the passage from Acts when the disciples have gathered, a question arises among them. So when they had come together, they asked him, "Lord, is this the time when you will restore the kingdom to Israel?" The apostles, with an understandable curiosity that is still part of the Christian experience, want to know just where they are in the unfolding plan of God. Such curiosity is often a frustration to the Spirit and a sign that folks need to wait on the fullness of time when it is appropriate for such matters to be revealed. "He replied, 'It is not for you to know the times or periods that the Father has set by his own authority.' " Needless to say there has been much theological effort thrown in to determine at just what point we are in God's unfolding intention for the world. Yet such a preoccupation is a frustration to the Spirit. A congregation so invested needs to sit down and reflect on the work of the Spirit in its midst. We are to be obedient to what God intends while not fully capable of understanding unfolding details of the plan of God.

The Acts passage warns against being transfixed by staring at the place where Jesus once was. It reminds me somewhat of any congregation that has been through a church fire. Often congregants will come for days immediately following the fire to the stare at the place where the steeple was, pondering whether the hole in the sky or in their souls will ever be filled again. The angels that appear push the apostles to move beyond staring off into the sky to the realization that Jesus will return again.

Many congregations in the mainline tradition seem to be staring off into the place where Jesus and they once were after the spiritual fire that many of them had experienced in previous years. The promise is that after the fire, Jesus will return. He may not return in the manner that we had previously experienced, as if his work was more to restore the past than lead us into the future. However, he will return with the same redemptive intention, "This Jesus, who has been taken up from you into heaven, will come in the same way as you saw him go into heaven" (v. 11). If you find yourself staring off into heaven, it is time to gather and wait on the Spirit who has more in store.

Ephesians 1:15-23
The letter reflects a close relationship between the writer and the people. "I have heard of your faith in the Lord Jesus and your love toward all the saints, and for this reason I do not cease to give thanks for you as I remember you in my prayers" (vv. 15-16). These are clearly folks with whom the letter writer has a close relationship and a deep affection. Sometimes it is very hard to pray for those with whom we are the closest. We are often afraid as they grow and develop that for one reason or the other we will lose the close relationship. A spirit of wisdom and knowledge may leave those who are closest to us in disagreement with us or ahead us of us in a way that they do not need us.

So what then should we pray for those who are particularly close to us? "I pray that the God of our Lord Jesus Christ, the Father of glory, may give you a spirit of wisdom and revelation as you come to know him" (v. 17). We do get very close to each other in church life and sometimes too close as we experience each others' foibles and are tempted to take each other for granted. Praying for each other becomes essential as the community of faith waits for the return of Jesus. It is one of the ground rules for Paul as he reminds his readers in several of his letters that he is praying for them. "I have heard of your faith in the Lord Jesus and your love toward all the saints, and for this reason I do not cease to give thanks for you as I remember you in my prayers" (vv. 15-16).

The readers of the letter to the Ephesians, by virtue of the example of the letter writer, are clearly urged to keep one another in their prayers. However, the reader is urged to offer a specific prayer. The author prays for the Ephesians that they be given a spirit of wisdom and revelation as they come to know Jesus. The prayer asks for a spirit that will give wisdom over human affairs as it anticipates the revelation of things that are hidden. Despite the nearly 2,000 years that have passed since the writing of this letter many churches find that, as they await the return of Jesus, they are in about the same place as were the Ephesians. As the "emerging church" comes into view what will be the practical consequences for "old first" mainline on the town square? How will the emerging church affect the use, renovation, or location of the church building? What will be the implications for church structure and organization? What will be the impact on those who were born into one form of church and who will now live out their days in a church context far different from the one they were born into?

Wisdom and revelation go hand in hand. One of the ground rules is to never separate the two. Without being attuned to the things that God is revealing, much of what we do in church feels like a desperate scheme to save ourselves from declining numbers and resources. On the other hand, there is nothing worse than the leader of the new wave of things who has no appreciation in human terms of what they are proposing.

When these two are held together, "... that, with the eyes of your heart enlightened, you may know what is the hope to which he has called you, what are the riches of his glorious inheritance among the saints" (v. 18). But separate the two and things are either hopelessly boring or depressingly impractical.

The Ephesians are reminded that if the spirit of wisdom and revelation are held together, they will understand the result as the work of the immeasurable power of God. The holding together of these two dimensions has carried the church up until now and will carry it into the immeasurable future until Christ returns.

Luke 24:44-53
Once again, Jesus directs his disciples to go to Jerusalem and wait until they are "clothed with power from on high" (v. 49). No doubt we are a bit uncomfortable with what appears to be a senseless repetition

of the scene recounted in the book of Acts. It certainly does not meet our standard for effective writing. Of course, by this standard much of scripture does not meet the standard of effective writing. Time and again we are walked through the same territory as the stories are retold with different emphasis and through different voices.

In this context, Jesus says to the disciples, "These are my words that I spoke to you while I was still with you — that everything written about me in the law of Moses, the prophets, and the psalms must be fulfilled" (v. 44). Jesus is the extension of the witness of the Hebrew Testament. No doubt, there were times for the early church when the waters did not part and it seemed that they were so far from the promised land that it was hard to believe that they were living out God's intention, which was rooted in the Hebrew story. As they faced the interim time between the ascension and Jesus' return it must have seemed hard to believe that. I suspect as we live in the interim time it is hard to believe it when the church seems so weak and vulnerable. Part of Jesus' teaching is to remind the disciples that he, too, has gone through a time of weakness and vulnerability, "Then he opened their minds to understand the scriptures, and he said to them, 'Thus it is written, that the Messiah is to suffer and to rise from the dead on the third day' " (vv. 45-46).

The Holy Sprit is bestowed on those who must live through this time. The end product, as it were, is that the disciples can bless God even in the time of Jesus' absence. Living in this time, we must come to terms with what the Spirit promotes and pushes for as well as what it does not provide for. A sermonic illustration from my context literally as an interim pastor puts it this way, "I have known a class of people over the years that never seems to be able to settle on a church. They always seem to be searching for the perfect church where 24 hours a day, 7 days a week, everyone agrees on everything and there is perpetual conflict-free harmony. Such an approach leads to a few years here and a few years there. Always something seems to come up that sets them off church hunting once again: the church paints the bathroom the wrong color, the youth group does something wrong, or they pick the wrong minister." I suspect that these are people who are really drowning, because they have stood on what they think is the safety of the shore rather than plunging right into the waters of life. Taking the plunge means choosing to make stumbling blocks the stepping stones. If you are searching for the perfect church, you certainly would have never found it in the Bible. Just read Paul's letters. The question to be asked if looking for a church is, "Does this congregation turn its stumbling blocks (and every congregation has them) into building blocks?" Do the stumbles get turned into prayer, into more open and honest conversation, into the ability to laugh at yourself among others? The Holy Sprit will not provide a perfect church but can turn the imperfections to the glory of God and the blessing of its members. No wonder the disciples were continually in the temple praising God.

Application

It is an irony of biblical proportions that Jesus' ascension into heaven results in the establishment of some ground rules as we await his return. There are times when the church must wait on the Spirit. During the interim time, the church must hold together the spirit of wisdom and revelation, and the church must be open to what the Holy Spirit pushes and promotes as it lives with what the Spirit will not provide. I believe that this is true for all churches whatever their denominational background or history, for we are dealing here with the one who is "far above all rule and authority and power and dominion, and above every name that is named, not only in this age but also in the age to come. And he has put all things under his feet and has made him the head over all things for the church" (Ephesians 1:21-22).

I recall that the official rules of major league baseball say that the game shall commence when the umpire shall yell play. Not ball but play. I rather suspect that we lose our playfulness when we do not know or are not ready to go along with the basic ground rules.

An Alternative Application
Luke 24:44-53. One cannot read these texts without having some apocalyptic gestalt. However, much of the misery of the Christian faith has come about as the result of various theories of the end time that not only say Jesus will return but predict his every movement. In some ways, the hole in the sky where Jesus was is filled for some by the certainty they believe they have found in their own apocalyptic scheme. Many who have been wounded or put off by such schemes resolve to lay aside any notion of Jesus' return.

This might be the Sunday to give a survey of the various apocalyptic options and their implications. I suspect that one of the strengths of the mainline experience may not be that it has either given lip service to the end time or sought to completely lay it aside. Can we do this and remain faithful in any sense to Luke's understanding as well as the vision of the Christian scripture?

Easter 7
Acts 1:6-14
1 Peter 4:12-14; 5:6-11
John 17:1-11
by Wayne Brouwer

Invisible link

Now and again, one of my students will come into class and I'll greet her or him but get no response. Sometimes I'll even walk up to the student when she sits down and make my presence obvious. Then she will look up startled, pull back her hood, and yank the buds out of her ears or turn down her iPod so that she re-engages the world in which I exist. When her recorded music was shouted in her ears, she became deaf to this world and alive to another.

In a sense, that is what each of today's lectionary passages wants to have happen in the Christian's life. Only when we are uniquely and overwhelmingly connected to the music of eternity, and live in the reality of God's glory, can we keep our purpose and identity true (Acts 1), avoid the wiles of the devil (1 Peter 4-5), and nurture a passion that shines with God's own glory (John 17).

Acts 1:6-14

The existence of the Christian church is rooted in several theological declarations. First, we believe that there is a God who created this world and uniquely fashioned our human race with attributes that reflect its maker. Second, through human willfulness the world lost its pristine vitality and is now caught up in a civil war against its Creator. Third, by intruding directly into human affairs for the sake of reclaiming and restoring the world, the Creator began a mission of redemption and renewal through the nation of Israel, shaped by the Suzerain-Vassal covenant formed at Mount Sinai and positioned at the crossroads of global societies as a witness to all peoples. Fourth, because of the inadequacy of this method of operations as the human race expanded rapidly, the Creator revised the divine missional strategy, and interrupted human history again in the person of Jesus, who embodied the divine essence, taught the divine will, and through whose death and resurrection established a new understanding of eschatological hope. Fifth, the coming of this messianic age was foretold by the prophets of Israel who called it the "Day of the Lord" and identified its three major aspects: divine judgment on the sins of all nations (including Israel), the sparing of a remnant from Israel who would be the restored seed community of a new global divine initiative, and the coming of the eschatological messianic age in which righteousness and justice would renew both human society and the natural order so that people could again live out their intended purposes and destinies. Sixth, Jesus split this "Day of the Lord" in two bringing the beginnings of its eternal blessings while withholding the full impact of divine judgment for a time. Seventh, the Christian church is God's new agent for global missional recovery and restoration for the human race.

Each of these themes is implied or explicit in the first two chapters of the book of the Acts of the Apostles. God and sin and the divine mission are all part of the fabric, while Israel's role in the divine mission, along with the changing strategies, is declared openly. Jesus is at the center of all these things, but the unique divine intrusion he brought into the human race is now being withdrawn, and the church must become the ongoing embodiment of Jesus' life and teachings so that it may live out the divine mission until the remainder of the "Day of the Lord" arrives when Jesus returns.

This is seen in the few, but packed, verses of today's lectionary reading. First, Jesus' disciples are beside themselves with new hope and confidence, since their rabbi has become a death-defeating powerhouse.

They see the future in a limited (mis)understanding of all the promises of the prophets — Israel restored, victorious over the nations, and re-established as the most glorious and wealthy society on earth. Jesus, however, reads history in a new way, marking the change of divine mission strategy from that tied to the geography of Palestine through Israel's national witness to the dispersion of the church among the nations of the earth.

Second, in Jesus' ascension there is a twofold word of promise. On the one hand, Jesus' disappearance is a vote of confidence in his disciples. He is affirming that the work he has begun will be in good hands when left with them. In fact, in the early church there was a parabolic teaching that said when Jesus returned to heaven, amid the triumphant praise of the angels, Gabriel asked his master what contingency plan Jesus had left on earth. "Oh," said Jesus, "I've spent a little time with some fishermen and social misfits and housewives, and they will take care of things now."

Gabriel was stunned. "That's not very encouraging," he said. "You were only with them for three years and most of them ran out on you when things turned tough. Now you leave the whole mission of God in their hands? I don't get it. What's the backup plan?"

But the early church knew Jesus' response. He shook his head slowly and with a smile, said, "There is no backup plan. They won't fail. They're my people, and I trust them. I trust them."

On the other hand, Jesus' ascension is stage-managed by "two men dressed in white" who announce the end already at the beginning, by promising the Lord's planned return. In this way, Luke communicates the message that the church lives under eschatological urgency. There is a job to be done: witnessing about Jesus. But those who are going to make testimony are on the clock, and the hours are ticking away. Furthermore, if Jesus is the "Day of the Lord," and his first coming inaugurated the blessings of the messianic age, his second coming will finalize the judgments of God on all that is evil and sinful. Therefore, the work to be done is critical in changing the eternal outcomes for all who live in these times.

Third, Luke spends a little time again on his grand theme of the fellowship of the worshiping community. In his gospel, Luke began with a scene of worship in the temple (Luke 1) and ended with a similar incident (Luke 24). Moreover, the early chapters of the gospel were filled with songs and prayers (Zechariah, Mary, the angels, Simeon). Now again, Luke introduces the great work of Jesus through the church by the power of the Holy Spirit with a scene of worshiping fellowship and prayer. What is interesting this time is that it does not take place in the temple. For good reason, of course — from this time forward the strategy of the mission of God changes. No longer is the divine intent to bring nations to Israel and the temple to view the glory of the creator there. Instead, the worshiping fellowship will be dispersed among the nations of the world and people will find God in these pockets of prayer and praise called the church.

Luke certainly wants to keep the focus on the events in this dimension. But it is also wonderful to use his ascension story to imagine what happened in heaven that day. Can you see the angels welcoming back their Creator who has become their ward under protection? Can you imagine the tear in the eye of the Father as the Son returns in humble triumph after changing the course of human history, as well as sealing the blessed fate of the stars and galaxies? Can you feel the resonant praise of celestial choirs in the celebration that reverberated to the far reaches of the expanding universe? Can you sense the awe of the archangel Michael as he touched the scars in the human flesh that was now forever wedded to the Son's divine nature? Chuck Girard's great song "Hear The Angels Sing" seems to fit the atmosphere of the occasion.

1 Peter 4:12-14; 5:6-11

Peter was probably aware of the great suffering that was about to unfold as the ominous winds of Nero's power whipped the Roman world. While he begins writing in powerful terms of the great salvation recently brought to humankind through Jesus, and irreversibly guaranteed, by way of Jesus' resurrection and ascension, for those who believe (1 Peter 1:3-12), he quickly moves on to an extended exhortation to holy living, because these believers in Jesus are God's special people (1 Peter 1:13—2:10), who follow in the footsteps of Jesus (1 Peter 2:11—3:12), and must face, with their master, the sufferings that will fall on all his disciples in these challenging times (1 Peter 3:12—4:19). The tone of Peter's letter is troubled. There is an ominous pall of suffering that clouds every perspective. Jesus suffered. You will suffer, if you are faithful. You must follow Jesus in and through suffering. New trials and greater suffering are coming.

Yet through the murky shrieks and dark valleys, Peter never loses confidence in God's sovereignty or care. This is the constant underlying theme. Especially in the verses of today's lectionary reading, Peter declares that God is judge of evil, faithful creator, and the chief shepherd who will soon bring untarnishing crowns of glory for those who remain true.

This is an important message, particularly in light of the warnings Peter issues about the wiles of the devil. Persistence often conquers resistance, especially as cunning as the evil one can be. Offering pleasures that appear harmless, they are usually ultimately deadly. Following the path of least resistance, as one person put it, is what makes people and rivers crooked.

We need to learn resistance in many ways in order to survive in life. When two Russian cosmonauts returned to earth in 1982 after 211 days in space, they suffered from dizziness, high pulse rates, and heart palpitations. They couldn't walk for a week. A month later they were still undergoing therapy for atrophied muscles and weakened hearts. In the zero gravity of outer space, their muscles had begun to waste away. Scientists had to design "resistance suits" to counteract the unseen predator. Only with resistance applied against the muscles of the body could they remain strong.

Ben Weir, in his book, *Hostage Bound, Hostage Free* (Westminster, 1987), translated this into spiritual terms. He documented the inner resistance that saved his life. During his many months of captivity in Beirut there was a constant nagging to give in to depression and give up to despair. Although his situation was excessive, far beyond that which we normally face, it condensed into eighteen months the wasting that can happen in any spirit over the years. Charles Darwin, who grew up in a strong Presbyterian home, said, in his later years, that he never rejected the Christian faith; instead, he said, it gradually lost its importance to him as he ceased to use it — no resistance, no resurgence — no test, no tensile — no effort, no energy.

Someone told me recently of a young man who was buying his own clothes in preparation for college. He asked a sales clerk what the tag meant when it said "Shrink Resistant." The clerk replied, "Even though that shirt doesn't want to shrink, it will!"

Most of us could wear a label like that on our souls. Only the disciplines of faith cause it to fall off as our resistance to the devil grows.

John 17:1-11

In many respects, this chapter can more appropriately be called "The Lord's Prayer" than the other familiar lines that usually go by that name. Here, Jesus bares his soul before his Father and his disciples in a truly powerful and passionate expression of love and commitment. There are two overarching themes throughout the prayer: unity and mission. Both of these come together in the word Jesus repeatedly uses: glory. The Father lives in splendid glory from before all time. Jesus shares the Father's glory. Jesus came to earth on a mission of revealing the Father's glory in the world darkened by sin, particularly to his disciples. Now Jesus is sending his disciples out to continue that mission and only the glory of God can bind them together and to heaven's purpose.

They will need Jesus' prayers; though their cause is great, the pitfalls are plentiful. Fred Craddock, retired professor of homiletics at Emory University, says we all have this glorious image of ourselves when we first stand up and confess Jesus Christ, like Jesus' own disciples. Craddock says that it is as if we have been given a brand-new starched and stiff $1,000 bill. We take it to Jesus and shout, "Here! Here's my life! Here's my wealth! Here's all of my being! Take me, Jesus! I give myself to you!"

Jesus takes our bright and shiny and crinkly $1,000 bill. But then he hands it back to us. "Go to the bank," he says. "Cash it in for nickels and dimes."

When we do that, coming home with buckets and baskets and wheelbarrows of coins, he says to us, "Now give me fifteen cents a day for the rest of your life."

All excited, we start out with a flourish. A nickel and a dime set aside each morning. But there are always so many other things to buy, so many other toys to play with, and soon the nickels and dimes are gone. So is our faith. And so is our uncompromising devotion. Like the beggars on the street, we walk around with limp hands and feeble hearts.

It's easy to love your spouse on the day of your wedding. It's easy to make commitments for a lifetime in the heat of passion. It's easy to soar on a blazing glory star of faith when you join the church. But the world around says: "You'll never make it. You'll never keep your vows. You'll never last."

Jesus knew this about the twelve he had gathered as his own. He also knows it about us and that is why John included this prayer in his gospel. We have to know how hard Jesus is wrestling for us and our passions. When Jesus asks us for a slow and steady devotion rather than a martyr's burst of passion, we often die inch by inch, a nickel and a dime at a time.

One mother tells this story about her son. He earned a little spending money every winter by shoveling snow from people's driveways. He walks up and down their street. One morning, after a heavy snowfall, he seemed awfully slow in leaving the house. She asked him if there was anything wrong. "No," he said, "I'm just waiting until people get started. I get most of my jobs from people who want to quit halfway through."

Jesus wants to make sure his disciples are going for the goal. He pleads with the Father that they won't drop out of the race. Jesus knows they will be knocked down by their own pride and passions now and again and sometimes by the storms of others. But Jesus begs for the power of God to get them up and running again, a nickel and dime each morning, and heading for the finish line of God's glory.

How does that happen? In a sense, Jesus wants to inspire them with the kind of "magnificent obsession" that author Lloyd Douglas wrote about in his novel of that name. The book is about a fellow named Robert Merrick. He's young. He's rich. He's drunk. Life is a game for him, a game of using people and tossing them aside. A game of playing with his toys in his self-centered world.

Then it happens: He's out on his yacht, the wind catches the sail and throws the boom at him, he falls into the water, unconscious, and is rescued, barely alive. At the same moment, a world-famous doctor, dedicated, devoted, a saver of lives, drowns in a freak accident just down the beach. Young Merrick lies in the hospital. His eyes are closed and everybody thinks he's unconscious. Two nurses stand over him and one shakes her head.

"What a tragedy..." she says. "A great man who saves lives [is] lost, and this fellow, who never did any good for anybody, [is] saved!"

Merrick knows it's true. He's alive but he's never really lived. He was pulled from the water but for no good reason. In that moment, in that instant of judgment, Merrick gains his "magnificent obsession." He'll go to university. He'll get a degree in medicine. He'll take the doctor's place. He'll save lives and begin to truly live himself.

A magnificent obsession! A purpose for which to live and a cause for which to die. That's the atmosphere that pervades Jesus' prayer. My Father! The glory of God! Jesus' magnificent obsession carries him and those who are his on from glory to glory (2 Corinthians 3:18).

Application

Richard Mouw, in his book, *Calvinism in the Las Vegas Airport*, mentions a conversation with an immigrant from eastern Europe. He had asked her where she was from, and she told him all about her former community, family, and especially her grandmother. When she turned the tables and asked him where *he* was from, he said, "Oh, a suburb of Los Angeles." But that meant nothing to her.

"No!" she said. "Where are you *from*? Who was your grandmother?" She meant to get at the culture that made him the person he was today.

So with these lectionary passages. The goal is to get our people to know who they are, *whose* they are, and to claim that identity as their primary point of reference in all things.

An Alternative Application
Acts 1:6-14. If you did not yet celebrate Jesus' ascension, today is the day to make use of Acts 1 and talk about Jesus' finished work, his coronation day in heaven, and the trust he bestows on his church as we carry on with the transforming mission of God's evangelistic grace.

Pentecost Sunday
Acts 2:1-21
1 Corinthians 12:3b-13
John 20:19-23
by David Kalas

The counterproductive sermon

This is Pentecost Sunday. Accordingly, our first reading is the familiar story of Pentecost from chapter 2 of Acts. And, accompanying it, we have two other passages that bring to light the work of the Holy Spirit. In 1 Corinthians 12, Paul discusses the gifts of the Spirit and in John 20, Jesus breathes on his disciples, saying, "Receive the Holy Spirit."

It would be natural enough, therefore, for us to conclude that we should preach this week about the Holy Spirit.

In so many of our churches, the Holy Spirit is the most unmentioned member of the Trinity. Of course, in other churches, he may be talked about quite a lot but that is probably more the exception than the rule in church history.

For those church folks who grew up reciting the Apostles' Creed, the poverty of their doctrine of the Holy Spirit is unsurprising, for the creed has almost nothing to say about him. There is a grand opening statement about God the Father, and then a detailed affirmation about God the Son. But God the Spirit? "I believe in the Holy Spirit" endeavors to sum it all up.

The Nicene Creed does a somewhat better job of elucidating just what it is we believe about the Holy Spirit, though it still comes up short in the face of the gaping void for so many Christians in this area. Most of our hymnals and songbooks, too, do a better job of explicitly instructing our people about the Father and the Son than they do about the Spirit.

So it seems not only appropriate but necessary that we should preach this Sunday about the Holy Spirit. Perhaps we will. And if we do, the selected lections will give us plenty of material to consider, exegete, and proclaim.

Acts 2:1-21

I had a friend in high school who was agnostic and liked to talk to me about my beliefs and experiences with God. I remember sitting and talking with him in his living room one evening, when suddenly he pointed to the fireplace. "If God would make fire miraculously appear in that fireplace," he declared, "I would believe in him."

This is standard fare for the skeptic, of course: The request for proof. In Jesus' day, it was the "demand for a sign" (see, for example, Matthew 12:38-39; Luke 11:16), but Jesus always declined and even condemned the request.

At some level, I suppose, there is something sweet about the skeptic's demand. After all, it may not actually be born out of antagonism; it may reflect a genuine, inner longing to believe. They just need some bridge to get them over the chasm between skepticism and faith. They think a miraculous sign would serve the purpose.

The miraculous signs, however, may be overrated in the skeptic's imagination. After all, see how people respond when they are confronted with such displays of God's power. Pharaoh's conversions are notoriously brief (see, for example, Exodus 8:28-32; 9:27-35). Jezebel was more infuriated than impressed by the spectacular event on Mount Carmel (1 Kings 19:1-2). The disciples were slow to believe and understand, even with miracles right under their noses (as in Matthew 16:6-11). The people who were antagonistic toward Jesus only channeled his miracles into their antagonism (Matthew 12:22-24).

Likewise, here in this scene of the Holy Spirit's manifestation among the disciples and pouring out into the streets, see the responses of the crowds. In Acts 2, Luke reports that they were "bewildered" (v. 6), "amazed and astonished" (v. 7), "amazed and perplexed" (v. 12), and "others sneered" (v. 13).

Are these the responses God craves? If he wanted amazement and astonishment, don't we suppose that he could wow the socks right off of us every day? And even in the face of the Spirit's presence and power, still there were some who sneered, chalking the whole thing up to "new wine."

Eventually, by the end of the episode, we discover that about 3,000 people were converted to faith in Christ that day (v. 41), but it was not in response to the miraculous sign; rather, it was the heartfelt response to the preaching of the word by Peter.

We are reminded of the real function of this phenomenal outpouring of the Holy Spirit on Pentecost. This is not spectacle for spectacle's sake. This is power with a purpose.

Pentecost was one of the annual festivals when the people of God were required by law to travel to the place of worship with an offering (see Deuteronomy 16:9-12). Accordingly, at this time Jerusalem was occupied by Jews from all over the Mediterranean world (see Luke's list in Acts 2:9-11). And so this divine enabling was to guarantee the instantaneous spread of the gospel across the empire. The Spirit came with power, indeed; but he came not to wow, but to witness.

1 Corinthians 12:3b-13

If Paul's first letter to the Corinthians were a record album, chapter 13 would be the hit single that goes platinum. Everyone knows 1 Corinthians 13. Much of the rest of the "album," however, is unknown to the general public that recognizes only the Bible's "Top 40."

But here is the cut that precedes everyone's favorite song by Paul. They all play chapter 13 at their weddings, but they've never listened to chapter 12. Yet, if I may presume to speak for Paul, they cannot really understand cut 13 until they understand cut 12. For the famous love chapter is only fully understood within its larger context. And that context is Paul's extended discussion of the gifts of the Spirit.

Paul begins with what might seem a strange proof of the Spirit to such a charismatic congregation. "No one can say, 'Jesus is Lord,' " Paul insists, "except by the Holy Spirit." And so the grand evidence of the Spirit is not a miraculous sign, mysterious wisdom, or unaccounted for knowledge. It is something spoken, though not even necessarily spoken in a strange tongue. It is a personal affirmation of Jesus as Lord. Though this may seem unspectacular within the context of the Corinthian congregation, it is consistent with other teachings in scripture (see, for example, 1 John 4:2).

In verses 4-6, Paul beautifully frames the whole discussion in Trinitarian terms. He recognizes that there are a variety of gifts, services, and activities, yet there is one and the same Spirit, Lord, and God, respectively.

In verse 7, with respect to the spiritual gifts, Paul identifies the interplay between God, the church, and the individual believer. God is the source of the gifts, he gives them to the individual, and he gives them "for the common good." We'll give more consideration to that interplay below.

The particular gifts identified by Paul are better suited for a study than a sermon or at least a sermon series, rather than a single homily. At a minimum, though, it is important to recognize a few fundamentals. First, the gifts are given by God. The source is important for, as we know from our currency, if it doesn't come from the right source then the product is ultimately worthless. Second, while given to the individual, the gifts are not given for the individual. They have a broader purpose. Third, the very metaphor Paul uses to explain the gifts' roles reminds us that we do not function in isolation but in community. Fourth, this list of gifts is not exhaustive, for Paul has slightly differing lists elsewhere (as in Romans 12:6-8; Ephesians 4:11).

Finally, we may also note Paul's use of the word "activate." *Energeo* is the underlying Greek word, with its obvious connection to our English word "energy" or "energize." The King James Version had translated Paul's word "worketh," though that did not lend itself as naturally to recognizing the relationship between a noun and the verb in verse 6. The NRSV does a better job by translating the noun (*energaymatone*) "activities" and the verb (*energone*) "activates."

We discover that Paul uses this verb twice, plus a related noun once, in this passage and so an understanding of the verb will shed light on the whole text for our listeners. The verb can be taken to mean "be at work," "be effective," "be operative," "to display one's activity," and "to show one's self-operative." This is the marvelous picture and prospect of the spiritual gifts: that God himself is effectively at work within us, displaying his activity through us. Lest we fall into the trap of thinking that our work on Christ's behalf is a function of our own human ability, or that his work is hopelessly handicapped by our personal limitations, we have this good news: "It is the same God who activates all of (the gifts) in everyone."

John 20:19-23

The gospel lection comes from Easter Sunday. But while "Easter" connotes early morning for most of our folks, this episode comes from later that evening. This is not the sunrise scene by the garden tomb; this is more of a sundown scene in a locked room.

The locked room is an interesting detail. Partly, of course, because it presents us with the fascinating post-resurrection ability of Jesus apparently to enter space without traditional human limitations. Beyond that, though, there is the compelling picture of a grave that is open but a house that is closed.

Following Jesus' crucifixion, we gather that the Jewish authorities, with the assistance of Roman guards, went to great lengths to seal Jesus' tomb. That was the site of a locked-up space and tight security. But by Sunday evening that confinement had been blown wide open.

Meanwhile, not far away, however, there was a different locked-up space, also motivated by fear. And just as easily and powerfully as Jesus had exited the first locked-up space, so now he entered the second. This lock, too, was to be eliminated, for "as the Father has sent me, so I send you." His followers were not to be cooped up and cowering, hiding in their locked-up house; rather, they were to go out into the world with the message of the risen Christ.

Jesus' repetition of the phrase, "Peace be with you," is unexplained. We may comfortably infer that the disciples were not at peace prior to Jesus' arrival, for they were locked up in a house "for fear of the Jews." They were likely a group marked, not by peace, but by grief, anxiety, and fear.

We are not told how the disciples responded when Jesus first — and suddenly — appeared and spoke to them. Perhaps the silence about their reaction is sufficient to portray their reaction: dumbfounded. It is only after Jesus shows them his hands and side that "the disciples rejoiced when the saw the Lord." Had they not seen him before? Perhaps not — at least not in the sense of recognizing and believing.

Knowing what follows, it is hard to read this passage and not feel sorry for Thomas. Apparently, he is the only one of the group that is missing on this occasion, which results in his infamous statement of incredulity. That, in turn, led to his terrible and undeserved nickname: doubting Thomas.

In fact, of course, Thomas' faith was probably indistinguishable from the rest of the disciples. We see plenty of evidence of doubt, fear, and uncertainty on every hand in the post-resurrection accounts of the disciples. Thomas' insistence that he wanted to see for himself Jesus' wounded hands and side was only a desire to experience what the others already had, for in verse 20 we read that "he showed them his hands and his side." It was after that bit of startling, physical evidence that "the disciples rejoiced."

In the last two verses of this passage, we are presented with two difficulties. First, since the disciples received the Holy Spirit here on this occasion, what different thing happened on Pentecost? Second, what precisely is the assignment or authority granted in verse 23? There are interpretations aplenty to be found in commentaries and they are too varied and in-depth to be explored here.

Finally, one of the hallmarks of the fourth gospel is the interplay portrayed between the persons of the Trinity. As we read the words of Jesus in John's extended Last Supper scene, for example, we discover so many references to the Son's relationship to the Father and to the Spirit. We further discover that the followers of Jesus are marvelously included in that interplay. Here we see that the Father sent the Son, the Son sends the disciples, and the Son gives the Spirit to those disciples.

Application

When I was a college student, participating in a weekly study and discussion group with other Christian students, I heard an interesting insight into the work of the Holy Spirit. These many years later, I don't recall who shared the illustration, let alone whether it was their original insight or borrowed from some other source. With apologies, therefore, to the first person to paint this picture, let me share the image with you.

In the analogy, we were asked to picture the Washington Monument. Most of the students in the group were from Virginia and so the image was a personally familiar one. The monument, we were reminded, stands tall, splendid, and unmistakable in the night sky for visitors to Washington DC. But it is the strong and trained spotlights at its base that actually make it visible at night. The spotlights, therefore, are essential to see the monument and they prompt you to look at and think about the monument, though not about the spotlights themselves.

Jesus, the analogy suggested, is like the Washington Monument and those powerful lights represent the Holy Spirit. The Spirit does not endeavor to draw any attention to himself: only to Jesus. We could not see or come to Christ apart from the work of the Spirit, yet the Spirit's role and will is to focus our attention on Christ, not on himself.

We see in our lections today the altogether selfless nature of the work of the Spirit.

We have observed that the dramatic advent of the Spirit in the Acts passage was not designed to wow the crowds into conversion but rather to enable the apostles to preach the good news to the multitudes gathered in Jerusalem. The expectation, it seems, was that the people would respond to the proclamation of the word, not to the manifestation of the Spirit.

Meanwhile, in Paul's discussion of the Spirit's gifts in 1 Corinthians, we noted that those gifts, by intent and design, are not self-serving. They are not given to an individual in order to elevate that individual. Rather they are given "for the common good." In this respect, then, we recognize that the Spirit's gifts reflect the Spirit's style and are thoroughly consistent with the Spirit's work.

On a recent Sunday morning, our church choir sang a piece that prompted our congregation to applaud. I was a bit surprised, for I noticed that the choir director had kept her arms suspended for several moments following the final chord — a technique, she once confided in me, to keep a congregation from applauding. Still, they applauded, and I could see in her face that she was disappointed. She is eager for the choir's anthems to be understood as worship rather than performance. She does not want applause.

I wonder, in the same vein, if the Holy Spirit does not want applause. I wonder if, perhaps, he does not want recognition and attention. If so, then perhaps he would be happier this week if we just preached about Jesus and let him do his selfless work at the base of the monument.

An Alternative Application
1 Corinthians 12:3b-13. "Read the tag." When the time comes to wrap Christmas presents each year, I surround myself with a predictable assortment of supplies: wrapping paper, tape, ribbons, bows, and tags. The wrapping serves to conceal the gift. The tag reveals all that can be known about the gift until Christmas Day: namely, the name of the giver and the name of the recipient.

Most of those tags have two blank lines. The one line is labeled "To" and the other line is labeled "From." The tag seems to be slightly different, however, on the gifts from God.

In 1 Corinthians 12, the apostle Paul teaches the Christians in Corinth about the gifts of the Spirit. They might suspect that they don't need to be taught about them because they had so abundantly experienced them. Still, there was much that they apparently did not understand, so Paul wrote to instruct them.

In verse 7, Paul places the "tag" on the spiritual gifts. On this tag, however, we find three lines instead of the usual two: "From," "To," and "For."

The "From" line is God. These gifts are not a reflection of the individual's power or significance. They are not tricks-of-the-trade to be learned or purchased, as Simon the magician cynically supposed (Acts 8:14-24). Rather, they are free gifts from God. They reflect his goodness, power, and purpose, not our own.

The "To" line features the individual believer. As in the familiar parable of the three stewards (Matthew 25:14-30), this master entrusts some of his great wealth to individuals. He does not hoard his splendor; he delegates it, enabling his servants to do his work. And that brings us to the pivotal third line on the tag.

In addition to the familiar "From" and "To" designations, there is also a "For" line. The gifts are given "for the common good," Paul writes. These spiritual gifts are not for self-satisfaction or self-aggrandizement. The person who is able to work miracles is not meant to prance about working miracles to impress others or to draw attention to himself.

We see this truth most beautifully embodied, of course, in the life and ministry of Jesus. He does not work miracles to meet his own needs (see Matthew 4:3-4; Luke 23:35-39), he resists the demands to perform signs that will prove his identity and (presumably) turn skeptics into believers (Mark 8:11-12), he shies away from publicity (Luke 5:12-15; 8:51-56), and he even deliberately chooses to work some miracles privately (Mark 7:32- 33).

Imagine giving Christmas or birthday gifts to children with tags that feature all three lines. "To Johnny," the tag reads, "From Daddy," and "For you to share with your little brother."

Such is the nature of the tag God has put on his gifts to us. We express our gratitude to him for what he has bestowed on us. We receive with delight what he has for us and we employ what we have received, not in our own service, but "for the common good."

Holy Trinity Sunday
Genesis 1:1—2:4a
2 Corinthians 13:11-13
Matthew 28:16-20
by William Shepherd

It was good

The more I listened, the more I heard desperation.

"It is possible for there to be light and darkness without the sun and the moon," she said as she launched into a long explanation gleaned from some dubious website. "And of course the days are not real days, but eras," she concluded.

"But the days are defined as alternating periods of light and darkness," someone replied. "Are you trying to tell us that there was darkness for thousands of years, and then light for another thousand?"

"That's one possibility," she said.

"But what about the sun and the moon?" someone else asked. "Weren't they moving at the same rate they are now? How could there be darkness for thousands of years, if the sun comes up every morning?"

"There's no light if there's cloud cover," she said. "The important thing to notice is that the order of creation is precisely what science prescribes: vegetation, ocean life, birds, mammals, and human beings."

I pointed out that this order was established by the very evolutionist thinkers she was opposed to and that the order of creation was different in Genesis 2. Besides, there's no mention of cloud cover in the story.

"Well, there could have been clouds."

So once again the attempt to turn Genesis into science collapsed into silliness, contradiction, and the death of a thousand qualifications. It is desperate; this twisting of ancient poetry into something it is not — a scientific treatise. Witness the recent "Intelligent Design Movement," which tries to strip creationism of all its religious trappings, as if it would even exist apart from a certain reading of Genesis!

Genesis presents us not with a scientific account, but a priestly one. Its true value is theological in the proper sense. It shows us who God is — a God who presides over nature as a priest over an altar, blessing, consecrating, and separating the holy from the profane. It presents God as our Creator, the one to whom we owe everything, beginning with our very existence. It validates not only our own lives but also the worth of every stone, river, and living creature, offering this pronouncement over all: "It was good."

Genesis 1:1—2:4a

The opening of Genesis is the preface not just to that book, but the whole Hebrew Bible. It introduces the hopeful, yet pessimistic, primordial history (1:1—11:32) that serves as a backdrop to the call of Abraham. It is similar to, yet refutes the theological claims of, the Babylonian creation story found in the *Enuma Elish*. Stemming from the time of Israel's interaction with Babylon, it takes a priestly point of view and may well have been used liturgically.

This first creation story is relatively abstract, spacious, and majestic (especially in comparison with the story found in Genesis 2, which concentrates on the garden). It moves from chaos to rest by means of constant repetition: "God said... let there be... and it was so... and God made... and God saw that it was good... and it was evening and morning." The symmetrical pattern reflects the serenity of the process. There is also an overall symmetry to the passage: three different realms are populated on three parallel days, with a final day set apart to be observed by God alone. The number seven represents completeness and figures prominently in the construction of the passage. Not only are there seven days in the week but seven repetitions of "and God saw that it was good." God is mentioned exactly 35 times and the story of the seventh day is recounted in exactly 35 Hebrew words (2:1-3).

The story opens with a temporal clause: "In the beginning when God created...." God presides over a primordial chaos, something dark and dangerous and worse than nothing (which may well have reflected the experience of the exiles who molded this story). As in Babylonian myth, God shows mastery over the unfathomable deep, that great subterranean reservoir that will later erupt in the flood (1:1-2). Into this chaos God introduces light with nothing more than a word (v. 3); creation will be purely a result of God's will and speech. Like a priest distinguishing the sacred from the profane, God separates light from darkness ("separate," a bit of priestly vocabulary, is used five times in the story). God responds to creation by naming it, thus evaluating it and discerning its place in the whole (vv. 4-5). This is not scientific language; day and night here are defined solely in relation to the purpose of God and have nothing to do with the (unheard of at the time) revolutions of the earth, and totally independent of the sun and moon, which are created later (vv. 13-18).

The picture of the earth itself is in no way scientific: a flat earth is coupled with a celestial dome to form a giant bell at the center of the universe, surrounded above and below by the deep. The dome that is the sky is a hammered-out slab (perhaps held up by pillars, cf. Job 26:11) designed to hold back the reservoir of sky-waters, just as the earth holds back the subterranean waters (v. 6). Again there is separation, the waters above from the waters below (v. 7), and then the seas from the land (vv. 9-10).

The first life is vegetation, seed-plants, and fruit-trees ("according to its kind," v. 11; note the priestly concern for separation and categorization). The seeds and fruit are ordained for the sustenance of humans and animals (v. 29). Like the vegetation, the animal kingdom is created and designated as "good" — even the sea monsters! (v. 21). Nothing in this creation stands outside of the purpose and will of God.

The pinnacle of creation is humankind. In saying "let *us* make humankind in our image," God includes the heavenly retinue in the creative process, just as God will make human beings creative agents. Creation is a dialogical and not monological act, which God shares with the created. Genesis asserts but does not specify the creation of humankind in the image of God and the heavenly cohort, except that it is both individual and plural, "him," "them," and "male and female"; human beings alone out of all creation are designated as created in this image. Sexual distinction is included as part of creation; God created sex, and then pronounced it good. The human beings are given "dominion" over the rest of creation; God gives the creation for human use, and humans are to exercise dominion as those who are in the image of the Creator (note this did not originally include permission to kill animals for food).

Finally God finishes and rests. This is a divine and not a human rest (the Sabbath law is not given until Exodus 16). While it may be seen (anthropomorphically) as an appropriate reaction to a hard week of work, it really indicates the nature of the God who made this good creation. There is in the heart of eternity a rest independent of all human notions of relaxation. In God there is a peace with creation that is expressed in God's rest.

2 Corinthians 13:11-13

We move into a very different realm of biblical literature with the closing farewell of Paul's letters to the Corinthians, but there are similar notions to be found here: the goodness of creation (here expressed in community) and the rest and peace to be found only in God. As in the primordial history in Genesis, there is a strong strain of hope in Paul, coupled with an obvious pessimism about human nature.

Paul has called the Corinthians to a rigorous self-examination in light of his upcoming visit. They need to deal with their contentiousness and their other communal issues. Paul, his relationship with them at an all-time low, resorts to the ancient rule that "any charge must be sustained by the evidence of two or three witnesses" (13:1; cf. Deuteronomy 19:15). This will be his third visit to them, and the third witness against them, unless they change. He sums up his desires for them in 13:10: "So I write these things while I am away from you, so that when I come, I may not have to be severe in using the authority that the Lord has given me for building up and not for tearing down."

The farewell (13:11-13) injects a ray of hope into this gloom. While it is a typically Pauline closing, it pithily sums up what the Corinthians need to do before he comes for his third (and perhaps final) visit. He exhorts them to put their communal affairs in order, listen to his appeal, agree with one another on the major issues, and thus live in peace (v. 11). The "holy kiss," given on the brow and shoulders among families, should not be without meaning among them. Paul reminds them that there is a strong community of believers ("the saints") who stand behind him (v. 12).

Finally, he gives his exhortation one last bit of theological backing (v. 13). This is one of the few explicitly Trinitarian formulas in the New Testament (cf. 1:21-22; Matthew 28:19), and it serves as a summary of sort. The grace that comes through Jesus proceeds from the love that God showed by sending him to us, and results in fellowship not only with his Spirit, but also the fellowship with one another that is enabled by that Spirit. Thus Paul brings to a close his exhortation on communal life with a reminder that the community, however contentious, is a gift from God.

Matthew 28:16-20

The closing section of Matthew's gospel picks up the thread of the story of the women at the tomb: true to Jesus' word (28:10) and the prediction of the angel of the Lord (v. 7), the eleven go to the mountain in Galilee (28:16). They join in worship of the resurrected Lord, though some doubt (v. 17). Jesus acknowledges that their worship is well-placed: "All authority in heaven and on earth has been given to me" (v. 18). The scene binds together two of Matthew's main images of Jesus: Lord and Teacher. The two cannot be separated; Jesus cannot be teacher without being Lord. On the mountain, Jesus is the all-powerful resurrected Lord. He is also the teacher (like Moses) who speaks his final words on the mountain of revelation. This is the climax as well as the end of the gospel: the royal Messiah, Son of David, Son of God, teacher of the law, is now enthroned as king. The disciples in turn are commissioned to continue Jesus' ministry.

The Great Commission is the final step in the disciples' training and preparation for their future mission. They are to become mirror images of Jesus in their own disciple-making: "Go therefore and make disciples of all nations, baptizing them in the name of the Father and of the Son and of the Holy Spirit, and teaching them to obey everything that I have commanded you" (vv. 19-20). The exhortation lands squarely on its main imperative: "make disciples." The other verbs in the sentence ("go," "baptize," "teach") are not imperatives in Greek but participles, used to stress the means by which disciples are to be made: "Make disciples, by going and baptizing and teaching." The disciples' main job is to replicate themselves; like their Lord, they are to gather around themselves students of his teaching. The time until the end of the age (v. 20) is to be spent making more disciples.

The mission includes community-formation and teaching. Baptism is the formation of a community "where two or three are gathered together" to be with the resurrected Jesus (vv. 19-20). The continued worship of these small communities is a crucial part of disciple-making. Matthew has not included baptism as a part of Jesus' teaching until now, apart from his own example of being baptized by John the Baptist. When Jesus was baptized, he told John it was to "fulfill all righteousness" (3:15); that is, to be baptized is thus a part of following the way of righteousness that Jesus teaches (5:6, 10; 6:33). Matthew assumes the practice of his own community in reporting this command, baptism being done in the name of the Trinity — Father, Son, and Holy Spirit.

Teaching is a necessary part of the worship gatherings. Again, the idea is to replicate the work of Jesus. The subject of the teaching is "everything I have commanded you." The goal is obedience (v. 20). Throughout Matthew's story, the disciples are presented as students of the Lord. They are good students for the most part; unlike the disciples in Mark, they seem to understand most of what Jesus has to say. At the end of his parable discourse, he asks if they have understood his teaching; they answer, "Yes" (13:51). When Jesus walks on the water, the disciples are not astounded (as in Mark 6:51-52), but they confess, "Truly you are the Son of God" (Matthew 14:33). Yet, there is one stumbling block Matthew's disciples cannot quite overcome: They do not understand his death (16:22-24; 17:23). The disciples are unprepared to stand by Jesus at the cross (26:56), being ill-prepared to understand his death, despite his predictions (16:21; 17:9, 22-23; 20:17-18). By the end of the story, however, most of the cobwebs have been cleared away (though some still doubt, v. 17). In becoming witnesses to his resurrection they are now finished with their training and are fully ready to take their places in the teaching mission. They are truly scribes of the kingdom of heaven (13:52).

The mission of disciple-making is to be universal: the disciples are specifically sent to "all nations" or "all the Gentiles" (*panta ta ethne*, v. 19). Here Matthew draws out the implications of the various hints laid down throughout the story: Wise Gentiles worship him (2:11) since he is the light to the Gentiles (4:15-16; 12:18-21), Gentiles have faith in him when Israelites did not (8:10), a Canaanite woman takes the crumbs from his table (15:21-28), and many will come from east and west to sit at that table (8:11-12). Ironically, even the Roman soldiers responsible for his death speak words that recognize Jesus as the Son of God (27:54). Jesus' prophecy to the Jewish leaders will prove true: "The kingdom of God will be taken away from you and given to a nation (*ethnos*) producing the fruits of it" (21:43, author's translation). At the end of his earthly life, and at the beginning of his resurrected life, Jesus' mission is extended beyond "the lost sheep of the house of Israel" (15:24; 10:5-6; cf. 9:36; 10:23; 19:28). These hints laid throughout the book are now given explicit fulfillment in the command of the resurrected Lord.

The gospel ends with the promise given at its beginning: Jesus is "God with us" (1:23). "Remember, I am with you always, to the end of the age" (v. 20). The NRSV translation of *idou* (an imperative of the verb "to see," normally translated "behold, look") as "remember" is perhaps idiosyncratic, as *idou* was generally used as a sort of exclamation point, drawing attention to what follows. But both "remember" and "look" point to the function of the disciple, preacher, and teacher. The ongoing job of disciples is to teach other disciples to "remember" the teachings of the master, but also to point out the ways ("look!") that the resurrected Lord is still at work in the community, still "Emmanuel," God with us.

Application

Despite all appearances, God proclaims creation good. The world is good, according to Genesis. Human community is good, according to Paul. The work of making disciples is good, according to Matthew.

The world has its counter-arguments. A giant wave is taken as evidence of evil in God's good world (as if there could be a world with no laws of nature, and as if death were the ultimate evil in this world). There is no end of bad people in any community. And why would people be lining up for the Lotto and Powerball, if working were such a good thing?

The response of faith has to do with the nature of God. God is first and foremost Creator. God created us in conjunction with others, "them" as well as "him," and gave us creative powers. That the act of creation was in fact work is shown by the seventh day of rest. If we share the image of God in creation, then we can affirm its goodness with God. In the end, faith will allow us to look at the world, at our own lives, and say with God, "It was good."

Alternative Applications
1) Genesis 1:1—2:4a; 2 Corinthians 13:11-13; Matthew 28:16-20. I long ago resolved not to inflict on any congregation one of those sermons that tries to "explain" the Trinity using a bad analogy ("the apple has a core, flesh, and skin, but it's all one apple"). Besides, it could be argued that preaching the biblical text has priority. The doctrine of the Trinity in its final form dates from long after the New Testament was

written and compiled, and for those who preach the texts, the best we can find are the hints that led later theologians to develop the idea of a Triune God. Throughout the Bible, there is compelling evidence of a communal element within God. In Genesis, God is willing to share the pinnacle of creation and the image in which humanity is created with the rest of creation, embodied in the heavenly host. In Paul, community proves to be at the heart of faith. For Matthew, discipleship is all but defined as making other disciples. Can all this be any surprise, if the nature of God is indeed communal?

2) Matthew 28:16-20. Matthew commends not evangelism but disciple-making and there is a difference. The disheveled young man told me that he had been booted from his orthodox Jewish household when he heard and accepted the Christian gospel from a Jew for Jesus. Now he did not know where to go.
    "What about your friend? Can't he help you?"
    "What friend?" He looked puzzled.
    "The Jew for Jesus who converted you."
    "Oh, he's not my friend, I just met him. I don't even know his last name or where he lives."
    The Jew for Jesus had practiced hit-and-run evangelism, leaving God to pick up the pieces!
    This is not what Matthew had in mind. Disciple-making includes not just "going" but also "baptizing" and "teaching." It is a long-term process of formation. This is what is so "Great" about the "Great Commission."

Proper 7
Pentecost 2
Ordinary Time 12
Genesis 21:8-21
Romans 6:1b-11
Matthew 10:24-39
by Wayne Brouwer

Family privilege

My daughters know the direct access code to my office phone. Not everyone gets that information, and most of those who do have it, use it sparingly, but that's not true of my daughters. They know they can call me anytime. When I see theirs as the incoming number, I answer my phone, even if I have others with me. My daughters have privilege. They're family.

Something of that family privilege is part of each of today's passages. Hagar and Ishmael lost family privilege in the household of Abraham but gained it in the household of God. Spiritual family privilege marks Paul's conversations about what resources we have available to us in order to do battle with the darker side of life. Jesus talks about the family resemblance that comes to those who are claimed by him as part of the family.

Family privilege is a two-way street, of course. It carries a number of benefits that are allowed only to those in the inner circle. At the same time, it expects a certain lifestyle that matches the family coat-of-arms. *Whose* I am determines *who* I am.

John Bowler remembers an incident of family privilege that gave him a lifetime of reflection on its meaning. In 1959, John watched intently as his little brother was caught in the act of writing in their father's brand new hymnbook with a pen. Suddenly their father walked into the room, and both brothers cowered; they sensed that the younger boy had done something very wrong when he scribbled across the length and breadth of the entire first page. Both boys were certain that a grievous punishment would follow.

But John's father picked up his prized hymnal, looked at it carefully, and then sat down without saying a word. Books were precious to him; he was a clergyman with several earned degrees. For him, books were knowledge. But more important, as this day proved, he loved his children. Instead of punishing John's younger brother, instead of scolding or yelling or reprimanding, John's father sat down, took the pen from John's brother's hand and then wrote in the book himself, right alongside the scribbles John had made: "John's word 1959, age two. How many times have I looked into your beautiful face and into your warm, alert eyes looking up at me and thanked God for the one who has now scribbled in my new hymnal? You have made the book sacred as have your brothers and sister to so much of my life."

Only a parent who has understood what it means to be a child of God could respond so profoundly to such a seeming disgrace and disobedience. There is, indeed, something important in family privilege.

Genesis 21:8-21

There are four major story cycles in the book of Genesis: the story of Origins (1-11), the story of Abraham (12-25), the story of Jacob (26-36), and the story of Joseph (37-50). Included within each of these there are many other little stories like the one we read today. But it is important to read each little story within the context of the larger story cycle in which it is found. For the nation of Israel, receiving the covenant at Mount Sinai (Exodus 20-24), each of these story cycles in Genesis asked and answered a fundamental question of identity:

- Origins story cycle (1-11): Why is God making this covenant with us? Because this world is the creation and kingdom of God and it is in civil war against God.
- Abraham story cycle (12-25): Who are we that God should come to us with this covenant? We are the descendents of the chosen son of Abraham, through whom the covenant was originated.
- Jacob story cycle (26-36): What is our character? We are tricksters and con artists like our father Jacob, but we are also "Israel" like him — those who wrestle with God.
- Joseph story cycle (37-50): But why were we in Egypt rather than in the land of God's promise to Abraham? Because of a famine and Joseph's protective care.

Thinking of the book of Genesis in this way helps us understand several things about the story in today's lectionary reading. First, Hagar and Ishmael needed to be separated from the family of Abraham, Sarah, and Isaac, because the covenant bloodline was being formulated. While Hagar and Ishmael received grace within the tents of Abraham, there was a larger drama being played out and they were a threat to it. We may argue the wisdom of this view, and debate the theological conundrums it causes, but the text is quite clear on this point. For Israel at Sinai, this would confirm their right in the battles ahead with the descendents of Ishmael.

Second, the "distress" of Abraham (v. 11) is evidence of grace. Although a separation between two sides of the family was demanded by Sarah (v. 10) and permitted by God (v. 12), it went against Abraham's nature and against the promises made to him in Genesis 12:1-3. This note of grace is echoed both in the speech of God in verse 13 and in the kindness of Abraham's actions in verse 14. For Israel at Sinai, this tenderhearted compassion would become a necessary part of the international mission and hospitality that the Sinai Covenant would lay upon the nation.

Third, God's direct care is found in the promises made (v. 18) and the provision offered (v. 19). For Israel at Sinai, the covenant would seek to instill this hospitable approach to life in its very character as a nation (cf. Exodus 23:9).

There is, in this story, the typical (and somewhat quirky) biblical upending of things: the first becomes last, the older is ruled over by the younger, the outcast becomes family and the family outcast. Yet neither first nor last, older nor younger, outcast nor family is ever far from grace. Dr. E. Stanley Jones told of an incident from his missionary days that illustrates the point. A young girl got tired of things at home. She longed for the freedom of the streets and the excitement of the nightlife. She ran away to a large city. It wasn't long before she fell under the spell of a pimp and was degraded into a prostitute.

The girl's mother was beside herself with anxiety. It was true that things hadn't been going right between them, but a mother's love is restless and protective, and she had to find her daughter again. She remembered the child who sat on her lap, and the daughter who whispered in her ear, and needed somehow to renew their bond of trust. Yet how should she begin the search? All she had heard were rumors about her daughter, thirdhand reports that she was now wasting her body in the red-light district. The mother went to the city and simply began to walk, hoping to stumble across someone who might know her daughter. Up one street and down the next she trudged, talking to anyone who would listen, hoping for a clue to follow, but to no avail. Her daughter didn't want to be found: shame, rebellion, spite — who can say what reasons mingle in our deceptive minds?

Eventually the quest tired even the mother. Before she returned home, she did one more thing. She carried a photograph that had been taken several years before, a picture of the two of them, mother and daughter, at a happier moment in both their lives. She got the photograph enlarged and made dozens of copies. Then she scattered those pictures around the area, hoping that one would catch her daughter's eye. On each photo she penned these five words: "Come home! I love you!" And one day the girl did see. She began to remember what love was all about. A holy restlessness gripped her soul, battering her resentment until she had to call her mother. The next day she was home.

Was she ever not her mother's child? Was Ishmael ever not his father's son? Are Abraham or Israel or we ever not the children of God? Perhaps only in our own minds and attitudes at times, but God maintains privilege with God's family.

Romans 6:1b-11

In a large outline, Paul's letter to the Romans can be summarized as Sin (1-3), Salvation (4-11), and Service (12-16). The plight of humanity (1-3) calls out God's redemptive care (4-11) that creates a new consciousness of what it means to be in God's family (12-16). Here Paul continues to redraw the family tree as he began in chapter 5. There (5:12-21) he said the original family tree had wilted and died under the influence of its patriarch Adam. Because God was not willing for the human race to deteriorate into extinction, God started over and grafted the old family onto a new patriarch root — Jesus (this theme is restated in Romans 11).

Now the implications of this transaction are recounted. The two realms of this world and the next, of earth and Hades, of life and death, have no legal connection. What happens here may influence the next world, but one cannot take anything from this world into the next. Metaphorically this is what happens to us: we were born sinners (5:12-21), but were then transferred into the family of Jesus. Because Jesus lived on our behalf, then died our death in this world, and finally came alive again, we are freed from the automatic links to sin that dogged us. Like Jean Valjean in *Les Miserables*, we have been given our same lives back again but separated from the sinful bloodlines of our past. The act of baptism (which means "to immerse," and was a common cleansing rite in many religious circles, including Judaism) powerfully pictured death (from the family of the first Adam and its sin-tainted bloodline) and resurrection (into the family of the second Adam and its redemptive bloodline).

From Australia comes a story of two brothers caught stealing sheep. A large "ST" was branded on each forehead so all would know that they were "Sheep Thieves" and not to be trusted. One brother immediately left town in shame. He couldn't abide the stares and isolation caused by this ignominy. He traveled from town to town in the outback, always trying to hide his telltale scar under the brim of a hat. But infamy and suspicion dogged him and without fail his evil deeds came to light. He died young, diseased, and feeble with alcoholism, lost forever from his family and home community.

The other brother realized he could never run from his past but he also believed that he had not been born a sheep thief. This was not his true character. He stayed in his hometown. It was not easy — stares, mockery, and gossip wove a shroud of isolation, but he believed his crime had been punished and the debt paid. He lived as if he had a right to the streets, a place at the diner counter, and the privilege of citizenship. Slowly, over the years, this brother's actions of care, consistency of good deeds, and partnership in the enterprise of the town won for him a new identity. One day a traveler passed through town and saw this old man walking the sidewalks with the scars looking like "ST" on his forehead. When he asked the clerk at the general story what had happened to the man, the clerk thought for a moment, shook his head, and then said, "I'm not exactly sure. I know there's a story behind it. Knowing the man, I'd guess that the 'ST' stands for 'saint.' "

So states Paul's exhortation in these verses. We were guilty sinners. God took care of the punishment for that sin in Jesus, and, from a theological perspective, we died in that transaction. Now we are part of the family of God and have been made free. Freedom has its privileges but it also has its responsibilities. How now will we live?

Matthew 10:24-39

These verses come at the end of Jesus' missionary commissioning of the twelve (10:1-5). Jesus makes a strong identification between the twelve and himself. They are part of the family and have family privileges.

Within the gospel as a whole, chapter 10 forms a bridge between the original work of Jesus and its ongoing expression in the life of the Christian community. Christians are privileged children of God. It is in the family character to live in the house of the master (v. 25), carry oneself with the confidence of the royal household (vv. 26-31), speak as an ambassador of the great king (v. 32), and live on the battlefield of the universe as a person clearly under the banner of heaven (vv. 34-39). These are all part of the family resemblance that follows through in our lives because of the life-giving grace of God.

Application

Fred Craddock tells a great story that provides an excellent application on these passages. Fred and his wife were on vacation in the Great Smoky Mountains of eastern Tennessee when they stumbled onto an out-of-the-way restaurant called the Black Bear Inn. It proved to be a good place to eat, besides offering the possibility of actually seeing one of those black bears. An entire wall of glass opened out onto a wild and rugged valley. As they sat at supper, quietly communing with nature and each other, their solitude was broken by a tall man with a shock of white hair who ambled over. They could see he was well along in years, probably past the fourscore allotted by the psalmist.

He was hard of hearing as well, since he rudely interrupted their quiet reverie with noisy and nosy questions at least twenty decibels too loud. When he found that Fred taught at a seminary he suddenly had a story to tell about preachers. Without an invitation he pulled up a chair and invaded their space. Nodding out the great glass window, he said, "I was born back here in these mountains." But the story was not to be a pretty one. "My mother was not married," he went on, "and the reproach that fell upon her, fell upon me. The children at school had a name for me and it hurt. It hurt very much." In fact, he said, "During recess I would go hide in the weeds until the bell rang. At noon hour I took my lunch and went behind a tree to avoid them. When I went to town with my mamma, all the grownups would stop and stare at us. They'd look at my mamma, and then they'd look at me, and I could see they were trying to guess who my daddy might have been. Painful years, those."

But something big was about to happen. "I guess it was about the seventh or eight grade," he continued, "when a preacher came to town. He frightened me when he preached, and he attracted me, all at the same time. Every time he preached he caught me with his words. I didn't want the people to catch me, though, so I never went to church on time. I'd sneak in just as he was getting warmed up. When he was finished I'd rush right out. But one morning I got caught. A bunch of women lined up in the aisle, and I couldn't get out, and I knew somebody was going to see me and say, 'What's a boy like you doin' in church?' Sure enough, suddenly a hand clamped down on my shoulder. Out of the corner of my eye I could see the preacher's face. 'Whoa, boy!' he said to me. He turned me around and looked me in the face. I could see he was trying to find the family resemblance. Finally he said, 'Well, boy, I can see it now...! I can see you're a child of... You're a child of... Wait now...' And he stared me right in the face. 'Yep!' he said. 'I can see it now! You're a child of... God! There's a striking resemblance!' He swatted me on the bottom, and he said, 'Go on, boy! Go claim your family inheritance!'"

The Craddocks were quite taken by the story the old man had to tell. Fred thought there was something familiar about it, so he asked the elderly gent, "Sir, what's your name?"

The man replied, proudly, "Ben Hooper!"

It was then that Fred Craddock remembered his daddy telling him the story of the time the people of Tennessee twice elected an illegitimate bastard boy as governor, and how Ben Hooper had done the state proud. Ben Hooper gained faith when a preacher told him he was child of God. He proved his faith when he carved a future of grace out of a mixed inheritance.

An Alternative Application
Romans 6:1b-11. The Pauline passage preaches well by itself. Scenes from Alex Haley's *Roots*, or the movie *Amistad*, might make for excellent expressions of the pain of slavery and the amazement of release. Two questions need to be part of the presentation: "How will you die?" and "How will you live?" The first gets at the need to become aware of the transaction that takes place in order for us to become children of God. The second focuses on behavior and lifestyle within the family of God.

John Perkins' story is a great illustration of these things. His journey from poverty and racism through skepticism and finally faith, and the rebirth of New Hebron and Mendenhall, Mississippi, under his new walk with God, are a profound testimony of how this transformation can happen.

The language of Paul in this passage indicates that the transformation from death to life, from slavery to freedom, from outcast to family involves at least three things. First, our consciences need to be reactivated. Under sin's slavery we can no longer think clearly. Spiritual resurrection begins when our consciences are renewed so that we begin to see our lost condition and also gain a taste for the life of freedom. Second, our vision needs to be broadened. We need to gain the eyes of the heart that can see the world from God's perspective. Third, we need to have our wills strengthened, since part of the transaction from slavery to freedom includes our own choices.

Proper 8
Pentecost 3
Ordinary Time 13
Genesis 22:1-14
Romans 6:12-23
Matthew 10:40-42
by David Kalas

Pick me! Pick me!

The children gather on the playground for a game: perhaps kickball, basketball, or touch football. All the eligible players line up in front of the two captains and then the great process begins picking teams.

Perhaps some of the kids stand quietly, even shyly, waiting, hoping to be picked. Not the eager ones, though. They do not stand quietly. They raise and wave their hands! "Hey, over here! Pick me! Pick me!"

If it's a football game, they will likely do the same thing out on the field. Eager for the quarterback to throw the ball to them, they will wave their arms and call, "Over here! I'm open! Throw it to me!"

The man or woman of God ought to have something of that eagerness: the readiness to be chosen and used by God. Raise your hand and wave your arms for God — here I am! Pick me! Use me!

The Christian who presents himself and his members to God; the disciple, along with the one who gives him a cup of water; Abraham: all available to God.

Genesis 22:1-14

Do you have caller ID on your telephone? Have you ever used it to determine whether or not you would answer a particular call? Would we answer if the caller ID tipped us off that the incoming call was from God?

God called Abraham, and Abraham answered. On the one hand, this was the same God who had forced him to leave his home and his kin to move to a strange land and live as an alien. On the other hand, this was the same God who had been Abraham's companion, provider, protector, and friend for so many years and so many miles; the same God who had made so many marvelous promises and who had miraculously fulfilled the most precious of those promises in the form of Abraham's beloved son, Isaac.

God called, and Abraham answered. That was a courageous thing to do, for it seems that every such contact with God was a life-changing one for Abraham. In chapter 12, the Lord spoke, and Abraham had to pull up his roots to leave his home in favor of a strange and distant land. In chapter 13, the Lord spoke, and Abraham was promised property as far as the eye could see, though he owned not an acre of it at the time and he lived and died as an alien in the land. In chapter 15, the Lord spoke, and promised Abraham a galaxy of descendants, though Sarah's scheme to help make it happen became a headache and a heartache. In chapter 17, the Lord spoke, and Abraham was given the (probably unwelcome) sign of circumcision. (Isn't there just a contract I could sign?) It was for him, for his household, and all of the yet unseen branches of his family tree. In chapter 18, the Lord spoke, and Sarah laughed. The Lord spoke, and an old man's life was promised to be changed forever, again. The Lord spoke, and divine judgment seemed imminent for Abraham's only kinfolk in the whole land. In chapter 21, the Lord spoke, and Ishmael was sent away from his home and his father.

And now, in chapter 22, the Lord spoke again. The Lord called, and Abraham answered. We could preach on Abraham under the theme, "Answering the Call."

It seems that Abraham couldn't answer a call from God without his life being disrupted. At this advanced age, wasn't he a little weary of having his life disrupted? Wouldn't he want just to be left alone?

God called. Abraham answered and a few moments later, he must have wished that he hadn't.

The Lord was requiring the unthinkable of Abraham: "Take your son... whom you love... and offer him there as a burnt offering." What loving parent would do such a thing? And what loving God would request such a thing?

The text reports that Abraham "rose early the next morning, saddled his donkey," and set out on his unthinkable journey. The immediacy of Abraham's obedience — "early the next morning" — seems to be characteristic of him. In Genesis 12, the Lord requires Abram to pull up his roots and move to an unknown destination, and one verse later we read: "So Abram went, as the Lord had told him" (12:4). No evidence of a hesitation or delay (cf. Lot and his wife in Genesis 19:16 and 19:26, respectively). Later, Peter, Andrew, James, and John will respond to the Lord's call with comparable quickness: no hesitation; they just dropped their nets and followed him. Abraham followed God's command — his unthinkable command — first thing the next morning.

How painful is this journey for this old man? A father and son should relish walks and trips together, but this poor father betrays his young son's love and trust by inviting him on this particular journey. Does little Isaac make innocuous, childish conversation, while Abraham silently carries the weight of a breaking heart within? And how much more painful when the innocuous conversation becomes a pointed question! "Where is the lamb for a burnt offering?" the innocent asked.

Abraham is losing two of the most precious things in his life. Shortly, he will forfeit his beloved son. Already he must have felt that he had lost his beloved God, for this God who requires the murder of his own gift cannot have seemed to Abraham like the God he had known and served before.

In the midst of it all, Abraham demonstrated an unblinking faith. "God himself will provide a lamb," Abraham confidently declared, even as his heart must have been breaking. Abraham was right. God did indeed provide a sacrifice. For Abraham, for Isaac, for you, and for me: God did provide.

Romans 6:12-23

We human beings seem to have a love-hate relationship with our bodies. We feed them, we rest them, we do all that we can to get them fixed when they are broken or diseased, and sometimes we cater to them at the expense of more important things.

On the other hand, we find we often resent both the limitations and the needs of our bodies. Our blemished and feeble flesh weighs us down. The spirit is willing, but the flesh — the poor, stupid flesh — gets in the way of what we might otherwise be and do.

As Christians, we are challenged to achieve and maintain a healthy balance in relation to our bodies. Our superficial culture is preoccupied with the body, exalting its appearance and its appetites above all else, as though your physique were the most important part of you. On the other hand, the spiritual focus of some folks' faith has historically led them to disregard, neglect, or mistreat their bodies as a temporary and disposable nuisance.

Paul's attitude toward the body is a study all its own. He identifies it as a temple (1 Corinthians 6:19), finds in it a meaningful illustration of the church (1 Corinthians 12:12-27), and affirms its resurrection (1 Corinthians 15:35-53). On the other hand, he is realistic about its relative importance (1 Timothy 4:8), as well as its fallenness (Romans 7:21-24). He knows that it is natural for us to love and care for our bodies (Ephesians 5:28-30), yet he warns about living to satisfy them (Galatians 5:16-21).

In this particular passage, Paul's attitude toward the body is a theologically pragmatic one: Your body is going to belong to someone and serve someone, so make sure that it belongs to and serves the Lord.

In our culture, we are so emphatic about personal freedom that we do not take easily to Paul's paradigm, for he assumes our slavery. We are not without a choice when it comes to our master, mind you, but that we will have a master — we will be enslaved to one thing or another — that is a given for Paul.

Paul's use of the term "members" in this exhortation to be "slaves to righteousness" rather than "slaves to impurity" is reminiscent of an earlier use of the same Greek word. When Jesus offers his pragmatic, though startling, teaching about cutting off a hand that causes one to sin or gouging out an eye that leads to sin, he employs the same term: "It is better for you to lose one of your members than for your whole body to be thrown into hell" (Matthew 5:29).

Paul concludes this passage with a famous and cherished affirmation: "The wages of sin is death, but the free gift of God is eternal life." It is a simple and picturesque statement of grace. "Wages" refers to what one earns, which stands in contrast to a "free gift" that is quite independent of what has been earned or deserved. My "wages" are what I have coming to me; in that respect, my wages are a reflection on me. A "free gift," by contrast, is not necessarily something I have coming and it is, therefore, much more of a reflection on the giver than the recipient.

Death is what I have coming to me. Death is what I deserve, for that is what I have earned by my sin. Eternal life, however, is quite separate from what I have earned or deserved; it is a gift, and as such it is a reflection on the grace, kindness, and generosity of the giver.

While this familiar statement is best employed as an explanation of what it means to be saved by grace, it might also be used to refute a rather common heresy afloat in our day. Many folks in our churches have borrowed from the surrounding culture a presumption about an afterlife. How we imagine that afterlife may differ from one person, one belief system to the next, but the basic assumption is quite common. And many Christians, in turn, have come to equate the generic notion of an "afterlife" with the biblical concept of "eternal life." If some afterlife awaits everyone, then it must be different from the eternal life Paul references here as "a free gift of God... in Christ Jesus our Lord" (v. 23).

Matthew 10:40-42

Jesus describes a two-way flow. The one way is conventional wisdom. The other way, however, is dramatic and new.

Everyone in the original audience for this brief message understood this first principle. When a potentate sends an emissary, that emissary is a representative of the one who sent him. He carries his king's message and the reception he receives is a plain demonstration of respect or disrespect for the one who sent him.

Several places in scripture we see this principle at work. King David, for example, takes as a personal affront the mistreatment that his emissaries receive at the hands of the Ammonites (see 2 Samuel 10). Likewise, the owner of the vineyard in Jesus' parable (Luke 20:9-18) reasons that his servants, messengers, and ultimately his son will be respected by the tenants to whom they are sent. And when they are mistreated, the owner responds with unmitigated vengeance.

When Jesus makes a correlation, therefore, between the sender and the ones sent, he is working within the framework of conventional wisdom. Everyone understood the vicarious role of ambassadors, emissaries, messengers, and such.

Of course, the implications for Jesus' missionaries — that is, literally, those who are sent out by him — are quite heady. We represent Jesus, who sent us, as well as the Father, who sent him. Our demeanor and our message, therefore, are nothing less than a reflection on God. And people's receptiveness and responsiveness to us is a form of receiving and responding to God.

The surprising part of Jesus' teaching is that the current also flows in the other direction. Just as the individual's response to a servant of God is, by extension, a response to God, so too, the reward that belongs to God's servant is also extended to the one who receives God's servant. That is quite remarkable.

Mistreat the king's messenger and your punishment is to be expected. But receive the king's messenger and, consequently, receive the king's messenger's reward? That is a dramatic twist and an uncommon generosity.

Set aside for the moment any speculation about what the rewards actually are. Let us think only in terms of human responsibilities and human compensation. The newspaper compensates the young men and women who deliver their papers to homes and neighborhoods. But will that newspaper pay the same wage to anyone and everyone who is hospitable or receptive to those paper carriers? It's an extraordinary proposition.

Yet, at the same time, it is also quite consistent.

In Matthew 20:1-16, Jesus tells a story of another vineyard owner. This one is hiring laborers to harvest his vineyard, and he hires them in several shifts throughout the day. When the work and the day have come to an end, he gathers all the workers to pay them, and he surprises them all by paying the same wage across the board. The ones who worked all day are rightly paid for a full day's work, and the ones who worked only the last and smallest stretch were also paid for a full day's work. The first group thinks the policy is unfair. Of course, the owner is not being less than fair to them; it's just that he is being more than fair to the others.

Such is the characteristic extravagance of God. This Lord doesn't just miraculously feed 5,000; he provides too much — there are leftovers! This Lord does not just faithfully lead his people through the wilderness; he also keeps their sandals good as new. This Lord does not just set his people free from slavery; he makes sure that they are laden with gifts and gold as they go. And this Lord does not just provide a good catch for the fisherman; he provides a catch that exceeds the boat's capacity.

It stands to reason, then, that he would be unreasonably generous. He doesn't just have rewards in mind and in store for his servants; he has rewards in mind and in store for those who treat his servants well.

Application

"Here I am." That's what Abraham says. He says it three different times in the course of the one episode from Genesis 22. It is Abraham's response when God spoke to him at the beginning. It is his response when his son, Isaac, raised a question. And it is Abraham's response when the Lord called out to stop him from sacrificing Isaac.

"Here I am." That is Abraham's response.

"Here I am" is what you say when you are willing to be found, willing to be interrupted, willing to be used. It is what Abraham says in this passage. It is what Isaiah said in his call scene (Isaiah 6:8). And it is, of course, the essence of what Jonah did not say to God, as he hightailed it to Tarshish "to flee... from the presence of the Lord" (Jonah 1:3).

The Hebrew behind Abraham and Isaiah's "here I am" is interesting. Literally, it is the interjection "behold" with the first-person, singular suffix tacked on the end.

The Lord asks, "Whom shall we send?" and Isaiah says, "Behold me!" The Lord calls to Abraham and he responds, "Behold me!"

It's a risky business to answer God's call. But the eager, obedient ones wave their arms and cry out, "Over here! Pick me!"

An Alternative Application

Genesis 22:1-14. "What kind of God is this?" I imagine a sermon comprised of two scenes, carefully drawn for the congregation with words. The first scene shows a father and a son, each one bearing a heavy load up a hill.

The son's heavy load is wood. Some of us know well how heavy a load of wood can by to carry for any distance. It's the wood for a sacrifice that they'll make at the top of the hill.

The father is not carrying a physical load like the son. The heaviness is found in his heart. It's a heaviness of dread, of grief, of love. It's the heaviness of a breaking heart. Many of us know how heavy that load can be to carry.

It turns out, of course, that the father and the son are carrying the same load: that is, the weight of the son's sacrifice. The son innocently carries the instrument of it; the father carries the knowledge of it. And who has imposed this terrible load on this father and son? The Lord God. He required Abraham to sacrifice his son, his only son, whom he loved.

Now comes the wondering aloud. What kind of God would ask such a thing? What kind of God promises a son, gives a son, and then takes that son away? What kind of God would break an old man's heart and needlessly steal a young man's life? And so on.

The second picture is a parallel. The Son carrying a load of wood up a hill, wood for a sacrifice, wood on which he himself will be sacrificed. The Father, meanwhile, bears the unspeakably heavy heart. But it is his doing. "It was the will of the Lord to crush him with pain... make his life an offering for sin" (Isaiah 53:10).

Then comes the wondering aloud. What kind of God would do such a thing? What kind of a God would offer his own son on behalf of sinners? What kind of God would bear an offense twice: the offense of human disobedience, and then the penalty for that offense too? "What wondrous love is this, O my soul, O my soul, what wondrous love is this, O my soul! What wondrous love is this that caused the Lord of bliss to bear the dreadful curse for my soul, for my soul, to bear the dreadful curse for my soul" ("What Wondrous Love Is This").

Proper 9
Pentecost 4
Ordinary Time 14
Genesis 24:34-38, 42-49, 58-67
Romans 7:15-25a
Matthew 11:16-19, 25-30
by William Shepherd

Covenant: the next generation

One of the central concepts of the Bible is the "covenant." A covenant is a contract-plus. Like a contract, a covenant is an agreement between two parties to behave in a certain way: I'll do this, and you will do that. Unlike a contract, however, the two parties are not necessarily equals; a king, for example, could enter into a covenant with his people, while in no way ceding power to the people. Further, you can't just walk away from a covenant. A contract, sure — just pay the penalties for breaking the agreement and you're off the hook. Covenants, however, frequently invoke curses on those who do not live up to their obligations. Certainly the biblical covenants of God with Abraham, for example, or the Sinai tradition embrace these ideas: they are covenants of unequals that cannot lightly be set aside.

Our lections this morning show that "covenant" was not an idea but a living tradition — not a concept that demanded assent, but a way of being that demanded a creative response to the vagaries of life. Thus, we find Rebekah re-enacting the part of Abraham as the covenant passes from one generation to the next. We find Paul explaining how the Sinai covenant can't do everything that has been claimed for it, and we find Matthew painting the covenant with Moses in the new colors of Jesus.

Genesis 24:34-38, 42-49, 58-67

While our lection takes snippets from the longest chapter in the book of Genesis, the preacher would do well to become familiar with the entirety of this leisurely told narrative that gives pride of place to speeches rather than events, using detailed repetition to push the story along and give it suspense and resolution. The story centers on the literary convention of the betrothal at the well (cf. Jacob and Rachel, 29:1-14; Moses and Zipporah, Exodus 2:15-22; there are parallels, also, in Ugaritic literature and John 4). The hints of humor along the way (for example, the avaricious portrait of Laban, or Rachel's hustling to water the camels) might provide a little spice for the sermon; sometimes the best sermon stories are those of scripture itself.

The story is in transition between Abraham and Isaac (cf. the similar transition scenes of Jacob in chapters 34-35 and Joseph in 47-50). The transition is spurred by three major events. The first spur is the death of Isaac's mother, Sarah, which leaves the position of clan matriarch open for Rebekah, whom Isaac will love as a mother-substitute (24:67). The second spur is the virtual deathbed scene of Abraham in 24:1-9. While Abraham doesn't actually die until 25:7-11, these are his last words in the story (and the original version may have recounted his death after v. 9 or v. 61). Clearly, Abraham has ceded the leadership of the clan to Isaac, who now owns all of his possessions (v. 36) and is called "my master" by Abraham's servant (v. 65). Isaac is on his own in the promised land, with no mother, no father, and no family, until Rebekah comes to complete the covenant with children. The third spur of the transition is their marriage.

The marriage of Isaac and Rebekah rounds out the Abraham cycle, recapping the promise and fulfillment of the covenant. The language of the original covenant (12:1-7) is reiterated in 24:1-9. The marriage will fulfill God's promise to Abraham of many descendents (vv. 7, 27, 50-51, 60). The theme of "blessing" moves from Abraham (v. 1) through his servant (v. 31) to the family of Laban and Rebekah herself (v. 60).

Another theme through the story is the prosperity brought to Abraham by God because of the covenant (vv. 21, 40, 42, 56). Further echoes of covenant language are found in the references to loyalty and fidelity (vv. 12, 14, 27, 49). It is actually Rebekah, not Isaac, who follows Abraham's footsteps in response to God's call, moving from the tent of her mother (v. 28) in Haran in upper Mesopotamia to that of her mother-in-law in the Negeb (v. 67). Rebekah's words of assent to the marriage (literally "I will walk," v. 58) echo the original command to Abraham to "walk" to the promised land (21:1), and the blessing her family uses to send her off echoes the blessing God once gave to Abraham (22:17).

The theme of divine providence is at the forefront of the story. The hidden hand of God is invoked again and again (vv. 7, 21, 27, 40, 42, 48, 56). The guiding angel that leads Abraham's servant to the well can be discerned only by faith (v. 40), and yet the human actors are also important in moving the drama along. The unnamed servant shows his wisdom and worthiness as he speaks, subtly persuading Rebekah's family by embellishing Abraham's prosperity (vv. 1, 35), omitting unseemly details in Abraham's original charge (such as his refusal to let Isaac himself travel to Haran, vv. 6, 38-40), and emphasizing Rebekah's desirable pedigree in the retelling of their meeting (vv. 46-47). Laban, too, propels the story along, taking one look at the jewelry given to his sister and saying, "Yes" (thus the narrator hints at his future role in the story as the greedy exploiter of Jacob).

But it is Rebekah herself who becomes the prominent character in the story. She is tested and proven true; her personal qualities of helpfulness, kindness, hospitality, care for animals, as well as her beauty and availability, commend her as a proper wife for Isaac, who indeed responds to her with love (vv. 14-21, 67). A hint of their future relationship is found not only in her forthrightness (v. 58), but also her Herculean camel-watering (the anachronistic reference to camels is quite amusing, since Rebekah would have really have had to hustle to bring enough water for ten thirsty camels in her little jug). In their marriage, Isaac would prove to be the most passive of patriarchs, while Rebekah would be pro-active in ensuring the family's future.

Romans 7:15-25a

Paul picks up the discussion of the covenant tradition at another major turning point: the giving of the law (or *Torah*) to Moses. What place did Torah have under the new covenant that Jesus initiated in his body and blood? Paul's contention is that Torah definitely has an important place in Christianity — just not the place many people thought.

Paul's thought here is perhaps obscured rather than elucidated by his use of an exemplary first-person style. Many commentators have tried to interpret this passage autobiographically, but the truth is that Paul was not talking so much about his personal experience as he was making an argument. Indeed, personally, Paul clearly saw himself as a good Jew, a commendable Pharisee who was able to observe Torah (cf. Acts 22:3; Galatians 1:14; Philippians 3:6). His use of "I" is not meant to be taken as personal history, but as part of the form of the particular kind of argument he makes in Romans. The "I" makes the argument less abstract, as if it were acted out on a stage rather than merely spoken about.

This section of the argument actually stretches back to 6:1, where Paul begins to take up objections to his theology and deal with them one by one. By chapter 7, he has arrived at the issue of Torah, which for Paul the Pharisee was perfect and holy (7:12). However, as a Christian, Paul had a problem with Torah, for it taught that Jesus not only lived as a sinner, but also died accursed (Galatians 3:13). How could such a man be Messiah? Obviously, the place of Torah in the life of a Christian must be re-thought. The problem was not with Torah *per se*, but with the claims made for it, in particular, that Torah could bring life. However, Jesus' death and resurrection prove this to be a false conclusion, because only God can bring life and God chose to bring it to one who was cursed by Torah. In fact, wasn't the notion of the ability of human beings to give themselves life by doing the works of Torah another instance of human arrogance before the God who is the sole source of all being? Torah has been over-sold as healing medicine; it can do no such thing. What then is the purpose of Torah? It is merely the diagnostician, not the healer.

Paul asserts in chapter 7 that Torah is not the problem; the problem is sin. Note that he almost always uses the word in the singular; we are not talking about peccadilloes but a power, almost personified, which is capable of reign and dominion (6:14). Sin is in fact a power that enslaves those it is able to trick and capture (6:15-23). The locus of this slavery is the "flesh," i.e., the human being in its natural condition (7:14), and the symptom of this slavery is death (5:21; 6:23). And though sin is powerful, it is dormant apart from Torah, which enables it to be known (4:15; 5:13; 7:8). The problem is that while Torah can reveal sin, it can do nothing to prevent it, and nothing to liberate those who have been enslaved by its power (which includes, Paul believes, all of us, 6:23). The commandments tell us what sin is, but they cannot heal us of it (7:7-13).

The only solution to the power of sin is to die to sin (7:1-6). Even if you keep Torah faithfully, as Paul did, life will not spring from Torah, simply because it is not to be found there. Life comes through Jesus Christ. Specifically, new life is established through death and resurrection, first and foremost Jesus' own death and resurrection (which prove that he is indeed the source of life) and secondly through the believer's own death and resurrection, the identification with Christ in baptism (6:1-14). Our sharing in his death and resurrection leaves us dead to sin and alive to God. It is our relationship with Jesus, not our relationship with Torah, that gives us life.

Our lection details the enslaving power of sin. Sin creates a divided self, as our minds move one way while our flesh (again, to be understood as the entirety of the human being) moves another. The mind acknowledges the goodness of Torah, but the flesh is enslaved by sin, and the power of sin is greater than intellectual assent to Torah (vv. 16, 19, 22, 25). Thus sin becomes a "law" or "rule" of its own, because it cannot be sidestepped (v. 21); it becomes "another law," an alternate Torah that exploits the weakness of human flesh to do its own dirty work (v. 23). So we end up living in a "body of death" (v. 24), which can be freed only by death and resurrection (v. 25). Paul sums it up: "So then, with my mind I am a slave to the law of God, but with my flesh I am a slave to the law of sin" (v. 25). Human beings are divided between the goodness we can recognize, and the evil we cannot help but act out. Paul's solution to human two-sidedness is elaborated in the next chapter: through God's gift of Christ, we have access to the power of the Spirit, which outranks that of sin, resulting in our liberation from slavery (8:1-4).

Matthew 11:16-19, 25-30

Matthew's take on the relation of Jesus and Torah is even more radical than that of Paul, because Matthew sees Jesus as the heir of Moses. Matthew clearly draws on biblical language about Moses. The declaration about the Father and the Son (11:27) is modeled on Exodus 33:12-13. The saying on rest (v. 29) reflects Exodus 33:14. Moses is called "meek" in Numbers 12:2 (cf. v. 29). But Matthew doesn't stop with painting Jesus to look like Moses. Matthew actually presents Jesus as the personification of Torah itself.

A section on John the Baptist has led the narrative into issues of reward and punishment. Matthew 11:1-19 covers John the Baptist, who, while identified as Elijah (v. 14), is clearly subordinated to Jesus (vv. 1-6). Although John the Baptist is marked as a turning point in salvation history (v. 1), he has been rejected by his contemporaries (vv. 16-19).

Both Jesus and John have actually been rejected by "this generation" (v. 16; cf. 12:38-45; 16:4; 17:17; 23:29-36; 24:34), an allusion to the wilderness generation (Deuteronomy 1:35; 32:5, 20). The issue is "eating and drinking," which is Bible-speak for "excess" (cf. Isaiah 22:13; Matthew 24:38, 49; 1 Corinthians 15:32). The mini-parable about flutes and funerals has two possible interpretations: most commentators see it as an allegory about John the ascetic and Jesus the party-goer, both of whom are dismissed as extremists by "this generation." An alternate and perhaps more likely view is that both groups of children stand for "this generation," who like ill-behaved children pout when neither John nor Jesus play the game they wanted. Ironically, these children claim to represent "wisdom," yet, only the children who accept Jesus will receive true wisdom (v. 25). The "little ones" are Jesus' disciples (cf. 18:6; 21:6, 9), who correspond to the "gentle and humble" Jesus himself (v. 29).

The end of the section about the Baptist contains the key to understanding what comes next: "Yet wisdom is vindicated by her deeds" (v. 19). Clearly, Matthew has Jesus equating himself with a personified Wisdom (cf. Proverbs 8-9; Wisdom 7-8); her deeds are his deeds (cf. 11:2-6). When you consider that Wisdom was equated with Torah (Sirach 24:43), Matthew's picture becomes quite extraordinary. Jesus is himself the *personification of Torah*. This is confirmed by a close examination of the rest of the passage. We have already noted the allusions to Moses. The language of revelation in verse 27 reflects Wisdom tradition, for only God knows Wisdom (Job 28:12-27; Sirach 1:6-9; Baruch 3:32), and vice-versa (Wisdom 9:1-18; 10:10). The saying in verse 28 is also modeled on sayings about Wisdom (cf. Sirach 24:19; 51:23, 26-27). And when Jesus speaks of his "yoke," he is using language that the rabbis reserved for Torah (vv. 29-30, cf. 23:4; Jeremiah 5:5; Acts 15:10); Torah was like the yoke used to guide and harness farm animals. Now Jesus himself offers that same yoke to those who would come to him.

Matthew thus draws Jesus as both Torah and Torah-giver, the new Moses and the substance of the teaching. Those who come to him will receive sabbath-rest, not because they will have leisure, but because they will be guided to their true purpose. The yoke of Jesus' instruction proves surprisingly light, because there is no friction: It directs us in the proper paths and distributes the weight evenly upon us. It is light and easy because it is the way of God, the way we were meant to be.

Application

There are many lenses through which to look at the Bible and many ways to perceive God's covenant. If it were not so, life would be dull indeed, and the Christian life merely a matter of repeating memorized tracts. Biblical theology does not necessarily fit together like a jigsaw puzzle and that is its glory. The multiple avenues of access ensure that the covenant remains a living tradition and not a dead and dusty regulation.

The living tradition of the scripture is clearly demonstrated in these very disparate lections. In Genesis, we view God's action on a historical scale, part of a larger narrative that looks forward even as it glances back. Paul allows access to God's point of view on a different level, not through narrative but through argument; he sees the covenant as pointing toward Jesus. Finally, Matthew gives us a completely new take on the covenant, as seen from the perspective of Jesus looking back. What he sees is indeed a living tradition, for it lives in him.

Alternative Applications
1) Genesis 24:34-38, 42-49, 58-67. Divine guidance is not incompatible with human freedom as far as the Bible is concerned. There is no doubt in Abraham's mind that God has led him thus far and would lead his servant to the next step: "The Lord, the God of heaven, who took me from my father's house and from the land of my birth, and who spoke to me and swore to me, 'To your offspring I will give this land,' he will send his angel before you, and you shall take a wife for my son from there" (24:7). The servant himself depends on divine guidance: "Then I bowed my head and worshiped the Lord, and blessed the Lord, the God of my master Abraham, who had led me by the right way to obtain the daughter of my master's kinsman for his son" (v. 48). Even the avaricious Laban can see that "the thing comes from the Lord" (v. 50). Yet, at each step along the way, human beings act under their own volition. Foremost among them is Rebekah herself, whose simple reply to the question says volumes about her: "I will walk" (v. 58).

2) Matthew 11:16-19, 25-30. Normally we expect Matthew to tell us homey little stories about sowers and seed, farmers and tax collectors. Here, however, he speaks with a voice we would be more likely to expect from the gospel of John: "All things have been handed over to me by my Father; and no one knows the Son except the Father, and no one knows the Father except the Son and anyone to whom the Son chooses to reveal him" (11:27). The verse is actually shared with Luke, however (cf. Luke 10:21-22). It is a reminder that linear schemes in history are usually inadequate; it would be a mistake to say that Matthew reflects a less-developed Christology than John. It would be more accurate to say that Matthew developed a different Christology for a different place and time; for the Jewish Christians who populated Matthew's church, it was important to understand the precise relationship between Jesus and Torah. Matthew showed them that there was nothing incompatible in their messianism, for Torah was properly understood only through Jesus, who was not only the true interpreter of Torah, but also the fulfillment and personification of it.

Proper 10
Pentecost 5
Ordinary Time 15
Genesis 25:19-34
Romans 8:1-11
Matthew 13:1-9, 18-23
by Wayne Brouwer

Living in unsafe neighborhoods

We vacationed recently on Hilton Head Island. It was a way to spend time with our daughter who is a student at the Savannah College of Art and Design nearby. One of the things that impressed us about Hilton Head Island is that if you don't live there, you don't know where things are or how to get to them. Traffic is tightly controlled, especially in residential areas. Most of the housing developments are "gated communities," with access only by way of a single entrance barred by security devices to all but the privileged owners, their guests, and those who serve their needs.

Gated communities, according to a recent article in *The Wall Street Journal*, are valued partly for their safety and partly for the status they connote. People can choose to live in neighborhoods where others are like them in social class, economic hierarchy, or ethnic background. Gated communities make us feel like we are in control by isolating us from "bad elements," however we might define that term.

Life, however, cannot be lived in a bubble. The movie, *Bubble Boy* some years ago poked fun at the insanity of trying to remain isolated from the world. Even those who live in medical quarantine because of compromised immune systems would declare such arrangements to be unusual at best and traumatic at worst, and the Bible concurs. We live in mixed neighborhoods, not merely socially, economically, or ethnically. We live in spiritually mixed neighborhoods, where good and evil mix in a murky gray haze, and every virtue is carried by people of vice.

It is not only around us, but within us. We are our own worst enemies, at times. We are caught in struggles of the soul that are merely the reflection of our divided hearts. We live in unsafe neighborhoods, and it is often because we have to live with ourselves.

The lectionary passages for today talk about unsafe neighborhoods. Isaac and Rebekah's twin boys made the world unsafe for each other, beginning a fierce battle before birth. Paul writes of spiritual struggles in unsafe neighborhoods that look a lot like our own restless hearts, and Jesus tells a good old farming story that hinges on fields being far less homogeneous in character than one might suspect when driving through America's vast plains states. No matter where we live, it is an unsafe neighborhood spiritually, and it calls us to remember where we find refuge.

Genesis 25:19-34

Genesis was composed out of several literary threads and with a couple of clearly obvious structural plans. The "Creation Story plus Ten Genealogies" (2:4—4:26; 5:1—6:8; 6:9—9:29; 10:1—11:9; 11:10-26; 11:27—25:11; 25:12-18; 25:19—35:29; 36:1—37:1; 37:2—50:26) is the most obvious. In this organizational structure each "genealogy" (Hebrew *toldoth*) carries a morally weighted value. At the beginning of the Jacob story the genealogy identifies two things: first, that Jacob will be the winner and will carry the continuity of the positive moral story initiated through Abraham. Second, this story will have negative dimensions that make it far less than a pristine hero story with unalloyed virtues. Jacob will be the winner of the special covenant relationship with God, the main character of Genesis. But Jacob will carry this reward in spite of himself and not because of it.

A second major literary structure guiding the development of the book of Genesis is that of major story cycles. Four major story cycles emerge, each giving a different "big picture" view: the story of Origins (chs. 1-11), the story of Abraham (chs. 12-25), the story of Jacob (chs. 26-36), and the story of Joseph (chs. 37-50). Included within each of these are many other little stories like the one we read today. But it is important to read each little story within the context of the larger story cycle in which it is found.

When these two literary structures are overlaid, some helpful interpretive ideas emerge for today's reading. First, since the nation of Israel lingering at Mount Sinai is searching for its identity, it must encounter the origins of its name. "Israel" emerges from "Jacob," and each of those names deepens its identity. Here, in brief summary, the character of "Jacob" is revealed. Jacob is a fighter (v. 22). Jacob is discontent (v. 23). Jacob makes his own way in life (v. 26). Jacob is quiet but shrewd (v. 27). Jacob is a "Mama's Boy" (v. 28). Jacob is cunning (v. 31). Jacob has no family loyalty (v. 33).

Regardless of how favored the nation of Israel might have felt in its recent release from Egypt and slavery, this story of origins must have caused them to pause. They were born of tainted stock. Deception and scrappiness was bred in their bones. They made every neighborhood in which they lived unsafe.

Second, the reality of God's special plan for Jacob's life was revealed already at birth. Despite opposition, despite second-son disfavored status, despite scrawniness, despite machismo, Jacob would carry the baton in the relay race of God's special blessing. So it is with Israel. Size is no guarantee of success (cf. Israel versus Egypt) but neither is scrappiness — Jacob does not get the prize on his own strength, no matter how cunning he may be. It is God's prize to offer and God's prize to give.

Third, carrying the baton in the relay race of the Genesis covenant story does not guarantee peace and delight. It actually brings Jacob into constant struggle, as evinced in his birthing battle with his brother. Jacob will not become "Israel" — one who wrestles with God — until Jacob has lived a long time on a very unsafe battlefield.

Romans 8:1-11

The Heidelberg Catechism, written by Oleveanus and Ursinus in the capital city of the Palatinate of the Holy Roman Empire in 1563, is a great resource for understanding Paul's letter to the Romans. Oleveanus and Ursinus used the structure of Paul's argument to shape their summary of the Christian faith. In large outline, each document is developed in three sections that may be headed sin (Romans 1-3), salvation (Romans 4-11), and service (Romans 12-16). The plight of humanity (Romans 1-3) calls out the redemptive care of God (Romans 4-11), which creates a new consciousness of what it means to be in God's family (Romans 12-16). In Romans 8, Paul brings great confidence to those he took through the dicey spiritual struggles of chapters 6-7. Now confidence rings out, not because we move out of an unsafe neighborhood into a safe one, but because the power of Jesus is greater than the power of evil that resides within us.

Paul ties spiritual growth and victory directly to Good Friday and Easter in the bookends of this passage (8:1-3, 10-11). A recent award-winning song plays out this theme in a rather down-to-earth way. In Tim McGraw's musical tale, "Live Like You Were Dying," the singer meets a man who was told that he has cancer and that his lifespan has just shrunk to less than a calendar. Instead of self-pity, the victim relates that he found a new lease on life. He began to live each day as if it were his last and only do the important things. The narrator in the song carries that thought ahead into a new place, telling what the important things of life really might be:

> The dying man first tells of some things he had just done that freedom from the fear of dying made possible, like sky diving, mountain climbing, and bull riding. But then he adds some more meaningful things he had done as well: "and I loved deeper and I spoke sweeter and I gave forgiveness I'd been denying." He goes on to say that he was finally being the husband, friend, and son that he should have been all along. He concludes:

*Well, I finally read the good book
and I took a good, long, hard look
at what I'd do if I could do it all again....*

Paul speaks of the battles of the spirit in each of us and the choices we have to make to live in ways that matter. We all live in unsafe neighborhoods (such as the battlegrounds of our own inner turmoil and the passions pulling at our hearts), but we still need to choose *how* we will live in those neighborhoods.

Matthew 13:1-9, 18-23

Jesus' parable of the four soils is sometimes misinterpreted. It is not about the sower or the seed; it is about the soils. A little understanding of first-century Palestinian farming technique is needed to understand what Jesus is saying. In many places of the world, a seedbed is prepared at the end of the previous harvest. Most farmland across the plains of North America are plowed or harrowed in the fall to break up the topsoil in anticipation of spring planting. Not so in ancient Palestine. Once the grain crops were harvested in late spring, the fields were left untouched. A series of events then unfolded that would make Jesus' words much more understandable.

First would come the gleaners. These were the poor people in the neighborhood who would gather stray stalks to reap leftover grain for their meal tables. Next, the cattle would be turned loose into the fields to sniff through the stubble and find kernels that had fallen. The cattle would be a kind of final harvest cleanup crew. Then, however, the fields would become a sort of regional public park where people could wander where they wanted. All people lived in villages or towns and the farmland they owned or worked ringed those villages and towns. During the growing season most were occupied with working the land, but once the harvest had been taken in, trading season began. The traders could travel between villages more directly if they created paths through the fields. Hence, hard-surfaced walkways emerged, and through the summer months weeds would grow wherever they could find moisture.

When winter arrived, and planting time came, the farmers would scope out the boundary lines between fields, scatter their seed, and then plow under all that was on the surface — regular soil, hard-packed path, and weeds.

Now the meaning of Jesus' tale becomes more clear. The sower scatters seed indiscriminately, even among weeds (which are about to be plowed under), even over rocks (which are not visible because of the stubble), and even on the path (because it is only a temporary traffic pattern). The sower is not wasting good seed but merely following the best farming customs of the region. When the seed has been scattered, the farmer will come through with a wooden plow harnessed to an ox, and drag open the soils to accept the seed while rooting up the weeds and the path.

All seeds have equal chance to survive, except that not all soils will nurture that life well. Some parts of the field have given themselves over to weeds that are not easily killed with a single pass of the plow. There the weeds, with their deep roots, will survive the farmer's tilling and will have a head start on the tiny roots that finally germinate from the recent seeding. Some parts of the field will have been packed too hard by the travelers' footprints, and the seeds will sprout quickly, but their fragile roots will not find the moisture of the earth because of a hardpan barrier lingering from the path. Some parts of the field will hide rocks that kill young plants even after they have gotten a promising start.

The meaning, said Jesus, is clear. We all live in unsafe neighborhoods like any farmer's field in Palestine. But, while the seeds and the soils connect in unalterable ways under the farmer's care, the spiritual seed given by God lands on hearts that can change their complexion. We can be our own worst enemies and stiffen up like the path, bouncing the seed elsewhere. We can be hypocritical and deceptive, like the rocky soil that promises more than it delivers. We can lack nerve or will, and twist with prevailing winds of culture, much as the soil still full of old weed roots was. We are the soil and we can choose to change. We control the relative safety of our own inner spiritual neighborhoods.

Application
A great application for all three of these passages is the story of the 1,000 marbles. It serves to remind each of us that we live in unsafe neighborhoods, but that we can choose to make them come alive with spiritual significance if we keep in step with the Covenant (Genesis 25), the Spirit (Romans 8), or the Sower (Matthew 13).

This is purported to be a conversation over a ham radio set one Saturday morning:

> "Well, Tom, it sure sounds like you're busy with your job. I'm sure they pay you well, but it's a shame you have to be away from home and your family so much. Hard to believe a young fellow should have to work sixty or seventy hours a week to make ends meet. Too bad you missed your daughter's dance recital." He continued, "Let me tell you something Tom, something that has helped me keep a good perspective on my own priorities."
>
> And that's when he began to explain his theory of "1,000 marbles." "You see, I sat down one day and did a little arithmetic. The average person lives about 75 years. I know, some live more and some less, but on average, folks live about 75 years.
>
> "Now then, I multiplied 75 times 52 and I came up with 3,900, which is the number of Saturdays that the average person has in his/her entire lifetime. Now, stick with me, Tom, I'm getting to the important part.
>
> "It took me until I was 55 years old to think about all this in any detail," he went on, "and by that time I had lived through over 2,800 Saturdays. I got to thinking that if I lived to be 75, I only had about 1,000 of them left to enjoy.
>
> "So, I went to a toy store and bought every single marble they had. I ended up having to visit three toy stores to roundup 1,000 marbles. I took them home and put them inside a large, clear plastic container right here in the shack next to my gear. Every Saturday since then, I have taken one marble out and thrown it away.
>
> "I found that by watching the marbles diminish, I focused more on the really important things in life. There is nothing like watching your time here on this earth run out to help you get your priorities straight.
>
> "Now, let me tell you one last thing before I sign-off with you and take my lovely wife out for breakfast. This morning, I took the very last marble out of the container. I figure if I make it until next Saturday, then I have been given a little extra time. And the one thing we can all use is a little more time.
>
> "It was nice to meet you, Tom. I hope you spend more time with your family, and I hope to meet you again."

The application naturally follows. In fact, it could be well illustrated by a jar of marbles and the encouragement for others to go out and buy some.

An Alternative Application
Matthew 13:1-9, 18-23. Jesus' parable of the soils begs to be treated by itself. Jesus gives a fine story and also interprets it for us. A fitting message could tease out four images, each related to one of the kinds of soils that felt the seed land on it.

The first image could be that of "historical faith" that shapes the life of one who grew up in the church, but only adopted it as a cultural expression and not as a personal belief. The second image could be that of "experiential faith" that is professed in the hyper-charged atmosphere of an emotional appeal (retreat or conference setting), but lost quickly when other cares and concerns set in. The third image could be that of "foxhole faith" that is declared in times of great crisis as a sort of bargaining chip with God but sounds hollow and silly after the crisis passes. The fourth image could be that of "saving faith" that is as natural to a person's character as crops are to good farmland and consistently yields a winning spiritual harvest.

Proper 11
Pentecost 6
Ordinary Time 16
Genesis 28:10-19a
Romans 8:12-25
Matthew 13:24-30, 36-43
by David Kalas

That's the way

Walter Cronkite, in his long tenure as the anchor of the *CBS Evening News*, was known for his closing line, "And that's the way it was...." It is a reporter's refrain. By and large, it's the best that a reporter can do — or any other human being, for that matter. We are not able to change the way it was; we can only recognize and recount the way it was.

God can do more, however. He is not limited to, or by, the way it was. So we find — in his word, and in his very character — that he is more a God of "that's the way it will be."

From the very beginning, we see this part of God's nature. The "let there be" pattern in his creation of the universe reveals a God who states in advance how he envisions it and how he wants it to be. That part of his nature is not thwarted or nullified by sin, for even in the very wake of Adam and Eve's disobedience, God is again making statements about how it's going to be — statements that consist of both warnings and promises.

It is central to the ministry and message of the Old Testament prophets that the Lord God calls his shots — that he says in advance how it's going to be. Likewise all along the way in both Old and New Testament stories, God assures and promises his people how it's going to be (see, for example, Genesis 15:13-21; Exodus 3:19-22; 2 Samuel 7:12-16; Jeremiah 33:6-9; Mark 8:31).

Our selected passages for this week affirm a God of "the way that it's going to be." The Lord shares his plans with Jacob — plans that are specific to Jacob and extend beyond the borders of Jacob's own existence. Paul reassures the Christians in Rome that how it is in the present is not the way it's "about to be," and Jesus tells a story of a farmer whose field illustrates both how it is and how it's going to be.

Genesis 28:10-19a

Jacob is running away from home. He is somewhat more dignified than the average runaway, for he has the imprimatur of his parents. But he, his family, and we all know that the ostensible errand to find a wife is a thinly veiled conspiracy to get Jacob away from his older brother's vengeful wrath.

Jacob, with the encouragement and aid of his mother, has just duped and cheated the other half of his family — Isaac and Esau — and he has become *persona non grata* at home. One wonders, as Jacob sets out alone toward a foreign land, whether he questions the worth of his trickery. He seems to be more pragmatic than principled — an "ends justify the means" kind of guy — and so his barely disguised exile may have made him wonder if his father's blessing was worth enough to endure his brother's curse.

His first overnight stop embodies his isolation. He is on the road between kinfolk and kinfolk, but he has to stop and stay where he knows no one and no one knows him. He is not staying with friends and family. He is not invited in by hospitable strangers. Instead, he is alone and exposed, sleeping outdoors with his head on a rock.

It seems to be a most undesirable place: a metaphor and a reminder of where his choices have brought him. But then, in his sleep, the place is transformed by a dream.

The dream, it appears, was an encounter with God. It may be a tacit indictment of Jacob that God was perhaps unable to communicate with him while he was awake. Still, it is a testimony to God's versatility the variety of ways that he speaks to people.

God initially identifies himself to Jacob by means of other human beings. He is "the God of Abraham your father and the God of Isaac." This method of introduction is not unique to this episode with Jacob. God uses the same technique with Isaac (Genesis 26:24) and with Moses (Exodus 3:6). It seems here to be God's way of introducing himself to someone who doesn't know him. It's as though God is saying, "You don't know me yet, Jacob, but we have some friends in common. Allow me to introduce myself...."

Jacob is ever the wheeler-dealer, as evidenced by his eventual response after awakening (28:20-22). Perhaps God spoke to him in a dream because then Jacob wouldn't talk back — at least not right away. God begins by laying out his plan and his promise for Jacob. We find that the arrangement God proposes to Jacob is substantially the same as what he had articulated earlier to Abraham.

That may be surprising, at first blush. Abraham seems to be a man of so much more character, understanding, and faith than Jacob. One would think God's plans for Abraham and for Jacob would be as different as the men themselves were. But this is the God who pays all the workers the same wage at the end of the day (see Matthew 20:8-15). He is not less than fair with anyone, but he is more than generous with many. Certainly he was with Jacob. And with me too.

Finally, as I read this episode from Jacob's life, I am reminded of a certain kind of guided prayer and meditation technique that I have seen used throughout the years in some churches, as well as in some curriculum resources. The individuals are invited to close their eyes and relax, while imagining themselves in a beautiful and peaceful place. Then, having set the pretty stage, they are invited to picture Jesus coming to meet and talk with them there.

I hesitate to criticize the technique, for I'm sure it has generated some meaningful experiences for numbers of people. What troubles me, however, is the fundamental biblical truth that is undermined by the process. Namely, scripture does not bear witness to a God who meets us in imaginary places. Quite the contrary, scripture reveals a God who meets us in very real — and often not-so-lovely — places.

This is the God who meets Hagar in the midst of her distress, who meets Gideon where he is hiding from the menacing Midianites and who meets Saul on his bloodthirsty way to Damascus. This is the God who meets a manipulative, deceitful scoundrel of a younger brother as he runs away from home, sleeping with his head on a rock in the middle of nowhere. It is a great testimony to his grace — and a great comfort to us in our ordinariness and our distress — that God meets us in very real places.

Romans 8:12-25

If your preaching style is verse-by-verse exposition, then this is a lection to salivate over. It is a rich vein for miners, a mother lode. As is so often the case in Paul's epistles, and particularly with some great passages in this letter to the Romans, the preacher is invited here to put on the lighted helmet, grab the pickax, and start working.

Because the space afforded here is too small for detailed exposition, I would encourage the exploration of any one of three major themes suggested by the passage. First, consideration of to whom or to what we belong. Second, an examination of the relationship between spirit and flesh. And, third, a comparison of our present condition and our future hope.

For my congregation and me, I would want to explore this central question: to whom do we belong? Paul notes that "you did not receive a spirit of slavery" but rather "a spirit of adoption." Both images — slavery and adoption — are relationship images. They speak of belonging to someone else, and that truth deserves our attention, our proclamation, and our application.

That we human beings will belong to something or someone is rather a truism in the New Testament. Our American congregations may be slow to embrace the truth, for we cut our teeth on independence and freedom, and so we reckon that we belong to no one. Still, an honest look at the underbelly of most human existence reveals that there is no such thing as human sovereignty. Voluntarily or involuntarily, human beings will always belong to something or someone else. Some poor souls belong to an addiction that becomes an oppressive tyrant in their lives. Many sell themselves to their appetites or ambitions. We choose to belong to friends and family. Universally, we belong to our mortality in the sense that we do not have ultimate say-so over our bodies and earthly existence.

If we can accept the fact that we will — and do — belong to someone or something, we can turn then to ask what sort of a thing it is that owns us. What is the nature of this belonging?

When it is sin that owns us, when it is the flesh to which we belong, then Paul contends that the relationship is slavery. We "belong" in the most undesirable sense. It is involuntary (though not without complicity, of course), it is exploitive, and it is destructive.

God wants to set us free from that slavery, but when we are set free, it is not some vague, vacuous emancipation. We are not set free to be on our own but to return to our rightful owner. Paul reckons this new relationship as adoption, and so we "belong" now in the most desirable and lovely sense. We are chosen, embraced, and loved.

What you are depends upon to what you belong. Where once we were sin's property, we have now become God's children. If property, then used and discarded. But if children, then heirs.

A second major theme that evolves in this passage is the relationship between spirit and flesh. That relationship is first introduced in scripture when God breathes the breath (or spirit) of life into the molded clay that became a man. From that day, human beings have lived as two-part compositions: breath and clay, spirit and flesh.

In this passage, "spirit" is used in three different ways. First, it seems that there is the spirit that is within us — "our spirit" in verse 16. Second, there is the Spirit of God, which helps us "put to death the deeds of the body" (v. 13), leads us (v. 14), and "bears witness with our spirits" (v. 16). Then there seems to be the spirits that we were and were not given — "a spirit of slavery" or "a spirit of adoption." Except for the reference to "a spirit of slavery," the use of the word "spirit" in this passage carries a positive connotation and it stands in contrast and opposition to "the flesh" and "the body."

Finally, the third theme that emerges in this passage is the juxtaposition of present condition with future hope. The present is characterized by sufferings, while the future hope is of glory. In the present, there is bondage and futility; in the future, there is freedom and glory. In the present, groaning and longing; in the future, redemption.

The notable difference between the present condition and the future hope, meanwhile, is that one is visible and the other is not. In our day, we say, "seeing is believing." Paul counters, "not seeing is hoping."

Matthew 13:24-30, 36-43

Here is an exercise that I have used with classes and congregations along the way. Begin by asking the folks how many parables they think Jesus told. (The average guess will probably be in the neighborhood of a dozen to twenty.) Then ask them to list the first five parables they can think of. (Individually, I have found that most church folks have to take several minutes to come up with five.) Finally, ask folks what is the central theme of nearly half of Jesus' parables. (Common guesses will be "love" and "forgiveness.")

The parables that are prominent and memorable for people, it seems, are the ones that are more stories than similes, and more relational than merely descriptive. People remember the good Samaritan, the prodigal son, and the lost sheep. It would be a rare congregation member indeed, however, for whom the parable in this week's gospel lection would spring to mind.

Scholars' conclusions vary slightly as to how many different parables Jesus told, for "parable" is a genre without precise definition. Between the three synoptic gospels, though, it's generally agreed that we have something in the neighborhood of forty parables. Of those forty, eleven are introduced explicitly as explanations of the kingdom (for example, "the kingdom of heaven is like" or "the kingdom of heaven will be like"). Two other parables, in their contexts, are implicitly explanations of the kingdom, and in the case of still three others, while the kingdom is not explicitly mentioned in the parable, it is referenced in the subsequent interpretation or application. In short, nearly half of Jesus' parables are parables about the kingdom.

The preponderance of that theme would surprise most of the people in our pews. Yet, while this particular parable is not likely to be prominent in their minds and hearts, it is typical of a large plurality of Jesus' parables: it is a description of the kingdom.

If asked to describe the kingdom of heaven, I suspect that most American Christians would speak about gates of pearl and streets of gold. The seeds-and-weeds material found in Matthew 13, therefore, offers a healthy corrective. Before the kingdom is sparkling and other-worldly, it is first of all very earthy. That is, quite deliberately, the nature of the kingdom. It is not merely a destination to which we go when we leave this world; it is a divinely planted and growing reality within this world.

This particular parable is highly allegorical and it is one of a handful that is accompanied by an explanation from Jesus himself. We do not need to decipher the symbolism in this parable because that task has been done for us. It seems appropriate that Jesus should offer an explanation of this parable, for the parable itself is an explanation.

In the picture of a field, Jesus explains the present and future condition of the world and of the kingdom. The Son of Man is the rightful owner of the field but not the only influence there. The image of an "enemy" personifies the evil and personalizes the attack. It is not accident or misfortune; it is deliberate, malevolent, and diabolical. An us-them paradigm is implicit in the picture, and yet there is no developed theme of active animosity between "the children of the kingdom" and "the children of the evil one." Rather, the parable illustrates the wisdom of God's delay in bringing his kingdom to final fulfillment. To make a dramatic, immediate move to eliminate the enemy's influence would be premature and destructive; instead, the farmer will let everything grow and develop until the time is ripe.

Jesus' followers, then and now, walk away from this parable with an understanding of why things are the way they are, an insight into the God who neither abandons his compromised field nor rashly purges it, and a picture of the harvest that is to come. "For the Lord our God shall come, and shall take the harvest home; from the field shall in that day all offenses purge away, giving angels charge at last in the fire the tares to cast; but the fruitful ears to store in the garner evermore" (Henry Alford, "Come, Ye Thankful People, Come," United Methodist Hymnal, No. 694).

Application

A woman was in my office the other day seeking some advice for her marriage. After seven years, it is not what either she or her husband had expected or hoped, and they were both disappointed and unhappy. As she enumerated the problems they were having, she had the sound of someone in despair. "If I just knew that it would be better someday," she said. "It wouldn't have to be tomorrow, or even this year, but if I just knew that it would be better someday, then I could go on."

Paul wrote that "the whole creation has been groaning." He was speaking, of course, about the larger matter of salvation history. But you and I know as pastors that, one person, one family, one situation at a time, creation continues to groan, longing for good reason to hope, but tending toward despair.

Central to our gospel message is the truth that our God has a plan. He has a plan for us as individuals and beyond us as individuals. He is not limited to, or by, present circumstances. His plan is ultimately good and victorious, and he is patient, deliberate, and strategic about bringing it to fruition.

For Jacob on the run, for suffering Christians in Rome, for a mixed and compromised field, and for a groaning creation: It may not be better tomorrow or even this year, but we go on with the assurance that it will be better — all better! — someday.

An Alternative Application
Genesis 28:10-19a. Jacob's epiphany at Bethel is expressed in two marvelous phrases: "Surely the Lord is in this place," and "I did not know it!"

The ancients had perhaps a somewhat more localized view of gods than we do today. "Omnipresent" is one of our core assumptions about the deity. We are not so likely to be startled by the thought of God being in any particular place — or every particular place, for that matter. But while we are not surprised by the thought of God in this place or that, we may well be surprised by the experience of God in this place or that.

Our human expectations of God will always be underestimations, and he continues to defy our expectations. There are those places where we expect to find him — places where we anticipate having a sense of his presence, having meaningful contact with him — and then we are blessed by the surprising encounters we have with him elsewhere, in unexpected places.

Jacob's experience is not an isolated incident. Moses was surprised to discover the Lord in the burning bush (Exodus 3:1-5), and Gideon was surprised to be discovered by the Lord in his hiding place (Judges 6:11-16). Hagar (16:7-14), Joshua (Joshua 5:13-15), Balaam (Numbers 22:21-31), Samuel (1 Samuel 3:1-10), Elijah (1 Kings 19:11-13), Cleopas and his companion (Luke 24:13-35), and Saul (Acts 9:1-6) were all met by surprise or in surprising places.

Jacob's experience is not an isolated incident: it is characteristic of our God, who is not limited by likelihoods or expectations. Instead, he meets us where we are — wherever that happens to be.

Proper 12
Pentecost 7
Ordinary Time 17
Genesis 29:15-28
Romans 8:26-39
Matthew 13:31-33, 44-52
by William Shepherd

"X" marks the spot

God works in hidden ways.

It's an oft-heard saying, perhaps a cliché, but there is a reason certain phrases become clichés. The Bible gives plenty of evidence of a God who works in hidden ways.

Our lections this morning give us three such pieces of evidence. In Jacob, God was at work to fulfill the promise given to Abraham that he would become a great nation — even in the trickery that kept Jacob in virtual serfdom for fourteen years. In the letter to the Romans, Paul speaks of God's work in a Spirit we cannot see, who speaks words we cannot hear, and the gospel of Matthew pictures the kingdom of heaven growing through hidden processes and surprising turns. The promise of all three lessons is that at the end of the road, everything will turn out for the good.

Just because it's a cliché doesn't mean it's not true.

Genesis 29:15-28

Jacob's personality as a devious trickster has already been well established (see Genesis 27:1-29). Laban now reenters the story, his personality only hinted at in chapter 24. But the man who took one look at the gifts lavished on his sister and said, "Yes, Isaac, please marry her" will prove to be as avaricious as we might expect and just as devious as Jacob. Even though he called him kin (literally, "brother," 29:15), Laban was willing to let Jacob work without pay for a month (his talk of Jacob's "service" is ironic in light of the prophecies that Jacob would be the one served, cf. 25:33; 27:29, 37, 40). In response to Jacob's precise, legalistic statement of what he wanted ("seven years," "younger daughter," "Rachel," 29:18), Laban's non-committal commitment will easily bend to his purpose (v. 19) — in a deal that is already much to Laban's favor!

Jacob has more than met his match in Laban and the punishment fits his own crime like a wool glove (cf. 27:16). Jacob ironically protests being "deceived," using the same word that describes his own treatment of his father (29:25; cf. 27:35). Jacob fumbled in the darkness, just as Isaac, in blindness. He again runs afoul of cultural standards regarding the rights of the firstborn and those of the younger (29:26; cf. 27:16, 32, 36). Jacob's treachery against Esau rebounds right back at him, and he finds himself trapped in servitude to his own dark alter ego, his father-in-law.

However, both trickeries work together for God's purpose. Laban's deceit plays into the hands of God, as did Jacob's. We are moving in covenant time here, toward the fulfillment of the promise given to Abraham of many descendents. The "reward" promised to Abraham (15:10) will turn out to be the progeny that issues from fourteen years of Jacob's "wages" (the same Hebrew root is used in 29:15). While the chapter represents another "betrothal by the well" scene (cf. 24:15-33; Exodus 2:15-22), the significant formal feature is found on a larger level of the narrative movement. The entire episode between Jacob and Laban (29:1—32:2) puts the birth of eleven children (all but Benjamin) at its apex, contrasting Jacob's arrival in Haran (29:1-14) and his return to Canaan (31:1-54) with his struggles with Laban over marriage

(29:15-30) and work (30:25-43), with the birth of the sons at the very center of the story (29:31—30:24). The point of Jacob's exile in Haran is thus shown to be the fulfillment of the promise that Abraham would spawn a great nation. Even the maids played a part (29:24, 29; cf. 30:5-13).

Laban's motivation is explained by his concern with public honor and shame. Blood may be thicker than water, but honor and shame trump both. It was actually more honorable in Laban's eyes to deceive Jacob than to violate the custom that specified the firstborn daughter must be the first to marry (v. 26). The wedding and marriage customs are assumed rather than explained including the requirement of the "bride price" (v. 18; cf. 24:53; 34:12; on the "servant's marriage" cf. Joshua 15:16-17; 1 Samuel 17:25; 18:17, 25), the lavish wedding feast (v. 22) and the weeklong nuptial period (v. 27), the veiled bride (implied in vv. 23-25), and the overwhelming importance of birth order in marriagability (v. 26). Marriage was strictly a property transfer, the woman practically bartered, but this was not necessarily incompatible with a love match (vv. 18, 20), so much so that the narrator can skip over the seven years of waiting, saying only that "they seemed to him but a few days because of the love he had for her" (v. 20).

Rachel's status as the favored wife will prove to be a factor in the ongoing story (cf. vv. 30-31). It's not clear whether Leah's eyes were defective or the narrator is damning her with faint praise, but in favor of the "defect" interpretation it can be said that she apparently had no other suitors in seven years! (Some ancient interpreters held that she had ruined her eyes with crying because her prospects were so bad, and she might even get stuck with hairy old Esau.) By contrast, Rachel was "graceful and beautiful" (v. 17), like Sarah (12:11) and Rebekah (24:16) before her. The contrast between Jacob's two wives-to-be is embedded even in their names: Leah means "wild cow," while Rachel means "ewe" (and the tribes descended from Leah were known as cattlemen, those from Rachel, shepherds).

The improbability factor has ranked high among interpreters, both ancient and modern. Where, for example, was Rachel all night? Was she herself tricked by Laban, as some rabbis maintained? Or was she part of the conspiracy, helping Leah to convince Jacob of her identity in order to preserve her sister from public shame? Some rabbis held that Leah herself played an active role in deceiving Jacob, answering to the name of "Rachel" when he called that night, and later justifying it on the basis that he had pulled the same trick on his own father. The truth is that neither woman would have had anything to say in the matter, which was strictly a business deal between the men.

But how could Jacob have let himself be deceived so? Wasn't it obvious that the woman was not Rachel? Some ancient interpreters blamed Jacob's wedding-night credulity on the veil, the darkness, or too much party wine. Others speculated that Jacob realized he was duped at once but waited until the morning to confront Laban. None of these explanations would have interested the original storyteller, who was content to leave the reader room to fill in the blanks. The important point was that God was at work despite all the shenanigans, fulfilling the promise even in the midst of the deception.

Fortunately for Jacob, he didn't have to wait another seven years (his sexual impatience is implied in v. 21, "Give me my wife that I may go in to her, for my time is completed"). He was able to take Rachel as his wife after the first wedding week concluded (v. 28); he had to *work* another seven years, but only *wait* a week. Laban may have been deceitful, but he wasn't totally sadistic.

Romans 8:26-39

In Romans 8, Paul continues his argument about the nature of justification by faith. Christian life is life in the Spirit, which gives us the power to overcome sin and live a new life of grace. Paul pulls out plenty of rhetorical tricks, including word-chain form (cf. 5:3-5), the citation of scripture (8:36, cf. Psalm 44:22), a hardship catalog (v. 35), the use of contrasting pairs (vv. 38-39), and rhetorical questions (vv. 31-39). The final section has the feeling of a legal closing argument, as Paul takes one last stab at persuading a sympathetic jury of Roman Christians.

This section of the argument focuses on the role of the Holy Spirit as intercessor. This is a practical as well as a theological concern; Paul's focus is correctly understood when we realize that "those who love God" (v. 28) is in the emphatic, first position in the sentence. The Spirit is given to help those who love God. The Spirit prays for us (v. 25), in fact "sighs" or "groans" for us (v. 26); this may refer back to the "groans" of the created order cited in verses 22-23, or the cry of "Abba, Father" in 8:15, or it may simply refer to *glossolalia*. Whatever form the Spirit's prayers take, their purpose is straightforward: to help us in our weakness (v. 26). The Spirit has a definite advantage here in light of its intimacy with God. The Spirit can bypass normal human abilities of communication, since "God, who searches the heart, knows what is the mind of the Spirit." Thus the Spirit's intercessions for us are "according to the will of God" (v. 27).

Paul also speaks of the role of Jesus as a model for the Christian life in the Spirit. Those who love God have a God-given purpose: to be conformed to the image of his Son (v. 29). Paul recaps the Adam/Christ contrast introduced at 1:23; Jesus is the new Adam who restores humanity to the image of God (cf. 1 Corinthians 15:49; 2 Corinthians 4:4; Philippians 3:21). Jesus Christ is literally "the firstborn among many brothers" (v. 29; cf. 8:14; Colossians 1:15; Hebrews 2:8-13). The hardships Paul lists are those that line us up in the image of Christ (vv. 35-36), a Messiah who suffered, he tells the Roman Christians, "for your sake" (v. 36).

Ultimately, God is the instigator and sustainer of this system of new life. God's saving work is the context of the oft-quoted verse 28, "all things work together for good for those who love God," which was not a *carte blanche* for material accumulation or a promise of a hassle-free life, but a promise of movement toward salvation — by "good" Paul clearly meant the good of salvation, the new life given through the Spirit on the model of Jesus. Paul traces this movement toward salvation through a series of verbs describing God's action for us: God "called" (vv. 28, 30), "foreknew," "predestined" (v. 29), "justified," and "glorified" us (v. 30). This is all one series of actions in God's time so that our future "glorification" can be spoken of in the same verb tense as our past "calling." God's faithfulness in bringing us life in his Son is the climax of God's work in history and in scripture (v. 32 echoes the Abraham story, cf. Genesis 22:16). The eloquent rhetorical climax (vv. 34-39) can preach itself as any additions from the preacher could only be anti-climactic.

Matthew 13:31-33, 44-52

Matthew's parable chapter is the third of five major blocks of teaching in the gospel. Its major theme is summed up in the parable (and interpretation) of the sower: the mystery of the acceptance and rejection of the good news.

Our lection omits a crucial transition section. Verses 34-43 change the setting of Jesus' teaching from public to private, introducing teaching for the disciples about the parable of the weeds and the final judgment (a theme which returns in vv. 47-50). Verses 44-52 continue this private teaching but constitute a single unit unified by the opening and closing mention of "treasure" and by the identical introductions of the parables. It is important to realize, therefore, that the parables of the mustard seed and yeast were delivered publicly to the crowds, according to Matthew, but the other parables are part of the private teaching, meant only for disciples.

The public teaching to the crowds pivots on the twin themes of growth and "hiddenness." The theme of growth has expanded to the point of hyperbole, as Jesus super-sizes ordinary occurrences. A mustard plant might grow quickly to ten or twelve feet, but it would never become a tree with room for birds' nests (vv. 31-32); the picture is akin to the cover of the Allman Brother's album, *Eat A Peach*, with a giant peach in a flatbed truck. Similarly, it would be a commercial baker, not an ordinary housewife, who would leaven three measures of flour (about fifty pounds), enough for 100 loaves — or one giant one! (v. 33). This tremendous growth, of course, was meant to be taken as a sign of the presence of God's kingdom.

The seed in the ground or the leaven in the bread expresses the hidden nature of the kingdom. We can't see the hyperbolic growth happening, only its results. Plus, the images are unexpected; we wouldn't normally think of God's work as a bush or a loaf, and "yeast" is usually used negatively (16:6), so Jesus' use of the image is a bit like saying "the kingdom of heaven is like a virus no antibiotic can stop." Both the kingdom and the teaching about it are unexpected.

The private teaching to the disciples sounds the themes of risk, surprise, and judgment. It is indeed a risky business to sell all that you have for one field — especially when there was no assurance that any treasure you might find there would be legally yours (v. 44; the laws on such finds were debated). Neither would a jeweler who sold his whole inventory to obtain one pearl be accused of good business practice (v. 45). Yet the value of the kingdom of heaven is worth such a risk, for it is the legacy of a lifetime, the spiritual equivalent of winning the state lottery, the Powerball, and the Publisher's Clearinghouse Sweepstakes all at once.

The kingdom is also a surprise, since no treasure map marks "X" as the spot. There were no banks with safe deposit boxes in those days, so it was common enough to bury one's goods to protect the assets — what a surprise it would be to dig a hole for your own stuff, only to find a pirate's chest! The pearl is found in the course of daily business, but it exceeds in value all the business the jeweler has ever done (as if a minor art dealer came across a Picasso in an attic). In the same way — surprise! surprise! — the kingdom of heaven is in your midst.

The final parable of the section recaps the theme of judgment (vv. 47-48). Fishing on the Sea of Galilee was done with a dragnet, weighted with rocks, tossed out of a boat or suspended between two boats. Needless to say, the net would not be picky about what was caught, so the inedible or ritually unclean seafood would have to be sorted out. Like the weeds (vv. 24-30), the bad is disposed of (it is not thrown back into the water!).

According to its conclusion, the parable chapter is intended as student/teacher training. Throughout Matthew's story, the disciples are presented as students of the Lord, who will in turn become teachers of others (28:18-20). They are to be "scribes trained for the kingdom of heaven," who are "like the master of a household who brings out of his treasure what is new and what is old" (13:52). What is old is the Mosaic tradition, which is not denigrated (cf. 5:17-20); what is new is the authoritative interpretation of it given by Jesus. That old/new teaching is to be handed on to further generations. Obedience to this tradition thus becomes a mark of community membership: to do the will of God as revealed in Jesus' teaching is to become part of his family (12:46-50).

Unlike the disciples as portrayed by Mark, Matthew's disciples understand what Jesus has to say. When he asks if they have understood his teaching; they answer, "Yes" (13:51). By the end of the story, they will finish their training by becoming witnesses of his resurrection (28:17) and will take their places in the teaching mission as scribes of the kingdom of heaven (13:52).

The training is intended for all followers of Jesus, not just an elite. Matthew designates the entire community, not just the twelve, as holders of the teaching office (18:18). Hierarchy is discouraged and the measurement for leadership in the community is service: "You are not to be called rabbi, for you have one teacher, and you are all students... Nor are you to be called instructors, for you have one instructor, the Messiah. The greatest among you will be your servant" (23:8, 10-11). Thus no one disciple, but all together, imitate Jesus in his teaching role. No one fount of wisdom that pours knowledge into the heads of the community, but a round table of scribes exercises the teaching office together. The ongoing presence of Jesus as teacher is to be found in the small community of two or three that has gathered around him, the family that does the will of God as he taught it (18:20; 12:46-50).

Application

"There's something wrong with every person who comes to this church." My friend was neither a candidate for clergy burnout intervention nor was he expressing cynicism about his congregation. He was simply reflecting on the wounds that had brought so many to his door. They came to Jesus, because only the sick need a physician.

"All things work together for good" is not a guarantee of health and wealth, but a deeper promise — one of salvation. We've seen God working this good in the story of Jacob, who forms a model for how God might redeem a dysfunctional family. We've seen it among the Romans: Why would they need the Spirit to groan for them, if there were nothing to groan about? And, we've seen it in Matthew, where the final sorting out of life must wait for the end.

In the meantime, we are called to be householders who ourselves bring good stuff out of things both old and new — scribes who, like Jesus, are well-trained for the kingdom of heaven.

An Alternative Application
Matthew 13:31-33, 44-52. "What's your pearl?" the preaching focus group asked. The student preacher stammered a bit. "What would you personally give up everything for?" the questioner persisted. "If you can't find something in your own experience that matches the gospel message, how can you possibly preach it to others?"

Over the years, I've become dubious about this assertion. I grant that some personal point of contact is necessary for effective preaching. The sermon is not a lecture; it must touch on something that is of ultimate importance to us at a personal level. An abstracted discourse on the nature of salvation is not the same as good news, and abstraction will never get our point across; it will just bore people.

That being said, I'm not sure that coming out and telling people my own pearl of great price is the proper function of the sermon. For one thing, I'm leery of sermons that tell us more about the preacher than the good news — and it may well be that any first-person revelation will distract from our message. For example, I recently told a story in a sermon about "my friend Tom"; after the service, I was asked, "Were you talking about Tom So-and-so?" (someone of whom I had never heard). It was the only substantive conversation I had with anyone about the sermon, and it left me feeling that they were so engaged with guessing games that the point passed them by.

My other concern is that talking about what one would give to obtain a pearl of great price might lead us into some deep waters. Giving up everything for one goal is not only a feature of religious conversion, it is also a feature of addiction. Do we really want to offer our own addictive behaviors, whatever they may be, as illustrations of the gospel?

In short, it may well be worth our while to consider the question, "What is my personal pearl?" Such reflection may yield insight for the sermon. It also may be much too personal to talk about.

Proper 13
Pentecost 8
Ordinary Time 18
Genesis 32:22-31
Romans 9:1-5
Matthew 14:13-21
by David Kalas

God in unexpected places

Early in the cherished 1965 movie *The Sound of Music*, we see the sisters at the abbey wondering about their whimsical novice, Maria. At the moment, no one can find her, and one of the sisters dutifully reports to the Reverend Mother that she has looked in all the usual places. "Considering that it's Maria," responds the wise, old woman, "perhaps you should look someplace unusual."

We do have a natural tendency, of course, to look in "usual" places. When we have searched high and low for something that is missing, we'll finally sigh, "I've looked everywhere and I can't find it." Clearly, of course, the latter statement belies the former, for if we had in fact looked everywhere, literally, then we would have found the item. But we so naturally limit our looking to usual places — that is, the places where we would expect to find the lost item.

Likewise when we're shopping. We go to the hardware store for power tools and the grocery store for bread, not the other way around. It's all about expectations: Where we reasonably expect to find, see, or get certain things.

That's all well and good, of course, until we begin to impose it all on God. For we limit him — perhaps even miss him — when we relegate him and his work to the usual places. He is not to be confused with the flighty and forgetful young Maria of the movie, of course. Still, considering that it's God, perhaps we should watch for him someplace unusual.

Genesis 32:22-31

We might take a moment to point out to our people the long-lasting significance of this event. After all, nearly 4,000 years later, there persists a nation on the world's map that is called "Israel." And that name traces all the way back to this moment in Genesis 32.

Even a sketchy knowledge of scripture confirms the importance of names. The name of God holds a place of mysterious prominence in the Old Testament. And in the New Testament, the name of Jesus becomes a key ingredient in our gathering, baptizing, preaching, healing, and praying.

The names of people, meanwhile, are likewise presented as a matter of symbolism and significance. The naming of Isaac, Samuel, the many sons of Jacob, Ichabod, the children of Isaiah and Hosea, and more all reflect the meaningful perspectives and testimonies of their parents. Then there are those babies whose names are not determined by the human parents, but assigned by God — John the Baptist is a notable example. Later in life, there are those individuals whose names are changed by God: Abram to Abraham, Simon to Peter, and here in our story, Jacob to Israel.

We will explore the significance of names in this passage in greater detail below. For the present, however, let us simply observe the context of Jacob's new name.

A person's name may come from his parents, but a person's eventual identity comes from how he lives. And, specifically, a person's identity and reputation are forged by how he comes through certain circumstances.

Reggie Jackson earned the nickname "Mr. October" because of his prolific play in the postseason. Ronald Reagan became known as "the great communicator" because of his capacity to speak so effectively to an audience, especially in very difficult situations. Conversely, athletes like Bill Buckner and Scott Norwood will, perhaps unfairly, always be known for their singular failures in big games.

So, here, see where Jacob gets his new name: in a wrestling match with God. And that man's new name becomes the nation's name. Their great patriarch Abraham was renamed by God, yet that good name — "father of a multitude" — is not the nation's identity. Their second patriarch, Isaac, was named "laughter" by his parents because he was the miraculous fulfillment of an improbable promise, yet his descendants are not known as the "Isaacites."

No, the people of Israel found their identity on a night when their most dubious ancestor wrestled with God. As we read their stories and their prayers — in Job, Psalms, Habakkuk, Jeremiah, and even in our selected passage from the apostle Paul this week — we see them wrestling with God, indeed.

Romans 9:1-5

This brief New Testament reading is only five verses long. But for our people to understand those five verses, we must help them step back to see those verses within their larger context. Specifically, we must take three steps back.

The first step back is to see this passage within the context of the larger epistle. The letter to the Romans is very much a letter of introduction. As such, it provides us with perhaps his most balanced statement of his understanding of the gospel — balanced since he is not writing to correct some bad behavior or errant doctrine within the congregation to which he writes.

In the preceding chapters, Paul has carefully explored the fundamental truths of sin and salvation and the pivotal roles of faith and grace in the latter. Meanwhile, interwoven with those universal themes there is the significant thread of the law. Paul's background was as a Pharisee and he must have lived most of his life with a sense of the significance of God's law in God's plan. Now in the light of the gospel, he investigates the exact relation of the law to our sin, salvation, and God's grace.

Throughout the entire discussion, of course, Paul is mindful that his audience falls into two categories. They are all Christians, but their personal histories with the law are not identical, for some are Jewish while others are Gentile. Some, therefore, were familiar with and had lived under the Old Testament law, while others had not. He repeatedly addresses the differences and similarities of those two contexts.

All of that, however, leads him to another topic, which no doubt causes him some pain. The subject of the Jews, Israel, and the law in relation to God's plan and salvation forces him to examine why the Jews had largely rejected the gospel and what would become of them.

The second step back, then, is to see this passage within the larger context yet of Paul's life and experience. One might think that with each step we take further back from the text, the more impersonal it becomes. On the contrary, it becomes more personal. This particular personal layer is summarized in verses 2 and 3 of our passage. "I have great sorrow and unceasing anguish," Paul writes. This is a dramatic statement, as the apostle searches for words to express the depth of what he feels. Indeed, each of the underlying Greek words, which we translate "unceasing anguish," appears only one other time in the New Testament. The term for "unceasing" is used by Paul in his second letter to Timothy (1:3), and the term for "anguish" is used by Paul in his first letter to Timothy (6:10). They are personal, heartfelt terms for Paul and he does not use them easily or lightly.

Another term Paul does not use lightly but uses here is "accursed." He uses it twice in his first letter to the Corinthians (12:3; 16:22) and emphatically in his angry letter to the Galatians (1:8-9). Interestingly, the only other usage in the New Testament expresses some persecutors' passionate determination to get rid of Paul (Acts 23:14).

In the end, the real issue — the personal issue — is captured in the phrase "my own people." That's the real heart of the matter for Paul. Jonah might stand indifferently, or even contemptuously, outside of Nineveh, for he is not one of them and he does not love them. Jeremiah, on the other hand, weeps over his misguided audience, for he is one of them and he does love them. Like Hosea, God's greatest ministers are those who share his heartache for the people. That is the personal context here for Paul.

Finally, the third step back is to see this passage against the much larger backdrop of God's plan and purpose. Paul recognizes that the Jews have been at the heart of God's plan — "to them belong the adoption, glory, covenants, giving of the law, the worship" in the past. He further observes that they have continued to play a central role even in the gospel: for "to them belong... the promises... and from them... comes the Messiah." And so he is persuaded that, even if the Jews have, for a time, rejected God's plan in Jesus Christ, God has not rejected them.

Matthew 14:13-21

This familiar story from the ministry of Jesus holds a distinctive place in scripture — one that our people might be surprised to discover. Apart from the resurrection itself, this feeding of the 5,000 is the only miracle of Jesus that is recorded in all four of the gospels. Matthew, Mark, and Luke each record and reference quite a number of Jesus' miracles. John is somewhat more selective and deliberate about the miracles he reports. But when the four gospels are set side-by-side, we discover that this is the only miracle of Jesus that all four of the evangelists included.

While this story is naturally associated with a very large crowd, that is not where it begins. On the contrary, the scene begins with Jesus seeking "a deserted place by himself." We in the ministry may well be encouraged to see that Jesus felt this need. And we may be challenged by the fact that he took steps to meet that need; yet still did not abandon the needs of the people.

The crowd, it seems, was relentless. Small wonder. Jesus was not only a riveting teacher; he was a powerful miracle worker and healer whose reputation had begun to spread far and wide. If a clinic opened in your state that boasted a 100% cure rate for its cancer patients, can you imagine how that facility would be flooded with individuals and families craving hope and needing healing? Well here was a man who had, apparently, cured every demoniac, leper, cripple, and paralytic that had come to him. So, inevitably, they kept coming to him. By the thousands they came. Even when he sought some solitude, he was pursued and greeted by the persistent and needy crowds.

That Jesus "had compassion for them" is noteworthy. The fallen and selfish instinct in his circumstance would be to feel sorry for himself. Instead, he felt sorry for them. I will know that my conversion has made significant strides when the latter replaces the former in me.

After what appears to have been a long day healing the sick, the disciples observe that the crowd has another need: food. The disciples' concern for the needs of the people, however, is conspicuously different from Jesus' concern for them. For while Jesus had gone into the crowd to meet their needs, the disciples suggested that he "send the crowds away" so that they might meet their own needs.

This is not the only time the disciples try to shoo away people that Jesus ultimately blessed. There is the infamous episode with the children (Mark 10:13-14), as well as the persistent Canaanite woman (Matthew 15:23). Similarly, there were folks, who themselves sought Jesus' attention and tried to keep others away from him (as in Mark 10:47-48).

Jesus' statement that "they need not go away" is profoundly beautiful. Given the immediate personal context that he had wanted to be alone, and given the severely limited resources available, his statement reflects his mercy and his power. Then his next statement was, at least initially, a puzzling one: "You give them something to eat."

I can imagine the disciples looking at one another in bewilderment. What is Jesus thinking? Say, Thomas, did you bring along some groceries none of us knew about? How much do we have in the treasury, Judas?

The disciples report their limitations to Jesus: "We have nothing here but five loaves and two fish." They mean it to be the proof that they can't do anything to meet the need. It becomes, however, the proof that Jesus can meet needs way out of proportion to the resources available.

"Bring them here to me," Jesus says, and that instruction would serve well as the caption beneath this scene, as well as so many others. Of the children, sick, and weary, Jesus says, "Bring them here to me." Of our sins and our needs; of our hearts and our resources; of our talents and our limitations; again and again, this is his gracious invitation, and this is our best policy: to bring it all to him.

And in the end, leftovers! What a testimony to the power and prodigality of our God. He does not just meet the enormous need; he oversubscribes.

Application

I have been troubled to find, in several church settings and resources through the years, an imagination-based approach to prayer. "Imagine yourselves in a quiet, peaceful, lovely place," begin the instructions. After we have mentally ensconced ourselves in some make-believe Eden, then we are invited to meet Jesus and talk to him there.

I'm sure that approach serves some need. I'm equally sure, however, that it misses the point. Ours is not a God who needs to be consigned to imaginary, happy places. A great, recurring truth of scripture is how he meets us wherever we are.

So it was with Jacob in our Old Testament lection. The great patriarch was not sitting crossed-legged on the floor imagining happy places and thinking peaceful thoughts. Neither was he privy to some glorious sanctuary or lovely chapel. No, he was anxious and alone, sleepless in the open air of a fretful night. He was haunted by a troubled past that was coming back to meet him. He was caught between an alienated father-in-law to the north and a bitter brother to the south. And whom should he meet there? The hands-on, face-to-face God who would bless and redeem him.

This was not placid Jesus in a picturesque garden of undisturbed beauty. This was on-the-ground, in-the-dirt wrestling — a sweaty struggle that lasted until dawn. It was God in an unexpected place.

So, too, in the gospel lection. Where do you go to find food? Certainly not that desolate place, the disciples observed. Yet the Lord provided for the multitude there, plus conspicuous leftovers after all were fed and satisfied. Jesus' followers figured the crowds should "go into the villages and buy food for themselves," but God fed them in that unexpected place.

Perhaps that was the crux of the problem for the Jews, whose rejection of Christ Paul laments in our selected epistle. Perhaps they had some usual place where they expected God's work, kingdom, and Messiah to be. But it wasn't a manger, it wasn't Nazareth, and it certainly wasn't the cross. That, above all, is God in an unexpected place.

Alternative Applications
1) Genesis 32:22-31. "What's in a name?" Names are a prominent part of our Old Testament lection. And given the larger symbolic and real importance of names throughout scripture, perhaps we might devote this Sunday's sermon to the role that names play in this story.

First, the anonymous wrestler asks Jacob his name. The last time we saw Jacob trying to get a blessing from someone, you remember, he did it under an assumed name. "I am Esau your firstborn," he lied to his father (Genesis 27:19). But now, in this encounter with divinity, he is not able to pull a stunt as he had done with blind Isaac. He is asked to tell his name, and for Jacob that moment of truth amounts to a confession. To tell his name was to admit not just who he was but what he was: a heel-grabber, a cheat, a usurper.

Then, graciously, the supernatural wrestler changes Jacob's name. God finds him as Jacob but does not leave him as Jacob. That's good news for all of us. Instead, the humiliating name and identity are exchanged for a grand and noble one, and the man who had been known for his manipulative and selfish dealings with men will henceforth be known for his encounter with God.

Next, Jacob asks his opponent to tell him his name. The mysterious visitor declines, asking, "Why is it that you ask my name?" The moment reminds us of the later encounter that Samson's parents had with an angel. They also inquired about his name, and "the angel of the Lord said to him, 'Why do you ask my name? It is too wonderful' " (Judges 13:18). In both instances, the human beings inquire about their visitors' names, and in both cases the response comes back, "Why do you ask?" The angel of the Lord in the Judges episode offers an additional explanation that may apply in Jacob's situation, as well.

Finally, Jacob gives a name to the place where his encounter had occurred. "Peniel," he calls it, which means "face of God." This is testimony to God's providence and grace. The more miles we travel with God, the more spots in our lives that are named for him — his presence and his work at critical junctures. To the outsider, the shores of Jabbok might not seem like much to write home about, but to Jacob they became a sacred place: a place touched by God and named for him.

2) Matthew 14:13-21. "Pictures of plenty." The story of the feeding of the 5,000 might be told in terms to two juxtaposed scenes.

In the first scene, the disciples bring to Jesus the tiny supply of food available to them — five small loaves of bread and two small fish. Perhaps one disciple holds the bread, while another has the fish. The rest of the disciples, meanwhile, stand empty-handed and clueless. This bag lunch in the face of a hungry multitude is the equivalent of the disciples pulling their pockets inside out to show that they have nothing but lint.

Then comes the second scene. The disciples are back before Jesus, presenting food to him again. This time, however, there are no empty hands. Rather, each disciple is using both his hands to hold a basket — a basket brimming with leftover pieces of bread and servings of fish. Twelve baskets in all and each one containing more food than they had at the start. In the background, the folks in the crowd lean back in their places, their stomachs all satisfied, their bodies all nourished.

This is the prodigal God, who created more stars than we can see, more species than we can catalog, and more plant life than we can discover. This is the God whose freed slaves are loaded down with their oppressors' gold and silver, whose fire survivors don't even smell like smoke, and whose house has many mansions. This is the one who "is able to accomplish abundantly far more than all we can ask or imagine" (Ephesians 3:20), who rewards with "a good measure, pressed down, shaken together, running over, will be put into your lap" (Luke 6:38), and who comes "that they may have life, and have it abundantly" (John 10:10).

We should preach the two scenes, therefore, for together they tell us a lot about him.

Proper 14
Pentecost 9
Ordinary Time 19
Genesis 37:1-4, 12-28
Romans 10:5-15
Matthew 14:22-33
by David Kalas

Hitting out of the rough

I grew up as a football-and-basketball guy, but the girl I married came from more of a tennis-and-golf family. The only golf I had played prior to vacationing with her family was the kind of golf that features windmills, bumpers, and loops.

Never having played on a real golf course before, I found it quite intimidating. As I tried to do what I had never done before, however, I gained a new appreciation for the skill of the people who were good at it.

At first, my natural admiration was for the folks who could hit a good shot off the tee. That's where a golfer is likely to get his greatest distance, and a good tee shot can be a beautiful thing to behold. Likewise, I was very impressed by the folks who could go long and straight off the fairway.

As I played more, I came to appreciate a different element of the game. The tough shot.

In golf, water hazards, sand traps, and roughs all come with the territory. If you land in the water, of course, you have to drop a ball somewhere on land. But if you wind up in the sand or in the tall grass, then you have to try to hit out of it. That's hard to do well and I have gained great appreciation for the golfer who is able to make a good shot out of a rough spot.

In life, too, we recognize that traps and roughs come with the territory. We come to admire the folks who are able to maneuver their way through and out of those places effectively and gracefully. And a part of what we affirm from scripture is that God has proven, time and again, how good he is at making a great shot from a tough spot.

Genesis 37:1-4, 12-28

The writer of this passage chooses to single out the sons of Bilhah and Zilpah, which recalls the earlier soap opera of Rachel and Leah's great baby race (Genesis 29:31—30:24). After Leah had given birth to four of the seven children that she eventually bore to Jacob, Rachel used her servant-girl Bilhah to bear children to Jacob on Rachel's behalf. Jacob and Bilhah produced two sons: Dan and Naphtali. Leah, meanwhile, took the "two can play at that game" approach and designated her servant-girl, Zilpah, for the same arrangement. Jacob and Zilpah also produced two boys together: Gad and Asher.

Jacob's youngest sons, Joseph and Benjamin, meanwhile, came later, out of Jacob's union with Rachel, his true love. His subsequent preference for Joseph and Benjamin was apparent to all — a somewhat surprising dysfunction for Jacob to introduce into his family since he himself had been at the short end of a father's preference for one son over another.

In the end, Leah had given birth to six sons, plus a daughter. Bilhah and Zilpah each bore two sons to Jacob, and Rachel gave birth to Joseph and Benjamin.

Jacob's clear favoritism did Joseph no great favor, at least not with his brothers. They had developed an understandable antagonism toward him. That pre-existent condition was further complicated by Joseph's precocious dreams — or at least his precociousness in sharing them. Then, in our selected passage, Jacob may further damage Joseph's relation to his brothers to whatever extent he relied on Joseph as a kind of informant. No sibling likes the tattler.

In verse 18, we read that Joseph's brothers saw him from a distance. At first blush, the image is reminiscent of the scene in Jesus' parable of the prodigal son, when the father sees his son "while he was still far off" (Luke 15:20). The responses in the two stories, however, are entirely different.

In the case of the prodigal son, the sight of him coming in the distance is like an answer to prayer, and the father hoists up his robe and hurries to embrace him. In the case of Joseph, however, the sight of him coming in the distance is an unwelcome and irritating prospect for his brothers. For the prodigal's father, the distance is shortened by a loving run. For Joseph's brothers, the distance is an opportunity to plot and plan.

In the end, the sons of Jacob prove to be embarrassing mascots for a certain kind of rationalizing to which we human beings are prone. When we do less evil than we would like to in a given situation, we confuse our restraint with actual goodness. I excuse myself for saying the harsh thing that I did say to this person because it was so much less than I might have said or wanted to say. An employee is self-congratulatory about the very little pilfering he does compared to what he could do. A libidinous husband thinks his pornographic habit rather noble because he isn't actually pursuing an adulterous relationship with some female coworker.

These half-brothers/full-scoundrels reason that they should not kill Joseph because he is, after all, kin. So the paragons of restraint think themselves quite reasonable and compassionate when they choose merely to sell Joseph as a slave and intimate to their father that he had been killed by an animal. Their mission to get rid of the annoying little brother is accomplished, they have not shed their brother's blood, and they make a tidy profit in the process. It's all in a good Machiavellian day's work.

Romans 10:5-15

The issue in this passage is part of a larger and common theme for Paul: the question of how we are saved and made right with God.

Earlier in this epistle, Paul deals with the subject as a central part of his explanation of his understanding of the gospel. In other letters — particularly the one to the Galatians — Paul covers the same material in the context of correcting misunderstandings and false teachings in the churches.

The controversy in the early church stemmed primarily from different understandings and assumptions concerning the role of the law and the old covenant between God and Israel. What was the continuing relevance and impact of the Old Testament law for Jews who had come to faith in Christ? And what was the relevance and impact of that law for Gentile Christians, for whom that old covenant was not a preexisting condition?

The subject rises to the surface again here in this passage because Paul has just been considering the response of his own people (Israel) to the gospel of Christ. He laments their resistance to "God's way of putting people right" (Romans 10:3 TEV), and then goes on in our passage to affirm what that way is, as well as the fact that it is for all people.

Paul's statement that "there is no distinction between Jew and Greek" is so axiomatic for us that our people may miss the import of what he is saying in its context here.

On the road I drive each day to take my daughter to school, I pass by a sign that reads, "The same God hears everyone's prayers." The statement is accompanied by both familiar and unfamiliar symbols representing an assortment of major world religions.

While the sign belongs to and promotes a local Baha'i community, it articulates a rather common paradigm in our day. And so, because we are more likely today to err on the far side of "there is no distinction," we do not operate from the same set of assumptions that would have characterized the pharisaical Judaism from which Paul came.

For Paul and the cloth from which he was cut, there was a distinction — a dramatic and divine distinction — between Jews and Greeks. We have a remnant of that distinction in our word "Gentile." It is a word that applies equally to everyone who is not Jewish. By contrast, we do not have a single word that means everyone who is not Irish, not Italian, or not Indian. But such a historical us-them paradigm has existed, on both sides, involving the Jews that a single word exists to convey "everybody else."

For the religious Jews of first-century Palestine, the distinction between Jew and Greek — or between Jew and everybody else — was one ordained by God. The Jews were, after all, God's chosen people. Furthermore, it was a distinction that they were called to observe and maintain — an obligation of purity, and we see numerous evidences of a struggle with that old, established paradigm in the accounts of the New Testament church (see Acts 10:1—11:18; Galatians 2:1-14).

Paul's constant assertion, however, is that all human beings — Jew or Greek, with the law or without it, circumcised or uncircumcised — all are put right with God the same way: by faith.

The way that Paul says people come to that saving faith has particular meaning for us as preachers. People cannot believe in, and call upon, one of whom they have not heard. They cannot hear about him unless someone proclaims him. That is where you and I come in: We are called to proclaim him.

Paul concludes this passage with a quote from the prophet Isaiah (52:7). Our congregations may be initially amused by the reference to beautiful feet. Still, deep inside, we understand the association. When we have received long-awaited good news from someone — a doctor, an employer, a spouse, or whomever — our gladness about the news does make everything beautiful. The person's face, the doctor's office, the handwriting on the envelope — whatever the source of the good news.

So it was for the people of Isaiah's day. If a messenger came with good news, the very sight of him coming over the horizon, and the very sound of his feet running along the road — it was all a thing of beauty.

That is our privilege, according to Paul. We are beautified by the news we bring and by the deep longing of the people to hear that good news.

Matthew 14:22-33

We are not privy to Jesus' thinking in this episode, but it seems clear that he was craving privacy. He dismissed the disciples and the crowds, and then we he went up a nearby mountain alone to pray. He had sent the disciples across "to the other side" of the Sea of Galilee in a boat, though it is unclear how or when he intended to rejoin them. Surely they didn't expect it to be when and where he did.

Evidently, Jesus prayed through the night by himself. The disciples, meanwhile, were encountering something of a storm out on the lake and the wind and waves conspired to make their voyage difficult. Then, in the midst of it, Jesus appeared nearby, walking to them on the water.

It is not explicit in Matthew's account what Jesus was intending to do. Was his purpose to join them in the boat? Did he intend from the start to calm the storm? Or was he merely taking the shortest route available to the other side of the lake?

Since walking on water is undoubtedly a miracle, and since there is no other evidence in the gospels of Jesus performing a miracle for his own benefit, we are safe to assume that he was coming to them on the water for the purpose of helping them. When they see him, however, the sight of what seems to be a ghost frightens them.

Jesus calls out his reassurance that they need not be afraid and that it is he, to which Peter responds with a remarkable request, "If it is you, command me to come to you on the water."

Peter can always be voted the one most likely to open his mouth. Whether it is his head-of-the-class confession about Christ (Matthew 16:15-19) or his big-mouthed misunderstanding of the Messiah's mission (21-23), whether making bold protests (John 13:4-11) or bold promises (Matthew 26:31-35), whether it is vigorously denying Christ (Luke 22:54-62) or boldly proclaiming him (see, for example, Acts 2:14ff, 3:11ff, 4:8ff), Peter is the disciple most likely on any occasion to open his mouth and say something.

So, here on this occasion, Peter is the one who speaks up.

Peter's walk-on-water episode is generally remembered as a failure since, in the end, he began to doubt, began to sink, and needed to be saved. But consider how remarkable Peter's statement and action was.

The disciples were perhaps already unnerved. They were out on the water in the middle of the night, which is a vulnerable experience and particularly in an age when nighttime was truly dark, without all of the artificial light that mitigates the experience of darkness for us today. In addition to the darkness, there was the wind. It was apparently a severe wind, which suggests rough waters, as well as great difficulty in trying to maneuver their boat to their destination. On top of all that, they must have been exhausted.

If the earlier episode of Jesus with the disciples on a boat in a storm (see Matthew 8:23-27) is any indication, a nighttime boat trip could have been an opportunity for rest. Surely these men needed a night's sleep, but instead they found themselves struggling against the weather out on the water in the middle of the night.

The stage is set: darkness, strong winds, rough water, tired men. Now enter the apparition, the unidentified walking object.

The disciples see a figure coming toward them on the water. Who wouldn't be frightened by that? Perhaps we blame the disciples for other occasions where their faith is little, where their understanding comes up short, where they are unnecessarily worried or afraid — but who can blame them for this?

It is in the middle of that scene that Peter gets out of the boat. The boat, we must recall, was the one place of relative safety in the midst of a storm. The boat is what you are eager to preserve, and where you are eager to stay, but Peter was volunteering to get out of that boat — if it meant going to Jesus.

Application

At the far end of Joseph's story, Joseph helps his brothers (and us) to see the provident hand of God in all of the circumstances of his life (Genesis 50:20). At the end of the particular episode that is our Old Testament lection, however, can we imagine how Joseph must have felt? How betrayed and abandoned, by God and family alike? How frightened, as a boy being taken away from home, forever, to an unknown fate in a foreign land? Unthinkable.

When Joseph awakened that morning, he was comfortable and secure at home. He was loved and cherished by his father and he lived with a sense of divine destiny. When he went to sleep that night, however, he was merchandise in the hands of foreigners. His own brothers had created this catastrophe and his father would never know about it. There was nothing to be done — he could not be rescued; he would not return. His life had changed completely, desperately, in one day.

How far away God's providence and help must have seemed — as far away as Joseph was from home — as far away as slavery in Egypt was from those dreams he had had.

Later still, Joseph would be imprisoned. How far is a prison from Pharaoh's chariot? How far are the inmates' chains from Pharaoh's own ring?

Such is the nature of God's providence and power that he can work in and through such circumstances. The best and most important shot that a great golfer may make during a tournament, after all, may be a shot out of a rough or a sand trap.

Time and again in scripture, we see God making great shots from rough places. It is true with Joseph. It is true of the Lord who walks on water and calms storms. And it is eminently true of the one who comes out of the tomb!

Alternative Applications
1) Matthew 14:22-33. "Scared of the one who loves us." We have described above the circumstances of the disciples — exhausted, in the dark, against the wind, in rough waters. And into that already difficult circumstance comes a frightening specter.

We recognized that the disciples' frightened reaction is understandable. The irony, however, is that they are frightened by the one who comes to help them.

I wonder how often that has happened to us. Not that you and I have often seen either Jesus or a ghost walking on the water. But, rather, I wonder how often we have misunderstood his presence; how often we have been afraid of something, not realizing that it was him, or at least from him.

We gather from the angel's word to Joseph (Matthew 1:20) that he was afraid. The reassurance came to him, though, that he did not need to be afraid to go ahead and wed Mary in the present circumstances, for God was in it. Those frightening circumstances were actually from God. At some level, too, that was one of the *post facto* functions of the judgment prophets. While sitting in exile in Babylon, defeated and tempted to despair, there was reassurance to be had in the news that God was in it. Better that the judgment was from him than the alternative: that the God of Israel had been impotent to defend and protect his people against the armies and the gods of Babylon.

This is the essence of the reassurance that is captured in the familiar hymn, "How Firm A Foundation."

> *When through fiery trials thy pathways shall lie,*
> *my grace, all-sufficient, shall be thy supply;*
> *the flame shall not hurt thee; I only design*
> *thy dross to consume, and thy gold to refine.*

2) Romans 10:5-15. "A God of up close and personal." The apostle Paul takes the words of Moses (Deuteronomy 30:12-14) and gives them a distinctively Christian interpretation. Whether in its original Old Testament context or in Paul's usage of it, however, the message is a compelling and needed one in every generation.

We are always being tempted to think of God as far off — distant and unreachable. In our modern recognition of the immensity of space and the seeming insignificance of earth; in our calculation of the relative brevity and puniness of any single human life; in our sense of guilt, unworthiness, and depravity; we are prone to think that God is far off.

It is always good news to hear of God's proximity. The God who has the hairs of our head numbered; the God who invites us to think of him as loving parent, as attentive shepherd, as faithful friend; the God who put on flesh to come and get us — this God is near and accessible. He is close and he wants to be closer.

Proper 15
Pentecost 10
Ordinary Time 20
Genesis 45:1-15
Romans 11:1-2a, 29-32
Matthew 15:(10-20) 21-28
by William Shepherd

It could happen to you

There is a chain of tradition. You can trace its links across the centuries and through the pages of the Bible. The chain connects seemingly disparate events to one overarching purpose — God's purpose.

This morning our chain takes us from the original promise of God to the patriarchs through the ultimate fulfillment of the promise in Jesus Christ. The promise to Abraham is still the promise for Paul and for Matthew, but neither New Testament author limits the promise to its original situation or beneficiaries. The promise of land and descendants becomes the promise of community and eternal life. While this may seem to some to be a sharp turn for the promise, Paul and Matthew have their reasons, which they argue cogently. Their treatment of the promise indicates that it is part of a living tradition that grows and changes rather than stagnates. They look back and see something that Abraham could not have foreseen, had he the ability to look ahead. The promise given to him is not only kept, it is expanded.

The living tradition means that the gift of God cannot be restricted to those who claim blood kinship to the dysfunctional family units of the Genesis narrative. Even a dysfunctional Pharisee appealing for money to a group of Romans he had never met can now claim to be a part of the family. Even a woman driven almost to hysteria by a strange illness can join the brothers and sisters of the promise.

Genesis 45:1-15

The preacher who focuses on today's reading from Genesis faces an initial choice: Do I tell the story or summarize? Last week's lection told the story of how Joseph's brothers sold him into slavery and next week's will pick it up again with Moses. The preacher could just wade in where the brothers left off with a few words about how Joseph made good in Egypt. But the story itself, the longest sustained narrative cycle in the book of Genesis, provides some roaring good sermon material. It begins with Joseph's favored status with his father, Jacob; his naive reportage of his dreams, and his brothers' angry and violent reaction; through Joseph's rise, fall, and rise again in Egypt. Joseph finds himself first a trusted aide to Potiphar, then in prison with a baker, and finally moving via the baker to the highest position in Pharaoh's court. His administrative and prophetic ability led him to high office, for he could interpret Pharaoh's dream about seven years of famine and also do something about it. The famine brought his brothers to his door in Egypt through a series of ironic encounters that culminate in the scene we read today. Only the preacher can decide how much weight to give this material but suffice it to say that it is more than mere "background," for without it, today's story would be the climax of nothing.

This recognition scene is in fact the climax of the Joseph story; the whole plot becomes clear at once. There is a reason it looks like a theophany scene, with its elements of self-identification, the command against fear, and the announcement of God's purpose (cf. 26:24) — this is in fact God's revelation of how the story holds together. When Joseph reveals himself, he reveals God's plan.

This is a human drama with a theological point. At issue is the covenant promise to Abraham of land and descendants. The land has been given and the descendants are living on it, but how will this land support them through the seven years of famine to come? God's solution involved the convoluted means by which Joseph went to Egypt to prepare a place for his brothers. Thus this scene is not only the climax of the Joseph story, but of the entire book of Genesis, because only here, in retrospect, does God's utter faithfulness to the promise become clear. Just as God rescued Noah (Genesis 6:8-22), just as God rescued Abraham and Lot (chs. 18-19), so now God is rescuing the whole people. God can even make use of the criminal actions of the brothers, even of the official deeds of the Egyptian Pharaoh, and even of the wayward naiveté of Joseph. When Joseph articulates the goodness of God's plan for the first time, it comes as a shock of good news, for it is revealed that they all have been a part of something larger than themselves (vv. 5-8). The personal drama of the family of Jacob takes on a national significance when the brothers are called to relocate to Egypt. A "remnant" of "survivors" will preserve the people of God, no matter what (v. 7; cf. Exodus 32:9-10; 1 Kings 19:17-19; Isaiah 4:3). Thanks to God's work in Joseph, the children of Israel will be able to graze their flocks in the land of Goshen, trading seven bad years in the dust bowl of Palestine for 400 good years in the fertile Nile delta.

Yet there is still a human drama at work here. The poignant speech of Judah discloses the change the brothers have undergone since they threw Joseph into a pit and sold him to slave traders. The Hebrew text begins a major section at 44:18, titled "And he went up" (an allusion to the Abraham story, 18:23). Like Abraham, Judah argues for mercy over judgment, but rather than appeal to the innocent minority (18:23-32), Judah does not even try to prove Benjamin's innocence of the charge against him. Rather, he offers himself in his brother's stead, for the sake of his father and his family. The irony here is that Judah, who had been the prime advocate of selling Joseph into slavery, now offers himself as a slave to Joseph in order to save the youngest brother. The special attention given to Benjamin, Joseph's only full-blood brother, is thus doubly poignant (vv. 13-14).

Joseph, prompted by the self-sacrifice of Judah, is overcome with emotion for the third and decisive time (cf. 42:24; 43:30-31) and clears out the servants and court functionaries in order to make the reunion a private, family affair (vv. 1-2). His first question is about his father (v. 3), even though he has already heard the answer (43:27-28). Joseph invites them to step closer and cross the official boundaries between Egyptian vizier and Hebrew brother, while cautioning them against negative emotions (vv. 3-4); his ascription of blame is muted, and he asks them for no penitence (vv. 4-5). Even though his prophetic dream about ruling his brothers has been fulfilled (cf. 37:5-11), and even though Joseph has taken no little pride in his own advanced achievements (vv. 5, 8), he is not going to give them any reason to be dismayed. Joseph breaks the brothers' conspiracy and the family's dysfunction by offering them forgiveness and renewed purpose. Where once they had been driven by fear and envy, Joseph offers them a new way of living together, in forgiveness rather than revenge. They can now do what they previously could not do: speak to their brother "in peace" (v. 15; cf. 37:4). How great a distance has been overcome is underlined when we realize that until this scene, he has spoken to his brothers through a translator ("it is my own mouth that speaks to you," v. 12; cf. 42:23).

Romans 11:1-2a, 29-32

Paul picks up where Genesis leaves off: Is the covenant promise still viable for Israel? His answer is a resounding, "Yes!"

Chapters 9 through 11 of Romans form the climax of Paul's argument about how God has made things right for humanity in Jesus Christ. The great problem for Paul's argument is this: If Jesus is the way God has chosen to make good the promise of new life through faith, why have the Jewish people not accepted him *en masse*? If he really were the Messiah foretold by the scriptures, would not the people of the "Book" embrace him without qualification? Paul's answer is that God's very way of making human beings righteous shows God's faithfulness to the covenant promise (3:26).

God shows no partiality (2:11), and yet the good news did come first to the Jews (3:1), even though they did not necessarily flock to it (3:3; 9:6). That the offer of new life came first to the Jews is in keeping with God's revelation in history. Further, God's continued faithfulness to Israel can be shown in the very scripture that details that history. In Romans 10, Paul shows how the Hebrew scriptures (particularly Deuteronomy 30 and Isaiah 53) can be interpreted so as to show that the story of Christ is already implicit in them. Had they read their Bibles closely enough, the Jews would have recognized the suffering servant, Jesus, as their Messiah. Why didn't they?

Paul has a number of answers. A remnant did, in fact, believe, as Paul himself illustrates — he is an Israelite, descendant of Abraham, of the tribe of Benjamin, and if there is even a remnant of one, then God's promise stands (v. 2). The remnant lives by grace; for example, everyone who receives God's gift of Jesus Christ becomes a part of the remnant (v. 5). Some, it is true, were hardened against God's gift (11:7, 25; an obvious allusion to the Exodus story). However, the rejection by Israel has had a positive result, in that it led to the mission to the Gentiles (11:11-12), who are like a wild shoot grafted onto the olive tree of Israel (vv. 16-24). In the same way, the mission to the Gentiles will eventually provoke Israel to jealousy (vv. 11-15), and eventually — in the "mystery" of the last days — will lead all Israel to God (vv. 25-29).

Thus "the gifts and calling of God are irrevocable" (v. 29; cf. 9:6). God's nature is not defined by the human response to it but solely by God's own sovereign will. Despite the human, "No" (a response not by any means limited to Jews), God keeps offering a "Yes." God gives mercy in the face of disobedience, in the hope that mercy will one day trump disobedience. The very thought of God's careful dealings with fickle human beings leads Paul into a doxology to the inscrutable and unsearchable God (vv. 33-36).

Matthew 15:(10-20) 21-28

Matthew works out in narrative form the theological issue of universality, that left Paul, particularly, in such doxological ecstasy. He follows the same theological path as Paul: the good news properly came first to the Jews, and only later to the Gentiles. The issue in Matthew's Jewish-Christian community was how to continue to be faithful to Jewish tradition while living in this new situation with Gentiles. Matthew's answer was to reassert the community's faithfulness to the Mosaic tradition, but only as interpreted by Jesus. That the message came first to "the lost sheep of the house of Israel" was regarded as a simple fact of God's work in Jesus, which could not be overcome by sentimentality (v. 26). The new community formed by Jesus was the fulfillment of the promises to Israel. However, Gentile believers were welcomed into the community, as long as they recognized the premiere and prior position of the Jews, which in no way would restrict them from claiming their own place in the economy of salvation. Matthew spells this theology out in narrative fashion, by showing Jesus first in a critique of the pharisaic tradition (15:1-20), and then in an encounter with the Gentile woman (15:21-28).

The washing of hands to avoid ritual impurity was not required for all Jews or even for all Pharisees; it was definitely above-and-beyond normal religious duty. Jesus' problem was not with the scriptural law, which he thought — in Matthew's view — to be eternally valid (5:17-20). The problem was the tacking on of human traditions that could move in directions contrary to the intent of scripture. The issue was the tradition of interpretation that had grown up around scripture, not the scripture itself. Matthew subtly edits his version of the story to preserve the priority of Jewish law for his community; for example, he omits the line in Mark's version that assures his Gentile audience that "Jesus declared all foods clean" (Mark 7:19; if Jesus had indeed been that clear on this matter, there probably would have not arisen the great debates in early Christianity over the issue, cf. Acts 10:14-15; Romans 14:19-21; Galatians 2:11-14). Further, Matthew introduces a question-and-answer session with the disciples that makes it clear that Jesus is only critiquing the pharisaic tradition (15:12-15). For Matthew, Christians do not throw out the Jewish law, but try to interpret it as Jesus himself did, in order to discern the greater righteousness inherent in it (cf. 5:20).

The prime example of tradition gone awry is not the relatively trivial matter of ritual hand washing (15:1-2), but the practice of declaring material goods as *korban* or "sacred," thus shielding them from the claims of others. The *korban* rule could be used to circumvent one of the most basic commandments, to honor one's father and mother by supporting them in their old age (15:3-9).

It is no accident that the story moves directly to the issue of Jesus' response to a Gentile woman. The disciples now know that mere contact cannot make them ritually or spiritually "unclean," since uncleanness comes from within and not from without. Armed with Jesus' demand that scripture be interpreted on a deep, rather than surface level, they can open themselves up to a representative of Israel's traditional enemy, the Canaanites. (This designation, along with the archaic reference to "Sidon," helps highlight the traditional enmity between Jew and Gentile. It is a bit like calling a German a "Kraut," as if we were still fighting World War II. Note that Mark 7:26 does not use either name.) Matthew's version of the story is edited in a way that highlights the theological movement of the story: the mounting suspense of Jesus passing by, the disciples' confusion, the woman's near-hysterical persistence, and finally her prayer and worship of Jesus that lead to an eloquent statement of faith.

That being said, Matthew does hold the Canaanite woman at a certain arm's length. The story can be read as if Jesus merely "came near" to the Gentile territory rather than entering it, as the woman "came out" to meet him (vv. 21-22). Certainly, Matthew did not picture Jesus as entering a Gentile house, as Mark did (7:24). The woman is much more emotional in Matthew's version, as she shouts and implores (v. 22). Yet she is theologically correct to call Jesus both "Lord" and "Son of David."

Despite her use of the correct Jewish terminology, Jesus refuses to engage her at all, walking right past her. At best he deals with her secondhand, through the disciples (who want to get rid of her whether the daughter is healed or not, v. 23). His word about "the lost sheep of the house of Israel" is spoken to the disciples, not the woman. When he does speak to her, it is only after she throws herself to her knees and stops him in his tracks, so that he can hardly avoid running over her. Despite her posture of prayer, he speaks dismissively to her, implying that she is a dog scrounging for food (v. 26). Her reply cannot be understood as the winning zinger in a rhetorical contest (which is what it looks like in Mark) but only as a statement of true faith. She recognizes the priority of the children of Israel, and yet claims Jesus as Savior for her own child (vv. 27-28). Her words encompass the universalism that Matthew has grounded in particularism: because Jesus is the Jewish Messiah, he is the Son of God, and therefore the Savior of all nations (cf. 20:18-20). The healing of her daughter provides yet another instance of the positive results of prayed faith (15:28; cf. 7:7-11).

Application

"Fairy tales can come true, it could happen to you...."

But it's no fairy tale.

Joseph really did lead his brothers into Egypt, Paul really did gather Jews and Gentiles into one church, and both Matthew and Mark agree that Jesus really did heal the daughter of a Gentile woman.

Yet each of these instances has become paradigm as well as event, a way of looking at the larger picture of faith. They each mean more than they say.

That's good news for us, because it means that each of us can find our own place in the tradition. We can fit ourselves in the paradigms, because they are flexible enough to allow for more than one way of looking at things. Their promise can become our promise, their Savior our Savior.

It *could* happen to you.

An Alternative Application

Matthew 15:(10-20) 21-28. This text can reduce squirming preachers to artful dodgers: Surely Jesus — the friendly, happy, helpful Jesus we all know and love — did *not* tell this poor woman who came to him on behalf of a sick child that she was no better than a dog!

Well, says the dodging preacher, Jesus didn't actually say "dog" but "doggie" — isn't that cute (Jesus the Nice Guy)? Or perhaps he was testing her faith, drawing her to the limits of her endurance in order to show her what she was made of before he did was he what going to do anyway (Jesus the Faith Therapist). Or Jesus was giving his disciples a case study in how *not* to treat people from other cultures (Jesus the Multicultural Guru). Or perhaps Jesus (the Sensitive Guy, Surprised by His Own Chauvinism) couldn't quite make up his mind at first and gives us a reason to be more decisive about helping out the needy. At the bottom of the barrel for the squirming dodger: Jesus the Stand-Up Comic (he didn't *mean* it!) rolling his eyes with his disciples as they clutch at their jiggling bellies.

Albert Schweitzer closed his famous study of the historical Jesus by noting that the original questers wanted to bring Jesus straight into the modern age as Teacher and Savior, but they found it impossible. "He does not stay," Schweitzer wrote. "He passes by our time and returns to his own." (Albert Schweitzer, *The Quest of the Historical Jesus: A Critical Study of Its Progress from Reimarus to Wrede* [New York: Macmillan, 1968, p. 399].) Similarly Jesus the Nice Guy, the Faith Therapist, the Guru, the Sensitive Guy, and the Stand-Up Comic must look on in confusion as the Jesus of Matthew's gospel walks right past them and back into Matthew's community, where Gentiles really were referred to as "dogs," and no one took that as a compliment. Only in their case, "Gentile" had become a way of referring to non-Christians, not just non-Jews (cf. 5:47; 6:7, 32; 20:25). Thus to be truly "Gentile" was defined in terms of faith, which knew no ethnic borders (15:28). If the dividing line between the faithful and the dogs seems a little rough, it is perhaps because we have politely papered over the line when we should have thoughtfully observed it.

The majesty of Matthew's theological narration is that it allows us to confront the one who is our teacher without the need to subsume the text under our own prejudices. Matthew reminds us that our own personal views and pet projects are never to be equated with those of Jesus. He speaks with the voice of an outsider, saying to us, "Listen to him" (17:5). Only then can we become scribes of the kingdom of heaven.

Proper 16
Pentecost 11
Ordinary Time 21
Exodus 1:8—2:10
Romans 12:1-8
Matthew 16:13-20
by Wayne Brouwer

People you can count on

Some years ago, a major research firm conducted a survey to determine what people would be willing to do for $10 million. The results were astounding. Three percent would put their children up for adoption. Seven percent would kill a stranger. Ten percent would lie in court to set a murderer free. Sixteen percent would divorce their spouses. Twenty-three percent said they would become prostitutes for a week or longer. Most astonishing was the category at the top of the list. One fourth of all surveyed said that they would leave their families for $10 million.

Everyone has a selling price at which he or she will step over a line of conduct and allow someone else to dictate the terms of behavior. It might be $10 million or it might only be one more bottle of wine. It might be a night in the spotlight or a night in bed. In Shusaku Endo's powerful novel, *Silence*, the missionary priest Rodriguez steps over the line when torture exceeds what his soul can bear, and he desecrates an image of Jesus. We all have our selling price.

Our selling price is linked to our identity: the stronger our sense of who we are, the higher our selling price and the deeper our character. There are, however, several identities that each of us wears. The first is the identity we receive from others. We get our looks and temperament from our parents. We garner our tastes and styles from our culture. There is even something mystical about us that we receive as a gift from God, unique to our personalities. Paul talks at length about these spiritual gifts in 1 Corinthians 12-14.

A second identity we have in life is the one we make. In the drama, *The Rainmaker*, the main character is a con artist who calls himself Starbuck. He travels from town to town during the "dirty '30s" scheming to get people to pay him to bring the rains for their parched fields. Young Lizzie Curry catches his eye and they spar with building passion. But Lizzie is no fool and she challenges him to come clean with her about his true name. It can't really be Starbuck, she knows. Starbuck admits that he was born a "Smith," but asks, "What kind of name is that for a fellow like me? I needed a name that had the whole sky in it! And the power of a man! Starbuck! Now there's a name — and it's mine!"

Lizzie tries to contradict him, telling him he has no right choosing his own name and giving up his family heritage. Yet he will not capitulate quickly. "You're wrong, Lizzie," he says. "The name you choose for yourself is more your own name than the name you were born with!" Starbuck is on to something. Much of what we see in people around us has to do with what they have made of themselves. When an English nobleman named Roberts was having his portrait painted, the artist asked him if he would like the lines and creases in his face smoothed over. "Certainly not!" he objected. "Make sure you put them all in. I earned every single wrinkle on my face!" He was a man who knew the identity he had made.

There is also a third and deeper human identity. It is the identity that transforms us from what we were to what we are becoming. The poet saw a friend clearly when he wrote:

> *And there were three men went down the road*
> *As down the road went he:*

The man they saw, the man he was,
And the man he wanted to be.

The person we each want to be when we find our truest selves in God is larger than either the identity we have received from others or the one we try to create. This is the thought that lies at the heart of each text today. Anything that sullies us by trying to define us on terms less than God's grace limits our best self. But those things that bring out God's character in us help us to be people that others can count on.

Exodus 1:8—2:10

The first half of the book of Exodus narrates what will become a pitched battle between Yahweh and Pharaoh. Both lay claim to Israel. Both seek obedience from the nation. Both demand recognition as deity. Both wield enormous powers. A drama is set in motion to determine who will be able to topple the other and take control of the territory and nation.

The animosity that drives this combat tale begins in today's lectionary passage. The opening verses declare the heart and perspective of Pharaoh: Israel is a chattel to be used and spent in building the wealth of Pharaoh's own house. There are several things to note as this message is unpacked.

First, there is a comparison of the character of each of these leaders. Pharaoh is forgetful (1:8), ungrateful (1:8), fearful (1:9), conniving (1:10), mean-spirited (1:11), harsh (1:12-14), ruthless (1:14), and murderous (1:15-16). Yahweh (whose name is not yet known — see ch. 3), meanwhile, is life-giving (1:17), kind (1:20), and encouraging and supportive (1:21). While this is all caricature, it is a deliberate introductory description designed to build antagonism toward Pharaoh and sympathy with the cause of Israel and Israel's God.

Second, the use of the Nile in determining the fate of the people is instructive. There is very little rain in Egypt. Yet life-sustaining water abounds because of the amazing flows of the Nile. The Nile and Egypt are symbiotically connected, and the life of the people depends upon the seasonal flooding and constant faithfulness of the great river. Because of this, the Nile gained a role of divinity for the Egyptians. It was a living thing and was honored by religious rituals spanning all ages and dynasties. Thus, when the Pharaoh declares that the male Israelite babies be thrown into the Nile, it is more than merely a death sentence; in effect the Pharaoh is making a sacrifice to the Nile, honoring it as provider for the Egyptians. At the same time, when the Levite family of chapter 2 floats a basket bassinet on the Nile currents, there is an incipient recognition that Yahweh rules over the waters of the Nile, and they cannot have a destructive power against Yahweh's people.

Third, when the Pharaoh's own daughter becomes part of the plot to defy the will of the Pharaoh, there is a premonition of the victory of Yahweh. Even the Pharaoh's own family recognizes the wrongness of the Pharaoh's outlook and ruling plan, while paying allegiance to the designs of Yahweh.

Romans 12:1-8

Romans 12 begins the third section of Paul's letter. In large outline the message of Paul in Romans can be summarized as sin (chs. 1-3), salvation (chs. 4-11), and service (chs. 12-16). The plight of humanity (chs. 1-3) calls out the redemptive care of God (chs. 4-11) that creates a new consciousness of what it means to be in God's family (chs. 12-16). Paul employs a ritual motif to explain ongoing and living devotion to God. The chapter itself flows in three literary sections: heart and mind transformation (chs. 1-2), realistic personal assessment (chs. 3-8), and divine flow-through (chs. 9-21). In the first two paragraphs of the chapter, morality is tied to an understanding of God and of ourselves.

The hardest thing for any of us to do in life is to maintain integrity. Even though we are not, by and large, evil people, sin has a way of playing around with our hearts. On the outside we appear rather nice and respectable. In fact, much of what we do is good, noble, kind, and wise. No one can deny that. The problem is that sin has a way of slicing our hearts with perforated lines. Before we are aware of it we have torn off a piece here and a section there, until we find ourselves fragmented.

It is not that we become blackened by sin in large strokes. Nor do we generally turn into some hideous monsters of greed and cruelty, dissolving the kind Dr. Jekylls of our personalities into dastardly Mr. Hydes. Instead, we keep most of our goodness intact while making small allowances in certain little areas. We shave our taxable income as we fill out our 1040s, maybe. Or we lose our peripheral vision when someone in need approaches. Or we compromise our communication so that we speak from only our mouths but not our souls.

The fragmentation of our lives makes us less than we should or could be. We strut on tiny legs, ants marching across the busy highway of life imagining that tires of destruction will skid around us. It is this diminishing of our hearts and characters that Paul seeks to address when he calls for whole-person transformation.

In Robert Bolt's play, *A Man for All Seasons*, Sir Thomas More stands at a moral crossroads. More has been a loyal subject of the English crown, supporting his king in both civil and ecclesiastical matters. Now, however, King Henry VIII is engaged in a devious plan that pits his own desires against that of the church. In order to pull off his scheme, Henry requires that all his nobles swear to him a personal oath of allegiance. Because the terms of the oath violate More's conscience before his God, he refused and is arrested and jailed.

More's daughter, Margaret, comes to visit him. She is his pride and joy, often thinking his thoughts after him. In their playful terms of endearment she is her father's "Meg," and Henry knows that More will do anything for her. That is why he sent Meg to plead with her father in prison. "Take the oath, Father!" she urges him. "Take it with your mouth, if you can't take it with your heart! Take it and return to us! You can't do us any good in here!"

In so many ways she is right, of course — how can More bless and protect his family if he rots in jail or dances with the executioner? And who will know if More coughs a testimony he doesn't fully believe?

Sir Thomas, however, has felt the creases in his heart and knows what will happen to him if he finds himself, rather than King Henry, the betrayer in the mirror. So he says, "Meg, when a man swears an oath, he holds himself in his hands like water. And if he opens his fingers, how can he hope to find himself again?"

When our lives begin to fragment, as Thomas More knew, we are left as though holding our lives like water in our hands. As the cracks between our fingers shift, even slightly, the water of our very selves dribbles away. We may look like the same people, but who we are inside has begun to change.

This is why Paul reminds us that we do not belong to ourselves, nor do we have the power of right living within us until we are fully sacrificed to God in the transforming power of grace. Then we begin to find our truest selves and can find a way to live that matters for both time and eternity.

Matthew 16:13-20

John Calvin said that there were two aspects to faith: *assentia* and *fiducia*. The first we often translate as "assent." It is in this dimension of faith that we acknowledge that something exists. *Assentia* is knowing something factually, or knowing about someone only from a distance. Calvin's second aspect of faith might well be termed "trust." It is a heart engagement, involving us personally in an emotional attachment with whatever we might have previously acknowledged only intellectually.

Take a chair, for instance. *Assentia* is our willingness to say that it could hold the person daring to sit on it. *Fiducia*, on the other hand, is the act of sitting on that chair ourselves, trusting its sturdiness to hold our bulk. Both are elements of faith. Both are important. But until the latter is added to the former, faith remains inert, distant, intellectual, and impersonal.

The interaction between Jesus and his disciples in Matthew 16 expresses both kinds of faith. There is a need to rightly understand who Jesus is (*assentia*). But there is also a need to trust that Jesus has authority to change life and eternity (*fiducia*). In the clarifications Jesus asks from his followers, we have the first. In Peter's declaration that Jesus is "the Christ" (that is, the anointed Messiah who brings deliverance to God's people), we have the second. For this reason Jesus can turn around the confidence that the disciples have in him to a corollary of confidence in them. Because of their *assentia* and *fiducia*, the disciples become people upon whom the earthly territory of God's kingdom can be built.

Application

Someone has suggested a powerfully illuminating analogy. When a ship is built, he said, each part has a little voice of its own. As seamen walk the passageways on her maiden voyage they can hear the creaking whispers of separate identities: "I'm a rivet!" "I'm a sheet of steel!" "I'm a propeller!" "I'm a beam!" For a while, these little voices sing their individual songs, proudly independent and fiercely self-protective.

Then a storm blows in on the high seas and the waves toss, the gales hurl, and the rains beat. If the parts of the ship try to withstand the pummeling independent from one another, each would be lost. On the bridge, however, stands the captain. He issues orders that take all of the little voices and bring them together for a larger purpose. By the time the vessel has weathered the storm, sailors hear a new and deeper song echoing from stem to stern: "I am a ship!"

It is the captain's call that creates the deeper identity. So it is in our lives as well. Minor stars in a world of glamour try to sing siren songs pulling bits and pieces of us from the voyage of our lives. Those who hear the captain's call are able to sail true and straight.

An Alternative Application

Matthew 16:13-20. The gospel passage is rich with meaning and may well be developed with the Exodus passage as a battle of the powers. Note that there is an important geographical understanding that informs Jesus' words to his disciples. In the region of Caesarea Philippi, on the rocky slopes of Mount Hermon, springs emerge from caves. These have been recognized as spiritually significant places from time immemorial. During Jesus' day there were many niches carved into the stone walls of the mountain fitted with images of gods and providing places for sacrificial gifts to be made. Furthermore, the caves that spewed fresh water were considered to be the gateways to the world of the gods. Jesus' words declare that no physical reality such as the rocks of Mount Hermon or its secret caverns can put one in touch with God; only the living testimony of Jesus can bring one into relationship with the divine.

Paired with the build up to the battle of the divine superpowers in Exodus, this theme of eschatological conflict takes on powerful significance and may well be illustrated with scenes from the *Matrix* trilogy or the *Star Wars* epics.

Proper 17
Pentecost 12
Ordinary Time 22
Exodus 3:1-15
Romans 12:9-21
Matthew 16:21-28
by R. Craig MacCreary

Choose your weapon

Weapon: "1) something (as a club, knife, or gun) used to injure, defeat, or destroy; 2) a means of contending against another." Now this seems to be something where Christian people ought to put a lot of distance between themselves and the whole idea of clubs, knives, or guns. Yet Paul reminds us that we are to fight the good fight, "Fight the good fight of the faith; take hold of the eternal life, to which you were called and for which you made the good confession in the presence of many witnesses" (1 Timothy 6:12). Paul according to the second letter of Timothy seeks to be remembered as one who has fought the good fight.

It is not without reason that many Christians have become gun-shy at the use of this image and metaphor to describe the central ethos of the Christian faith. I am a graduate of Elon University formally known as the "Fighting Christians": In part a reflection of its founding by members of the Christian church as in the Christian side of the Congregational Christian Church stream of the United Church of Christ. I remember the logo as a sort of clergyperson in a boxing posture. At the time, folks probably thought it was cute but now the thought occurs, "What were they thinking?" All this has long ago been exchanged for the currently more culturally acceptable Elon Phoenix rising from the ashes. Elon sports teams are now cheered on by a rising although very determined and somewhat seemingly angry, phoenix logo.

No doubt, there are plenty of valid reasons for the cultural shift that finds the phoenix more appealing than a leprechaun-like clergy boxer. The change in ethos no doubt makes it unlikely that anyone would today publish a book titled *The Manhood of the Master* as Harry Emerson Fosdick did in 1913. No doubt the fighting image was conducive to cultivating faith in the age of empire and especially when Christianity was the official religion of the empire.

Yet each of the lectionary texts for Proper 17 present us with the culturally uncomfortable image of conflict that will end in bloodshed, the loss of human life, and a faith community that does have to deal with its enemies. In the Hebrew testament we are presented with the beginning of Moses' call to lead the Israelites from slavery to freedom. The reader knows that this will not be accomplished without a serious confrontation with the Hebrews battling their way through the hardness of Pharaoh's heart pursued by the Egyptian army.

Paul writes to the Romans, "Let love be genuine; hate what is evil, hold fast to what is good... Bless those who persecute you; bless and do not curse them" (Romans 12:9, 14). This need to instruct his readers suggests that some in the early church are finding it hard to do the Christian walk in relationship to some of the opposition that they are facing. The Matthew text reflects the difficulty that Peter has with the coming denouement in Jerusalem where Jesus will have to suffer and die on the cross. James Carroll's 2002 book *Constantine's Sword* delineates how an excessive reliance on the cross as the central entry point into Christianity has resulted in persecution of Jews and the justification of the imperial ambitions of many Christians.

Taking up weapons even for the good seems problematic for most Christians. There is a dynamic in these texts that is different from the usual fights we take on. While for the most part our battles are shaped by strategic considerations for the protagonists in these texts, the battles that we fight are chosen on the basis of the weapons they have rather than choosing the battles and finding suitable weapons.

Exodus 3:1-15

Up to this point we have in Moses' story the tale of a person for whom in large part religion has been an irrelevant factor. Certainly his origins, his fall from the ruling house of Egypt, and where he landed reflects a divine plan that the reader is aware of, but one that Moses does not yet see — a divine hand leading. We should not be surprised that it does take a burning bush that is not consumed to get Moses' attention. It is important to note that more like a secular scientist than a religious devotee Moses says to no one in particular, "I must turn aside and look at this great sight, and see why the bush is not burned up" (v. 3). Moses is far from jumping on the theological bandwagon. Rousing his curiosity rather than his faith God is ready to move on to the next level, " 'Come no closer! Remove the sandals from your feet, for the place on which you are standing is holy ground.' He said further, 'I am the God of your father, the God of Abraham, the God of Isaac, and the God of Jacob.' And Moses hid his face, for he was afraid to look at God" (vv. 5-6). It must have been a comfort, though not for Moses, to the returning exiles that the liberator God and the one who has restored them to their homes is continuous with the God who has made them a people. This gives some comforting assurance as to what the divine is up to in their lives.

We hear in one breath, "I have come down to deliver them from the Egyptians, and to bring them up out of that land to a good and broad land, a land flowing with milk and honey..." (v. 8). Yet in the next moment we read, "So come, I will send you to Pharaoh to bring my people, the Israelites, out of Egypt" (v. 10). Out of this dichotomy Moses responds, "But Moses said to God, 'Who am I that I should go to Pharaoh, and bring the Israelites out of Egypt?' " (v. 11). Here is the fundamental question that the text wants us to ask of ourselves. Who are we? The answer that is given is not in a psychological or political understanding but through an invitation to a theological consultation about by what name God shall be called. For the most part, the heavy-duty social planning and political change by most of the human beings I know does not begin with a conversation. Perhaps there is the routine opening prayer or closing benediction where the name is assumed, the theology taken for granted. Such moments are not about becoming theologically adventuresome but it is time for Moses. This is all a new business where he will have to have the details filled in. Well-tuned theology is not exactly the weapon that many of us want to carry into battle.

However, take into account the actual situation of the first readers of these words. These texts have been collated by the postexilic community to help them adequately understand their experience. Rather than preparing for battle, the community is seeking to understand the conflict and convulsions that they have been through. These are people trying to make sense of the past as they venture toward the future. Furthermore, the text makes the claim that our slavery is a matter of worshiping a false God as was the exile of the Hebrews.

The Hebrews' downfall is attributable to, in part by, not taking their God seriously enough as one who has woven the justice and mercy into the very image, which is violated only at their risk. On the other hand the Hebrews have been led astray by taking their own understanding of God too seriously. Is this not what Jesus meant when he said, "Do not presume to say to yourselves, 'We have Abraham as our ancestor'; for I tell you, God is able from these stones to raise up children to Abraham" (Matthew 3:9). In our day perhaps we are enslaved by a literalism, habit of thought, and a history when we were at the center of an empire that has left us presuming too much and trusting too little. This might not seem to be the beginning place as we confront the current political, social, and economic challenges. However, I would hate to face the battle ahead without such a conversation.

Romans 12:9-21

"Let love be genuine; hate what is evil, hold fast to what is good; love one another with mutual affection; outdo one another in showing honor" (vv. 9-10). Elsewhere in the letter to the Romans Paul writes, "No, 'if your enemies are hungry, feed them; if they are thirsty, give them something to drink; for by doing this you will heap burning coals on their heads' " (v. 20). To a community that is under siege from within and without he writes them to take up arms in a most unusual way. He does not anticipate his opponents to be running around in pain with singed scalps. Rather, he writes in hopes that the Romans will have taken up a weapon that will overcome the usual defenses that most of us have against developing the kind of loving relationships that God calls us to share.

I suppose that we could laud Paul for taking a prudent ethical stance in the context of the early church and come away from this text admiring his reasonable approach to things. Yet the early church did not outlast all the ethical prudence of its day by exercising common sense and thoughtfulness. The pouring of hot coals on the head rather than appealing to the sensibility of their opponents demanded a people who themselves were on fire with the love of God that had been poured into their hearts.

I remember coming out of the theater after seeing the movie *Gandhi*. I should say more accurately that I staggered out of the theater. Like the rest of the audience, I felt that a hot coal had been poured on my head and that it had quickly made its way to my heart. That is what Paul is appealing to here, a life that will pour it on and bring it on in a way that will break down the defenses of the world.

I do not often remember much of what my mentors have said to me over the years. I do recall a number of life-changing pieces of advice. However, what I can never forget is the number of times that I felt in their presence like hot coals that could burn through my pretensions and foolishness were being poured on my head — "Let love be genuine; hate what is evil, hold fast to what is good...." I imagine it must have been like that in some way for Peter when meeting the risen Christ after Peter had betrayed him. Seeing the look on Jesus' face when he knew things more in a human way than in a divine mode, and when he perhaps rightfully so had great pretensions to leadership was found to be one of little faith. He was only to discover in such moments that he was standing before one whose love was genuine. If that does not burn within you, I don't know what does.

Paul clearly chooses to live in a way that most people do not. "Rejoice in hope, be patient in suffering, persevere in prayer. Contribute to the needs of the saints; extend hospitality to strangers. Bless those who persecute you; bless and do not curse them" (vv. 12-14). Whatever your partisan claims, I wish the president of the United States would attend fewer prayer breakfasts and make his speeches and press conferences more of a prayer. I suspect that would have more to do with altering the balance of power than anything else he might do. However I suspect that the shift might not be in the direction he intended.

"Live in harmony with one another; do not be haughty, but associate with the lowly; do not claim to be wiser than you are. Do not repay anyone evil for evil, but take thought for what is noble in the sight of all. If it is possible, so far as it depends on you, live peaceably with all. Beloved, never avenge yourselves, but leave room for the wrath of God; for it is written, 'Vengeance is mine, I will repay, says the Lord' " (vv. 16-19). I rather suspect if the weapons that Paul enjoins us to use in the struggles of life were brought into play we would have quite a different understanding of the United Nations, our international responsibilities, global warming, and our own estimate of national self-hood. I am not entirely confident that our current understanding of the road ahead will pave the way for what God wants or what we desire. I rather suspect that we are not the best in choosing the weapons that we will use to deliver the kind of hot coals that will heal and repair the world.

Matthew 16:21-28

In this lesson, Jesus comments on the marked difference between him and Peter as to how they would handle the road ahead. In a sense Peter is crippled as he faces the journey ahead, "And Peter took him aside and began to rebuke him, saying, 'God forbid it, Lord! This must never happen to you.' But he turned and said to Peter, 'Get behind me, Satan! You are a stumbling block to me; for you are setting your mind not on divine things but on human things' " (vv. 22-23). In no small measure, Peter is locked into how he will calculate the next move and every move after that in the days ahead. This seems obvious as the way to go. Then again, as much as Peter, we are caught up in setting our minds not on divine things but on human things. This is not to say that we have looked entirely to those things that debase and debauch. Many of our schemes have been noble and reflected the best of common sense. However, too many of our thoughts about shaping the world have not been about laying down our lives and lifting up the cross of getting to know our neighbor who lives in Darfur, who walks the streets of Palestine in fear, whose understanding of American power comes from what they see Americans drop from the sky.

I am continually struck by the fact that I can strike up a conversation in the grocery store and have an answer for the world's problems from people who have no knowledge of the world's people. Lest this observation seem to tip toward the liberal side of the equation, I have had similar experiences in classrooms of all stripes and sizes. We too often seem to be more devoted to solving problems than practicing the presence of God in the world that renders us to being transformed by what we experience.

Jesus' words, "For what will it profit them if they gain the whole world but forfeit their life? Indeed, what can they give in return for their life?" (Mark 8:36-37). Make no mistake about it, we will get pretty far on setting our minds on human things rather than on divine things. In most people's books, gaining the whole world is not such a bad thing. As a matter of fact, most of us settle for something slightly less than the whole enchilada. A threshold is crossed, however, when gas prices cross $4 a gallon as if it were written in the heavens that we were never to share the world's fate or have to deal with the reality that we have run the string on all the thanksgivings that we offered up gratitude for having been born in a land that has been blessed with so many natural resources. It is a land that now does little manufacturing and is dependent on the economic assistance of China to pay its debts, where France builds its airplane tankers, whose leading trading partner is Canada because it is our leading supplier of oil and natural gas, and whose currency now trails Europe and Canada in value. We have to deal here not merely with physical realities but with the new spiritual reality of our place in the world.

There has been talk in recent years of how the church can no longer play the role it once did in the old imperial scheme of things that placed our nation at the center. Certainly it will be a long time before we can no longer flex our muscles. Yet behind these realities of the daily headlines there are new spiritual needs. It is time we throw something new into the mixture and "weaponize" around the ways of God.

Application
In the seventeenth through the nineteenth centuries, one of the methods that was fairly effective in keeping the male population down was the relatively deadly practice of dueling. The most notorious American example is the killing of Alexander Hamilton, former secretary of the treasury of the United States by the then vice president of the United States, Aaron Burr, on July 11, 1804. Despite attempts to outlaw the practice, Hamilton's own son would be killed in a duel. The trick in dueling was that the one challenged had the choice of weapons. If you were really smart, you chose something like pillows or jelly beans at fifty paces, which could make a mockery of the whole business and send everyone happily on their way. Of course, many did not make the right choice of weapon.

Long before we have a strategy in place, the most important question is what weapon we choose that will shape how we respond to life. Through Moses, the Hebrews are asked to escalate their theological capacity. Paul reminds the Romans that given their context they should choose the weapons of love. Jesus calls us to consider whether our choice reflects more the ways of God than of human beings. What are your and your congregation's weapons of choice?

An Alternative Application
Romans 12:9-21. Paul writes rather blithely about how the Christian community should live together and work out its differences. "Contribute to the needs of the saints; extend hospitality to strangers. Bless those who persecute you; bless and do not curse them. Rejoice with those who rejoice, weep with those who weep" (vv. 13-15). Easier said than done. In many ways, it seems that we barely have time to weep for the tangle that we get our lives into or even to laugh at ourselves. Yet we have a serious way of robbing the grave of its power when we love. To find something or someone to love in the way that Jesus loved is to draw out hormones and enzymes in the human body that renews and revitalizes.

Love makes a way where there is no way — beyond the stale aridness that comes when a church is not able to bless when persecuted, or able to have enough energy and commitment to laugh and weep together, or when in the mood for revenge more than redemption, or not have enough faith and joy in its life to "hate what is evil, hold fast to what is good..." (v. 9).

In short, the fundamental question that a church must ask of itself is: How is its love life? Paul is not asking how much love we feel or how much love we feel for others, but do we feel the love of God sufficiently as it pours through us?

Proper 18
Pentecost 13
Ordinary Time 23
Exodus 12:1-14
Romans 13:8-14
Matthew 18:15-20
by William Shepherd

School days, school days

Good old golden rule days. The children will be going back to school this week, if they aren't there already. Yellow school buses reemerge from their hidden garages; crossing guards don their white shoulder belts and pick up their stop signs. Parents stock up on spiral notebooks and highlighter pens, while teachers give themselves bouquets of freshly sharpened No. 2 pencils. You can just smell the chalk in the air.

The lections this week send us back to school. Just in case we've forgotten over the summer, we begin with a review of some basics. Exodus reminds us about... well, the Exodus. Romans looks back to the time of Moses, too, as it instructs us on the proper meaning of the Ten Commandments, and Matthew teaches us what it means to study together as a community. These three lessons are not just of antiquarian interest, however, they prepare us to move forward to the next level.

There will be a quiz next time. And the next. And the next.

Exodus 12:1-14

We begin, however, not with the fall semester, but at spring break.

While the Jewish New Year begins in the month of Tishri (which covers September and October), the Jewish liturgical year begins in Nisan (March/April). "This month shall mark for you the beginning of months; it shall be the first month of the year for you" (Exodus 12:2). With the Exodus, each month of the year takes on a number, so that every time the people look at a calendar, they will remember, "This is the Nth month since God redeemed Israel from slavery in Egypt."

The Exodus story interrupts the account of the tenth and final plague (11:1-10; 12:29-32). Not only does this create suspense in the narrative, but it also puts the historical story in a liturgical context, which puts it outside normal history into God's history. The entire section (12:1—15:21) is framed by liturgical material (12:1-27a; 15:1-21), and the two blocks of narrative material (12:29-39 and 13:17—14:29) are themselves encapsulated by liturgy (including the institution of both the Passover and the Festival of Unleavened Bread). The effect of this combination of story and liturgy is to make God's action in every generation "Exodus-shaped." The Passover ritual doesn't just ward off the tenth plague but establishes a pattern of redemption for all people.

Not only has the event been given a liturgical cast, the liturgy has shaped the account of the event: The liturgy precedes the account of the event, so that the event itself is liturgy. This is so much the case that history is in some sense obscured by liturgy. There are two views of the Passover to be discerned in this account. In one, God slays the Egyptians and the blood on the lintels and doorposts is a sign of God's grace in "skipping over" the chosen people (v. 13). In the other view, God comes with a demonic "destroyer" (vv. 22-23, 27; cf. Genesis 19:13-14; 2 Samuel 24:16; 2 Kings 18:35; 1 Chronicles 21:15) and the blood actually wards off this demon (perhaps following an older shepherds' rite, where the blood was thought to have magical powers). Thus some scholars translate the verb "pass over" as "protect" (as it is used in Isaiah 31:5). But the narrative has no interest in the pre-history of this obviously ancient ritual, only in its future history — first, the immediate future of Israel's redemption from slavery in Egypt, and second, of the future perennial commemoration of the event that continually reshapes present reality for those who remember.

This is the first command of the law of Moses, given even before Sinai. Its timing corresponds to another major ritual that takes place on the tenth day of another month: the Day of Atonement (12:3; cf. Leviticus 16:29; 23:27). The lamb is taken either from the sheep or the goats (vv. 3, 5); since animals were valuable commodities in that culture, they must be shared with those who cannot afford one of their own (v. 4). As in most sacrifices, the lamb must be without blemish, a year old (v. 5; cf. Leviticus 1:3, 10; 22:17-25; Deuteronomy 15:21; 17:1; Malachi 1:6-8; Numbers 28:3; 29:2). It must be roasted to consume all the life-giving blood that is not used in the ritual (v. 8); in fact it must be consumed completely (vv. 9-10). And it must be eaten in haste (v. 11; some Arabic Jews still observe Passover in this fashion) since there is not time even for dough to rise (v. 8).

The blood of the lamb painted on the lintels and doorposts has symbolic value as the essence of life (Genesis 9:4; Leviticus 17:11, 14). Blood has been a crucial motif in the larger narrative, since Moses shed the blood of an Egyptian in defense of his people (2:11-13); later the blood of circumcision saved his life (4:24-26); a plague of the Nile turning to blood astounded all (7:17-21); and now finally we learn of the plague that will take the blood of Egypt's firstborn. The punishment is harsh, but no harsher than the slavery the Hebrews had been subjected to (symbolized by the bitter herbs, v. 8; cf. 1:14). Ultimately, the plague is given a theological justification: it proves the Lord's superiority to the gods of Egypt (v. 12; there is an ancient tradition that during the plague, the idols of the Egyptians were actually smashed). The political abuse of the Hebrew people was backed by an ideology, which was actually and literally idolatry. The gods of the empire sanctioned the abuse of this people, and it is these gods and their callous worshipers who are ultimately judged.

Romans 13:8-14

The schoolteacher Paul has already asked us to transform our minds: "Do not be conformed to this world, but be transformed by the renewing of your minds, so that you may discern what is the will of God — what is good and acceptable and perfect" (Romans 12:2). Christians are called to renew and transform their *minds*; learning about God is presented as a primary task of faith. Only with this correct knowledge can faith be practiced; it is necessary to "discern what is the will of God" according to what has been learned. Now Paul comes full circle, closing out his chapters of exhortation by asking us to "put on the Lord Jesus Christ, and make no provision for the flesh, to gratify its desires" (13:14).

To "put on Christ" reflects the actual practice of the early Christians; the baptismal candidate would be given a new white garment as a symbol of the new life in Christ. The expression became quite common (cf. Romans 6:3-4; Galatians 3:27; Colossians 3:8-10; Ephesians 4:22-25; James 1:21; 1 Peter 2:1). Any doubt about the connection to baptism is dispelled by Paul's exhortation to "put on the armor of light"; "light" was another metaphor for baptism (cf. Ephesians 5:8-10, 14; 1 Peter 2:9; 2 Timothy 1:10; Hebrews 6:4). The exhortation to transform one's mind by the teachings of Jesus is a reminder of the pledge to follow Jesus that is made in baptism; the disciple is, if nothing else, a student.

The master of mixed metaphor draws on both baptismal and military imagery, urging the Romans to wear their Lord like a "chain-mail" baptismal gown armor against the insidious desires that flow from the font Paul calls "the flesh" (*sarx*, cf. ch. 7). By *sarx* Paul does not mean the physical being as opposed to the spiritual, but that entire pattern of human life that has hardened itself against God. Modern congregations may speak of "sins of the flesh" as if it were a matter of the body and not the spirit. Paul's use of *sarx* is quite different from this; for him, *sarx* is everything in the human being that rebels against God. It is the root of idolatry and sin, a malign arrogance that thinks it knows better than the one true teacher (cf. Romans 1:3; 2:28; 3:20; 4:1; 6:19; 7:5, 18, 25; 8:3-9, 12-13; 9:3, 5, 8; 11:14; 13:14). He names some of the symptoms of the *sarx* (v. 13): reveling, drunkenness, debauchery, licentiousness, quarrelling, and jealousy. Drunkenness and sexual sins are given no exalted place in this pantheon; the "flesh" can be manifested just as well in the petty conflicts that rage out of control among us.

To walk in the flesh is to walk in the darkness (v. 12), when the actual time, Christologically speaking, is just before dawn, when "salvation is nearer to us now than when we became believers" (v. 11). This could be said by any Christian; of course our time gets shorter as we get older. Paul's language intensifies the thought by drawing on conventions and metaphors associated with apocalyptic thought. He refers not to chronological time, but rather *kairos*, a special "time" or "season" that is urgent and compelling. The *kairos* time is metaphorically just before daybreak, as Paul draws in the metaphors of waking/sleeping and darkness/light (cf. 1 Thessalonians 5:1-11; Matthew 24:42-44, 26:45; Mark 13:33-37; Luke 12:35-46, 21:36; Ephesians 5:8-16, 6:18). Paul exhorts the Romans to wakefulness in light of the coming dawn when his gospel mission will find its completion (cf. Romans 8:18-23; 11:15). Even the vices he warns against are those associated with the darkness; Christians are to learn to walk in the daylight (v. 13).

The Lord Jesus is like a new set of clothes that makes love the fashion (vv. 8-10). Paul has moved from a discussion of literal debt (v. 7) to the metaphorical debt we all owe to God, which is love (v. 8). "For the one who loves has fulfilled the law" says Paul (this is a more natural reading of the Greek than NRSV), the "other law" being the four commandments that Paul cites in verse 9, which represent the whole of the law of Moses. Love fulfills the entire law, because it encompasses the true meaning and ultimate purpose of the commandments. Again, Paul comes full circle, because the ultimate example, model, and enabler of love is Jesus; once we put him on, we are wearing the coveralls of love.

Matthew 18:15-20

Matthew's school is a bit different from the others, because there is no head of the class in this schoolroom. "But you are not to be called rabbi, for you have one teacher, and you are all students" (Matthew 23:8). The disciples are supposed to learn from Jesus alone: "Nor are you to be called instructors, for you have one instructor, the Messiah" (23:10). Their subject matter is the kingdom of God (cf. ch. 13).

But even though they are to learn only from Jesus, they themselves, by the end of their training, become, if not teachers and instructors, then scribes: "every scribe who has been trained for the kingdom of heaven is like the master of a household who brings out of his treasure what is new and what is old" (13:52). The purpose of their training is to reduplicate themselves: they "make disciples" by "teaching them to obey everything that I have commanded you" (28:19-20). Like their master, they are to gather around themselves students of his teaching. These small teaching communities (as few as two or three, 18:19-20) are crucial in fomenting the "greater righteousness" that Christ taught (5:6, 10; 6:33).

No one is called "teacher," then, not just because Jesus alone deserves that title but also because the entire community is given the teaching office. They are called to "bind and loose" (16:9; 18:18), which in this context obviously refers to community judgments concerning offenders (vv. 15-17), but the terms are also used in the Jewish rabbinic tradition to signify the entirety of what the law allows and forbids. In other words, to "bind and loose" signifies teaching authority; the disciples are given authority to teach in the tradition of Jesus. No one disciple takes on the role of Jesus; but rather, all together imitate him as teacher. There is in the community no one fount of wisdom who pours knowledge into the heads of fellow disciples, but a round table of scribes who hold the teaching office together.

There is a problem, however, because the schoolroom can become an unruly place under these circumstances. It's one thing for everyone to be teachers at a round table of two or three gathered together, but what happens when the community swells in size? If too many cooks spoil the meal, how many teachers does it take to turn the classroom into cacophony? To put on our baptismal robes at such — that is, the garment that is the Lord Jesus himself, if Paul is to be trusted — it must seem that we should indeed be wearing chain-mail armor. Or at the least, a good coverall smock, since the children are about to get into a rather messy finger-painting project.

Matthew does not resolve the messiness of a faith where all sit at the feet of Jesus together and attempt to discern the ongoing meaning of his teaching — debating, disagreeing, and drawing differing conclusions. However, Matthew does make provision for the inevitable conflicts that will arise in even the smallest communities. We are dealing with relationships between "brothers and sisters" (v. 15; the NRSV translation "another member of the church" is interpretively correct but misses the flavor of the kinship language used). As we know, families quarrel, and Matthew depicts the church as a family (12:46-50). What is required is a system for dealing with such quarrels.

Matthew sets forth such a system, which has the advantage of dealing with the petty and the trivial before it escalates into major bitterness among community members. No one is going to call in two or three witnesses for any trivial offense, much less the entire assembly (two or three witnesses was the minimum standard of evidence in Mosaic law, cf. Deuteronomy 19:15). Long before the erring member is expelled from the community ("let such a one be to you as a Gentile and a tax collector," v. 17), the community will "regain" the member (v. 15); the church's primary role is to reconcile and not condemn an offender. However, if the offense is serious enough, and the wronged brother or sister wishes to pursue it further, Matthew provides a workable if rigorous implementation of community discipline. It is unfortunate that so few Christians bother to take even the first step Matthew suggests, which would solve about 95% of all congregational issues.

Clearly the church is not acting in its own name, but that of its Lord, when the two or three gathered together do their binding and loosing. This may go against the grain of modern individualism, but so much the worse for the modern world. Rather than allowing Christians to walk away from brothers and sisters who prove to be not like-minded, Matthew requires us to engage them, call them into the wider community, and if necessary correct them as a community. It is no less than what Jesus would do. If the church is truly a people called by God to make disciples by teaching what Jesus taught — if the church is "the Body of Christ," to use Pauline language — then that teaching authority must also recognize Jesus' role as impartial judge (cf. 25:31-46; 28:18).

Application

What have we learned at the blackboard by the end of this period? In the book of Exodus, we learned to celebrate God's saving action in history. From Paul, we learned the ultimate importance of love, and from Matthew, we learned how to do that love within a real flesh-and-blood community.

Are we ready, then, to graduate? The answer must be, "No," simply because this is not the kind of school where you move from grade to grade until you have reached the top. It's more of a one-room schoolhouse, where teachers rotate with the students in a lifelong learning project. No one ever gets to leave the school, because no one is ever finished. The celebration is a perpetual one. Love is never finished but always in progress. The community requires constant attention lest it disintegrate.

What to do? Nothing but smile, put on our Jesus-smocks, and wade into the next activity.

An Alternative Application

Exodus 12:1-14. It may seem that the Passover is an archaic, neglected, and forgotten ritual for Christians, but it is not so. While many Christians celebrate the Passover with Jewish friends, or enact their own version of a Passover meal at a weekday educational event, this is not the extent of the Christian Passover tradition. Passover is not neglected but transformed in Christian tradition, in that it is represented in the liturgies of Maundy Thursday, Good Friday, the Easter Vigil, and Easter Day. It is also represented in the Holy Eucharist itself. Maundy Thursday celebrates Jesus' final Passover meal, along with his instruction to his disciples to follow his example in giving themselves for others. Good Friday represents Jesus' sacrifice as the true Passover lamb. The Great Vigil of Easter celebrates God's action in history from the foundation of the world through the deliverance and foundation of the people of Israel to the ultimate fulfillment of God's promise in Jesus Christ. Of course, Easter celebrates the new life given to all the people through the risen Lord. When we meet him in the bread and the cup, we do it not only in remembrance of him, but also through God's entire work in bringing him to us.

Proper 19
Pentecost 14
Ordinary Time 24
Exodus 14:19-31
Romans 14:1-12
Matthew 18:21-35
by David Kalas

Life on the inside

I attended two schools in the state of Virginia. I did my undergraduate work at the University of Virginia in Charlottesville and my seminary work at Union Theological Seminary in Richmond.

At the center of the University of Virginia's campus is a long rectangle of grass, called "The Lawn." It is surrounded by buildings that were originally designed to serve as classrooms and residences for both students and professors. Those buildings face inward, making "The Lawn" a truly picturesque environment.

Union Seminary, meanwhile, also has at the heart of its campus a grassy rectangle of lawn surrounded by various buildings on all four sides. In the case of Union's design, however, the buildings face outward. Unlike the University of Virginia, what you see as you walk through the quadrangle at Union is the back of the buildings. The seminary's buildings are oriented to face the outside world, you see, as a testimony to the school's mission.

We do well in the church to be reminded of that mission. It's easy to turn inward, often to the neglect of the world to which we are called. Yet for all of the soul saving and need meeting to be done out in the world, it is appropriate, from time to time, to stop and consider together our life on the inside. That is what our two New Testament lections invite us to do this week.

Exodus 14:19-31

The parting of the Red Sea is one of the most famous miracles in scripture. It clearly was a pivotal event for that immediate generation, and it continued to be a cherished memory as part of Israel's national testimony. And still to this day, when people think of biblical miracles, the parting of the Red Sea comes near the top of the list.

The event challenges us to be precise about our definitions, however. Just what do we mean when we call something a miracle? For at first blush, this occasion may not match the conventional assumptions about miracles.

First, many of our people may be surprised to discover that the event was a process. Typically, people think of miracles as instantaneous events — such as, the immediate, on-the-spot healing of a blind man or a paralytic, Jesus walking on water, or the widow's son being raised from the dead. However, in this episode, God did not instantly part the water; and this may stand in contrast, incidentally, to the three occasions when the Jordan River was parted. On this more famous occasion, however, the biblical account reports that it was a process that took all night.

Second, in most people's casual thinking about the meaning of a miracle, there is an assumption that the event is supernatural rather than natural. In other words, the several-week mending of a broken arm that has been set and put in a cast by a doctor is not typically considered miraculous, while the unexplained, instantaneous cure of a diagnosed but untreated condition is called "a miracle." If the Israelites had physically torn down the walls of Jericho, it would not be heralded as miraculous, for it would be a case of natural cause-and-effect. Yet here, in this story, we are offered a natural cause for the dividing of the water: "a strong east wind... turned the sea into dry land."

I don't want to be misunderstood on this point. I am not proposing that we withdraw the event at the Red Sea from our catalog of miracles. Rather, I want to encourage us to rethink our definition of miracles, so that we might properly broaden it to include a wider, more marvelous variety of the works of God.

Meanwhile, though God himself is clearly the star of this scene, it is worth taking a moment to observe some of the supporting cast. Specifically, I'm thinking of the Egyptians. After being effectively barred by an apparently supernatural spectacle until the completion of a most improbable escape route, the writer reports that "the Egyptians pursued" the Israelites, "and went into the sea after them."

At this juncture, one has to stop and ask, "What were they thinking?" After watching their country and their people being pummeled by the devastating series of plagues, one wonders why the Egyptians would bother chasing after the Israelites in the first place. We might observe, in a rare moment of admiration for the Philistines, that they were faster learners than the Egyptians, for they did not pursue the Ark after capturing and then returning it (1 Samuel 5:1—6:18).

Yet after all of the battering of the plagues, the tragedy of the Passover, and then the spectacle by the Red Sea, why would the Egyptians pursue? Why would they go down into the sea after the Israelites? How obtuse can these people and their leaders be?

Perhaps these questions are akin to the bewilderment of the psalmist, who asked, "Why do the nations conspire, and the peoples plot in vain?" (Psalm 2:1). It is, indeed, in vain to oppose the Lord and his purpose. But that has not stopped countless fools from the endeavor, beginning with Lucifer, including the hell-bent Egyptians of this episode.

It is only after the Egyptians find that their chariot wheels are clogged in the mud — hardly, we should note, the most impressive display of God's saving power that they have witnessed — they belatedly realize, "The Lord is fighting for them against Egypt."

It's a terrible thing to realize God's truth too late. It was true of those Egyptians whose bodies washed up on the shores of the Red Sea. It has been true of others, too, including the skeptical captain in Samaria (2 Kings 7:1-20), the foolish virgins (Matthew 25:1-12), and perhaps the centurion at the foot of the cross (Mark 15:39).

Meanwhile, equally terrible is the ironic conclusion of the passage. When the saved-yet-again Israelites "saw the great work that the Lord did," they "fear the Lord and believe in the Lord and in his servant Moses."

That's great, of course, only so long as it lasts. It did not seem to last long with those Israelites. The same congregation that was so in awe at the end of chapter 14 was complaining by the end of chapter 15 (v. 24) and had become completely unglued by the beginning of chapter 16 (v. 3). Indeed, in the four brief chapters between the episode at the Red Sea and the theophany at Mount Sinai, we witness a disturbing pattern of complaining and disobeying. Like so many of God's people since, the Israelites' dramatic experience with God did not seem to translate into daily faithfulness.

Romans 14:1-12

Paul begins chapter 14 of his letter to the Romans with an imperative: "Welcome." Specifically, it is an exhortation to welcome "those who are weak in faith," but it is not until two verses later that Paul gives the real reason for the instruction: "for God has welcomed them."

We might recognize this sort of parallelism as somewhat characteristic of Paul (see, for example, Philippians 3:12). Beyond a mere linguistic technique, however, this balance of instruction and rationale reveals an important scriptural principle: Namely, we do what we do because of what God does.

From the first command to be holy (Leviticus 11:44) to Jesus' command to be perfect (Matthew 5:43-48), this is the pattern: God's people are to do and to be in response to what God does and what God is. It is implicit in the parable of the unforgiving servant (Matthew 18:21-34) and explicit in Jesus' new commandment (John 13:34). It was the experience and policy of Peter in regard to the Gentile believers (Acts 10:47-48; 11:17). And John makes it our fundamental testimony and ethic: "We love because he first loved us" (1 John 4:19).

Meanwhile, Paul makes a fascinating observation about certain types of conflict among believers. He urges the Roman Christians to welcome the folks who are weak in faith "not for the purpose of quarreling over opinions." The fact, of course, is that Paul can be forcefully dogmatic about certain things (see, for example, Galatians 1:6-9; 2 Thessalonians 3:6-15). Yet we misunderstand Paul if we think of him as rigid and unbending in all things. Rather, he sets a healthy example for us by making a distinction between matters of essential truth and matters of personal opinion. It's so easy in the church for the latter to be treated like the former. Earnestness and zeal tend to inflate the value of everything they touch, and so believers end up "quarreling over opinions," which certainly neither pleases God nor edifies the church.

The broadmindedness of Paul is still more explicit in verse 6 ("those who eat, eat in honor of the Lord... while those who abstain, abstain in honor of the Lord"). As the parent who steps in between two fighting children, each convinced he is right and the other is wrong, Paul surprisingly concludes, "You're both right!"

Of course, to apply this approach too broadly leads to all sorts of mischief and is not true to the larger body of the apostle's instructions to the churches. The following verse may provide the key that clarifies this, and every, situation. Paul writes, "If we live, we live to the Lord, and if we die, we die to the Lord."

The simple statement is reminiscent of his more personal reflection on his own circumstances in his letter to the Philippians (1:20-26). Beyond that, it reveals what is the essential underlying principle for Paul: namely, orientation. As followers and servants of Jesus Christ, we have been completely reoriented, so that now everything about us points toward him. While we formerly lived for ourselves or for others, we lived according to the flesh or like the world, we lived toward our human goals or personal ambitions, but now we live and die exclusively for and to the Lord.

Finally, Paul offers the ultimate antidote to the judgmental inclinations of some in the Roman church. "Why do you pass judgment on your brother or sister?" He reasons, "for we will all stand before the judgment seat of God." This is the trump card. I am relieved of any necessity to play the part of judge because I am assured that that role has been filled. Moreover, I humbly shrink back from my judgmental reflexes when I am reminded that I don't sit on that seat; I myself stand before it.

So long as you and I are both living to the Lord, therefore, we give each other space on matters of opinion, knowing that "each of us will be accountable to God."

Matthew 18:21-35

If your Sunday worship is like mine, then you and your congregation will, at some point during the service, pray together the Lord's Prayer. Perhaps we might begin this Sunday's sermon with a reference back to that prayer. For when Jesus taught that prayer during the Sermon on the Mount (see Matthew 6:9-13), he made an interesting choice about what needed elaboration.

The Lord's Prayer is full of significant themes and truths. Yet when he had finished reciting the model prayer, see which theme and truth Jesus returned to in order to offer further teaching on the subject. Not God's name nor God's kingdom; not God's title as Father, his provision of daily bread, nor his protection from temptation and evil. No, he let all of those monumental issues be, electing instead to complement the prayer with a reiteration of the forgiveness principle: "For if you forgive others their trespasses, your heavenly Father will also forgive you; but if you do not forgive others, neither will your Father forgive your trespasses" (vv. 14-15).

That forgiveness principle, which we recite routinely in the Lord's Prayer, is at the heart of this teaching of Jesus from later in Matthew.

The teaching has a context. It is not abstract and theoretical. Rather, it is an answer to a question, perhaps even a situation. "How many times should I forgive?" Peter asks. Then he suggests an answer of his own: "As many as seven times?"

The assumption, of course, is that there has to be a limit. You can't just keep forgiving a person indefinitely, after all. At some point, the forgiveness wears out; the policy changes. It's as though forgiveness is like holding one's breath underwater: something we find difficult to do, but we can manage for a limited time. Peter wants to know how long he must do it.

We share Peter's concern. We think there is a great injustice to bottomless mercy and there is an impractical vulnerability that comes with blank-check forgiveness. We have a situation in our own lives — or we surely know of people who have such situations — in which we're certain there must be a more productive alternative to forgiveness.

Peter asks the question for us. At what point do we say, "Enough"? How many times do we have to forgive this habitual offender?

Jesus changes the entire equation. It's not merely a matter of his larger number ("not seven times, but, I tell you, seventy-seven times"). For the real calculation, it turns out, is not how often we ought to forgive an undeserving person, but rather how much God has forgiven us.

We can readily appreciate the principle of the parable in its purely financial terms. The Greek talent is sometimes reckoned as having had a value of approximately 5,000 denarii. Given that estimate, we see the proportions suggested here by Jesus: that the debt of the "fellow slave" was just a tiny fraction of what the first slave had owed to his master. Specifically, thinking in terms of our currency, Jesus would be portraying a man who had just been forgiven a half-million dollar debt, only to go ballistic over a guy who owed him a dollar but couldn't pay it.

It's a preposterous suggestion, of course. But then, from heaven's perspective, apparently it is equally preposterous for you and me to behold the cross and yet be unwilling to forgive some fellow human being.

Peter begins with one question of quantity, and Jesus' final answer is about a different sort of quantity: It's a case of how many vs. how much. We want to know how many times we must forgive. Jesus wants us to consider how much we've been forgiven.

Application

This week's epistle and gospel lections invite us to stop and consider life on the inside. They do not encourage us, of course, to encumber ourselves with the trivial inward-focused stuff that so often preoccupies churches. This is not about carpet colors, music styles, or budget battles. No, this is the larger and deeper matter of how we treat one another and live together in gracious, humble fellowship. When we learn to do that well, then everything — from our budget battles to our beyond-the-walls missions — will go better.

The gospel lection is Jesus' marvelous parable about forgiveness, born out of Peter's personal inquiry. The noteworthy thing is that Peter's situation involves "another member of the church" who sins against him. This is a slice of life on the inside.

Likewise, the passage from Romans concerns the harmony and fellowship of the church: thorny issues of judgmental people, theological and ethical disagreements, differing interpretations and practices.

Neither lection, you see, assumes that everything is all peaches and cream on the inside. But both passages suggest a similar paradigm for resolving the struggles. Namely, the perspective that comes to our lateral human relations when we keep in view our vertical relationship with God. In Jesus' parable, he is the master who has forgiven and to whom we will answer for our begrudging and unforgiving spirits. In Paul's letter, he is the judge before whom one day we will all stand. When I see him clearly, then I will see my "fellow slave," the other church member, much more clearly too.

An Alternative Application

Exodus 14:19-31. "In over their heads." I have heard it said that most people who drown don't drown because they can't swim; they drown because they panic. (Personally, speaking as one who can't swim, I think that if I were to drown, it would be equal parts of both.)

Of course, in some terrible instances, the panic is appropriate. We all know stories of people who drowned because — literally and figuratively — they got themselves in over their heads. They went into a situation where the water was too fast, the tide too strong, or the ice too thin and they were not able to survive it. It's too bad in those instances that they didn't feel appropriately panicked while they were still on dry land.

I am reminded of the truism about panicking and drowning when I read the Exodus account of the event at the Red Sea. We know, of course, that in the end the Egyptians drowned. Earlier in the account, however, we discover that they also panicked. Specifically, the writer reports, "At the morning watch the Lord in the pillar of fire and cloud looked down upon the Egyptian army, and threw the Egyptian army into panic" (v. 24).

It's worth noting at what point in the story the panic occurs. The Egyptians had already experienced the Lord's victories on their own home field — ten plagues that accumulated to devastate the land and its people. They weren't sufficiently panicked by it all, however, to just let the people of God go. Then, there at the Red Sea, the Egyptian army had been held off all night by a supernatural pillar, an angel running interference for the Israelites. Still no sign of panic among the Egyptians, however. Later, when the pillar is removed, the Egyptians see that a dry path had been made for the Israelites to cross over; yet that astonishing sight did not make them panic. No, it is only after the Egyptians have chosen to pursue the children of Israel through that dry path that the Lord throws the army into a panic.

I wonder if this is not a story of missed grace. After all, was God not able to smite the Egyptians there in the desert, even as they were on their way to catch up to the Israelites? Yes, he could have, but he did not. He put a barrier in their way: a barrier, I suggest, that protected both the Israelites and the Egyptians.

The point is that the Egyptians panicked way too late. They should have feared the Lord back in Egypt. They should have gotten a clue in the shadow of the pillar. They should have turned back when they saw the miraculous parting of the sea. Like so many tragic drowning stories, the Egyptians didn't drown because they panicked: They drowned because they panicked too late.

Proper 20
Pentecost 15
Ordinary Time 25
Exodus 16:2-15
Philippians 1:21-30
Matthew 20:1-16
by David Kalas

Of grease and squeaky wheels

Conventional wisdom says that it's the squeaky wheel that gets the grease.

That makes sense with wheels, of course, but the setting in which the phrase is most often used in our day has nothing whatsoever to do with wheels. Rather, the squeaky wheel has become a metaphor for a complaining person. And so for the squeaky wheel to get the grease means that the complainer gets what he or she wants.

Certainly we have seen the phenomenon played out time and again. When my wife worked as a server in a restaurant, she saw the principle at work almost every shift. The person who had a good attitude about something that wasn't quite right — a long wait, a mistake in the order, an unsatisfactory bite — received no benefit. But the person who complained? That customer was fawned over by the manager and oftentimes he was rewarded with some expense being taken off the final bill as a way of compensating for his dissatisfaction.

We have seen it elsewhere, too, haven't we? We have watched parents give in to their whining children. We have seen the peace-loving spouse cater to his or her volatile, demanding mate. We have witnessed the dynamics in a church where decisions are made — and unmade — in response to some vociferous, complaining minority.

In two of our selected lections for this week, we encounter squeaky wheels. The hungry children of Israel have a complaint in the desert. And the exhausted, sweat-soaked laborers in Jesus' parable also have a complaint. We will give some consideration to squeaky wheels — and to God's grease — this week.

Exodus 16:2-15

Complaining is something of a theme in this passage. The word appears here, in one form or another, seven different times, and that is par for the course, for complaining is something of a theme throughout the Exodus experience.

Not all complaining is equal, however. There are times when complaining is at least tolerated by God and sometimes even answered. That seems to be partly the case in this instance where the Israelites' complaint is met by God's provision of manna. On other occasions, however, God does not tolerate complaining (see, for example, Numbers 11:1-3; 14:26-38; 21:4-9), and it is not really endorsed here.

One of the interesting dynamics of complaining in this passage is the object of the complaints. At the outset, we read that the Israelites "complained against Moses and Aaron." Later, however, we see Moses deflecting their complaints: "What are we, that you complain against us? ... Your complaining is not against us but against the Lord" (vv. 7-8).

At a purely human level, of course, the phenomenon is a familiar one. In all areas of life, either cowardice or deviousness can prompt a person to misaddress his complaint. Perhaps the Israelites were too frightened on this occasion to presume to complain against the Lord and how he was doing things; perhaps it seemed easier, safer to lay the blame at the human feet of Moses and Aaron.

Also at a human level, we like to be able to personify blame. We want to know — and we want to say — whose fault it is. In our eagerness to blame, perhaps we have sometimes blamed innocent people. We call them scapegoats, and they are familiar victims in politics, sports, and business. Likewise with the Israelites: They may have wanted to identify a villain, a person to blame, and Moses and Aaron were the logical candidates.

Meanwhile, however, Moses' corrective to the people strips away a false veneer with which we may be more comfortable. It's easily palatable for us to walk around with some grudge, issue, or complaint against another human being. But when that misapplied blame is stripped away, we may discover that our argument is actually with God, and we don't want to discover that.

God took the occasion of the people's complaining as a double opportunity: that is, both a chance to provide for their needs and a chance to "test them, whether they will follow my instruction or not" (v. 4).

Both the provision and the test came in the form of a flay substance that came to be called "manna" (based on the people's inquiry in Hebrew, "What is it?"). The provision was an ample daily supply of food in the desert. The test was whether the people would trust God for that daily supply.

God's instruction was that the people should "go out and gather enough for that day." It's a picture of daily trust and daily providence that we echo whenever we pray The Lord's Prayer: "Give us this day our daily bread" (Matthew 6:11). And yet, truth be told, we are not satisfied with "enough for (this) day." We also want to be able to store some away for a rainy day. We want to have a contingency fund. We want to plan for the kids' education and for our own retirement. Gathering only enough for today seems imprudent. Yet gathering more for future days was, there in the wilderness, a manifested lack of faith in God and his reliable, provident care.

In the end, therefore, both the complaining and the over-gathering (which occurs just beyond the scope of our passage in 16:20) are different manifestations of the same root cause: a lack of trust in God. For the Israelites to complain was to doubt God's care and attentiveness to their needs; and to try to store away the manna was also, at another level, to doubt God's care and attentiveness to their daily needs.

Philippians 1:21-30

Personal mission statements have become rather fashionable in recent years. Following a trend in the business world and elsewhere, individuals have taken to drafting mission statements for themselves.

Such a statement can be a great clarifier. It defines purpose and determines priorities. It articulates for a person his or her own *raison d'etre*. Here is why I get up in the morning. Here is not only the reason why I do what I do, but why I do it the way that I do it. Here is the measure I use to judge whether I am succeeding or failing in life.

For myself, if I were to adopt such a personal mission statement, I would give serious consideration to Paul's dramatic opening line in this passage. "For me, living is Christ and dying is gain."

That sounds to me like Paul's personal mission statement, as well as his strategy for experiencing a great many blessings that elude most people.

While sitting in prison, Paul writes this letter that has since been nicknamed and known as "the joyful epistle." Paul had an uncommon joy, contentment, and fearlessness, and all of it, I believe, is rooted in this mission statement. His life was all about Jesus. And, at the same time, his life was nothing to be worried about, protected, preserved, or prolonged, for when life is all about Jesus, then death is an advantage, a promotion.

We have seen ample statistical evidence in our culture of how many people wish they were dead. There are the obvious cases of suicide. Then there are the unreported attempts. And then there are all those poor souls whose suicide is a slower self-destructiveness of lifestyle. But the bottom line remains: so many people do not care to go on living. It's a desperate state.

In contrast, see Paul there in prison. Has he been cruelly beaten? Is he unjustly locked up in some foreign country? Is he a million miles from the comforts of home that he might have enjoyed had he just stayed put in Tarsus, Jerusalem, or Antioch?

As he sits, bleeding in someplace bleak and dank, he ponders his life. He is torn. He wants to go on living — thinking of others, confident of "fruitful labor," and living for Jesus. At the same time, he wants also to die — but not as escape. His desire to depart this life is not because this life is meaningless, painful, and empty for him. Rather, his desire to depart this life is rooted in the very one who has brought meaning, joy, and fulfillment to this life, and so his "desire is to depart and be with Christ."

In the meantime, until we "depart to be with Christ," our calling is to "live your life in a manner worthy of the gospel of Christ" (v. 27). That's a tall order and it may be something of a reversal of our common understanding and application of the good news.

For some of us, the emphasis we have heard — and perhaps proclaimed — is the truth that the gospel of Christ accepts and embraces us even in our unworthiness. All have sinned; no one is worthy — these are among the first principles of our salvation. And it may happen that we do not take the next step in our understanding, emphasis, and proclamation: that having been saved by him, we are to live lives that are worthy of that gospel of Christ.

Finally, Paul's physical context lends credibility and power, then, to his remarkable statement near the end of the passage: "For he has graciously granted you the privilege not only of believing in Christ, but of suffering for him as well" (v. 29). For most of us, "privilege" and "suffering" only go together with sarcasm. Apart from that, it seems, they share nothing in common.

Yet this is rather a prevalent theme in the New Testament. Jesus introduces it in that beloved set of paradoxes called the Beatitudes (see Matthew 5:10-12). It is a truth also echoed by Peter (e.g., 1 Peter 4:13-16) and repeated elsewhere by Paul (cf. Romans 8:17-18; 2 Corinthians 1:5-7; Philippians 3:10; Colossians 1:24). This is no shallow "look at the bright side" approach. Rather, Paul — along with Jesus, Peter, and others — invites us to a sincere and profound appreciation of suffering: not as a good in itself, but as an avenue to a great many good and blessed things in, with, and for Christ.

Matthew 20:1-16

Trace the family tree of the workers hired first and I suspect that you will find in their lineage two characters from other parts of scripture.

First, those workers must be related to the older brother. In Jesus' familiar parable of the prodigal son, the older brother is the dutiful one. He works hardest and longest, while his younger brother comes and goes. He is not, so far as we can tell, deprived of anything by his brother's prodigality. Yet, clearly, he feels somehow cheated by his father's extravagant treatment of his brother.

Likewise, the workers hired first were not deprived of anything that they had coming to them. Still, the owner of the vineyard is extravagant in compensating the Johnny-come-lately workers who did not labor long through the heat of the day, and those who worked hardest feel cheated as a result.

In both parables, it is the character representing God — the owner of the vineyard and the father of two sons — whose bottom line is diminished by extravagance. Yet it is someone else, in each case, who feels unfairly treated.

The other obvious ancestor on the first workers' family tree is the Old Testament prophet, Jonah. He is not eager to go to Nineveh in the first place, but having gone, Jonah is eager to see its judgment. He watches and waits for some time, keeping a vengeful vigil over the city, but his worst fears come true in the end. "O Lord! Is not this what I said while I was still in my own country? That is why I fled to Tarshish at the beginning; for I knew that you are a gracious God and merciful, slow to anger, and abounding in steadfast love, and ready to relent from punishing" (Jonah 4:2).

Jonah's complaint reads like a testimony, and as such it is part of the same genre with the complaints of the prodigal's brother and the workers hired first. All these characters are angry with God. At the core, however, it is important to note that they are not angry about how badly God has treated them. He has not. Rather, to their great discredit, they are angry about how generously God has treated someone else: someone undeserving.

At a human level, this is the familiar stuff of sibling rivalry. This is the wandering eye of envy, always checking out what the other guy has, always comparing my lot to his. It may also be the issue that lies at the heart of the tenth commandment, for coveting seems to be something other than mere greed. The context of the tenth commandment is not merely that I want more, but rather that I want what my neighbor has. And what he has in the commandment, please notice, is nothing unusual. The mandate does not point to something rare and pricey that my neighbor has, like some expensive foreign sports car. No, but rather the commandment mentions my neighbor's house and my neighbor's wife. The implication and assumption are that I also have a house and a wife. These are common blessings, not uncommon possessions. But the posture of coveting is to peer over the fence, to see his house, and to prefer it to mine. I should have that, not him.

The workers hired first had peered over the fence into what later workers were paid, and when compared to their own wages, they were displeased by what they saw.

Also at a very human level, there is our native instinct for fairness. Again, the issue here is not so much greed as it is justice. The workers hired first were not initially discontent with their proposed compensation. It was only when workers who worked much less were paid the same amount that their fairness gland began to secrete wildly. From the time we were children, we had this capacity for indignation, and we complained to our parents, "That's not fair!"

Our complaint, of course, was seldom on behalf of some sibling whom we thought was being shortchanged. Rather, for most of us, our sense of fairness began as an entirely self-centered reflex and concern. It's only when it escapes that particular cocoon of self-interest that it becomes a beautiful thing that is useful to God.

Beyond the ordinary, human level, meanwhile, there is also a spiritual business here. The complaint of the first workers — and of the older brother and the prophet Jonah — is not really with some human authority, economic system, or fate. These characters all file a complaint with God. They do not like his policies. Just as surely as it seems unfair if I am given less than I deserve, it seems unfair if someone else is given more than he deserves.

And God is rather in the habit of doing precisely that: giving people more than they deserve.

Application

There's a great fallacy in the squeaky wheel policy. What works with an actual wheel we may commonly misapply with people.

In the case of a wheel that squeaks, the grease stops the squeaking. In the case of complaining people, on the other hand, giving them what they want seldom cures the complaining. Indeed, in the case of children — and, arguably, in a great many adult whiners, as well — the catering to their complaining only serves to reinforce the behavior. It becomes their tried-and-true method of getting what they want.

The misapplication of the squeaky wheel analogy, then, is this: the grease is actually what the squeaky wheel needs, but who can say what the squeaky wheel wants? With children — and perhaps the rest of us, as well — the complaints should be met not necessarily with what we want, but with what we need.

So it goes for Israel in the wilderness. They do a great deal of complaining along the way. Sometimes what they need is provision — bread, meat, water. Sometimes what they need, however, is correction — chastening, perspective, and gratitude.

Likewise the workers hired first. When the payroll checks were cut, they did a bit of squeaking, dissatisfied with what they perceived as a great injustice. In their case, they didn't actually need anything more in terms of provision or compensation — they received what they had agreed to and what was sufficient. They were not given what they wanted; they were given what they needed: an insight into how the owner does things. And so, too, the examples of Jonah (Jonah 4:10-11) and the older brother (Luke 15:31-32) demonstrate God's relationship with his creatures.

An Alternative Application
Philippians 1:21-30. Any of us who have been in ministry for more than a few years likely have been surprised to discover the pain and emptiness with which some folks are living. We suddenly learn about it in a counseling session, or when we hear that so-and-so has checked himself into a rehab center, or that so-and-so killed herself. Who knew?

On any given Sunday, therefore, as we look out over the well-dressed and cheerful facades that American churchgoers customarily wear, we may be assured that there are desperate people in some of those pews. A message of hope is never out-of-season.

Perhaps some soul in your congregation or mine will find new hope and encouragement in the example of Paul. At some level, that soul may relate to a part of Paul's condition — darkness, pain, bondage, suffering, and the like. And yet, he or she may be brought to a recognition that Paul seemed to experience his prison differently. He was characterized still by a sense of purpose, hope, and joy. How can that be?

While the investment advisor may urge diversification, Paul found his peace, joy, meaning, and purpose by putting all his eggs in one divine basket. For him, to live was Christ, and that simple formula gave him an unflinching purpose in life, an unimpeachable joy and an impervious peace.

In 1741, German pastor Johann Schewdler expressed the truth in a hymn: "Ask ye what great thing I know, that delights and stirs me so? What the high reward I win? Whose the name I glory in? Jesus Christ, the crucified. Who is life in life to me? Who the death of death will be? Who will place me on his right, with the countless hosts of light? Jesus Christ, the crucified" ("Ask Ye What Great Things I Know").

You and I have people who, though physically in our pews, are suffering in some prison. They have been taught about believing in God, but they have not yet discovered living for Jesus. The story and message of Paul may be just what they need to hear.

Proper 21
Pentecost 16
Ordinary Time 26
Exodus 17:1-7
Philippians 2:1-13
Matthew 21:23-32
by William Shepherd

By what authority?

The church doorbell rang insistently. "We want to speak to the pastor!" they yelled over again through the intercom.

I met them at the glass doors and asked how I could help them.

The tall thin one with the long hair, granny glasses, and floppy leather Bible announced that they had a message from "Our Lord Jesus Christ" (the other one was small, tubby, short haired, but the same floppy Bible).

"That's nice," I said, "but I'm afraid I'm rather busy right now." (I probably had an *Emphasis* deadline.) "Why don't you call ahead for an appointment next time?"

After I had to say that the third time, I shut the door and walked away. Behind me the tall guy kept tapping on the glass with his keys and shouting, "Our *Lord* Jesus Christ!"

A week later the same two guys yelled at the church organist until he threatened to call the police.

Having read this week's lections, I wished I had asked them, "By what authority do you dare speak in the name of our Lord Jesus Christ?" I don't imagine the question would have stumped them, but it might have been interesting to hear the answer.

Exodus 17:1-7

The issue was Moses' authority. The people did not realize that when they quarreled with Moses, they were quarreling with God. "Why do you quarrel with me? Why do you test the Lord?" (v. 2). In questioning Moses, they are in effect questioning God: "Is the Lord among us or not?" (v. 7).

The wilderness stories (Exodus 15:22—18:27) trace the transition of Israel from Egypt to Sinai, from slaves to people whom God has instructed. Israel is on a journey somewhere between promise and fulfillment; the wilderness becomes symbolic of their progress in faith, which is slow at best. The standard pattern in these stories (as in today's lection) is the complaint: The people are needy and they make an accusation against Moses, who prays and receives instructions that resolve the issue, at least temporarily. Here the names of the stops along the wilderness route are said to reflect the "complaining" and "testing" of the people. The issue in the wilderness is that Israel continues to confuse God with Santa Claus; a deity who does not produce on demand must be an absent deity or a non-entity. This attempt to manipulate God, to treat the Lord as a manifestation of their own will, is a precursor to the idolatry of the golden calf.

The Lord is leading the people, though Moses gets the blame when the water runs dry (vv. 1-2). This is ironic since their salvation came via the sea — yet in the wilderness, they think that God has no command of the water. "Why did you bring us out of Egypt, to kill us and our children and livestock with thirst?" (v. 3). At least slavery had its benefits! Moses' cry in response, "They are almost ready to stone me" (v. 4) is also ironic, in light of the subsequent command to strike a stone. The action itself is somewhat ludicrous — how could simply striking a rock produce water? — but the point is not the magic of the rod but the faithfulness of God (and since some claim that there are water channels to be found in the rocks of Sinai, the action may be ludicrous only on the face of things, literally). God has promised to provide for this people; despite their lack of faith and ingratitude, God will give them all they need.

Exodus points to the future when it describes "the rock at Horeb" (v. 6). Israel has not yet reached the mountain of God but it looms over the story. God's provision will prove to be part of a covenant established with Israel, which is itself God's provision of life. Just as water flowed from the rock, life for Israel will flow from God's law. Both the gift of life that is water and the gift of life that is God's instruction come from the same source.

Philippians 2:1-13

Paul also takes up the theme of authority when he writes to the Philippians. His model of authority is quite different from the one-up/one-down approach found in Exodus and Matthew, and he reinforces that model by using a number of examples. He's not above using himself as an example (see 3:20—4:1). He also uses his colleagues Timothy and Epaphroditus as models (2:19—3:1). But most of all, he invokes the example of Jesus (2:5-11).

Philippians is a letter about friendship and possessions and how one expresses the other. Paul writes to his friends to thank them for their monetary gift (1:7; 4:10, 15-18); it is not going too far to say that Philippians is one long "thank-you" note! In Greco-Roman society, it was a common notion that "friends share all things," and Paul rightly takes their gift as a sign of that kind of friendship. His exhortation to them is to live out the implications of their gift of friendship by sharing their hearts and minds (vv. 1-4). "Make my joy complete: be of the same mind, having the same love, being in full accord and of one mind" (v. 2). Such a mindset will regard the interests of other members of the community before self-interest; humility rather than selfish ambition is the watchword for the church (vv. 3-4).

Most scholars see verses 5-11 as an early Christian hymn inserted by Paul into his letter as support for his exhortation to communal harmony. This is certainly possible: the unusual and poetic vocabulary may not be Paul's own, and the structure is reminiscent of Hebrew poetry in its stress and parallelism (it is usually thought to be influenced by Isaiah's Servant Songs, though some scholars see its primary background in the story of Adam's fall in Genesis). However, the themes and even the language are well within Paul's rhetorical repertoire, so he may have written this ode to Christ himself.

There is some debate over exactly how Paul invokes the example of Christ. The elliptical introduction to the hymn reads literally, "This think in you (pl.) which also in Christ Jesus" (v. 5). The verb must be supplied in the second half of the sentence. Traditionally, the simplest translation has been preferred, with the verb "to be" (so NRSV, "Let the same mind be in you that was in Christ Jesus"). This implies that the point is simply ethical imitation, and the life of the community should parallel the life of Christ ("in you" is best understood as "among yourselves," specifying not individual inner disposition but group character). However, this translation does not quite capture all the nuances of Paul's expression "in Christ," which indicates a state of union and power that goes beyond mere aping of actions. So we might translate the phrase, "which is yours as those who are in Christ," or "which you think as those who are in Christ" (supplying the verb from the first half of the sentence). The sentence could be taken in a number of ways, as paradigmatic (Christ providing the model mind), mystical (the mind shared in union with Christ), ecclesiastical (the mind of those who are the Body of Christ), or soteriological (the mind that comes from being "in Christ"). These different ways of understanding the introductory sentence are not necessarily contradictory, however — in fact, they are quite complementary. Following Jesus is not merely imitating his example, but participating in his life, and being energized by his power. It is not just that we follow Christ but that we are in some sense sharers in Christ's nature and power, which the hymn specifies.

The hymn moves in two directions: first downward in humility, then upward to glory. Traditional interpretation has seen here a reference to the pre-existence and incarnation of Christ, who came down from heaven to take human form and then returned from whence he came. But an equally good case could be made that the poetic language imagines no pre-existence, and the entire tale is told of the incarnate Christ, who humbled himself in service to others. Both interpretations fit the hymn (though I incline to the traditional one).

The "one mind" the Philippians believers are to share is the mind of Christ, who was, first of all, in "the form of God." This could be understood as a reference to the divine Christ's pre-existence, or it could refer to his human form, as Adam was created in "the image of God." In either case, he did not regard that form as *harpagmos*, "something to be seized, grasped, robbed," such as, booty or plunder (v. 6). The poetic idea here is that Christ chose not to use his gifts to his own advantage; he did not take the opportunity that they presented for self-promotion. Note that this is possessions language and that the possessions symbolize a spiritual state, a notion that probably would not be lost on a congregation that had so recently sacrificed their own goods for Paul's mission.

Rather than looking out for himself, Christ "emptied himself" or stripped himself of the privileges that came with his status (like a reverse Adam). He took on the identity of a slave, much like Isaiah's servant (the hymn uses several synonyms for "form" and "likeness," all of which are poetic variants of the same idea). He did not thereby cease to be in the form of God, but by doing so defined that form — it is that of a slave (v. 7). The slave is humble and obedient (here the stark contrast to Adam), and Paul takes the logic of his argument to its obvious conclusion: the ultimate emptying and humbling is found in a death on the cross (v. 8).

Having reached the bottom, the movement is reversed (v. 9). The humble Christ is exalted and given "the name that is above every name" for example, either the name "Jesus" (v. 10) or more likely "Lord" (v. 11). This leads to a cosmic proclamation, in which "every knee should bend, in heaven and on earth and under the earth, and every tongue should confess that Jesus Christ is Lord, to the glory of God the Father" (vv. 10-11). The entire universe is thus brought under the lordship of Christ.

On the basis of this declaration, Paul will launch further into his exhortation, which includes not only the request for good works, but the promise of God's assistance (vv. 12-13). The final verses encapsulate the paradox of Christian life and responsibility: the way of salvation has been set forth by Christ and is the gift of God, not anything that we can seize for ourselves. And yet the community is called to "work out your own salvation with fear and trembling" (v. 12). The well-being or "salvation" of the community depends on a certain amount of cooperation (otherwise Paul's exhortation would be meaningless and downright silly). The community works because "it is God who is at work in you" (or better, "among you," since the focus throughout the section is the community and not the individual). God's active goodwill demands our response but exists independently of us.

Matthew 21:23-32

When Jesus rang the doorbell at the temple, the chief priests were well within their rights to ask him where he got his authority. He had entered Jerusalem to the praise of the throngs, he had tossed the moneychangers out of the holy precincts, and he had cursed the fig tree that traditionally stood for Israel (21:1-22). What authorization did he have for these brazen acts, who gave him the power to do these things, and to teach in the center of religious life?

The reader already knows the answer to the question: Jesus had been commissioned by God (1:18-25; 3:16-17) and given "all things" by his Father (11:27). Indeed, the story will end with a bald statement of Jesus' authority (28:18). The story actually does more to characterize Jesus' opponents than to tell us what we already knew. The debate over Jesus' authority introduces a series of five stories of controversy, in which we see that Jesus' opponents in the religious establishment are not merely uninformed on the subject, but willfully opposed to the work of God that Jesus has initiated. Matthew shows us what Jesus will later announce that these religious leaders are hypocrites and blind guides who do not practice what they teach (see ch. 23).

Their brief dialogue with Jesus characterizes his opponents as being at cross-purposes with themselves. The implication of their question is that Jesus has no formal authority; he certainly cannot claim to speak for God without training or certification. Nevertheless, he proves himself to be quite comfortable within the role, as he uses a standard rabbinic technique, the counter-question (v. 24). The opponents, far from relying on any God-given authority of their own, take an informal poll of their constituents and conclude that the only way to win is not to play. They cannot speak against John, due to his popularity, but to admit his divine authority would mean that they would be giving up their own (presumably none of them had actually been baptized by John). So they keep quiet. Jesus has out-maneuvered them; where they had hoped to trick him into some sort of actionable blasphemy, all that has happened is that they fall into their own trap and admit not only their ignorance but also their lack of authority. Jesus owes them no answer.

The parable of the two sons (vv. 28-32) is obviously to be read in light of this conflict. On the level of the story about Jesus, the religious leaders fare poorly in contrast with prostitutes and tax collectors who precede them into the kingdom. On the level of Matthew's own story, even a church with Johnny-come-lately Gentiles as members is better than a pure Jewish community that rejects its Messiah. And, on the level of the community that continues to read Matthew's story, those who pat themselves on the back that they are not like those hypocrites standing over there can do so only if they themselves have reported to work in the vineyard that morning. The trap is still laid bare for any who carelessly stumble toward it, for even a Bartlebyesque "I do not wish to" that is taken back is better than an "I go, sir" that is never taken up.

Lest we assume that the tax collectors and prostitutes are any better off these days, we might ask ourselves what would happen if one of them — or any obviously "unsuitable" person — might deign to show up in our own congregation one morning. A true story: a homeless man was found sleeping in the bushes outside a seminary library one morning. The librarian called the dean of the seminary to ask if she should report the incident to the police. "Oh yes," the dean said, "we can't have *that kind* hanging around." Almost puts you right back at the gate of the temple, doesn't it?

Application

My mentor, Fred Craddock, famously wrote a book titled *As One Without Authority*. Despite a certain evolution in his thinking that can be detected in his later works, Craddock is vilified in some circles as the man who made preaching interesting but wimpy (one homiletical opponent pointedly titled his own work *As One* With *Authority*). Indeed, some of my preaching students were dismayed that their supervisors had told them to drop my class, because they didn't want anyone in their churches preaching without authority!

But on what authority does one dare speak for God and what would that authority sound like? Could it be that a couple of anonymous but rude door-ringers might actually have a message from God? Or does such authority require some sort of ecclesiastical imprimatur? And would authorization by the higher-ups guarantee that the word spoken with authority is in fact authoritative?

It seems to me that anyone who claims to work under the authority of God as revealed in Jesus Christ ought to reflect the source. That is, if you claim Jesus as your backer, you ought to look like Jesus; as Paul clearly believed, authority can be taught by example. Jesus' example in the temple is instructive; when questioned about his authority, he refused to assert it. He did not claim to be speaking for God, because he did not flaunt his credentials. Instead, he cut to the heart of the matter. The entire story of the Messiah points to a brand of authority that does not assert itself or seek to grasp its own importance but empties itself, taking the form of a servant, serving in both life and death — even death on a cross.

There is a sense in which we should speak as one both with and without authority. We do claim to speak for God, as revealed in Jesus. But we are to speak while deeply aware of our own inadequacy for the task, our own misappropriation of the authority, our own pride in thinking that we could ever put words in

God's mouth. The two extremes are certainly wrong: we can neither be the milquetoast who wears a sign on his rear that says "Kick Me," nor can we tap our keys on glass doors in hopes that our voices will carry over our own arrogance. It's a balancing act, definitely — a high wire spectacle.

That's why preaching is hard work. That's why being a Christian is hard work. Without God's grace, we would surely fail at both tasks.

An Alternative Application
Exodus 17:1-7; Philippians 2:1-13. "Is the Lord among us or not?" The question posed by the people of Israel did not have an obvious answer. The Israelites considered the lack of water to be a sign that God was not with them. Moses, on the contrary, considered their doubt a test of the Lord, which the Lord had no need to pass. God was with them, whether they realized it or not. The water was merely the sign that God had been there all along.

So too, the Philippians needed to understand the way in which Jesus was present to them as a community. If he is really risen, that means he is still alive. But he is with us in the Spirit rather than in the flesh. That Spirit is manifest in the mutual love of the community that lives by his example. Note that none of the verbs or pronouns are singular; it is always "you" plural (a distinction that cannot always be made in translation, but is clear in the Greek). You can't be a Christian alone; you have to have a neighbor to love as yourself.

Proper 22
Pentecost 17
Ordinary Time 27
Exodus 20:1-4, 7-9, 12-20
Philippians 3:4b-14
Matthew 21:33-46
by Wayne Brouwer

On beyond perfection

On Beyond Zebra! Remember the book by Dr. Seuss? Some people learn the alphabet, starting out at "A is for apple," and when they get all the way through to "Z is for zebra," they think they are done. But not Dr. Seuss! Twenty-six letters might be good enough for most people, but it's only the beginning for Dr. Seuss. One of his great "little people" takes us on a tour of life *On Beyond Zebra!* — a whole new world of creatures most of us have never seen before. It's a world where things run on different time schedules and where life itself has a very different feel about it.

This seems to be the case in our reading for today as well. The encounter between God and Israel at Mount Sinai was a lesson about living life in the right way. The Ten Commandments are no mere checklist for meeting up to everyday mediocrity — they are the building blocks of a better society. Similar, too, is Paul's take on things in Philippians 3 — the morality of a religious code by itself cannot bring hope, happiness, and health; he paints a canvas with deeper hues and brighter lights than mere morality can offer. And certainly Jesus' parable of the tenants makes the point that ethics and morality are rooted in more than just what we can get away with. We are entering a world beyond life as we know it; we are peeking into the meaning of *life* itself, way beyond social conformity or ethical accuracy. It is the world "on beyond" perfection.

Exodus 20:1-4, 7-9, 12-20

Although most of the people we speak to today know of the Ten Commandments, few know how the Ten Commandments came into being. Hollywood has its cinematic version, with Charlton Heston as Moses. But the biblical record itself gives us telltale signals that evoke a much richer drama that only preachers can play out with purpose and power.

Exodus 20-24 forms a single literary unit that is crafted in a clear parallel to other covenant documents forged between rulers and their peoples in the ancient near east. A number of elements were typically found in these covenants, including:

• A *preamble* giving the particulars of the authority giving expression to this treaty.
• A *historical prologue* explaining the background that has led to this treaty.
• *Stipulations* that lay out the mutual demands on the parties of this treaty.
• *Blessings and curses* that describe life in harmony with this treaty and the consequences of defiling it.
• *Witnesses* who are called upon to ensure the appropriate ratification of the treaty.
• *Ratification and renewal* clauses that tell of the ratification itself and describe how this treaty will be remembered and renewed.

Each of these six elements of ancient covenant literature is clearly represented in Exodus 20-24. Yahweh gives the *preamble* (20:1) and *historical prologue* (20:2) that sum up the book of Genesis and the international politics of Exodus 1-19. The *stipulations* are summarized in 20:3-17 and then broadened in 21:1—23:19. *Blessings and curses* are explained in 23:20-33, while chapter 24 includes both the *witnesses* (the elders and representatives from the tribes) and the *ratification* ceremony itself.

This literary understanding of Exodus 20-24 helps to put the Ten Commandments in their proper place and perspective. Rather than being considered merely some ancient list of important behaviors, or the residue of an arcane legal code, the Ten Commandments are actually the life parameters of Israel's identity as the rescued and restored nation of Yahweh. There is an old life (in Egypt) that carried a moral dehumanization (slavery) and from it only Yahweh could rescue Israel. Now that Israel belongs to Yahweh and not Pharaoh, Yahweh outlines the character of society in this new political order.

It begins with divine/human relations. Egyptian myths explained human life as the unfortunate degrading of appendages of the gods. Natural and spiritual realities were co-terminus and both evil and good were eternal tensions within the system. Yahweh's declarations, however, explained a world-order in which the Creator stood exalted (so there is no need to play around with petty powers — *first commandment*) outside the system (thus making all attempts at conjuring the deity up by way of tangible things a silly waste of time — *second commandment*). More than that, Yahweh had created all things by way of speaking and naming, so people must be careful about how they name either God or other things named by God (*third commandment*). Furthermore, the goal of Creation was to establish a relationship between God and God's people that blossoms in time and social interaction and are not reduced to animal drudgery (*fourth commandment*).

Similarly, in the makeup of human society, there are boundaries that safeguard human dignity (*fifth*, *sixth*, *seventh*, and *ninth commandments*) and the livelihoods of free people (*eighth* and *tenth commandments*). Although these boundaries are absolute in their moral character, they are not clearly defined by way of all ethical practices in the Ten Commandments proper. Only with the expansions and case studies of Exodus 21-23 do they begin to take moral shape.

This perspective on the Ten Commandments helps to define the ongoing role they play in human society, even after the demise of ancient Israel. If there is a continuous covenant relationship between God and God's people (this is the language of the Bible in both its Testaments), then the human understanding of God that is expressed in the first four commandments and the moral boundaries that safeguard human dignity in the last six commandments remain normative through all ages of human/divine interaction. At the same time, those who live outside of that covenant relationship generally do not understand the implications and ramifications of biblical covenant history, and therefore cannot presume to use the Ten Commandments as definitive outside of its biblical context. In other words, the Ten Commandments do not belong in the courtrooms of any national judicial system as normative to that system. They may be displayed as examples of meaningful ethical codes, but their function is different.

One more thing that may help to bring out the homiletic value of preaching on the Ten Commandments is the ancient Hittite practice of writing two copies of the covenant documents and keeping one in the king's palace and the other among the people at a distance from the capital city. Representations of the Ten Commandments today often picture two tablets of stone (based upon the statements of Exodus 32:15-16) with the first four commandments on one and the last six on the other. This is incorrect. The full covenant (or its summary, like the Ten Commandments) would have been written on each of the stone tablets. The amazing thing about the biblical record was that instead of these two copies ending up at different locations (one in heaven with God and the other in the tabernacle/temple among the people), they are kept in exactly the same spot! In other words, the Ark of Yahweh, with its mercy seat and guardian sentinel cherubim, was the portable throne of God that symbolized God's choice to move in with God's people. Both copies of the covenant could be kept in the same place because God and Israel were living together!

Philippians 3:4b-14

Credit is a slippery thing, as Paul notes in this passage. You may want it, but if you mention that, you won't likely get it. In fact, you might even get blacklisted instead. Earlier in his life he was trying to rack up credit based upon accomplishments he was able to tick off, even pointing to things that took place before he was born (in God's chosen family — "of the people of Israel"; from a clan that remained faithful to the Sinai covenant — "of the tribe of Benjamin"; and having pure Hebrew pedigree on both sides of the family — "a Hebrew of Hebrews") and to actions taken by others on his behalf (circumcision was a requirement, but to be "circumcised on the eighth day" was to obey both the spirit *and* the letter of the law). By the time Paul took charge of his own life he was a type-A general of the most obnoxious kind (see the rest of his list in 3:5-6). It sounds a little like the repartee of Gilbert and Sullivan when they have their captain of the *H.M.S. Pinafore* proclaiming his eminent worth in their operetta of that name. Behind him a chorus declaims and defames: "He is an Englishman! For he himself has said it, and it's greatly to his credit, that he is an Englishman!" All the while, of course, the audience is laughing at his buffoonery.

That is where Paul goes himself — scoffing at his previous predilections. Then he turns to find credit elsewhere. It is a kind of credit by association. In the last years of his life, composer Louis Antoine Jullien dreamed of writing one final work. He said he would like to set the words of the Lord's Prayer to music. Wouldn't it look wonderful, he asked his colleagues, to have a title page that read: "The Lord's Prayer": *Words by Jesus Christ. Music by Jullien*? Paul is headed in that direction. What if the script of his life could be written by Jesus, and then played through the melodies and harmonies of Paul's unique character?

The best credit, in that sense, is neither earned nor grasped; it is imputed. This is the morality of the gospel. A story about Abraham Lincoln's Illinois days as a young lawyer serves well to capture it as a parable. An angry man stormed into Lincoln's office demanding that he bring suit against an impoverished debtor who owed him $2.50. "Make him pay!"

Lincoln didn't want anything of the sort to happen. The debtor couldn't pay the $2.50, the creditor didn't need the $2.50, and society shouldn't be run by either such greed or such insensitivity. So Lincoln declined the case.

Unfortunately the man kept pressing and since Lincoln was the only lawyer available, he was forced to serve the suit. First, though, he charged the man $10 for legal fees. Then he brought the defendant in, gave him $5.00 for his time, and asked if the charges were accurate. He readily agreed and out of his newly gotten $5 paid the $2.50 he owed. Everyone was satisfied, including the irate plaintiff, who never realized that he spent $10 to collect $2.50!

Now turn that story around and think of it from this angle: A man with no credit is burdened by a debt he could never repay. Along comes an advocate he can't hire to resolve a matter he can't win. Suddenly, in a transaction he could never accomplish, the debt is gone, the creditor has disappeared, and he has money in his pocket! All he had to do was agree to the terms.

So it is in the strange economy of God, says Paul. Don't try to figure it out and certainly don't claim credit for it. But when morality that lives on beyond perfection is there, you'll know it and so will others!

Matthew 21:33-46

To catch the full impact of these verses we need to understand two things. First, the gospel of Matthew presents Jesus as king. He is identified as a royal scion of David in chapter 1, recognized as international king in chapter 2, declares the contours of the kingdom in chapter 13, assumes a right to the kingly palace in chapter 21, and declares his royal rule in chapter 28. Throughout the gospel, Jesus is the king — sometimes cloaked and sometimes evident, but always ruling.

Second, chapters 21-22 set up a deliberate contrast (see vv. 12-13) between royalty as expressed through the administration of the religious leaders of the day who count themselves as caretakers of God's kingdom (notice that the conversations in 21:12-16 and again from 21:23—22:46 are deliberately framed as occurring between Jesus and "the chief priests and the teachers of the law/elders") depicted by Jesus. The chief priests don't know how to properly care for the house of God/palace of the king/temple (21:12-17). They don't recognize the source of Jesus' authority (21:23-27). They present an outward obedience to divine authority that lacks inner love and commitment (21:28-32). They refuse to join the coronation of the king's anointed (22:1-14). They quibble about dual allegiances (22:15-22). They scoff at eternity as if time were theirs to manage and no exams or final grade were to be handed out in evaluation of their deeds (22:23-33; note — the "Sadducees" include the priest and Levite families). They play games with rules and regulations for behavior while missing the point of ethics and morality (22:34-40; note — the "Pharisees" were considered the "elders of the people"). The entire passage comes back to where it began in 22:41-46 — what is the source of Jesus' authority?

At the heart of this longer literary unit comes the story of the tenants. While several of the gospels relate this parable in various forms, here in Matthew's gospel it is clearly pointed at the priests and elders/Pharisees (see 22:45) — the religious leaders of the day. In a theme picked up from the Old Testament, Israel, as a whole, is the special garden or vineyard planted by God in Palestine and tended lovingly there from the time of the Exodus on (see, for example, Psalm 80, Isaiah 5). Those who were given the mandate to nurture health and spiritual depth in Israel on God's behalf were the priests and prophets. They, however, failed God and the people and usurped their authority for social or financial advancement. The dark days of the northern kingdom and its ungodly demise (see 2 Kings 17), as well as the whimpering end of the southern kingdom and its exile were brought about because the administrators left to care for God's vineyard thought they could possess it for themselves.

Now, in God's last-ditch effort to rescue the estate, God is sending the heir to heaven's throne, the Son himself. And on the Monday or Tuesday of Holy Week, when Jesus first spoke these words, the last administrators of the vineyard were about to kill the Son out of the deluded fantasy that suddenly the world would belong to them.

Jesus, in telling this story, seems to be giving the priests and elders, the Sadducees and Pharisees, one last opportunity to give up their petty ethics among thieves and learn again the morality of the kingdom. And even if they don't take to the lesson, we ought to give it another listen.

Application

In *What Is the Kingdom of Heaven?* Arthur Clutton-Brock tells a powerful story of his childhood. He was out for a walk with his sitter, traipsing along a country lane. At a house just before them, three children were romping through the yard, playing games and laughing delightedly. They had climbed a small sycamore tree, gathering leaves and tossing them into the air. They broke off the tender branches from the top of the tree, covered at the time with blazing bronzed leaves, and carried them in a bundle like a bouquet of flowers.

When Arthur and his sitter passed by, the children ran out into the lane and danced about them. Then they presented the bouquet of branches to Arthur in a ceremony of great pomp. It was a magical moment of grace and beauty.

But for some reason, said Arthur, whether from fear or from pride, he refused the gift offered. He ran after his sitter and when they were shortly down the path he turned round to look at the three. He saw them standing in the middle of the road, faces suddenly dragging on the ground. The laughter was gone and all the pretty flowers they had made were spilled around them in the dust.

Looking back on that moment, Clutton-Brock said, "I felt, in that moment, that I had turned my back on the kingdom of God. Something had been offered to me in love, and I hadn't taken it!" He also said that the sight of those three disappointed faces has haunted him all his life.

The haunting of our lives is the gap between what we know to be truly significant and our own actions that betray days lived by secondary values and systems. Like Israel on the run from Pharaoh, like Paul shifting his theological sights from law to grace, like religious leaders in Jesus' day who were so busy taking care of business that they forgot what business they were in, we need to be haunted back to God.

So it is with faith. The words we speak in testimony mean little until our feet carry us home. That is why the Bible is so insistent on behaviors that go beyond legalism to faith, beyond law-keeping to covenant living, beyond mere morality to something radical "on beyond" perfection. What we believe is written in a story penned anew each day. The test of our relationship with God is not the bent of our theology but the grace with which we receive flowers of the kingdom and the attitude we bear toward all God had made.

An Alternative Application
Exodus 20:1-4, 7-9, 12-20. While the Ten Commandments are often taught or preached by way of a series of messages on each topic, today might be a good day to help people see the whole as a single unit, and dig into the covenant purposes that gave rise to its expression in the first place. There is enough material above to warrant focusing on just the Ten Commandments and how they form a powerful link between God and God's people, not just in terms of behaviors, but reflecting a cosmic world-and-life view.

Proper 23
Pentecost 18
Ordinary Time 28
Exodus 32:1-14
Philippians 4:1-9
Matthew 22:1-14
by David Kalas

Under the circumstances

As I was driving home from the office the other day, I was waiting at a traffic light downtown when I saw one of my parishioners cross the street in front of me. It's still my first year in my present appointment, and it occurred to me that I had never seen him outside of church. He is in church quite faithfully, but I had never seen him outside of that context. The sight of him in more casual clothes... chewing gum... and coming out of a store reminded me of a ridiculously simple fact: He has a life outside of that pew where I am accustomed to seeing him each Sunday morning.

That our people have lives outside of church, of course, is no great revelation. It may be an important reminder to some of us, however, since the church context is such a huge percentage of our lives.

I wondered for a moment what last Sunday's sermon could mean to that man as he walked down the street, shopping and chewing gum. And what would this coming Sunday's sermon mean to him?

I do not know all the circumstances of all the people in my congregation. I can't. But I am well served to remember that they have all sorts of circumstances — some quite ordinary, even mundane; and some extraordinary, either by reason of great difficulties or great blessings. And they come on Sunday mornings needing, in part, a faith that applies to all the circumstances of their lives.

The Exodus episode and the words from Paul to the Philippians combine to provide wisdom and insight for people who need faith under the circumstances.

Exodus 32:1-14

What's taking so long? This is the tortured question that we ask time and again, perhaps almost every day. When we're stuck in traffic, when we're waiting for a response from someone by phone or by email, when we're eager for some order to be delivered, when we're standing impatiently in a line that's not moving, we ask, "What's taking so long?"

The Israelites, camped at the base of Mount Sinai, looked up at the mountain each day for weeks. Their eyes strained to see some sign of Moses coming down, returning from his rendezvous with God. Day after day passed with no sign of Moses and the people became worried and impatient. What's taking him so long?

The experience of waiting presents us with a test of character. What will we do while we wait? Waiting suggests that circumstances are, for the present, out of our control. We don't like that. What will we do about it?

I remember occasions when my dad would pick me up from school. He would almost always arrive at the school before I got out of the building, and so he would wait for me. If he had nursed impatience within himself, then he might have nervously drummed his fingers, repeatedly checked his watch, and allowed a mounting urgency to grow inside. Under those circumstances, I would almost certainly have been greeted by that impatient protest that masquerades as a question: "What took you so long?"

Instead, however, my dad would always have in the car with him something to read and a pad to write on. And so he would redeem the time with work, reading, and correspondence, making it almost a matter of indifference to him whether he waited for me two minutes or twenty.

So the question of character is: What do we do while we wait? Do we grumble and complain? Does our impatience give birth to rudeness? Do we doubt and despair?

Jesus, anticipating the wait his followers would experience until his second coming, told parables about servants whose master was away for an indefinite time. How those servants were judged in the end was a function of what they did while they waited.

What the Israelites did while they waited for Moses reflects badly on them.

Perhaps you've been stuck in the kind of traffic jam that prompts you to go ahead and shift your car into park. I have. And I've concluded that there's no point in my sitting here with my foot on the break and my engine running and so I've shifted and turned off the car.

That represents a moment of resignation that the Israelites were loath to reach. They did not want to be parked indefinitely out there in the wilderness. They had children and flocks to worry about. The resources seemed limited. Their destination was known, but not familiar, and the trip forward was daunting, particularly without Moses' leadership. And so, unable to move forward, and unwilling to stay parked, the people decide to shift into reverse — into idolatry and debauchery.

The human dependence on a human agent and representative in our relationship to God is manifested here at Sinai. It is ostensibly Moses' disappearance that concerns the people; yet their response is to make new gods for themselves (see 32:4). Is Moses' absence the same as God's? Have they no faith in or relationship with God apart from Moses as the mediator?

God says of the people, "They have been quick to turn aside from the way that I commanded them" (v. 8). I am enough of a sports fan that "quick" sounds mostly like a virtue to me. But it depends, doesn't it, on what we are quick to do?

It is a charming thing to be quick-witted. It is not so pleasant, however, to be quick-tempered. We are grateful for people who are quick to respond, but we're burdened by folks who are quick to judge. In the case of the Israelites in the wilderness, they were quick to turn aside. What is my quickness? What are you and I quick to do?

The conclusion of this passage features a dramatic instance of human intercession and God changing his mind. In my experience, people are often troubled by this story, for they are uneasy with the thought of God changing his mind — or, worse yet, the thought of a human being changing God's mind.

In fact, of course, we are quite impossible to please on this subject. If there is no changing God's mind, then we chaff against the impression that everything is pre-determined and we wonder about the point and purpose of prayer. On the other hand, when presented with this powerful illustration of the point and purpose of prayer, we resist the prospect.

Yet here is this thematic truth, like it or not. The God who creates a world and then leaves us in charge of it, the God who entrusts the saving message of his love to human messengers, and that same God invites our intercession and our persistence. And so from Abraham on behalf of the unnumbered righteous in Sodom (Genesis 18:16-33) to the ever-hopeful gardener (Luke 13:6-9); from the Canaanite woman who would not take, "No," for an answer (Matthew 15:21-28) to Moses in our passage; our God invites, welcomes, and responds to our persevering faith and to our dogged prayers.

Philippians 4:1-9

One of the standard tricks of the trade for mothers whose children like to make ugly faces is to offer this warning: "Be careful! Your face might freeze like that!" In the short term, of course, the superstition is unfounded. Over the long haul, however, I expect the warning has its wisdom. We have all known people whose eyes and lines reflect years of either smiling or frowning, bitterness or beatitude.

Whenever I read this passage from Paul's letter to the Philippians, I am reminded of that old maternal warning. We don't know what was going on between Euodia and Syntyche there in the church at Philippi. We don't know anything about who they were. But we surmise from Paul's brief reference that there was some quarrel between them.

You could probably identify two people in your church just now who are separated by some disagreement. It is unfortunate, to be sure, but it is not uncommon. And yet the names of these two otherwise unknown women of first-century Philippi are still known and read around the globe 2,000 years later. And like the lovers frozen in mid-flirtation in Keats' "Ode on a Grecian Urn," so Euodia and Syntyche are frozen in mid-quarrel. It's as though history caught them making an ugly face and their faces did, indeed, freeze like that.

That Paul exhorts those two women personally in the midst of his letter to the congregation as a whole suggests something about Paul's emphasis on unity. We certainly see evidence of that priority in other letters (as in 1 Corinthians 1:10-13; Ephesians 4:1-16; Titus 3:10), and it is particularly striking here. We might be inclined to shrug off a two-person dispute. What can it hurt? Besides, aren't such things inevitable when dealing with human beings? Paul maintains a higher view of the Body of Christ, however, and higher hopes for the church. As William Barclay observes, "He thought no effort too great to maintain the peace of the church. A quarreling church is no church at all, for it is one from which Christ has been shut out. No man can be at peace with God and at variance with his fellow-man."

Later in the passage we find one of the most familiar phrases from the entire Pauline corpus, as well as one of the emblem statements of this particular letter, "Rejoice in the Lord always; again I will say, Rejoice."

If this were scribbled on a postcard from the Bahamas where Paul was lounging on a beach, his words might seem shallow and unconvincing. But Paul wrote to the Philippians from prison and that context makes his exhortation to rejoice — and his own manifest joy — quite remarkable. We cannot easily dismiss Paul's words because of our own difficulties when we see the circumstances from which he wrote and in which he rejoiced.

"Rejoice," which appears twice in the verse, is rendered as a plural imperative in the original Greek. The word is a healthy reminder that rejoicing is a verb, not merely an emotion. It is something we do; not necessarily something we feel. And Paul commands the people of Philippi to do it.

That's a strong word for us in our day and in our circumstances. It is neither a pale "cheer up" nor a heartless "get over it." Rejoicing is something you and I can do. I can choose to do it just now as surely as I can choose to blink, snap, or walk. And Paul urges me to do it, and to do it always, at all times.

Matthew 22:1-14

Jesus introduces this parable about a wedding banquet with a familiar introduction. As "once upon a time" is to children's fables, so "the kingdom of heaven is like" is to Jesus' parables. They are not all explicitly parables of the kingdom but the kingdom is clearly a prevailing theme.

This particular parable offers a strange mix of moods.

On the one hand, there is the festive context: a wedding banquet. And it is not any ordinary celebration, for this is no less than the banquet being given by the king for his own son on the occasion of the son's wedding. This is big stuff: regal and opulent, joyful and personal.

On the other hand, the festive quality of the parable seems somewhat diminished by the recurring judgment theme. This king does not just send out invitations; he also sends out his troops. He seems to welcome all comers, but then he violently evicts one in the end.

It's a strange mix of moods but one that is consistent with our understanding of the eschaton. Just as "the day of the Lord" had two sides to it in Amos' day (see Amos 5:18-20), so the New Testament's picture of the end of time features a mixture of both judgment and joy.

Unlike the people of Jesus' day, we in the United States do not live in a context of kings and princes. We have witnessed some royal weddings in our time, however, and so we have some sense for the fanfare of the occasion. Even the weddings of ordinary people were big events in their communities in that day. And so it would no doubt have been a great honor and privilege to be invited to attend the wedding of the king's son. Accordingly, the way that the invited guests decline the big, special event — probably in favor of much lesser fare (see v. 5, and, in Luke's version of the parable, 14:18-20) — seems ridiculous to us. Yet truth be told, every time we decline any invitation from God, it is a ridiculous preference for lesser fare. We have, as Charles Wesley sings it, "sold for naught (our) heritage above."

It is noteworthy — and sobering — that among those who missed the great banquet were folks who did not choose bad places, just ordinary ones. Jesus said that one went to his farm and another to his business. Those are reasonable destinations, plausible priorities. Yet when they interfere with the king's invitation, suddenly they change from neutral to negative. The old adage says that the road to hell is paved with good intentions. And we can easily see why if that is the road we sometimes take just to get to our farms and our businesses.

At the end of the parable, Jesus describes the unceremonious dismissal of one of the attendees. Earlier, the invited guests had "made light of it and went away." And now, at the end, one man who did come "was not wearing a wedding robe." Thus we discover that there is more than one way to take lightly the invitation of God. Just as declining his invitation is an unworthy response, it is also possible to accept his invitation unworthily.

Application

The circumstances were unfavorable for the people of our passage from Exodus. They were out in the middle of nowhere — some distance from the place they had involuntarily called home for the past four centuries, and a still greater distance from the foreign land that was their final destination. They were in the wilderness with supplies that seemed to be no match for demands. And their leader — the one whom God had used to bring them out of Egypt and whom God was presumably going to use to lead them to the promised land — was missing in action.

What do you do under such circumstances?

Paul, too, wrote from unfavorable circumstances. He was in prison, no doubt unjustly, and probably after having been treated cruelly. Also, his future must have seemed uncertain. He was often misunderstood by some of his own Christian brethren, he met with mounting Jewish opposition almost everywhere he went, and even the civil authorities in certain places were intolerant of him, his work, and his influence.

What do you do under such circumstances?

The responses of Paul in prison and the Israelites in the wilderness could not be more different.

The children of Israel despaired in the midst of their circumstances, and they looked for help and for hope in improper places. The apostle Paul wrote the "joyful epistle." The Israelites were "quick to turn aside." Paul said, "Stand firm in the Lord." The Israelites worried about Moses, food, and water. Paul wrote, "Do not worry about anything." The Israelites complained. Paul rejoiced.

Side by side, the Israelites and the apostle present us with examples of how we might respond under the circumstances of our lives. We might despair and complain, be filled with worry, and be tempted to turn aside from the truth and the righteousness that we have known. Or we may stand firm, trust and rejoice in the Lord, and be assured that "the peace of God, which surpasses all understanding, will guard your hearts and your minds in Christ Jesus."

An Alternative Application
Philippians 4:1-9. Among the many compelling scenes in the 1975 movie *Jaws*, there is a late-night episode in which two characters, Hooper and Brody, slice open the carcass of a shark to discover what he

has eaten recently. The question at hand is whether he is the shark that recently killed two victims there at Amity, but the graphic depiction gives us a broader glimpse into the consumption of a shark, including a Louisiana license plate. With both its suspense and its grim realism, the scene invites the audience to ponder the feeding habits of a shark.

What if it were possible for us to perform such an exploration of the human mind? What if there was something we could open and all that our mind has consumed in the past week would spill out on the floor for all to see? What kind of mental diet would we see?

After this introduction, the sermon would have two major sections. First, some consideration of the unwholesome stuff that may fill our minds: worries and anger, bitterness and grudges, ambition and lust, unkind judgments and worthless trivialities. And then, having explored and examined some of what may presently fill our minds, we can turn to Paul's "think about these things" list.

The list deserves exposition at three levels. First, consideration of what these several words — true, honorable, commendable, just, pure, pleasing, excellent, worthy of praise — mean. Second, some cheerful imagining of what difference it would make in a life if our mental diet changed from worries, grudges, and trivialities to things honorable, pure, and worthy of praise. Third, a congregation might benefit from a concrete proposal — for example, to focus on a different word (emphasis) in Paul's list each day of the coming week as a way of training our minds.

Finally, it should be noted that Paul's list stands in stark contrast to the fare that is offered on television and in so many magazines. His list may also be quite far removed from the thoughts that come naturally to us or that we cultivate as a matter of habit. If we want our minds to be filled with these things, therefore, we may have to feed in different waters.

Proper 24
Pentecost 19
Ordinary Time 29
Exodus 33:12-23
1 Thessalonians 1:1-10
Matthew 22:15-22
by William Shepherd

Show me your ways

I have to admit that I have absolutely no interest in preserving the institution of the church. The community, that's another thing.

Institutions are idolatrous. That is, by their very nature they demand total allegiance, for they exist solely through the investment of their members. They have no life of their own but derive their existence from the life of the human beings who take part in them. They brook no rivals; they demand conformity. Institutions are humorless because if they do not take themselves seriously, they will cease to exist. Give your life to an institution, and it will take your life away from you.

Communities, on the other hand, are life-giving. Communities exist for the sake of their members. Rather than taking your life, they remind us that life is bigger than any one of us. They demand not conformity but diversity, since it is in encountering those who differ from us that we learn to accept that life is not our own but derived from an ultimate source. A community can look at itself and laugh at the absurdity of its diversity, because it holds itself loosely, recognizing that it exists not in and of itself but for a larger purpose. A community is created by God and, in the case of the church, exists to acknowledge that God. The church as a community differs from the church as an institution in that the one reflects for us the image of God, while the other pretends to be God.

Our lessons today trace a path out of idolatry into the service of a living God, who cannot be contained by any created thing, let alone an institution. In each lesson, the community plays a vital role in calling human beings away from idolatry and toward God but the moment communities become institutionalized, they pull the other way. We will never escape idolatry without the help of other people; we will always have to resist the tendency of communities to re-form themselves as idolatrous institutions.

Exodus 33:12-23

The story of Moses begins shortly after the people of Israel made the vital mistake of trying to institutionalize their community in the shape of a golden calf (cf. Exodus 32:1-35). Not content to be a community-in-waiting, they convinced Aaron to fashion a substitute for the living God whom Moses had gone up the mountain to meet. In the absence of any certainty, they attempt to create their own. It was Genesis 3 redux — the pattern of sin, dialogue, and new covenant is quite similar to the Bible's opening chapters. In some ways, Israel was in an even more precarious position than Adam and Eve, because their existence as a people was predicated on being the people of the Lord; without the Lord, they were no people.

Moses takes on the role of intercessor, as the one person who has "found favor" with God. Note that the usual rule in the biblical writings goes by the wayside in God's address to Moses; more often than not, the second-person pronoun "you" in the Bible is plural, reflecting God's commitment to the community rather than the individual, but here God speaks to Moses personally, omitting any reference to the community. "I will do the very thing that you have asked; for you have found favor in my sight, and I know you by name" (v. 17). This distresses Moses to no end, for it indicates that the community has lost its binding principle, its election by God. God has gone so far to call Israel, "Moses' people": "Go, leave this place, you and the people whom you have brought up out of the land of Egypt, and go to the land... I will send an angel before you... but I will not go up among you, or I would consume you on the way, for you are a stiff-necked people" (vv. 1-3). Moses realizes that if the peoples' leadership is delegated to an angel, Israel will no longer be unique, it will have lost the primary mark of its existence: "If your presence will not go, do not carry us up from here. For how shall it be known that I have found favor in your sight, I and your people, unless you go with us? In this way, we shall be distinct, I and your people, from every people on the face of the earth" (vv. 15-16). In his objection, Moses emphasizes not just his own closeness to God, but identifies himself with the people.

Rather than deny his close relationship with God, Moses seeks to capitalize on God's "favor" for the sake of the people (vv. 12-13, 16-17, 19). He asks God to lead Israel personally and not through an unknown intermediary: "See, you have said to me, 'Bring up this people'; but you have not let me know whom you will send with me. Yet you have said, 'I know you by name, and you have also found favor in my sight.' Now if I have found favor in your sight, show me your ways, so that I may know you and find favor in your sight. Consider too that this nation is your people" (vv. 12-13). The narrative moves forward via the keywords "favor," "see," "face," and "know." English translations tend to obscure the subtlety of Moses' intercession, as he attempts to get God to "see" (*r'h* variously translated as "see," "consider," and "show," vv. 12-13, 18) that God's "face" (*paneh* sometimes translated "presence," vv. 14-16) is crucial to Israel's existence, for it is the face that Israel presents to the world (v. 16). Moses wants to translate God's intimacy with him (expressed by the verb *yd'* "to know," vv. 12, 17) into confirmation both for him ("show me" in v. 13 reflects *yd'*) and the world (*yd'* again in v. 16, "How shall it be known that I have found favor in your sight, I and your people, unless you go with us?"). God finally relents and agrees to lead the people as a result of Moses' persistence (vv. 14, 17).

Moses isn't done yet: "Show me your glory" (*r'h* again, v. 18). Moses wants to see the essence of God. This is not an unreasonable request, because it has already been granted once when Moses and the leaders of Israel "saw the God of Israel. Under his feet there was something like a pavement of sapphire stone, like the very heaven for clearness. God did not lay his hand on the chief men of the people of Israel; also they beheld God, and they ate and drank" (24:10-11). However, Moses is asking for an even greater intimacy that cannot be granted — for safety's sake! "You cannot see my face (again *paneh*); for no one shall see me and live" (33:20; the contradiction with 24:10-11 is never fully resolved). Moses is personally denied the very "face" he had requested for Israel, as a reminder that the "favor" (*hen*, vv. 12-13, 16-17) he has been given is the sovereign gift of one who is by nature "gracious" (the cognate *hnn*, "to show favor," v. 19). Moses cannot see God's "glory," but only God's "goodness," as embodied in the divine name (v. 19). This is symbolized by God's care to shield Moses from his "face" and reveal only his "back" (vv. 21-23; the promise but not the action is narrated). As close as Moses is to God, there is a differentiation between creature and creator that cannot be bridged. No created thing can substitute for the creator without harm to creation.

1 Thessalonians 1:1-10

Paul writes to those who have "turned to God from idols, to serve a living and true God" (1:9). The Thessalonian church was composed primarily of Greeks, who needed instruction concerning exactly what it meant to worship God rather than idols. In pagan religion there was little connection between religion and morality (in comparison with Judaism); they were two separate spheres of existence. Even the worship of idols was not considered pejorative in Roman circles, as it was in Judaism; for a pagan audience, it would be news that there was a difference between idols and a living God (v. 9). Thus there was nothing in the Thessalonians' background that would prepare them for life as Christian believers. Paul and his colleagues must provide it for them in person or by letter.

Thus Paul, Silvanus, and Timothy take an existing literary form, the letter of friendship, and transform it for Christian purposes. The transformation is not limited to a Christianization of the opening greeting (v. 1); ancient letters often began with a prayer for the reader's well-being, along with a thanksgiving and supplication to the gods. Here the convention is changed to emphasize the spiritual condition of the recipients, reflecting the main themes of the letter, including the importance of the community for a continued life moving away from idolatry and toward God (vv. 9-10); the significance of the works produced by faith and love (cf. 2:1-16); the response of witness that comes with being chosen by God (cf. 2:17—3:13); the importance of moral exemplars for Christian growth (cf. 4:1-12; 5:12-24); and the ultimate reality of judgment and salvation in God's long-term time frame (cf. 4:13—5:11).

The multiple authorship is crucial to Paul's exemplary purpose. We tend to speak of "the letters of Paul" as if he did not explicitly and specifically acknowledge his co-writers, in this case Silvanus and Timothy. Paul worked as part of a team and we should take the multiple authorship of his letters seriously. It is "we" and not "I" who directs thanks to God for this community (v. 2). It is "we" and not "I" who acknowledge God's choice of these people (v. 4). Most importantly, it is "we" and not "I" who serve as moral examples of the Christian life (v. 5), because it is the whole community and not just the individuals who reflect the glory of their Lord (v. 6). Thus the Thessalonians, who imitate not just the apostles but also their Lord, can be examples to others (v. 7).

The primary focus of imitation, however, is not moral but evangelical. Their example, in which they follow that of the apostles, is "the word of the Lord has sounded forth from you" (v. 8). This is their "work of faith and labor of love," the indication that "he has chosen you, because our message of the gospel came to you not in word only, but also in power and in the Holy Spirit and with full conviction" (vv. 4-5). Thus their report (about the Lord and their own community) goes out throughout the region (vv. 8-9). The message about the messengers confirms their message.

The letter opening does not neglect the prominent eschatological theme that reverberates throughout (cf. 2:19; 3:13; 4:13-18; 5:1-11). The logical consequence of the turn from idols to a living God is to recognize that the risen Lord is still alive and scheduled for return (v. 10). The purpose of the return is to "rescue us from the wrath that is coming" (cf. 2:16; 5:9), and the purpose of the community is to "wait for his Son from heaven" by working to become the people of God. This end-times focus probably explains the reference to "persecution" (v. 6, literally "in deep tribulation"). This probably does not refer to any organized persecution of the Thessalonian church but to the inherent cultural and personal discomfort that comes with moving from idolatry to worship of the living God; they were moving to a new way of being and at odds with their neighbors. Such "tribulation" was commonly thought to be a sign of the end (cf. 2:2, 14-16; 3:3-4; cf. Matthew 24:9, 21, 29; Mark 13:19, 24; Revelation 7:14), but in fact it came with the territory of believing in a dying, rising, and living Lord (cf. John 16:33; Romans 5:3; 8:35; 12:12; 2 Corinthians 1:4, 8; 2:4; 4:17; Philippians 1:17; 4:14; 2 Thessalonians 1:4, 6; Hebrews 10:33; Revelation 1:9; 2:9-10). Distress and persecution follows from the imitation of Christ and it represents a share in the suffering of Christ; the new converts in Thessalonica would need a reminder that this too is part of following the example of their Lord.

Matthew 22:15-22

The situation is much more dangerous when the leaders of the community are those who have turned from the living God to idols. In the case of the Pharisees and the Herodians who tried to entrap Jesus, the idol was clearly the institution that had come to substitute for the community. In their attempt to preserve the institution, they failed both the community and the God who formed it. Having nothing to contribute to the community, they can do nothing but try to bolster an empty institution the best they know how — by giving their lives to it and demanding Jesus' life to preserve it.

Though the Pharisees present themselves as extremely poor models for imitation, they nevertheless have disciples of their own and in Matthew's version of the story, they send these poor lambs into a verbal joust with Jesus. The Herodians who accompany them are otherwise unknown, but presumably were followers of that Jewish leader. (There is no particular evidence for the hypothesis that the Herodians would have been invested in the opposite side of the issue as the Pharisees, for example, that they wanted to hear Jesus say "It is lawful," while the Pharisees believed "It is not lawful.") The irony here is that the question is not one of Jewish law at all; they simply ask Jesus his opinion on a political issue, in hopes that he will trip up — it is the original "Gotcha" question, along the lines of "Have you stopped beating your wife yet?" The unpopular Roman poll tax amounted to a day's worth of forced labor for the Romans (on top of all the other local and imperial taxes levied) and were Jesus to affirm it, his status among the people would be compromised. But it was a greater danger to deny it in public, since that could be taken as open sedition by the Romans. The mini-Pharisees think they have Jesus in a difficult situation.

But Jesus exposes their hypocrisy simply by asking for the coin used for the tribute tax, a silver denarius bearing the image and title of the emperor. They produce one from their own pockets (Jesus and his disciples conspicuously traveled without cash). If it were unlawful to give tribute to the emperor, why were they carrying his graven image? Did not their possession of his coinage signify their participation in a spiritual realm where the emperor was considered to be the Son of God? The coin would have burned their hands if their question had been in any way honest. Jesus can handle the coin, however, because he sees it for what it is — a created thing that takes its value from those who wield it. For Jesus it is relatively insignificant; he can hand it back to the emperor without any loss to himself. More important is to give back to God that which belongs to God.

"Give therefore to the emperor the things that are the emperor's, and to God the things that are God's" (v. 21). The pronouncement is hardly to be taken as guidance for political philosophy. It serves rhetorically to stop the conversation and shut the mouths of the insincere (v. 22). For those who have ears to hear, however, it does not end the conversation but opens it up. The issue of what belongs to the emperor is clear enough; it can be held in the hand or put in the change pocket. The issue of what belongs to God is less clear since there is no prop or visual aid. What does belong to God? It would be more to the point to ask if there is anything that does *not* belong to God. In effect, Jesus is inviting his listeners to turn from idols — which can consist in any created thing to which we give our allegiance — to the living God.

You may have seen the proposed simplified IRS form; it has two lines, the first of which asks, "What is your income?" while the second says, "Send it in." Jesus' answer turns the joke on its head. The truth of the matter is that no matter what you try to hold back, you always end up sending all of yourself. The choice is clear enough: Will you send what you have to the emperor (or whatever creature holds your interest that day), or will you send everything that is you to God? Only one choice is life-giving, because we can never truly belong to a created thing but only to the God who gives us life and breath and being.

Application

Idolatry and faith are not two separate conditions but different places on the same continuum. As created beings, we are always oscillating somewhere between these two poles. Being creatures and not the Creator, we will always be in need of something outside of our selves to make ourselves complete. Ideally, we will find our center in the Creator, the one who made us with the God-shaped hole in the heart. However, the problem with grasping the Creator is that there is nothing to grasp. Like Moses, we find ourselves staring at God's backside, seeing a fleeting glimpse of goodness were we hoped to find a confirming glory. The face of God eludes us. How much easier to grab creation that which can be seen and held and counted.

The gross idolatry of the glutton or the miser or the "sexaholic" may not appeal to the refined tastes of religious folk, however. We are more than aware of and on guard against the sins of the flesh. We may fail to realize, however, that the things of the spirit are our own creations too. We may attempt to accumulate for ourselves attitudes and attributes of our own making so that we come to trust in our own righteousness, virtue, and intellectual accomplishments. Any created thing can become an idol. Yes, even the church itself.

There is no easy fix for idolatry, and its subtler forms are even harder to fight against. But the very nature of idolatry precludes our ever escaping it completely. Faith is therefore a process. We choose the living God over the idol, again and again, one day at a time. We find ourselves looking down at Israel from the mountain, oblivious to the golden calf we hold in our own hearts. We smirk at the retreating Pharisees until we look down to see that the emperor's idolatrous image is still in *our* hands. We stumble, we confess our sins, and we get back up. We turn from idols to worship the living God. This is the life of faith.

This is where the community is so crucial to the process. You remind me, by the simple virtue of being you, that I am not God. God has called you, a fellow creature, to be in community with me, even though we may not agree on theology, politics, social issues, or much of anything else. Our agreement may be an institutional concern, but it is not a communal concern. Our difference is our gift to one another; it calls us away from the worship of our "creatureliness" by reminding us that God made us all to be different. God cannot be contained by any one creature. Simply looking at you calls me out of idolatry and toward the living God. This indeed is the life of faith.

An Alternative Application
Exodus 33:12-23; 1 Thessalonians 1:1-10. Prayer is a powerful force. God was ready to leave Israel to its golden calf. Moses, however, would not let the people go. He capitalized on his own favor with God in order to call God back to the people. He appealed to God's own nature as gracious and merciful, counting on God's own self-identification: "I will be gracious to whom I will be gracious, and will show mercy on whom I will show mercy" (Exodus 33:19). If God is sovereign in this favor and mercy, then there is no reason that God could not extend it to those who had proved themselves unworthy of it. Moses' example proved to subsequent believers, like Paul, Silvanus, and Timothy that intercessory prayer was worth a try.

Proper 25
Pentecost 20
Ordinary Time 30
Deuteronomy 34:1-12
1 Thessalonians 2:1-8
Matthew 22:34-46
by Wayne Brouwer

Testimonies

In Susan Howatch's novel, *Absolute Truths*, the main character is a rather perfect man. Oh, to be sure, Charles Ashworth had his little peculiarities in his younger years and he needed the guidance of Jon Darrow to help him understand himself. But all in all he is a portrait of humanity at its best — sound and sleek in body, steady in temperament, keen in intellect, faithful in relationships, and unwavering in morality. He is the consummate churchman. It is no accident of fate that has placed him in the high post of Bishop of Starbridge.

Just as he faces off against those in the church and society who seem to be changing the morals of culture, his wife suddenly dies of a blood clot in the brain. Charles is with her at the time and watches in horrified helplessness as she slumps lifeless to the floor.

Bishop Ashworth's world is shattered. Still, no one will hold him accountable for his depression and excessive drinking since these are the normal temporary responses to such a loss. He is still a perfect man, perfect even in his grief.

Then as he finally clears their bedroom of his wife's clothes and cosmetics, Charles discovers her journal. For some years she had been penning her secret thoughts. It began as an attempt at prayer, providing a means by which Mrs. Ashworth tried to sort through the turmoil inside in order to present herself to God honestly.

Some of the pages of the journal retrace the minutia of life — meetings and schedules, changing seasons, weather and fashions. Woven throughout, however, is a remarkable analysis of Charles' own psyche. He was not aware that she knew him so perceptively. More than that, he did not realize that there were flaws in his own character that kept her and their two sons at a (dis)respectful distance. Formally his life was in tune with the "absolute truths" of Christian behavior. Yet somewhere in the firmness of his propriety he had failed to grasp the one essential absolute truth of God: It is grace that drives love and not pedantic obedience.

Moses, Paul, Jesus. Part of the reason they stand with us and above us as spiritual leaders is because they each knew this. Their lives stand as testimonies of God's grace and that is why they are remembered.

Deuteronomy 34:1-12

When Erik Eriksen wrote his famous biography of Martin Luther he observed that all of us endure similar experiences of life, but what makes some people special is their ability to ferret out their truest selves through those adventures. In Luther's case it became a matter of "Greatness Finding Itself," and that's what Eriksen titled his study.

Eriksen said that one of the main crises of life was the quest to hang onto integrity. It is very hard, he said, for us to keep ourselves together. Even though we are mostly good people, we tend to break little pieces of our hearts off here and there, thinking we will serve some greater good in the long run. We may never destroy ourselves in some heinous crime or gross violation of decency. Still we frazzle the edges of our souls through compromise in a dozen minor matters.

Moses' life is a case in point. Raised at home in a hostile environment (imagine other families seeing how Moses' parents got to keep their baby while they had drown their own children!), Moses was then carried away to an entirely different culture to live out his teens and early adulthood. He was always the outsider. Then, just at the point of finding a mate and some political or business success, he was driven from Egypt as a murderer at the age of forty. Talk about being disenfranchised! Next, he manages to settle into nomadic seclusion for four more decades. Finally, just at the point of old age and retirement, he is abruptly visited by a strange God communicating with him in strange ways and is required to give up his peace and tranquility to take on the greatest political and military power of the day. When he finds the courage to confront Pharaoh and wins the "battle of the ten plagues," Moses rushes out of Egypt at the head of a column of misfits and slaves who then turn on him and make unrealistic demands. Moses lives out the last third of his life as single parent to a multitude of crying babies (we call them the "children of Israel") and gets blasted by God for getting upset with them. Now, after 120 years of schizophrenic readjustments to a changing life, Moses gives his last will and testament (the book of Deuteronomy) to the next generation of Israel and dies accompanied only by the God who has haunted, goaded, and loved him these past forty years.

Eriksen's review of Martin Luther could probably be rewritten for Moses' strange life story in this way: *Obscurity Transformed into Greatness*. No one could write a fiction more fanciful than Moses' true story. And none would be able to pen a finer eulogy than the words captured by the one who brought Moses' tale to a close in Deuteronomy 34:5-12. What Malvolio said in Shakespeare's *Twelfth Night* could well have been spoken of the life of Moses: "Some are born great, some achieve greatness, and some have greatness thrust upon them."

1 Thessalonians 2:1-8

Paul's Thessalonians correspondence was written early in his career. The book of Acts does not help us much with a background to this letter, only telling us that Paul stopped briefly in the city on his second mission journey and spent at least three weeks speaking in the synagogue before the city erupted in a riot against Paul's presence and message (17:1-9). In the few verses of today's text Paul adds some of his own recollections to the tale, and what emerges is a picture of graciousness that won the hearts of those who began to see a living testimony of God's goodness (see also 1 Thessalonians 1:4-10).

Graciousness is a rare commodity. Cecil Rhodes, the nineteenth-century expansionist, South African statesman, and financier, was known for his precise manners and impeccable dress code. Yet he wore these with a considerate heart. When Rhodes was hosting a formal dinner at his Kimberley home, for example, one of the guests was unable to arrive until the very moment of seating and had no time to change his travel-stained and rumpled clothes. The young man's obvious discomfort in this company of glittering women and dapper gentlemen was made more acute because Rhodes, usually so punctual, delayed his appearance at the table. The dusty fellow felt like pig in a hen house, surrounded by clucking criticism.

But when Rhodes finally entered the room to greet his guests and begin the meal, they were taken aback. Rather than sporting formal attire, he was clad in a shabby old blue suit! Now it was the young man's turn to feel at ease while the others wondered at their being over-dressed.

Only the household servants ever knew the whole story. Rhodes had been descending the stairs as the last guest arrived. Noting his guest's travel-weary look, Rhodes had returned to his dressing room, removed his black tuxedo, and quickly slipped into the sorriest suit he could find in his closet. It was his way of politely declaring the misfit to be welcome at his table. In this, Cecil Rhodes had class.

While we would all commend graciousness as a valuable social grace, Paul elevates it to the level of divine witness. What makes it so?

Maybe it has to do with the fact that a considerate person takes thought of others. Will Durant, the famous philosopher and historian, was asked for advice by one of his grandchildren. He summarized all his wisdom in "ten commandments." At the heart of them is this advice: "Do not speak while another is speaking. Discuss, do not dispute. Absorb and acknowledge whatever truth you can find in opinions different from your own. Be courteous and considerate to all, especially to those who oppose you."

But maybe graciousness is more than just thoughtfulness. Stan Wiersma, writing under his pen name "Sietze Buning," explored the religious roots of being considerate in his collection of folk poetry titled *Style and Class* (Orange City, Iowa: Middleburg Press, 1982). Much of what we display in life, said Sietze Buning, has to do with "style" — we watch how others dress or act, and then we try to imitate those we admire. But "class" is living out of the nobility of your inner character, said Sietze. He tells this little story to illustrate what he means:

> *Queen Wilhelmina was entertaining the Frisian Cattle Breeders' Association at dinner. The Frisian farmers didn't know what to make of their finger bowls. They drank them down. The stylish courtiers from The Hague nudged each other, pointed, and laughed at such lack of style, until the queen herself, without a smile, raised her finger bowl and drained it, obliging all the courtiers to follow suit — without a smile* (p. 17).

Sietze Buning ends with this note of judgment: The courtiers had style, but Queen Wilhelmina had class.

While that makes for good storytelling, Sietze Buning takes it one surprising step further. He links style to the wisdom of the world and class to the wisdom of heaven. The former tries to get us to fit in with the right crowd, looking the right way and eating the right foods, while driving the right vehicles. That's style.

But class — *real* class — happens to us when we realize that we are children of God. If God is king, we are nobility — princesses and princes in the realm of the great ruler! Children of the king do not need to prove themselves, nor do they need to flaunt their status. If they have learned well at home the true worth of their lives, they can treat others with courtesy and respect. They can be gracious and considerate. It is a religious thing, as Paul notes in these verses.

Matthew 22:34-46

Why can Jesus interpret the law of Moses as he does here? There are several possibilities. First, Jesus could do so since it was the prerogative of any Jewish male to wrestle with scripture. Second, he could do so because he was identified as having some wisdom (cf. the appellation "Teacher" given to him by his interrogator). Third, he could do so because he has a commanding authority; the gospel of Matthew presents Jesus as king throughout and comments on Jesus' teaching prowess on several occasions (cf. Matthew 7:28-29). Fourth, Jesus can interpret the law of Moses because he is, in fact, the author of that law by way of the divine Trinity.

This was, of course, the self-aggrandizing (from their perspective) assumption the Pharisees were looking for. Jesus had already silenced their opposing socio-political/religious leadership counterparts, the Sadducees (v. 34), and now the Pharisees attempt to corner and humiliate this charismatic leader. But Jesus merely allows Moses to speak for himself. Jesus quotes Moses to interpret Moses, showing how in Deuteronomy 6:5 and Leviticus 19:18 Moses himself clarifies the matter.

Then Jesus moves to the offensive. He becomes the questioner, seeking clarification of David's comments in Psalm 110. Matthew identifies Jesus as a descendent of David (cf. Matthew 1), something commonly known (see Matthew 9:37; 12:23; 15:22; 20:30-31). Matthew 21 opens with Jesus' arrival in Jerusalem, being praised as "The son of David," which was a genealogical designation and a religio-political appellation for the Messiah. Here Jesus throws back at his adversaries the charge they leveled against him:

If Messiah is to be a son of David, Jesus has a right to that position.

There are few passages with more power than Jesus' summary of the law in verses 37-40. It is not intended to be a checklist but rather a worldview. How do we see ourselves, others, and God in this wild ride we call life? Jesus reminds us of the basics found in love.

There is much that pretends to be wise in our world, but nothing can match the profound wisdom and strength of true mercy. Can we love others without finding that love first in God? Can we love God without it coming to expression in our care for others? Perhaps the reason the Pharisees challenged Jesus' authority in verses 41-46 was because his testimony robbed their own of power.

Application

Here is the greatest rub for those who are mature in life and faith. It is so easy to presume that strength of character and moral uprightness are the goals of faith and life. Certainly they are admirable and obedience to God is a high value. But there is something about love that stands just above them. A dear friend once explained it like this: in a dream he saw a marvelous apparatus of yellow silk billowing in the breezes next to a cliff. It was a transportation device of some kind, though he couldn't see either engines or supports. Like a magical tent, it floated in space.

Inside was a man whose face seemed so familiar and friendly my friend knew immediately that this was an intimate acquaintance. However, he could not seem to remember how they were associated nor the man's name. The man, with a smile of warmth, invited him to step off the cliff into the contrivance and be carried on a delightful journey in the yellow tent.

But my friend was so intrigued by the device itself that he wanted to try it on his own. *He* wanted to pilot the magical airship. So when he entered the craft he fought the man for control and pushed him out onto the cliff. Unfortunately, just as my friend felt the power of flight swell in his commanding grasp, the entire yellow tent began to collapse in on itself and plummet to disaster below. No matter what he did, my friend could not make the "machine" fly. He cried out for help and suddenly the man he had pushed out reappeared at his side. In that exact moment the airship began to billow and slow its freefall. Soon they were soaring together.

Without a further thought my friend knew that the strangely familiar man was Jesus. He also knew why Jesus said to him, "Don't you know that the power to fly is not found in the 'machine,' nor in your skills as a pilot, but in me?" Our testimonies only make sense when they point to Jesus.

An Alternative Application

Deuteronomy 34:1-12. The story of Moses' death begs to be treated by itself. One way to convey the character of Moses would be to have people go through an exercise in which they write their own eulogies or obituaries. Garrison Keillor says it is too bad we miss our own funerals because people say such nice things about us and we miss it by three days. But if we were able to attend our own funerals or had the opportunity to write what we believed others should know about the meaning of our lives, what would we say?

If we were goaded into that exercise in a meaningful way, how would we seek to live our lives in order that the eulogies we wrote about ourselves would be fact, not fiction? In other words, what does it take to live like Moses in such a way that our lives are, in fact, testimonies to God's character and grace?

Reformation Day
Jeremiah 31:31-34
Romans 3:19-28
John 8:31-36
by R. Craig MacCreary

Don't miss out on the coming reformation

Reformation Day always seemed to be the odd day out on the church calendar. It was one of those days, and there are many in church life, when we tried to say one thing with our mouths but when the words came tumbling out we were pretty far from our intentions. Reformation Day in my youth was a self-congratulatory festival where we celebrated why we were not Catholic and how through the gifts and insights of the enlightenment, we had advanced well beyond primitive religiosity. Perhaps the reason Reformation Day has in many ways gone by the boards is that many became aware as they were growing up that the only church around that seemed engaged in massive reformation was the Catholic church. The life and actions of Pope John XXIII had ignited a spirit of renewal that could only spark the envy of many Protestants, replacing the austere visage of Pius XII. John XXIII's demeanor seemed to reflect the humanism that was behind much of the motivation of the original Reformation.

As it was presented to us, the Reformation was very much an event that took place in the past. Yes, there was some lip service to the notion that reformation should be a continuing event but as one looked around, you did not see much evidence that the Reformation was a continuing event that challenged central dogmas and that had implications for the way we worshiped or governed ourselves.

If anything, the events and personalities that were changing church life were coming from outside the church rather than from within the church. Civil rights, the women's movement, Vietnam were all doing something more to liturgy, polity, theology, and pedagogy than anything taking place within or initiated in the church. Yes, there was the "God is Dead" movement that managed to place its claims on the front page of *Time* magazine. Yet this does not seem to be the stuff of which reformations are made, as evidenced by the fact that there are few who can remember what the movement was about or name any of its protagonists.

By the time my generation of Christians came along, the Reformation had been reduced to a fairly narrow personal struggle over one's own salvation. One could come away believing that Luther was dealing with his own private existential struggles. Gone were the political and social consequences that came as the result of a shift in theological understanding. Our understanding of the Reformation did little to prepare any of us for the development of "liberation theology" that generated a new understanding of poverty and the role of religious institutions in creating the kind of attitudes that maintained poverty. This should not be entirely surprising in a community that was clearly part of the "haves."

In many ways, our celebration of Reformation Day was a bust. What we missed out on is something that each of these texts embody. "The days are surely coming, says the Lord, when I will make a new covenant with the house of Israel and the house of Judah" (Jeremiah 31:31); "Then what becomes of boasting? It is excluded. By what law? By that of works? No, but by the law of faith" (Romans 3:27); "They answered him, 'We are descendants of Abraham and have never been slaves to anyone. What do you mean by saying, "You will be made free"?'" (John 8:33). All of the texts remind us that reformation is something that God initiates. God is free to initiate in the church or from outside the church. The real Reformation comes when, despite all evidence to the contrary and our certainties, we are open to what God will initiate.

Jeremiah 31:31-34

"It was the best of times, it was the worst of times." So opens Dickens' novel *A Tale of Two Cities*: the story of the French Revolution and its horrors and the glories of human beings in the face of massive change. As much could be said of the Hebrews' return from exile and their rebuilding of their faith community. At a recent church council meeting, a member of the council remarked that a good church fire is not the worst thing that can happen to a church. His point was that a good fire can be a worst of times/best of times sort of moment. Yes, there will be plenty of hard work to do to recover from the destruction. On the other hand, such times can be the occasion for the rediscovery of what church is primarily about, as the members plan for the future in real time as opposed to a theoretical proposition. A pastor/colleague remarked that the best thing that could happen to his church and community would be the start of a new church in his relatively small community. It would be a good test of the party line that soccer and other activities had overtaken Sundays so people had plenty of reason not to go to church.

What do all these events have in common? Each of them cries out for a return to the primal events and understandings of what a faith community is about in order that "... but those who wait for the Lord shall renew their strength, they shall mount up with wings like eagles, they shall run and not be weary, they shall walk and not faint" (Isaiah 40:31). The recondition for the flight of the eagles is a return, a reenactment, an engagement with those times when the community experienced God's leadership. In my tradition, heavily influenced by the writings of Phillip Schaff, it is important to note that renewal is defined before anything else as return so that there might be reformation. There is some evidence in the writings of Dianna Bass and others that the spiritual hunger of the current generation is not so much a longing for a break with the past but a curiosity and thirst to know where Christians have come from and what is usable from the past to build on. The culmination of scripture is in the affirmation of things past, "And the one who was seated on the throne said, 'See, I am making all things new.'" Also he said, "Write this, for these words are trustworthy and true." Note that the text does not say, "I make all new things." God makes things that *are* new.

This is what the prophet Jeremiah is proclaiming when he writes, "But this is the covenant that I will make with the house of Israel after those days, says the Lord: I will put my law within them, and I will write it on their hearts; and I will be their God, and they shall be my people." What is new here is that the covenant will become an internalized reality for God's people where the rhythm and beat of sabbath becomes the guide to planning and work. That would be quite a significant reformation. What occurs here is not the abolition of the law but its internalization into the life of the community. God will do this; not votes or resolutions but openness to the activity of God will make this possible.

The prophet makes clear that this reformation will involve everyone. The common experience of all, sharing in the sabbath/shalom pattern of life, and the equal playing field that it establishes will be the primal source of the Hebrews' renewal as they remember the law to the point that it is written on their hearts. This is the best of times if the work of God is accepted. There are difficult times ahead if the Hebrews reject the God that is reaching beyond all the betrayals and rejection to yet again enable God's people to enter into the primal experience of the new covenant based on the law.

Romans 3:19-28

One of the trends that has brought the church to a place of reformation in the last few years has been the hunger for authentic religious narrative and experience. On the part of many there is a feeling that they can no longer internalize the narrative of their youth. A narrative that was suitable when religious authority was accepted is no longer operative in a world where individual experience is the measure of truth. In a sense, the Reformation and the counter-Reformation was a battle fought over the same ground. "What would be the teaching of the church regarding salvation in the world to come?" The current Reformation shifts the ground to "What is the experience of salvation in the world that is?" For moderns, the rallying cry is less about what shall be taught about Jesus and more about "How may I have an encounter with Jesus?" Clearly, the Reformation is something less to be taught than to look forward to in our day.

As in the first Reformation, three central things stand out as a feature of the change that is happening. The emerging church movement, like the first Reformation, betokens new understandings of power in its core elements: the need for experiential meaning, the need to see the movement in continuity with the historic church, and the desire to impact the world in redemptive ways. This has led to the breaking of historic form and patterns of worship as the movement mixes various historic elements of the church. One could find themselves at a Pentecostal Congregational church in which icons play a central role as they seek to redeem the neighborhood.

The current Reformation, like the first, reflects a new focus on what it means to be a human being. The first Reformation was fueled by a shift toward a more Augustinian existential point of view. The new Reformation focuses on biology as a source of insight regarding faith and religious experience. David Brooks, in a *New York Times* article titled "The Neural Buddhists," illustrates the conversion of several elements of the new Reformation: human beings are wired to have a self-transcending religious experience, moral instinct is universal, and human beings are to be defined relationally rather than substantially or existentially. God is what weaves together all these elements.

The third element of the new Reformation is like the first Reformation in that the canon has shifted in its emphasis from Paul to Jesus, as evidenced in the writings of Marcus Borg and others.

What does all of this have to do with a preacher standing before a congregation on Sunday morning looking out at faces who have come to know whether the fundamental story is true or not? Part of the problem is that some will come as a result of the first Reformation and the others will come so the new Reformation can get under way.

Paul, who had his own personal encounter with Jesus, does have some advice that might prove helpful: "... All have sinned and fall short of the glory of God." This is a helpful reminder that seems to have been thoroughly ignored by the first Reformation. The world seems to have found plenty of excuses to do some bloodletting in the midst of our current crises without the religious/spiritual community adding to the misery. While few in the pews on a Sunday morning seem ready to lead the charge in a holy war, I have attended enough seminars on the writing of Marcus Borg and others to know that quite a few are *not* ready to be liberated by the new Reformation in scriptural understanding. Don't participate in reformation unless you have a good leavening of humility in the strengths and weaknesses of your position.

Paul also writes to the Romans, "... the righteousness of God through faith in Jesus Christ for all who believe. For there is no distinction, they are now justified by his grace as a gift, through the redemption that is in Christ Jesus." Paul is saying that if there is any truth in us as human beings it is because without distinction we have been graced by God. God has used many forms of the church to further the building of the kingdom, leading to the conclusion we can neither reject any expression of the church nor fully embrace any form of the church as final. This always leaves the door open for reformation. God has passed over the sins of all previous reforms and will redeem all reforms of the future.

John 8:31-36

What could partake more of the struggle over reformation than these words from the gospel of John, "They answered him, 'We are descendants of Abraham and have never been slaves to anyone. What do you mean by saying, "You will be made free"?'" Here is the struggle between those who have been shaped by the tradition and one who wants to shape the tradition. The key question here, whether we see the activity of God through the Holy Spirit, is an ongoing work of the risen Christ. Was Luther right in concluding that the church is always reforming and that this is the work of God? Many rightfully ask that if the answer is yes then does that make us free or does it make us slaves to a never-ending pattern of change and uncertainty that we must learn to live with? Given the convulsive changes that we have had to live with in many areas, I can sympathize with those who have found themselves gun-shy in the reformation department. I appreciate the complaint of those who cannot take one more change to their favorite hymn or one more new authoritative biblical translation. The truth is that Jesus and the early church lived in a changing world: the destruction of Jerusalem and the temple, the inward turning of Judaism, the early persecutions of the church. Yet John's community had staked itself on the kind of religious reforms that would lead to its separation from Judaism.

However, as the text makes clear, it is Jesus who makes us free through the reform. It is crucial to see the change as a result of his work to liberate and make free. It does mean agreement with all change or the denial of any change. It does mean that reformation was the work of Jesus himself on earth. It makes all the difference whether we see that as the ongoing work of the resurrection. It challenges us as to what we mean by free and slave. Jesus does say in chapter 14, "Very truly, I tell you, the one who believes in me will also do the works that I do and, in fact, will do greater works than these, because I am going to the Father."

If nothing else, Jesus invites us to a conversation around the meaning of reform. As a good Congregationalist/UCC pastor, I believe in that conversation we will hear the voice of Jesus.

Application

The questions for the preacher as he or she approaches this day fall into three categories: Does the preacher come down on the side of full speed ahead on reformation of the church? Is the congregation that the pastor serves so wounded by change and reformation that it needs healing? Has the pastor's congregation never undertaken the work of extensive reformation in its life so that it sees no need to undertake this work? I suspect that in the first Reformation there were congregations that were ready to lead, some to follow, and others who were going to stay put. The pastor needs to ask of themselves where they and their congregation are on Reformation Day.

An Alternative Application

John 8:31-36. One of the things that often seems to block the process of reformation is that we are so unfamiliar with our own tradition. My hunch is that it would be quite an eye-opener for most congregations to discover what their ancestors in faith actually believed was happening in communion or in the meaning of having a sabbath rhythm of your life or in the importance of hearing and discussing the preached word. This might be the day to help lay people understand what those who previously occupied the pews meant by faith — by taking a lay point of view of the previous Reformation. It might be the day to help your parishioners understand that things may have changed over the years in more ways than the average congregation realizes. "Very truly, I tell you, the one who believes in me will also do the works that I do and, in fact, will do greater works than these, because I am going to the Father."

All Saints Day
Revelation 7:9-17
1 John 3:1-3
Matthew 5:1-12
by Timothy Cargal

The church triumphant

A little knowledge can be a dangerous (or at least a humorous) thing. Occasionally people will hear a word or expression whose meaning seems obvious, but actually has a specific, less-than-obvious, technical meaning that leads in a quite different direction. As a result, they will use the expression in inappropriate contexts with quite unintended consequences.

For a number of years I regularly drove past a sign with a theological example of this phenomenon, and it never failed to amuse me. A congregation had chosen to adopt the phrase "The Church Triumphant" as its name. Obviously they had heard the expression used somewhere and thought it captured an important aspect of their mission. In a society that was not only increasingly secular but perhaps also perceived as openly hostile to Christian faith, this congregation refused to feel beaten down or defeated. They would gladly herald their joyous and victorious life to all who passed by. And so they had erected a billboard along a major thoroughfare that read, "The Church Triumphant, Next Exit."

The expression "Church Triumphant" is, of course, one half of the pairing "Church Militant" and "Church Triumphant." The terms have well-established meanings in the long history of Christian theology. The "Church Militant" is that part of the Body of Christ in this world still struggling to realize the fullness of God's reign in cultures and societies distorted by human sin. The "Church Triumphant" is the remainder of the Body of Christ already united with God through death. They have in their personal lives triumphed over evil through God's grace, and they are the seal and the promise of God's ultimate triumph over evil.

Each time I saw the sign, "The Church Triumphant, Next Exit," my mischievous mind could not help but conjure an image of a cemetery and chuckle at how far removed that image was from the image of a vibrant and active church that that congregation no doubt had in mind. It also reminded me of the unintentionally ironic line from a song I heard a number of years ago: "But the church triumphant is alive and well."

Yet sometimes even misunderstanding leads the way to insight. After all, the affirmation of belief in the "communion of the saints" in the Apostles' Creed relates to the conviction that the "Church Militant and Triumphant" is together the one Body of Christ, united across time in the physical and spiritual realms. All Saints' Sunday is a good time to remind ourselves of the unity of the "Church Militant" and the "Church Triumphant" within the "communion of the saints."

Revelation 7:9-17

One of the sources for the "Church Militant and Triumphant" imagery is no doubt this vision within the Revelation. It expresses the paradoxical idea (in terms of the usual human norms) of people who triumph in death by depicting those who have been martyred during the apocalypse's period of tribulation ("they who have come out of the great ordeal," v. 14) with palm branches — symbolic of victory and culturally associated with triumphal processions (e.g., "Palm Sunday"; see John 12:13; 1 Maccabees 13:51; 2 Maccabees 14:4) — in their hands (v. 9). Like the lamb whom they worship, this multitude that bears the scars of death has nevertheless conquered and triumphed over its enemies (cf. 5:5-14).

This innumerable multitude "from every nation, from all tribes and peoples and languages" represents a clear expansion of those redeemed beyond the "one hundred forty-four thousand, sealed out of every tribe of the people of Israel" (7:4). The point is not, however, that there are limits on those redeemed from Israel but not on the redemption of Gentiles. The symbolically representative character of the 144,000 is clear both from the fact that it is the product of 12,000 multiplied by 12 and from delineation of exactly 12,000 sealed from each tribe (vv. 5-8) despite their different relative sizes. Nor should those "sealed out of every tribe of the people of Israel" be too quickly identified with the church as a new, spiritual Israel. Quite likely the point of setting side-by-side a definite number "sealed" from Israel with an innumerable multitude "from every nation" is to show that God's consistency in keeping covenant with Israel is proof that God will also keep covenant with those newly brought into relationship with God through the work of Christ.

What unites this innumerable multitude in all its racial, cultural, and linguistic diversity is the common purpose of worshiping the one on "the throne" (a circumlocution for referring to God out of reverence for the divine name) and "the lamb." Moreover, the mixed mass of humanity is joined in its worship by "all the angels... the elders and the four living creatures" (vv. 9-12). By focusing on a unity of purpose, the totality of creation is able to join in a single song of praise to the Creator. It is a vision of hope and a model to be followed by all those who seek to build genuine unity that nevertheless respects the rich diversity of God's creation.

One of the characteristic features of Revelation is its construction of images that stand the usual human conceptions and values on their heads. Among these is the assertion that the white robes worn by the redeemed multitude have been made "white in the blood of the lamb" (v. 14). Then as now, the normal expectation was that blood would permanently stain fabrics. Yet within this vision, blood cleanses the robes rather than fouling them, using blood-soaked garments that would naturally be thought of as symbolic of death as symbols of eternal life instead. Those who have had the spiritual realm unveiled before their eyes come to recognize that the apparent triumph of evil in the world is an illusion, for God ultimately triumphs through what appears to be defeat. God's values overturn the values of a sinful world.

In yet another of these paradoxical images, "the lamb... will be their shepherd" (v. 17). Clearly the statement that this shepherd "will guide them to springs of the water of life" is intended to call to mind Psalm 23. But the allusion is triggered by the verbal connections with Psalm 23:1-2 and not limited to them. Just as the Lord shepherds the psalmist through "the valley of the shadow of death" and "prepares a table... in the presence of... enemies" (Psalm 23:4-5) so the lamb has led this multitude through a martyr's death (having suffered the same himself) and into God's eternal presence. The ultimate victory of those who have appeared to be the victims of evil is represented by the absence of hunger, thirst, suffering from harsh natural environments, and even "every tear from their eyes" (vv. 16-17).

1 John 3:1-3

One of the most striking features of this brief passage is how the author still seems somewhat amazed at the greatness of God's love and what it means for us to be the recipients of that love. The enthusiasm of the statement is born out by the somewhat awkward syntax of the Greek: "Behold what love the Father gave to us, so that we might be called God's children — even we are!" The very awkwardness may account for the absence of that final interjection in some manuscripts but the exuberance of the author comes through the struggle with inarticulateness. Such love is always amazing and should never be taken for granted.

This love should also be truly transforming in its effects upon us. It should, the writer maintains, make us as incomprehensible to those dominated by the value system of the world as Jesus himself was (cf. John 1:10). Moreover, this transformation is not just some distant hope. "We are God's children now" (1 John 3:2a), those who recognize this truth "purify themselves, just as Christ is pure" (v. 3).

Yet even though we are already transformed, the transformation is not yet complete. The reason for this on-going change is that we have not yet seen Christ fully revealed. The very process of incarnation has veiled something of the eternal Christ even as it has revealed the divine through human form. Only when we "see him as he is" in the fullness of divine glory (what later theologians would call the "beatific vision" in reflecting on passages such as the companion lectionary text from Revelation) can we become like him and so reveal the complete transformation that God's love is accomplishing in us.

Matthew 5:1-12

Matthew begins the "Sermon on the Mount" with a series of nine Beatitudes. Each of these pronouncements begins with the Greek adjective *makarios*. Traditionally translated into English as "blessed," some more recent translations have sparked mild controversy by rendering the word into English as "happy" or "fortunate." More is at stake in the choice between these competing options than just a concern for a less archaic, more colloquial sounding translation.

Makarios was used in both the common Greek of the period and some instances within the New Testament to describe a favorable emotional state arising from a person's particular circumstances and so would equate with the normal uses of English "happy" or "fortunate" (see as examples Luke 23:29; Acts 26:2; 1 Corinthians 7:40). The more customary use in Greek, however, was as a reference to a favorable emotional state arising from circumstances resulting from divine favor. Within Greco-Roman culture, this use might be associated with the notion of "one on whom fortune has smiled." Within a Jewish or Christian context, however, these circumstances would be associated not with an impersonal "fortune" or "fate" but with circumstances arising from actions on one's behalf by God. It is this origin in divine activity that is marked by the translation into English as "blessed."

The translation issue here in the Beatitudes is determining which of these two uses is intended. As Danker has recently commented, "the transl[ation] O, the happiness of or hail to those, favored by some... appears to be exactly right for the Aramaic original (=Hebr[ew] *'ashrey*), but scholars have disputed whether it exhausts the content that *makarios* had in the mouths of G[ree]k-speaking Christians" (Bauer, Danker, Arndt, and Gingrich, *A Greek-English Lexicon of the New Testament and Other Early Christian Literature* [3rd ed.; Chicago: University of Chicago Press, 2000], p. 611). In this case, the question is whether the English translation of Matthew should reflect the linguistic character of its Greek text ("blessed") or that of the Aramaic probably originally spoken by Jesus ("happy," "fortunate").

Within the context of the Beatitudes, however, the English translation "blessed" has more to commend itself than just longstanding tradition. It is clear that the favorable circumstances set out in the explanatory clause of each of these nine affirmations are intended to be understood as the result of divine action. Only God can grant the "kingdom of heaven" to the "poor in spirit" (v. 3) and those "persecuted for righteousness' sake" (v. 10). Notice particularly the use of the passive voice in four of the Beatitudes ("will be comforted," v. 4; "will be filled," v. 6; "will be given mercy," v. 7; and "will be called God's children," v. 9). The passive voice was frequently used in early Jewish and Christian writings to avoid explicitly naming God as the one performing an action (the so-called "divine passive") lest one inadvertently "use God's name in vain." If these are affirmations of divine favor, then the use of the English word with that specific connotation ("blessed") is justified, whether or not the Aramaic word may have had that specific meaning.

In terms of relating the Beatitudes to the liturgical context of preaching on All Saints' Day, two points deserve particular attention. As already noted, the second of the Beatitudes employs a divine passive construction. To say, "Blessed are those who mourn, for they will be comforted," is a far more specific affirmation than simply that mourners will find some source of comfort either in themselves or in the solace offered to them by others. It is to promise specifically that God will comfort those who mourn. This promise does not diminish the importance of the care that we provide to one another in times of grief and loss, but it does insist that even comfort is ultimately grounded in God's promise and activity in conquering death. Because this life is not all that there is, there is divine comfort available to us in our mourning.

Second, like the passage from Revelation, the Beatitudes overturn conventional human wisdom. They assert a vision of reality in which those who are despised by the world are affirmed as the recipients of divine favor. There are even specific parallels between the promises here in the gospel and the vision related in Revelation. Those who "mourn... will be comforted" (v. 4) for "God will wipe every tear from their eyes" (Revelation 7:17). Those who "hunger and thirst... will be filled" (v. 6; cf. Revelation 7:16). Those who are "pure in heart... will see God" (v. 8; cf. Revelation 7:15). Those who have been "persecuted for righteousness' sake" will receive a great reward in heaven (vv. 10-12; cf. Revelation 7:13-14).

Application

The origins of All Saints' Day are rooted in the early Christian practice of remembering and celebrating the lives of the heroes and martyrs of the church on the dates of their deaths. Over the centuries the number of such festivals observed throughout the church and in specific, local regions multiplied to the point that there literally were not enough days in the year to commemorate all the martyrs. Additionally, there was broad consensus that there were many more Christians who deserved to be honored for their faith and service but whose stories had simply been lost to the church. All Saints' Day was established as a general day of commemoration and was associated with November 1 by at least 835 AD. Since its beginnings All Saints' observance has been about the remembrance of those who have died in the faith.

Yet the core theological conviction of Christianity is belief in the resurrection. There would be no church were it not for the resurrection of Christ as the first fruits assuring the ultimate harvest of all souls united with Christ into God's eternal life (cf. 1 Corinthians 15:13-14, 20). In whatever context Christians gather to reflect on those who have died in the faith, there must therefore be an emphasis on bearing witness to the resurrection. The final truth regarding every Christian is not the grave but eternal life in the blessed presence of God.

It is this realization that strips the irony away from the statement that "the church triumphant is alive and well" (even if it doesn't exonerate the songwriter's misunderstanding of the phrase). What has always been most true in the Christian theology of the Church Triumphant is that it is eternally alive with its Lord, "the living one" who "was dead" but is "alive forever and ever" and has "the keys of death and of hades" (Revelation 1:18). The ultimate triumph of the Church Triumphant is indeed its victory over death, the ultimate consequence of sin.

The focal point of All Saints' observance then is not really in the past, but in the future. Its proper images are less the fires and tortures of martyrdom and more the songs of praise sung by the innumerable multitude caught up in the rapture of the beatific vision of God and the Christ. As the Church Militant, we still struggle with the consequences of sin in this world, among them our own grief in mourning for loved ones who have died. Yet as the communion of the saints makes clear, there really is only one church militant and triumphant. And some day we too will change our ranks. Today the battle cry; tomorrow the victor's song.

Alternative Applications
1) 1 John 3:1-3. Much of the Protestant Christian tradition has moved away from the veneration of the saints. Historically this development is rooted in the positive emphasis of the Reformers upon the "priesthood of all believers" and in their negative reaction against perceived excesses of the formal canonization process in the Roman church. Recently there has been some reassessment of what may have been lost in the liturgical abandonment of iconography and the exemplary function of the saints. In the midst of such debate, this brief passage from 1 John serves as a reminder that whatever may distinguish "all believers" from the "exemplary saints," it is not a result of some being more loved by God than others. We are all

"children of God" by virtue of God's great love for us. We need to look to the lives of the great women and men of faith not to find who were God's favorites, but to find models of what it means to be transformed by God's love.

2) Revelation 7:9-17. Part of the vision of the future glory of the church is the unity it finds through worship and song in the midst of its broad diversity. It is more than a little ironic, then, that a number of writers have begun speaking of "worship wars" breaking out in congregations with diverse memberships in terms of age, culture, ethnicity, and so forth — and that these "wars" tend to break out over music styles more than anything else. Maybe the problem is that we have made different forms of worship a part of our identity and self-expression. If worship is going to be a unifying rather than a dividing force, then the focus must be kept on the one who is being worshiped and not on those who are doing the worshiping. Who knows? Maybe if we can get God at the center of worship lives rather than our desires for self-expression, we will also be able to unite other aspects of our communal life around God as well.

Proper 26
Pentecost 21
Ordinary Time 31
Joshua 3:7-17
1 Thessalonians 2:9-13
Matthew 23:1-12
by David Kalas

Help wanted

A friend, who was about to become a father, asked me about the relationship I had with my father when I was growing up. My friend sensed that my relationship with my dad was a good one and that I regarded my dad as a good father. This friend of mine, however, had grown up without a father and so as he anticipated becoming a father himself, he found that he was without a good role model. He hoped to be able to borrow one from me.

My friend was deliberately seeking what we all crave, more or less consciously. In whatever area of life, we need and long for role models — someone who will show us how it's done, whatever "it" may be.

This pursuit becomes a public one in the buying of books written by people who have been successful. Whether the author has made it big in business, sports, or whatever, thousands — perhaps millions — of people will manifest their desire for a role model by buying his book.

You and I do the same in our field. Although folks like to say that we learn more from defeat than from victory, it's not the defeated pastors and preachers who have lost hundreds of members and who lead struggling churches, who write books and lead seminars. Rather, we seek out colleagues who have enjoyed remarkable success and we borrow them and their methods as models for ourselves and our ministries.

Our two New Testament readings this week remind us of the need that we — and our congregations — have for role models in the faith.

Joshua 3:7-17

Every death leaves some sense of vacancy, of absence. And some deaths leave in their wake a very great void for the people left behind. The empty chair at the dinner table or in the living room; the voice that is missing; the presence, the humor, the influence, the love... all elements of some great and beloved person's absence.

In our family settings, of course, a part of our grief is simply that absence. No one sits, now, where father used to sit, and we all know that no one can replace him. In most circumstances, no one tries. Or at least not right away.

In the larger context of our Old Testament passage, however, that is not the case. A great and beloved person had died, and there was immediately someone there to try to take his place.

Moses had died and his absence must have left an immense void for the children of Israel. No one among them (except, arguably, Joshua and Caleb) had ever known life without Moses. Just as a generation of Americans who grew up in the '30s and '40s didn't know any other president besides Franklin Roosevelt. The Israelites who grew up in the wilderness had never known any other leader than Moses. He was always there, he was always in charge, and he was, literally, a radiant presence in their midst.

Moses had been God's agent of deliverance in Egypt, God's spokesman for the people of Israel, and God's friend. But now Moses was gone and who could possibly sit in his chair at the table?

That unenviable responsibility fell to Joshua. From early on, Joshua had been Moses' right-hand man (see, for example, Exodus 17:8-9, 14; 24:12-13; 33:7-11). But the much-appreciated back-up quarterback is not necessarily the guy you welcome as the new team leader when the beloved star quarterback retires.

So God, in our selected passage, does a favor for Joshua. Indeed, it seems to be a calculated effort by God to help establish Joshua in Moses' place. When the children of Israel came to the Jordan River, the Lord caused the river to pile up in the north so that the people could cross over on dry ground. Like a variation on a motif in a musical composition, God reprises his water-parting miracle from a generation before. Just as God had parted the Red Sea for Moses, so now God parted the Jordan for Joshua, and thus he began "to exalt (Joshua) in the sight of all Israel" so that they would know that "I will be with (Joshua) as I was with Moses."

A part of Joshua's assignment at the Jordan was to "select twelve men from the tribes of Israel, one from each tribe." There, too, we see a symbolic promotion of Joshua. A generation earlier, Moses had selected twelve representatives from the tribes (Numbers 13:1-16) and Joshua was among one of those selected. Now, forty or so years later, it was Joshua doing the choosing.

While God was promoting and protecting Joshua, however, Joshua was not promoting himself. Notice how he introduces the parting of the Jordan River to the people: "By this you shall know that among you is the living God...." Faithfully, Joshua directs the people's attention to God. He does not say, "By this you shall know that I am the rightful successor to Moses," or some such self-proclamation. Rather, he makes the miracle always and only about God. It is a great virtue in God's leaders if we leave it to God to establish us, while we make it our only business to proclaim and point to him, not to ourselves.

Finally, though the parting of the Jordan River is certainly — and deliberately — reminiscent of what God did through Moses at the Red Sea, it is worth noting that the method of the miracle is not the same. At the Red Sea, God instructed Moses to "lift up your staff, and stretch out your hand over the sea and divide it, that the Israelites may go into the sea on dry ground" (Exodus 14:16). At the Jordan, by contrast, God told Joshua to instruct the priests, "When you come to the edge of the waters of the Jordan, you shall stand still in the Jordan." Hence, "when the soles of the feet of the priests who bear the ark of the Lord... rest in the waters.... the waters of the Jordan flowing from above shall be cut off."

We do God and ourselves a great disservice if we forget what he has done in the past. But we also err when we limit him to what he has done in the past — or limit him to how he has done it. God provided dry ground for his people on both occasions, but while the result was the same, the method was not.

1 Thessalonians 2:9-13

Paul's first letter to the Christians in Thessalonica is thought to have been written not long after his first visit there (a part of what we commonly identify as Paul's Second Missionary Journey, which took him beyond Asia and into Europe for the first time). Paul and his companions had been forced to leave Thessalonica by Jewish factions that were jealous of the gospel's reception among the people there (see Acts 17:1-10) and that opposition eventually chased Paul out of nearby Berea, as well (17:13-15).

The nature of Paul's missionary work was such that he planted seeds in one place after another, but he did not or could not stay to cultivate the fragile young plants, nor could he be assured that they were thriving and bearing fruit. He relied on letters and personal reports to learn how the Christians and churches that he had left behind in a given place were doing. Evidently, Paul had recently received such a report from Thessalonica, and he gave thanks for the good word about the Thessalonians' faith and faithfulness.

What cultivating and nurturing Paul could do at a distance, meanwhile, he did through his letters. Right on the heels of giving thanks for all that the Thessalonian Christians were, he moved on to encourage them in what they should be. That encouragement, in large measure, took the form of a reminder about the example Paul and his companions had set for the Thessalonians during their time together.

Within the larger context of this epistle, we see Paul's emphasis on working and earning a living. It's a theme revisited, we discover, in his second letter to the Thessalonians, as well (2 Thessalonians 3:6-12), suggesting that this was something of a continuing issue within that congregation. Paul repeatedly cites the example set by him and his companions — working diligently, supporting themselves, and keeping their motives for ministry unalloyed.

Both Paul's example before the Thessalonians and his challenge to them are of the highest order. His example was "pure, upright, and blameless." The calling was to "lead a life worthy of God." These are not modest goals. They are not part of the contemporary shoulder shrugging so common in American Christianity, where "nobody's perfect" seems to be an "article of religion." No, but rather they are no-nonsense reminders that the gospel deserves a certain kind of representative and that God deserves a certain kind of people. That does not narrow or limit the invitation of God's grace, mind you. It simply clarifies the proper response to that grace.

Finally, Paul commends the Thessalonians for receiving "the word of God that you heard from us... not as a human word but as what it really is, God's word." God's message through human messengers; God's word in human words — this is God's strange choice and our high calling.

The Second Helvetic Confession addressed the matter: "Wherefore when this Word of God is now preached in the church by preachers lawfully called, we believe that the very Word of God is preached, and received of the faithful... (and although the preacher) be evil and a sinner, nevertheless the Word of God abides true and good."

And so we are challenged to be pure vessels for the word we contain and transmit. The word deserves that, and the world to which we preach desires it. Yet even when we are not, the word remains "what it really is, God's word" "true and good."

Matthew 23:1-12

Focus groups are monitored to discover their gut reactions — positive and negative — to candidates, slogans, products, policies, and more. If we could thus monitor the people in our pews during the reading of the scripture, I suspect that we'd find an interesting reversal of reputations from Jesus' day to our own.

While the prevailing attitude of Jesus' contemporaries toward the Samaritans was aggressively negative, for example, our people have connected "Samaritan" with "good." Meanwhile, though the people of Jesus' day had a native respect for the scribes and Pharisees, the mention of those groups among American churchgoers elicits a negative reaction.

It's a shame that we think of the scribes and Pharisees as the bad guys, for the people of first-century Palestine assumed they were the good guys. And while they clearly did not universally deserve the favorable reputation that they had, our people are at a disadvantage in understanding many of Jesus' teachings without something of a prejudice in favor of those Pharisees and the scribes.

This section of Jesus' teaching is the kind of passage that creates and perpetuates our negative connotation of "scribes and Pharisees," for it is highly critical of them and exposes their hypocrisies. Still, for the sake of understanding the passage — and applying it! — we need to begin where Jesus' audience did: with a prejudice in favor of these religious leaders.

Jesus says that those religious leaders "sit on Moses' seat," which is a picturesque way of identifying their authority and responsibility. Those two things — authority and responsibility — almost always go together, and in the case of the role played by the scribes and Pharisees, we naturally think of James' caution: "Not many of you should become teachers, my brothers and sisters, for you know that we who teach will be judged with greater strictness" (James 3:1).

As men and women of the pulpit, expounding the word of God to the people of God, you and I may be among those who "sit on Moses' seat" today, and so this passage may be particularly important reading for us.

For example, I certainly recognize the phenomenon of passing along to people heavy burdens that are hard to bear. At its best, I call that challenging teaching and preaching. I wonder how much challenge some souls can take, though, before it becomes a heavy burden. I suspect it is "ought-heavy" preaching (as in, "you ought to...") that has given the words "preach" and "sermon" their unfavorable connotations in the culture outside of the church (as in "don't preach at me," "I didn't mean to sound preachy," or "I don't need a sermon about...").

The later admonition about being called "rabbi," "father," and "instructor" is also a difficult word for us as clergy. In different denominations, and in different regions of the country, different appellations for clergy prevail. Here among Wisconsin Protestants, "pastor" seems to be the title of choice. But I wonder, as "pastor" means "shepherd," if Jesus might not also say, "Nor are you to be called pastors, for you have one shepherd."

In the end, it seems, the real issue is not the titles but the misplaced honor that accompanies them. Earlier in Matthew (20:25-28), Jesus explained to his followers that they were to function differently than the world around them — not to be menacing, self-serving authorities, but rather to be servants of all. And while that earlier teaching juxtaposed how the Gentiles do things with how his followers were to do things, this teaching uses the scribes and Pharisees as the negative example of how his followers should not be.

Finally, Jesus' observation that the scribes and Pharisees "do all their deeds to be seen by others" is a sobering word to all of us. The attention and admiration of people is an intoxicating thing, and when we have tasted a bit of the applause for our good and godly deeds, our motivation for doing them becomes contaminated. While we may not live in a world where piety is generally applauded, it remains a risk within the church. If I let my motivation for serving God slip just a bit so that I am, partly, endeavoring to please people, then I have left myself vulnerable. For what will I do when the paths of pleasing God and pleasing people separate and they require different things? If my entire motivation has been to please God, then I will hardly notice as the human approval comes and goes.

Application

Most of what we have learned along the way, we learned from watching someone else. From tinkering in the garage to cooking in the kitchen; how we converse, how we carry ourselves, how we do our relationships... all of these can be traced back to one or several persons who were major influences on us along the way. Sometimes we deliberately seek a role model for ourselves in some area of life. Other times we adopt our role models rather unconsciously, and it's only in retrospect that we come to recognize the flow of influence and imitation between ourselves and our role models.

The two New Testament lections for this week present us with the reality and importance of role models in righteousness.

In the Thessalonians passage, we see evidence of Paul's emphasis on role models. Here and elsewhere, he is unapologetic about holding himself up as a model to be considered and imitated (see also 1 Corinthians 4:16, 11:1; Philippians 3:17; 1 Thessalonians 1:6; 2 Thessalonians 3:7-9). It stands to reason that, since human beings learn by example, Christians also learn by seeing and imitating the examples of other Christians.

In the Matthew passage, meanwhile, Jesus warns about the example set by the scribes and Pharisees. They are held up as a kind of anti-role model: "Be careful not to imitate them" is the thrust of Jesus' message to his followers.

And so, between the words of Paul and the teachings of Jesus, we are presented with several sobering prospects. First, our high calling is to be examples worthy of imitation. Second, the human likelihood that, whether we promote ourselves as exemplary or not, our example is an influence on others. Third, that some men and women of God ought not to be imitated, for their example is a misleading one.

Our calling, then, is twofold.

First, to be discerning and deliberate about our role models. Let us select, consciously and carefully, men and women of God whose examples we can follow as we endeavor to live lives pleasing and serviceable to God.

Second, to be mindful of our own responsibility as role models. "I would be true," Howard A. Walter wrote, "for there are those who trust me; I would be pure, for there are those who care." You and I do not necessarily know who those people are. We do not know, at any given moment, who is watching or who may be influenced by our example. But that is a part of the human reality and it becomes a part of our spiritual responsibility.

An Alternative Application
Matthew 23:1-12. "Daddy, watch me!" My wife and I have three little girls — ten, four, and two years old. They are at different stages, to be sure, but they are all still young enough that they want to be watched by their daddy. Whether it is the two-year-old who repeats some little stunt that got a laugh the first time, or the four-year-old with her nascent cartwheels, or the ten-year-old with her assorted tricks in the pool, they all call out, "Daddy, watch me!"

There is something sweet, natural, and wholesome about that part of childhood. The question, however, is how that "watch me" instinct will evolve as children grow into adults.

I imagine a fork in the road and both choices are natural extensions of what we have been and known as children. Will my daughters grow up in such a way that they will always want some *human being* to watch, approve, and applaud? Or will my daughters grow up in such a way that they always will want some *father* (as in divine Father) to watch, approve, and applaud?

The scribes and the Pharisees, according to Jesus, were men who lived for a human audience. "They do all their deeds to be seen by others." Like children, still, they want other human beings to see what they do and to be impressed.

The call of Christ, however, is to live for a divine audience. "But whenever you pray, go into your room and shut the door and pray to your Father who is in secret; and your Father who sees in secret will reward you" (Matthew 6:6). We are still like children, but now it is our heavenly Father's approval and applause that we seek. And no one else's.

Proper 27
Pentecost 22
Ordinary Time 32
Joshua 24:1-3a, 14-25
1 Thessalonians 4:13-18
Matthew 25:1-13
by David Kalas

On high alert

If the pitcher spends too much time fingering the rosin bag or peddling the dirt on the mound or looking in at the catcher and shaking off signs, the batter is likely to ask the umpire for a timeout. Some of that is just gamesmanship, of course. At the same time, however, the batter may genuinely need to step out of the batter's box for a moment. It is, after all, a difficult thing to maintain for a long time the intensity of waiting for a pitch.

Likewise in a track meet. The runners are not expected to stay in their starting stance for a long period before the starter gun sounds. There's a focus and tension that come with that posture: the readiness to explode off the blocks at any moment. The body is poised, the muscles are taut, and the ears are attuned to the sound that means "go!" The trigger on the starter's gun is the trigger on the athletes' muscles, as well.

It seems unreasonable that a sprinter should be asked to wait indefinitely in that starting stance. Or that the batter should stand, focused and perspiring, while the pitcher delays the pitch for minute after minute. Who can maintain that constant state of readiness? Who can live their lives on high alert?

Yet, it may be that is precisely what God expects us to do. Since the disciples watched Jesus disappear into the sky, with the angelic reassurance that "this Jesus, who has been taken up from you into heaven, will come in the same way as you saw him go into heaven" (Acts 1:11), his followers have been living on high alert.

Joshua 24:1-3a, 14-25

Every salesman has a technique, an approach, a hook. Some come from the "soft sell" school, while others take a "hard sell" approach. Then there is Joshua. He is the anti-salesman.

This episode comes from the end of Joshua's book and, we gather, near the end of his life. He had lived in bondage in Egypt as a young man. He had traveled with the first generation of liberated slaves from Egypt to the border of the promised land. He had been part of the twelve-man reconnaissance team that first explored the land. He had paid the price of his people's sin, living through their forty-year death sentence in the wilderness. He had led the next generation across the Jordan and through Canaan's hills and valleys waging war against the powerful and plentiful inhabitants of the land. He had seen the people fret at the Red Sea, defile themselves at Sinai, balk at the border, and complain their way through the wilderness. And now, as Israel stood on the verge of a new chapter, and as he prepared to go the way of all flesh, there is no question about what he wanted most of all.

Joshua's heartfelt goal was that the people should live in total devotion and careful obedience to God. He wants them to sign again on the dotted line of their covenant with God, and yet he does not urge them to do it. Indeed, on the surface, it seems that he urges them not to.

His approach is "hard sell" inasmuch as he pushes the people to make a decision. "Choose this day," he insists, perhaps knowing the diabolical appeal and effect of postponing some decisions. This decision is too important to put off until another day. It must be made today. Right now. So, with a tent-evangelist's-altar-call urgency, Joshua appeals to the people to "put away" the accumulated gods of other people and to make a once-and-for-all choice.

The distinctiveness of Joshua's altar call, however, is that, while he himself stands at the altar rail, he seems to point the people out the door. "If you are unwilling to serve the Lord, choose... whether the gods your ancestors served... or the gods of the Amorites." Joshua's invitation is not merely to commit to the Lord now. No, he is challenging the people to make some choice now, whether for the Lord or not.

His technique is effective. Presented with the expressed possibility of serving other gods, the people retort, "Far be it from us that we should forsake the Lord to serve other gods." So Joshua has them where he wants them, right? Wrong. Now he becomes the evangelist who seems to turn people away from the altar! "You cannot serve the Lord," he says, "for he is a holy God."

Here is the unusual car salesman that tells you to go away. "You can't afford this make and model," he insists, "so you might as well go elsewhere and select a car from one of the cheaper brands." It seems as though he doesn't want to make the sale that is precisely his purpose.

Of course, what Joshua wants the people to do is very familiar to the followers of Jesus Christ. He wants them to count the cost. He does, indeed, want them to sign on the dotted line of their covenant with God, but not lightly, not carelessly. Nonchalance is not the proper posture for making vows.

In the end, the people respond to Joshua's discouraging altar call, and he gives them a two-part instruction: First, to "put away the foreign gods," and second, to "incline (their) hearts to the Lord."

Perhaps I shall preach my own altar call sermon this Sunday, asking the question, "How many steps does it take to get to the altar?" According to Joshua, it takes these two steps: that we put away those competing allegiances that draw us away from God and that we so reorient our hearts that the Lord himself becomes our inclination.

1 Thessalonians 4:13-18

Paul states his purpose at the outset. He does not want the Christians in Thessalonica "to be uninformed... about those who have died." We might devote a Sunday morning to that same goal, for I suspect that the brothers and sisters continue to be largely uninformed — or misinformed — on that subject.

Our great and ongoing challenge, of course, is that the people in our pews are more the product of the surrounding culture than they are of God's word. In the absence of biblical knowledge and theology, most American churchgoers are left to create their own potpourri creed and most of the ingredients come from questionable kitchens.

On the subject of "those who have died" for example, our culture operates with some broad-brush assumptions that there is some sort of afterlife; bodily resurrection is an absurd notion easily stupefied by natural decomposition, cremation, organ donation, and such; and that, if there is a heaven, all good people go there (and all but the most notoriously despicable characters qualify as "good").

Consequently, the folks in so many of our churches have carelessly confused "eternal life" with "afterlife"; have abandoned any serious consideration of what the resurrection means, reducing it to a kind of natural order of things, like flowers in the spring and buds on trees; and have lost sight of the profound meaning of God's costly effort to save us (as well as replacing the Bible's strong understanding of "good" with our world's tepid connotation of it).

We would do well, therefore, to embark on a doctrinal mission this Sunday, so that our brothers and sisters would not "be uninformed... about those who have died."

Of course, Paul's mission was as much pastoral as doctrinal. The Christians of his generation faced a very genuine faith crisis. What would become of those dear friends who died before Christ returned (which the people clearly expected would be any day)? So much of what Jesus had said would happen — his going to Jerusalem, his suffering and death, his rising from the dead, and the coming of the Holy

Spirit — had happened in fairly short order. His promised return, therefore, was reasonably expected posthaste. But now some believers had died prior to his return and those left behind didn't know what to make of it.

A part of Paul's pastoral mission was that the Christians in Thessalonica would "not grieve as others do who have no hope." It is not entirely clear whether Paul's point was that they would not grieve at all, unlike those who have no hope, or that they would not grieve in the same way as those who have no hope. Other passages of scripture (such as Jesus himself weeping at Lazarus' tomb) encourage me to believe that we do rightly continue to experience grief in the midst of our loss but that our grief is profoundly different, because of the hope that we have in Christ. Indeed, how could it not be? For the believer's loss is not eternal and his good-bye is not final. Our grief, therefore, is framed by joy and victory.

The juxtaposition of "those who have died" with those "who have no hope" is a fascinating one.

In the first place, we commonly associate hope with probability. When the doctor offers a favorable prognosis for this loved one, we feel hopeful. When the prognosis is grim, however, we lose hope. Human hope tracks the same line on the graph as likelihood. Hope, it seems, is a matter of odds. And once the person has died, well, that's that. Once it's raining, after all, there's no more point in forecasting that there is a 60% chance of rain. And so from a strictly human standpoint, there's no more talking about hope once the person has died.

From a Christian standpoint, however, death is precisely the juncture at which to talk about hope. At the very moment that the world pulls the covers up over hope, we stand up and proclaim the great hope that we have in Christ.

The other interesting thing to note about Paul's juxtaposition of the dead and the hopeless is that they are not the same people. Ironically, the hopeless ones in this passage are folks who are still alive. The dead in Christ, by contrast, are not at all the ones "who have no hope."

Paul says that the Lord will descend "with a cry of command." He does not specify what that command will be, but given the context, I am personally rather attracted to some variation on "Lazarus, come forth" (John 11:43 KJV). The accompanying fanfare also includes "the archangel's call" and "the sound of God's trumpet." It's a remarkable set of actions from heaven and they are met by an equally remarkable set of reactions from earth, as "the dead in Christ will rise" and "then we who are alive... will be caught up in the clouds together with them to meet the Lord in the air" (v. 17).

Finally, at the end, we see again that Paul's purpose is not merely doctrinal or didactic, but pastoral: "Therefore encourage one another with these words." The promise of the Lord's return is not the stuff of theorizing and speculation; it is comfort, hope, and joy.

Matthew 25:1-13

Earlier in Matthew's gospel, we read an assortment of parables that begin with the phrase, "The kingdom of heaven is like..." (such as 13:31, 33, 44-45, 47; 20:1). Now, in this episode, Jesus has changed his tense. In every previous instance, the introductory phrase was *homoia esti* — *homoia* is an adjective meaning "like" or "of the same nature as," and *esti* is the third-person singular present active indicative form of the verb "to be." In our selected gospel lesson for this week, however, Jesus introduces this kingdom parable with the phrase *tote homoiotheysetai* — *tote* meaning "at that time," and *homoiotheysetai* being the third-person singular future passive form of a verb, meaning "it will resemble" or "it will be like." Previously he had focused on the present reality of the kingdom but here he speaks deliberately of the kingdom as a future reality.

While the introductory language sets this kingdom parable apart from earlier ones in Matthew, the future-looking quality is absolutely consistent with the immediate context of the collection of teachings found in chapters 24 and 25. At the beginning of 24, Jesus makes a provocative statement about the one-day destruction of the temple, which later prompts the disciples to question him about "the sign of your coming and of the end of the age" (24:3).

In response, Jesus teaches the disciples about some signs of the times — about which claims to ignore and which signs to heed. He uses the example of the fig tree (24:32-33) to illustrate his point. Even so, there is no clarity about the precise timing of events (v. 36) and what will be preceded by signs will still come as a surprise (vv. 37-45). Then come four different teachings that illustrate elements of the surprise. The unfaithful servant (24:45-51) is unhappily surprised by his master's sudden arrival after a long delay. The ten bridesmaids in our passage, likewise, are surprised by the delay and the arrival. The third of the three servants (25:14-30) is surprised by his master's response to his conservative stewardship. The goats (25:31-46) are also surprised: not, however, by his sudden arrival at the end of time, but rather by his unrecognized presence in the meantime.

Interestingly, while falling asleep is itself seen as a failure elsewhere (as in Matthew 24:43; 26:40-46; Luke 12:35-38), the wise, as well as the foolish, bridesmaids all fall asleep. That is not condemned in this context but perhaps only serves to indicate the bridegroom's long delay. What separates the wise from the foolish, instead, is the preparedness symbolized by the extra flasks of oil. Even so, in the end, "keep awake" (v. 13) is the imperative of being on high alert.

Jesus' use of the repetitious phrase "lord, lord" puts the foolish bridesmaids in undesirable company. The phrase appears three other times in his teachings. Earlier in Matthew's gospel, he twice attributes that phrase to people who will not necessarily enter the kingdom (7:21-22). Then, in Luke, he asks, "Why do you call me, 'Lord, Lord,' and do not do what I tell you?" (6:46). So for Jesus to put "lord, lord" in the mouths of the bridesmaids is to paint them as somehow well-meaning but ultimately inadequate.

The phrase may be a sobering one for us. After all, the problem with the foolish bridesmaids — and the other members of the "lord, lord" chorus — is not that they are overtly unrelated to Christ. No, in each case these are folks who identify themselves with him, who have responded to the invitation, and who expect to be included in the end. These poor souls, therefore, who appear at the end of the parable as shut out and unwelcome, are not evil people. They are not antagonistic unbelievers. They were not among those who opposed Jesus. They were simply unprepared for his arrival and that makes them frighteningly recognizable. The people in our pews will not easily relate to King Herod, who tried to kill the baby Jesus, or to the Good Friday soldiers, who scourged him when he was a man. But they will relate to five people who expected to be part of the party but who were caught by surprise when the bridegroom returned. After all, most of us would be surprised today, too, wouldn't we?

Application

What the batter and the runner are not expected to do, you and I are. Jesus' end-of-times teachings suggest a kind of perpetually poised posture for his followers.

The first-century Thessalonians were apparently surprised that Jesus had not yet returned. We, so many years later, might be surprised if he did return anytime soon and that may put us in the unhappy company of the foolish virgins. Heaven forbid that the runner should be sitting and relaxing when the starting gun sounds or that the batter should be preening and scratching when the pitch comes across the plate.

The great difference, of course, between Christ's followers and the two kinds of athletes described is that our waiting is not that kind of "on-pause" posture. The faithful servant, after all, is the one whom the master finds doing his work when he arrives (Matthew 24:45-51), and Paul urged the Thessalonians against idleness (2 Thessalonians 3:6-13). Joshua's admonition to the ancient Israelites may be apt for us, as well: "Serve (the Lord) in sincerity and in faithfulness" (24:14). Our waiting is not a certain kind of pausing; rather, our waiting is a certain kind of living.

An Alternative Application
Matthew 25:1-13. "Not a surprise party." All of us have probably, at one time or another, been involved in a surprise party... perhaps as guests; perhaps as the nervous and secretive organizer. Perhaps even as the

startled guest of honor. In a standard surprise party, of course, the surprise is meant to be a happy thing. The friends and family gather in the dark, they wait quietly and eagerly, and then they gleefully yell out, "Surprise!" when the loved one arrives. It's happy stuff.

Jesus' parable of the ten bridesmaids is, at its core, a story about a festive occasion, a party. And it includes some surprises. But it is not a happy surprise party.

The unhappy surprises occur to the five bridesmaids whom Jesus identifies as foolish. They were evidently surprised, first of all, by the long wait for the bridegroom to arrive. We gather that from the fact that they were clearly unprepared for such a long wait. Then, when they had to depart the scene in order to fetch more oil for themselves, they were unhappily surprised again — this time to discover that the bridegroom had disadvantageously arrived while they were gone and that the door was closed to them when they returned.

The scene is reminiscent of the startling news that the prophet Amos declared to the people of Israel in the eighth century BC (see Amos 5:18-20). They had happy expectations about the day of the Lord, but Amos warned that they would be unpleasantly surprised by that day. This was true also for the bridesmaids. They expected a festive and happy occasion, but it became an occasion of judgment and exclusion for them.

The juxtaposition of the five wise bridesmaids with the five foolish ones — like the sheep with the goats later in the same chapter, or like the two house builders earlier in Matthew (7:24-27) — eliminates all excuses. If no one had anticipated that more than a "lampful" of oil would be needed, each individual's failure would be understandable, perhaps even justified. But because a whole group did anticipate and was prepared, the others are left with no excuse.

So, as we preach this parable, we can extend a warm and wonderful invitation to our people. There is a festive event coming — a party thrown by God himself — and we are invited to be part of it. But it is not meant to be a surprise party. We should not be surprised that the guest of honor has taken a long time to arrive (see 2 Peter 3:9). Nor should we be surprised if he comes suddenly at any moment (see 2 Peter 3:10). Accordingly, we are called upon to be doubly prepared: prepared to wait for the long haul, on the one hand, and prepared to welcome on short notice, on the other.

Proper 28
Pentecost 23
Ordinary Time 33
Judges 4:1-7
1 Thessalonians 5:1-11
Matthew 25:14-30
by Wayne Brouwer

Midterm exams

At the college where I teach in the religion department, we are just past midterm exams. I enjoy the excitement of my students each fall as they seem energized for another year of college life. By late September, however, absenteeism climbs and some students drag themselves to class for a little nap. Life in this unreal campus world has taken on new dimensions: dating, parties, sporting events, roommate spats, dietary choices, and a host of other opportunities and maladies conspire to turn college commitments away from academics and toward all sorts of more wonderful and infinitely weirder dabblings.

Then it is time for midterm exams. Suddenly students wake up in class and ask questions — often not so much out of thirst for knowledge but rather in fear of judgment. Notes and review become more important. Textbooks emerge from their forgotten places of stopping doors and holding open windows or life at the bottom of the backpack. A rustling of purpose shakes most students back to reality... but not all!

Some undergrads have begun to live a lie. They believe their own superiority, their own invulnerability, their own inflated sense of capacity. They have found college life a terrific alternative to whatever the world was like where they came from and here they own their time, they own their desires, and they own their habits. In the words of Billy Joel: "This is my life! Leave me alone!"

So the test papers are passed and the hour ticks by in maddening swiftness. The accumulated wisdom is thrust onto the page, sometimes with gleeful regurgitation, sometimes with struggling banality, and sometimes with defiant b—s— that rivals God's creativity in bringing brand new things out of nothing.

But professors are called to be judges at some point and we get the last word. My heart wants to make every student a valedictorian but my mandate requires a measure of realism. Sometimes I have to weigh the words of the students in the balance and find them lacking. Though they come to me later with wailing and gnashing of teeth, explaining some illogical implications of statements they made that really meant the opposite, judgment day has come, and there is no turning back.

The lectionary passages for today carry with them this theme. College life (or whatever substitute you might wish to choose) is wonderful. It allows students to experience many freedoms and express many passions. But, like most things we do, it has its boundaries and assessments. Some are ready for judgment day and some are not. That doesn't make judgment day wrong; rather, it reminds us that we are not gods and must answer to limits, norms, and the true God. Those who make certain choices will find their midterm exams to be as delightful as sharing in the construction of a magnificent cathedral and sensing that God lives in the place. Of course, those who make other choices have every reason to fear midterm exams.

Judges 4:1-7

The book of Judges has three main literary sections: chapters 1:1—3:6 explain the promise, hope, and expectation that should be carried forward from the Israelites' entrance into Canaan that was recounted in the book of Joshua; chapters 3:7—16:31 tell tales of woe interrupted by mixed-signal victories as Israel presses toward self-destruction; chapters 17-21 form an appendix that documents how far degradation can suck a nation. The overarching theme of the book seems to be the reverse of that of Joshua. There the land of promise came within reach of God's people; here in Judges it is slipping away from their grasp. The condition that separates the two movements is covenant faithfulness.

The covenant created between God and Israel at Mount Sinai, on the way from Egypt to Canaan, was phrased in the form of a Suzerain-Vassal treaty, with historical prologue, stipulations, witnesses, and a section commonly called "curses and blessings." This rehearsal of woe and weal projected future welfare dependent upon fidelity to the character of the covenant relationship. In effect, the book of Judges explains the logical outcome of Israel's covenant unfaithfulness: curses abound.

Within each horror story there is a countervailing hero tale. While Israel forgets her marriage to God, God will not forget his marriage to Israel. Twelve times a strong (and often flawed) marriage counselor appears on the scene to do crisis management and then to moderate a time of vows renewal. The story of Othniel in chapter 3 standardizes the five-part typical "judge" (we don't really have a good English term to describe these people; "deliverer" is probably better than "judge," although the judgment dimension ought not to be neglected in our retelling and understanding of these stories) saga pattern: 1) Israelite sinful waywardness, 2) divine judgment in the form of a political threat, 3) a passionate prayer for deliverance, 4) the rising star of a divinely appointed deliverer, and 5) the conflict miraculously resolved in favor of Israel leading to a peaceful aftermath.

The tale of Deborah (and Barak) ought to be told in its entirety (Judges 4 is the prose, Judges 5 is the earlier poetic version), but today's lectionary intent is fulfilled when the preacher gets at the "exam day" feel of these stories. Israel is tested along the plumb line of the covenant; the invaders are judged as threatening God's plans; and the leaders themselves are assayed for their reluctant, ill-fitted, and corrupted response to God's challenging call. Homiletically, the point of connection ought to raise questions about such assessments in our own churches and cultures.

1 Thessalonians 5:1-11

Paul's Thessalonians correspondence was written early in his missionary career. The book of Acts does not help us much with a background to this letter, only telling us that Paul stopped briefly in the city on his second mission journey and spent at least three weeks speaking in the synagogue before the city erupted in a riot against Paul's presence and message (17:1-9). A theme that clearly emerges is Paul's perception that Jesus would return very soon to finish God's work of redemption. It seems that Paul's preaching focused so strongly on the awe-inspiring message of Jesus' resurrection and the promise of Jesus' imminent return, that two responses set in after the little missionary troupe moved on. First, some in Thessalonica became stargazers. They gave up their daily jobs and responsibilities in order to sit and wait for Jesus to come and rescue them. They lost their sense of purpose in this world and became spiritual space cadets — too heavenly minded to be any longer of earthly good.

Second, some who experienced deaths in the family following Paul's leave began to question whether Paul's message was true. If, in fact, Jesus had conquered death, why did death still rear up its ugly head? Why should Jesus-followers have to die anymore, if Jesus was stronger than death? Moreover, did their dead friends and relatives miss out on all the promises of God simply because they had died too soon?

To each of these challenges Paul gives a stirring response in chapter 4, and here in chapter 5 Paul outlines briefly an ethic for the waiting times. Paul uses metaphors of surprise (vv. 1-3) and darkness/light (vv. 4-10) to call for appropriate behaviors: constant preparedness and lifestyles that can pass the scrutiny of the exams that are coming.

Both metaphors can be mined effectively for sermons. Historians of the *Titanic* disaster, for instance, tell that when Captain Smith knew the gravity of the situation, he did not have time to teach his crew how to act. Months of training and years of British naval heritage came together, however, in his single command to his staff. "Be British," he told them. In those words they were instructed to go about their tasks with the firm confidence of seamen who had lived always on the edge of the great exam. Throughout their years of briny experiences they had prepared themselves for this possible eventuality, and now it was here. They did not have time for handholding or refresher courses or counseling sessions. "Be British," said Captain Smith and his crew knew how to conduct themselves in the crisis of the night. In a similar vein, Paul might be overheard in this passage, saying, "Be Christian!" (meaning, "Be ready!").

The darkness/light metaphor as well is rich with homiletic "preachability." From Plato's cave-dwellers' parable in *The Republic* to Steven Spielberg's *Star Wars* movie saga, darkness and light come to represent two world orders, two vantage points, two ways of living. The darkness seems natural to those who have known only it (see, for instance, George MacDonald's powerful short story "The Day Boy and the Night Girl"). But once one is introduced to the light, life itself is transformed. It is not merely a matter of being able to "see," but a whole new way of life that emerges. This is Paul's message in these verses.

Matthew 25:14-30

Jesus is nearing the end of his ministry. He is in Jerusalem (ch. 21) for the final week before his crucifixion. In Matthew's telling of these days, Jesus' teachings are extremely pointed (21:12—22:46) and often judgmental (chs. 23 and 24). The apocalyptic vision of chapter 24 ends with a call to watch and be prepared (24:36-44) because exam time (judgment day) is approaching and the outcome for each person will depend on preparation and awareness (24:45-51).

Chapter 25 is made up of three parables that have the same basic theme and together will crystallize the opposition against Jesus (see 26:1-4). The recurring motif is Jesus' question of readiness for the imminent divine exam time that is coming. The parable of the ten virgins (25:1-13) focuses on watchfulness and resources. This parable of the talents (25:14-30) explores attitude, and the following tale of the sheep and goats (25:31-46) investigates ongoing lifestyle in its connection with eternal outcomes. In effect, Jesus is constantly telling people to be ready for the exam but he is also making it clear that readiness for the divine examination is not something one can cram for, nor something that one ought to fear. Instead, the awareness of a coming assessment should help us think through why we are here and how our lives can reflect a purpose that has eternal significance.

That is certainly true in today's gospel reading. The parable of the talents is told in a slightly different way in Luke's gospel (19:11-27). There it follows the story of Jesus and Zacchaeus and includes elements that seem to echo the actual travels and commands of Herod within the remembered time. Here the parable is divorced from contextual referents and clearly calls the hearers to be prepared for the day of divine assessment. But fear is not an option. Fear causes spiritual paralysis and this is no virtue. Only those who live expectantly (with an emphasis on both those words — *live* and *expectantly*) will find exam day a good experience. To paraphrase Martin Luther's thoughts: As long as you are going to live anyway, you should live boldly.

Jesus calls us to a kind of active patience. We need to wait, because exam day has not yet arrived. But we need to be active in the waiting, since exam day will require of us things that only can be gained through the living of these days (cf. Harry Emerson Fosdick's great hymn, "God of Grace and God of Glory").

Application

A friend of mine was awakened suddenly on a Saturday morning by a telephone call across three time zones. His brother had been injured and was hospitalized in the critical care unit with a cracked skull and a swelling brain. My friend languored in helplessness. No airplane could get him to his brother's side before either the injury might prove fatal or the swelling would subside and the emergency pass. Enforced patience drummed him with nervous fret, a burden he did not want to bear.

Patience is a tough virtue, slipping from our grasp in the moment of demand. It always races with Road Runner while we are stymied in the dust with Wile E. Coyote, never catching up no matter what Acme technology we employ. Stephen Winward says that at his mother's knee he learned a poem that has proved perennially true:

Patience is a virtue: possess it if you can!
Seldom in a woman, and never in a man.

My own parents used to tell us, "All good things come to those who wait." While that may have been true in the past it hardly seems to apply any more. We seem systematically to have beaten the need for waiting. We buy instant foods, and "nuke" them to serving temperature in microwave ovens. Our satellite dishes and internet search engines bring immediate access to news and information from around the world. We pop painkillers to evaporate our aches, so we don't even have to deal with the whys of our hurts. If we see something we like, instant credit grants us immediate possession.

Still there are things that we can't control and these keep the fires of desire burning the paper house of patience in our souls. The church in first-century Thessalonica was trying to be "patient until the Lord's coming," and Paul had to tell the people to get back to work rather than constantly scanning the horizon.

Throughout history people have tried to run ahead of patience by pretending it wasn't needed and that the world would end before they did. The Millerites and the Seventh Day Adventists announced Judgment Day watches several times over. People climbed trees and sat on rooftops in all-night vigils, but starry skies never split with angelic celebration and the dreams died with graying dawn. So, too, did the patience.

A neighboring farmer in my boyhood community was captured by one of these millennial preachers. He sold his farm, bought a motor home, and traveled with his family in a caravan with a dozen others chasing the preacher on a whirlwind tour of North America, spreading the news of kingdom come. Six months later they circled the motor homes in Texas and waited. And waited. And waited.

When Jesus refused to do a command curtain call on their schedule (as in Matthew's gospel reading for today), the motor homes began to drift away. The prophetic band broke up, disillusioned with a near-sighted preacher, and our neighbor sneaked back to Minnesota in shame. He died a short while later tired of patience that gave out before promise.

This is the religious dimension of patience that we find hard to manage. Our world is imperfect, with corners that bump knees and scorpions that poison hands. We get lonely, we get pained; we struggle to survive and are old in body before our youthful ideals get a chance to catch up. We try to find a little comfort and come away addicted to work or booze or drugs or sex... always far short of heaven.

The patience of waiting is tied to our understanding of how time will get resolved into eternity (so the book of Judges). If there is no God outside the system, we are stuck with cycles of repetition, crushed beneath recurring tasks and tedium that never ends. But if there is a God who has promised to interrupt history with healing and hope and harmony, we wait with expectation.

My friend's brother died from his head injuries. Now my friend waits with the patience of Paul's instructions to the Thessalonians for the coming of Jesus. He is confident that then he will see his brother again, according to the promise of scripture. Without that promise he could not be patient. In an impatient world his is a remarkable hope. A religious hope. A patient hope.

An Alternative Application
Judges 4:1-7. The story of Deborah in Judges 4 can be preached on its own if it is told in its entirety. It is not necessary to read both Judges 4 and 5, but it might be good to bring some of the poetry of chapter 5 into a homily on the themes of chapter 4. Preaching the story of Deborah, Barak, and the time of the judges

requires developing an extensive history that reviews Israel's identity from Egypt to Canaan (especially the covenant at Mount Sinai), and also gives a religious apology for Israel's right to the "promised land." This cannot be phrased merely in terms of "divine promises" or "the spoils of conquest." Rather, it should be seen in the framework of Palestine's unique geographical location in the ancient world. This tiny strip of land forms the bridge between three continents (Africa, Asia, and Europe) and was the high-traffic road for virtually all conquest routes, trading caravans, communications links, and nomadic wanderings.

If the creation no longer knew its Creator (Genesis 1-11), it is understandable how the Creator would work with a community (Genesis 12-50) to nurture a unique identity (Exodus through Deuteronomy) and place that community in the most strategic spot of territory in the world of its day (Joshua) in order to be a witness to all nations. If, however, that community began to lose its distinctiveness (as in Judges), there would be no reason for its continued existence, and the wars of Judges might well wipe it out. But that would be to deny the Creator's purposes and so the tales of Judges begin to make sense. Israel gets divine deliverance in its battles not so much because of its special piety but in spite of its constant undermining of its special task. The judges (like Deborah and Barak) are not Israel's heroes but God's heroes. They do not stand as a witness of Israel's great strength but of God's covenant tenacity. Hence the celebrations that reverberate through the poetry of Judges 5.

Christ the King (Proper 29)
Ordinary Time 34
Ezekiel 34:11-16, 20-24
Ephesians 1:15-23
Matthew 25:31-46
by R. Craig MacCreary

Ride on in majesty?

As the ship made her way down the channel, there was hardly a dry eye among those watching. Certainly, there was none after Her Majesty began to publicly well up at the sight of one of the last vestiges of English royalty being decommissioned. An era had ended with the final sail of *HMS Britannia*, the royal yacht. Those not used to living under monarchy may find such deep emotions a bit odd, but even in the more democratically inclined parts of the world, there is a sad feeling that the tide may be running out for old forms of authority. Nothing seems to be treated as majestically as it once was. Never again will an American president be able to hide a health condition in the way Franklin Roosevelt hid his polio from the public. No president, governor, or mayor in a post-Watergate world can count on much slack from the press. Judging by the dearth of clergy discounts, it seems that clergy are not treated quite as royally as they once were. The internet has done much to dethrone the medical doctor as the sole source of health advice and guidance.

Then along comes Christ the King Sunday inviting us to consider that Jesus is not only friend, brother, fellow traveler, prophet, and priest... but king as well.

I think we clergy are in trouble here. The royal tide certainly seems to be running out: not only in the secular world but in the theological and religious sphere as well. For a while it seemed that no author could go wrong in selling the theory that the church through the centuries has been too tied to the ways of empire. Even the pope no longer wears a crown. Few congregations would tolerate the *Herr Pastor* style of pastoral care that thrived in the more imperial nineteenth century.

We bring a culturally and theologically inbuilt skepticism when we approach the lectionary texts for this Sunday. Most Americans are of democratic spirit. How can we understand the promise of a new David, and the gift of the one whom, being above every rule and dominion, has all things under his feet? We are much more comfortable with God dwelling with us than enthroned above us delivering humans to their final destiny.

Yet some of Jesus' followers did ask by what authority Jesus cast out demons. While many academically minded are reluctant to line out how it will all end, the literally gifted make millions explaining the final judgment in excruciating detail. The battles rage in our nation over where it is appropriate to place the commandments that Moses brought down from on high. The tide may not have run out on the ideas that linger in these texts. Indeed we may be running against the tide if we fail to honor them.

Ezekiel 34:11-16, 20-24

Certainly, for Ezekiel and his contemporaries, there was good reason to believe that the tide was running out on monarchy. Thoughts of how the old system had failed were bound to creep up on them as the Hebrews noticed Babylonian empire words creeping into their children's vocabulary, or found their daughters trying out the Queen Esther beauty cleanse, or seeing their sons thinking about a career in the Babylonia civil service. There is no doubt that for the moment the tide is running out for the old monarchy system as Judah experiences its low ebb.

The receding tide reveals a sad deep truth for Ezekiel. Judah has found itself in exile because of failed leadership that has tended more to its own needs than the needs of the people. In verse 8 preceding the lectionary reading, Ezekiel denounces a leadership that has left the people exposed in the desert to be plundered by wild animals.

Granted, Ezekiel seems to have been prone to wild visions but don't we recognize the feeling of being left high and dry to be devoured? Have not we felt the hot breath of ravenous beasts devouring pension funds while company CEOs tend to their perks and financial packages? Vultures with their schemes show up pecking away at vulnerable widows. All too often elephants and donkeys trample the truth as they leave political scandal in their wake. Good pasture needs to be secured for the lambs because some have fed off future generations leaving them exposed to financial debt and environmental bankruptcy.

Such ideas leave Ezekiel and us wondering if those who are exposed and hung out to dry to the point of being bare bones shall live again. How do people wander off so far from home to the point of such vulnerability? No doubt many of us can find a variety of things that have caused the sheep to go astray, including the mindless stupidity of the sheep themselves. However, for Ezekiel, it is failed leadership that is at the root of what has happened. Nonetheless, it is not failure of nerve or lack of training and skill. The flock has been exposed because of the false worship of the leaders who were charged with tending the sheep, not with tending the false god who has been enthroned in the temple.

One suspects that most of us can readily find the false gods that have been enthroned in our lives. It is not the free market but its enthronement and adoration as god that will lead us astray. It is false worship that leads us to believe that our help is in something other than the name of the Lord. Not a few churches have found themselves scattered and at their wits' end by the careerism of their clergy. It is often the self-adulation of true believers that diminishes truth by turning it into an all-encompassing ideology. The eighth chapter of Ezekiel is clearly the fork in the road where blue state and red state thinkers may find themselves diverging as to just what were the abominations that so repulsed Ezekiel as he viewed the goings on inside the temple. Just what they were we may never fully understand. However, it is how the preacher makes up his or her mind as to what is going on in the temple that will determine their application of this text to our current context.

For Ezekiel, the unraveling of the mess, the restoring of the community, and the returning of this people to their rightful place will be the activity of God. Whatever else it means, it involves God's identifying who has been left behind, exploited, and depleted to the point of leanness. It will require the establishment of new leadership as the result of God's shepherding and in the movement of God we will recognize what true leadership is.

Ephesians 1:15-23

One of the more intriguing works by my artistic wife is a reproduction of a catacomb painting depicting the scene where Jonah is finally tossed from the ship toward the ravenous sea monster that awaits his arrival. So good is the reproduction, that you almost want to reach out and grab the ancient peeling paint. What must it have been like for the early Christians to see this story so graphically depicted? They must have seen and felt their own story in the tale of the one who was being pitched overboard into the darkness. The sense of things closing in around them and then sucking them under must have been all too familiar as they went about worshiping on the first day of the week while others were getting themselves into high gear for the week ahead. It must have been hard to hold onto the belief that they were riding the wave of the future as they went underground and found their status, standing, career, and scaling the heights of the local social scene all cast overboard. All for the sake of below-ground living with children asking, "Are you sure that this is the way ahead — the wave of the future?"

In the midst of the controversies over circumcision and the inclusion of the Gentiles, the author of Ephesians writes, "I have heard of your faith in the Lord Jesus and your love toward all the saints, and for this reason I do not cease to give thanks for you as I remember you in my prayers" (v. 15). Given "red state/blue state" battles on just about everything, given questions of who can be an equal part of the church community, and fundamental questions of church and state knocking at the door, I, too, am thankful for anyone who sees in the church something that looks like the wave of the future! As with Jonah, the ship seems to pitch up and down in a never-ending squall that has left some of us seasick and pitched some of us out into a dark sea of doubt and depression.

In the catacomb depiction of Jonah, the figure cast into the ocean is balanced by the mast that, highlighted in gold, depicts the cross. When the eyes in your head are telling you that we are about to go under, seeing the church as the wave of the future giving one courage is clearly the work of the "eyes of the heart."

The eyes in the head see the might of Rome, the eyes of the heart see that the power to kill is not the same as the power to bury, as Pilate discovered. What is required to see with the eyes of the heart is the spirit of wisdom and revelation the letter writer prays that his readers will have. It is this spirit that says at the graveside service what we have here is not mere closure but what God may open in us through the life for which we give thanks. It is this spirit that, in the face of death, considers that the human task is less to hold on than to hand on the life that we have received. It is this spirit that sees the potential for new life even at the places where we are at cross-purposes.

Wisdom and revelation were, in the ancient world, thought to be the particular provinces of kings and emperors — Caesar and Solomon. However, the below-ground crowd who sees themselves being pitched overboard finds themselves seeing with the eyes of the heart that they just might be riding the wave of the future. They see things this way because they partake of the royal power of the Christ who is, "above every name that is named, not only in this age but also in the age to come." These folks, viewed with the eyes of the heart are a royal priesthood, a holy nation.

Matthew 25:31-46

All my life I have been at less than my best whenever I get to the business of mathematics. I can be reduced to something of subhuman proportions any time I start down the road of balancing checkbooks, calculating cost benefit ratios, or determining budgetary consequences of my latest passions. For most of my life I have lived close to the seacoast where calculating the rise and fall of the ocean tides has been an important matter. Occasionally, my eyes drift in wonderment to the newspaper column that gives the rundown of the comings and goings of the ocean in and out of the capes and coves up and down the coast. Just what mysterious formulas lay behind these predictions remains an impenetrable mystery to me.

The truth of the matter is that people have been in many ways trying to predict with a singular lack of success when their boat would arrive on the incoming tide. The movie, *The Graduate*, predicts that we will be swept up in a rising tide of financial prosperity from "plastics." As a child I watched Disney versions of the "Atomic Age" to come. The 1964 World's Fair featured the "Futurama" ride at the General Motors pavilion that clearly demonstrated that we would all, by now, be riding in cars that operated from tracks in the road. Needless to say, we have come up somewhat short in the human ability to predict the future and adjust our lives accordingly.

Jesus' prediction of the future also remains enigmatic. It seems that neither the sheep nor the goats know what they are doing. Both are caught up in surprise results that come from the kind of lives they have lived. If there is a difference between them, it lies in the calculation of those who go into eternal punishment that it was not the wise move to meet the needs of the hungry, the thirsty, the naked, the strangers, the sick, and those in prison.

It comes as a surprise to those who did connect to those on Jesus' list that anything was more at stake in what they did than the needs of the ones that they met. "And the king will answer them, 'Truly I tell you, just as you did it to one of the least of these who are members of my family, you did it to me' " (v.

40). Without calculation but acting out of connection with the plight and personhood of these least, they found themselves responding with clothes, drink, fellowship, and healing gifts.

Much is made of whether this story comes in defense of the needy in general or should the members of Jesus' family be understood as those who are his avowed followers? How quickly we get into trying to calculate what is precisely meant rather than enter into the story's emphasis on the lack of calculation by those who inherit the kingdom prepared for them from the foundation of the world.

Matthew has used chapter 25 to talk about what it means to stand before the ultimate final judgment. Verses 1-13 cover a domestic situation as a family goes through the motions of a wedding feast. In verses 14-30, Matthew deals with the ultimate judgment that should be applied to our economic life. The final section of this chapter indicates that the royal judgment favors those who operate more out of their connectedness to the needy than their calculations that it is best not to respond. One wonders to what degree our system of governance favors this judgment. In domestic, economic, and political life we face the demands of and experience the grace of God.

In Canada, the final step in the lawmaking process comes when the governor general, as representative of the monarch, gives the royal ascent by a mere nod of the head. In this text we have the ultimate "royal" ascent by the representative of the "monarch" — prophet, priest, and king.

Application

Many of us are, no doubt, gun-shy at the notion of finding gospel in anything that sounds like "Christ the King Sunday." Machiavelli suggested in *The Prince* that it was better for the ruler to be feared than loved. Perhaps that makes for good politics but for most of us it makes for bad religion. It does not seem to be what Jesus had in mind when he said "let the little ones come unto me and do not hinder them." While we may be a little sheepish about pledging all for "king and country," what we have enthroned as central and authoritative in our lives and country does matter. Ezekiel raises the question: What values have our rulers enthroned as worthy of their and our worship? Does the state grant the benefit of the doubt to the kind of judgment that is made in chapter 25 of Matthew? If it does not, do we have the courage to ride the wave that perhaps can only be seen with the eyes of the heart even though it may mean being tossed out of the boat in which everyone else is riding? I suspect that in many congregations it might be good preparation for the coming Advent season to raise the conversation to the discussion of law, rights, and royalty. After all, Joseph will have to consider whether he will take advantage of his full rights under the law in regard to Mary's unique situation. Herod's claim that all he wants to do is worship the newborn king is called into question. Many of the issues posed by Christ the King Sunday will be developed in the Advent season to come.

Alternative Applications

1) Ezekiel 34:11-16, 20-24. The Ezekiel passage, like Psalm 23, speaks of how the sheep are made to lie down. It does not say they were invited to lie down or that they were asked to lie down. Perhaps we are a bit uncomfortable about being forced to do something rather than being asked or invited. Yet this does not always seem to be how God works with me as I drop to my knees in awe at the beauty of the night sky, or my congregation makes sure that I take my full vacation, or I drop with the kind of exhaustion that comes from trying to burn both ends of the candle. When friction builds up in human relationships from the daily grind, when heat builds up from being out of touch with the things that sustain me, when I am given a wakeup call to my own stupidities or suddenly the light comes on, God may be more than suggesting that I lie down.

2) Ephesians 1:15-23. Both Ephesians and Ezekiel raise the question: What are the forms of worship, prayer, and praise that will support the mission of the faith community? In the sweeping issues with which the texts deal, we understand worship to be more than something that just makes people feel good. Worship should help people gain a feel for what God is doing and will do. Is the failure of those who are not sufficiently connected [to God, to the Body of Christ] the result of misdirected worship?

Thanksgiving Day
Deuteronomy 8:7-18
2 Corinthians 9:6-15
Luke 17:11-19
by Bass Mitchell

God is so good

"God is so good, God is so good, God is so good, God's so good to me." So go the words to a popular praise song and one of my favorites. In fact, I often find myself beginning each day singing it. It is a way of reminding myself of the tremendous blessings God has poured into my life, my need to be thankful, and also to be generous in my sharing of the blessings God has given me with those in need.

I have been blessed to have many wonderful teachers in my life. My first one, in Sunday school, taught me lessons I will never forget. One of them is always to be thankful to God. She said that each day she picks one of her blessings and all day whenever she thinks about it she says a prayer of thanks to God for that blessing. That is a practice I, too, have tried to continue and it has helped me to realize constantly just how good God is to me.

I don't know about others, but one thing I try to do, especially when preparing for worship on Sunday morning, is sit quietly and just count my blessings. I find that nothing places me in a better mood or frame of mind to worship than that — naming God's blessings, remembering God's goodness.

Our readings today could easily be under the title of "God Is So Good." In Deuteronomy 8:7-18, Moses reminds the people to sing that same song each day so that they might stay thankful to God. The reading from 2 Corinthians 9 is Paul's teachings about being generous because God has been so generous to us and that in such giving, we receive blessings. In the gospel reading from Luke 17 about the ten lepers, we see the one who returned to give thanks as a model of gratitude for all God has done for us.

Deuteronomy 8:7-18

A friend of mine told me that before he left for college, his parents sat down and told him, "Remember who you are." That could be a good title for the book of Deuteronomy, for in it, Moses, trying to prepare the people for the new land and life ahead of them, in essence says, "Remember who you are and whose you are." Today's passage continues that very theme.

Verses 7-18 should really be seen in light of verses 1-6. There Moses reminds the people of Israel of the wilderness wanderings they have just endured. It was a time of testing and of want and need. Yet God provided for them all they needed (see Exodus 12:37—17:16). Moses sees this time as a kind of disciplining, like that of a parent and child. The lessons were that God could be trusted and that they needed to depend on God. They were taught that God was faithful, whether or not they kept faith with him and whether or not they observed his commandments. Moses doesn't say it here, but the wilderness period was largely a time of faithlessness on the people's part. In fact, they were wandering because of their disobedience. We know the rest of the story — their sojourn in the promised land, in spite of all Moses tells them here, is often also one of disobedience and unfaithfulness.

Now, in verses 7-18, Moses tells them they will face another time of testing. But unlike the time in the wilderness when the issue was a lack of food and water (which God provided), the coming test would be one of abundance and blessings. The test simply was, "Will you continue to trust in and obey God, giving God thanks and credit, or will you grow haughty and proud, as if you were the sole reasons for your blessings?" Moses raises the theme here that times of plenty and blessings are as much a test as are times of famine and scarcity.

Verses 7-10 describe some of the blessings that await the people in the promised land. Moses seems to be describing paradise. Indeed, it was paradise compared to where they had been. What he chooses to mention first are the simple, everyday blessings — land that is fruitful, plenty of water, good crops, ample materials for making tools and all the people needed, bread always on the table. For them, this must have sounded too good to be true. These things had never been in abundance for the generations that had grown up in the wilderness. They would now be able to plant wheat, barley, vineyards, and be assured of a variety of food (not just manna and quails). Yes, they will have to earn them by the sweat of their brows, but these things are actually the gifts of a loving God.

As I write this, we are in the midst of a serious drought in many places in America that has caused many of us to think about and give thanks more for this simple, yet profound, gift of water that God so graciously gives. For we, like these ancient Hebrews, are every bit as dependant still on God's goodness.

In verses 11-18, Moses warns his people to make sure in the midst of their prosperity to keep on loving, serving, and giving thanks to God, for there are dangers in being prosperous. Moses plainly tells them that they are going to become so prosperous that they have land and food and all they need. The danger is that they will forget God and in fact begin to believe that they have earned these things and that they are not the gifts of a good God to them. In fact, Moses once again reminds them of all God has done for them and of the tough times God had seen them through. It's only because God did that and kept his promises made long ago to Abraham that they will be enjoying such prosperity. Far from causing them to stand in haughty pride, their blessings should keep them on their knees in praise and thanksgiving.

2 Corinthians 9:6-15

In Paul's letter to the Galatians (2:6-10) we read of how the leaders in Jerusalem recognized and blessed the ministry of Paul and Barnabas to the Gentiles, but they asked that Paul, in his work among the Gentiles, remember the poor there in Jerusalem. Paul latched onto this idea and put much effort into it. Why? It was the right and Christian thing to do to be generous. Also, it might help bring the Gentiles and Jewish Christians closer together. They had been suspicious of one another, especially Jewish Christians toward the Gentiles, who were not keeping the law as they themselves did. So Paul encourages all the Gentile churches to be generous in their giving for the poor. He intends that this be collected and taken to Jerusalem as soon as possible.

This is not the first time Paul speaks to the Corinthians about the collection. He does so in 1 Corinthians 16:1-4 as a reminder and no doubt had first shared it with them when he had visited them. Second Corinthians 8 also deals with the collection. In fact, it seems that Paul begins again about the collection in chapter 9, which has led some scholars to suggest that this passage may be part of another letter.

Verses 6-7: Paul lays down some principles for giving.

First, it is a lesson from nature itself that the farmer who sows sparingly also reaps sparingly. No farmer is going to sow just a few seeds and then expect a large harvest. The same is true in the spiritual realm. We tend to reap what we sow. Life has a way of balancing out things. The point Paul is making is not so much that they need to sow so they can reap, but that giving is good for them.

Second, giving is a personal matter, a matter of conscience. Each person should give this careful consideration (first part of v. 7). The point is that they should not have to be compelled to give. It should come freely from their hearts.

Third, Paul, quoting perhaps Proverbs 22:9 and Deuteronomy 15:7-11, says that God loves a cheerful giver. If one has to give grudgingly or because someone had forced them to, it is better not to give at all. God sees the heart of the giver. A heart given to God and neighbor first of all is a heart that is cheerful and joyous at any opportunity to help others.

Verses 8-10: Just as Paul uses the self-giving of Jesus on the cross as an example of generosity (see 2 Corinthians 8:8ff), so now Paul uses the giving goodness of God as their model. God has abundantly blessed them all. They have more than they need, due to the goodness and love of God, for God is the greatest cheerful giver of all. And one reason God gives so much is that they too might be such givers. Be as cheerful and generous as God has been to you.

Verses 11-13: Paul seems to be saying here that not only is giving good for us and others, it is also good for God. Why? Because it leads others to be thankful to God and to glorify God. "Just think of the joy, thanksgiving, and praise those in Jerusalem will render to God when they receive your generous gift," Paul tells them. Of course, the Christians in Jerusalem will also feel kindly toward the Corinthians as well and even sing their praises. But for Paul, the highest goal of all is always that praise and thanksgiving be given to God from whom all blessings flow.

Verses 14-15: Here Paul reminds them once again of the incredible goodness of God on their behalf. He does this by talking about "grace," a topic never far from his heart and mind. This grace is God's greatest gift. When it is truly understood and received for what it is, God's unmerited favor and acceptance through the cross of Christ, then one of the results of that is a generous, giving people.

Luke 17:11-19

Jesus is on his last journey to Jerusalem. He is near Samaria, probably not too far from the Jordan River. Samaria, as we know, was a land hated by the Jews. No Jew would pass through it, lest he become contaminated by the soil itself. Jews and Samaritans had hated one another for a long time.

As Jesus neared a village, he was confronted by lepers. In the Bible, "leprosy" covers a number of skin ailments. The classic leprosy is called "Hansen's Disease." It slowly but surely maims and disfigures until a person ceases to look like or feel like a human being. Lepers had strict laws they had to follow (see Leviticus 13-14). For example, lest someone walk up on them, they had to cover their upper lip and cry out, "Unclean! Unclean!" They were outcasts who were cut off from their families, their community, the worshiping community, and even, many thought, from God. They were the walking dead. Indeed, a common saying among the rabbis was that it was "easier to raise the dead than cure a leper."

So this group of lepers, ten in number, call out to Jesus. Leper colonies were all too common. They craved fellowship and community so they found it in one another. But after hearing about Jesus, they cry out to him to "have mercy" on them.

Verse 14 is wonderful in that it says that Jesus "saw them." Most people ignored lepers or fled from them. Not Jesus. They had not ceased to become persons for him, individuals of worth and value. He heard them. He knew their pain at every level, especially their feeling so abandoned and separated from God and the community.

Jesus simply tells them to go show themselves to the priests. According to Leviticus 14, lepers had to be under the care of priests who would verify if a leper had been cured, thus being restored to the community. Is Jesus telling them that they are none of his affair but that of the priests? Is he dismissing them? I think not. Maybe Jesus is seeing if they will have the faith to do what he asks of them, knowing that they cannot be fully healed, fully restored until the priests confirm it.

They do as Jesus directs and discover on the way that they have, in fact, been cured. Most continue to the priests to do as Jesus had said. But one, a Samaritan, returns on bended knee to give thanks to God who he sees being present in Jesus. This strongly suggests that the others were Jews. Their disease had brought them together, Jews and Samaritans, in a way that nothing else had been able to. They had found a common bond greater than their past differences. This Samaritan, a member of a group usually hated and avoided by Jews, would be unclean even if he didn't have leprosy. But now he becomes a model of faith and thankfulness (as does one in the parable Jesus tells about the good Samaritan). A "foreigner," a man from a despised land, becomes the model of appreciation and thanks, gaining in his humble response a blessing from Jesus even greater than his healing. His faith, not just expressed in his cry for help, but more so in his recognition of gratitude for God's mercy, brings him an inner spiritual healing.

Application

Recently I was eating with my wife in a popular restaurant in Harrisonburg, Virginia. I had not eaten there in a long time. It has changed a lot — for the better. There was a line out the door already and it wasn't even noon. When we finally did get inside and seated, the waitress brought us some plates, as they served food buffet style. I must say, I have never seen a larger buffet. There were at least five different sections. I had a terrible time just deciding what I wanted!

Over to the left was all the bread — bread of every kind.

Next to it were the veggies — every veggie you have heard of and some you haven't.

In the middle were the meats — from fish to roast beef, chicken — you name it.

Beside it were the soups and salads — clam chowder, vegetable, potato, and several others. The salad bar had everything on it you could possibly want.

Then came the dessert section. I can't even describe all they had there....

Boy, was I getting hungry!

We got our food and went back to the table. I noticed that the line had gotten longer and wasn't surprised. That line grew the whole time we were in there.

Then we bowed our heads to say the blessing and something happened in my heart.

That blessing became a lot more than just a mealtime ritual that day. From somewhere in the depths of my heart I felt this tremendous surge of gratitude and thanksgiving. It so overwhelmed me that I felt tears coming into my eyes.

For, you see, the thought came to me that all this food, in such abundance and variety, came from the good earth God has given to us all. I watched as the line of people got longer, but there was always more than enough food for all who came.

The thought came to me that this was but one group of people in one tiny restaurant. There are thousands of other restaurants also serving food, and millions of homes where day after day families sit and eat.

I became aware that day as I never have before of just how blessed I was, we all are especially in this country. But we often take it all for granted as if we deserve or earn being here. We keep saying or praying, "God bless America," when we should be far more often on our knees thanking God for all the blessings we have already been given!

Another aspect of this is that most often God gives blessings in order to become a blessing. We would be hard pressed to find a country with more blessings than America. "To whom much is given much is required." There are so many places in the world with people in the most desperate of need. Surely one of the reasons we are so blessed in this country is so that we can share those blessings with others.

Sharing them also is a way of showing that we are grateful to God for them. Although we are doing much around the world, there is still much to be done.

This might be a good week to identify a cause, a need somewhere in the world and lead your church in helping to address it. Also it's a good time to celebrate and share with the people the things your church and/or denomination's already doing at home and around the world to share the blessings of the Lord.

Alternative Applications
1) 2 Corinthians 9:6-15. A minister is preaching to his new congregation about his vision of the church. "With the help of God almighty, there will come a day when this church will no longer crawl, but will stand up and walk!"

"Make it walk, Rev, make it walk," responded the congregation.

"And when this church has learned how to walk, God almighty will cause this church to leap up and run!"

"Make it run, Rev, make it run!"

"And when this church has learned to run the race set before it, God almighty will cause this church to take off and fly!"

"Make it fly, Rev, make it fly!"

"And for God almighty to be able to make this church fly, it's going to take a lot of money!"

"Let it crawl, Rev, let it crawl!"

Paul knew that if the Corinthian church was ever going to truly "fly," it was going to have to give more. But money was only part of it. What he was most wanting from them and what they needed were cheerful hearts and generous spirits. Had they had these, many of the problems among them would not have arisen or would have been resolved. Paul knew that the church never soared higher or closer to Christ than when it reached out in generous giving to those in need.

2) Luke 17:11-19. When the lepers appealed to Jesus, they kept their distance, as the law required. But when Jesus responded to them, he bridged several "distances," including social distance, emotional distance, moral distance, and the distances caused by hatreds, traditions, and taboos. Jesus still bridges those distances today.

About the Authors

Wayne Brouwer teaches Religion, Theology, and Ministry Studies at both Hope College and Western Theological Seminary in Holland, Michigan. He holds degrees from Dordt College (A.B.), Calvin Theological Seminary (M.Div., Th.M.), and McMaster University (M.A., Ph.D.), and spent three decades as a pastor and international missionary teacher. Along with hundreds of published articles, Wayne Brouwer has authored thirteen books, including *Covenant Documents: Reading the Bible Again for the First Time* (Cognella), *The Literary Development of John 13-17: A Chiastic Reading* (SBL), and *Being a Believer in an Unbelieving World* (Hendrickson).

Timothy B. Cargal currently serves as Associate for Preparation for Ministry with the General Assembly of the Presbyterian Church (USA). For some twenty years he combined pastoral ministry with teaching biblical studies in universities and seminaries. He is the author of two books, including Hearing a Film, Seeing a Sermon: Preaching and Popular Movies (Westminster John Knox Press), and has contributed to several other books, study bibles, dictionaries, and journals in the areas of New Testament studies and preaching. He holds a Ph.D. in Religious Studies from Vanderbilt University.

David Kalas is the pastor of First United Methodist Church in Green Bay, Wisconsin. Before moving to Green Bay, he pastored churches in Whitewater, Wisconsin; Appleton, Wisconsin; and Hurt, Virginia. He also led youth ministries in Cleveland, Ohio, and Richmond, Virginia. David earned his undergraduate degree from the University of Virginia in Charlottesville and his Master of Divinity degree from Union Theological Seminary in Richmond, Virginia. He has also done coursework at Pittsburgh Theological Seminary and Asbury Theological Seminary.

In addition to the present volume, David has also contributed to other preaching resources published by CSS, is a regular contributor to *Emphasis: A Lectionary Preaching Journal* (CSS Publishing Company, Inc.), and has also written curriculum materials for the United Methodist Publishing House. David and his wife, Karen, have been married nearly 30 years and have three daughters, Angela, Lydia, and Susanna.

The late **R. Craig MacCreary** was pastor of South Congregational Church, United Church of Christ in Newport, New Hampshire. He held pastorates in Pennsylvania, West Virginia, and Massachusetts. He earned degrees from Elon University (B.A.), Lancaster Theological Seminary (M. Div.), and Hartford Seminary (D. Min.). His work appeared in *Colleague*, *Pulpit Digest*, and *The United Church News*. He was a guest on National Public Radio and was a contributor to *Candles in the Dark: Preaching and Poetry in Times of Crises*, edited by James Randolph.

Mark Molldrem has served as a pastor in the Evangelical Lutheran Church in America for 37 years. He has had parishes in Cobb/Edmund, Wisconsin; Beaver Dam, Wisconsin; Mondovi/Modena, Wisconsin; and Saginaw, Michigan. Currently he is Senior Pastor at First Lutheran Church in Beaver Dam, Wisconsin. Molldrem has written previously for CSS. He has authored numerous articles in various national magazines and journals. He received his Master of Divinity and also his Doctor of Ministry degrees from Luther Theological Seminary, St. Paul, Minnesota. He is very involved in his community, supporting People Against a Violent Environment (domestic violence) and developing community leadership through the Chamber of Commerce. Throughout the years, he has enjoyed art glass, martial arts, landscaping, preaching and teaching in the Lutheran Church in Liberia (West Africa), playing with his grandchildren, and vacationing with his wife, Shirley, with whom he has raised two children.

William H. Shepherd is an author, teacher, biblical scholar, and Episcopal priest who currently serves as an Interim Ministry Specialist in the Diocese of Connecticut. In addition to 19 years of experience in parish ministry, he has taught preaching and biblical studies at Candler School of Theology, Virginia Theological Seminary, George Mercer Memorial School of Theology, and Immaculate Conception Seminary. Shepherd's writing has appeared in *Christian Century, Anglican Theological Review, Emphasis: A Preaching Journal for the Parish Pastor*, and several other publications. He is a graduate of the University of Georgia, Yale Divinity School, and received his Ph.D. in New Testament studies from Emory University.

If You Like This Book...

Please go to **www.csspub.com** or call **800-241-4056** to order any of the below titles.

David Kalas contributed to each of the following books: *Sermons on the First Readings, Series II, Cycle A* (978-0-7880-2451-1) (printed book $37.95, e-book $29.95); *Sermons on the First Readings, Series III, Cycle C* (978-0-7880-2619-5) (printed book $37.95, e-book $29.95); *Sermons on the Gospel Readings, Series I, Cycle C* (978-0-7880-1968-5) (printed book $38.95, e-book $29.95); *Navigating the Sermon, Cycle B* (978-0-7880-2670-6) (printed book $39.95, e-book $29.95); and *Navigating the Sermon, Cycle C* (978-0-7880-2676-8) (printed book $34.95, e-book $29.95).

Craig MacCreary has pieces from **Emphasis** published in *Navigating the Sermon, Cycle B* (978-0-7880-2670-6) (printed book $39.95, e-book $29.95) and *Navigating the Sermon, Cycle C* (978-0-7880-2676-8) (printed book $34.95, e-book $29.95).

Mark Molldrem wrote *The Victory of Faith, New Testament Sermons for Lent and Easter* (978-0-7880-1005-7) (printed book $11.95, e-book $8.95) and pieces from **Emphasis** published in *Navigating the Sermon, Cycle C* (978-0-7880-2676-8) (printed book $34.95, e-book $29.95).

Timothy Cargal has pieces from **Emphasis** published in *Navigating the Sermon, Cycle B* (978-0-7880-2670-6) (printed book $39.95, e-book $29.95) and *Navigating the Sermon, Cycle C* (978-0-7880-2676-8) (printed book $34.95, e-book $29.95).

Wayne Brouwer wrote *Humming Till the Music Returns, Second Lesson Sermons for Advent/Christmas/Epiphany, Cycle B* (978-0-7880-1506-9) (printed book $17.95, e-book $9.95), contributed to *Sermons on the Gospel Readings, Series II, Cycle A* (978-0-7880-2453-5) (printed book $37.95, e-book $29.95), pieces from **Emphasis** in *Navigating the Sermon, Cycle B* (978-0-7880-2670-6) (printed book $39.95, e-book $29.95), and *Navigating the Sermon, Cycle C* (978-0-7880-2676-8) (printed book $34.95, e-book $29.95).

William H. Shepherd Jr. wrote *Without a Net: Preaching in a Paperless Society* (978-0-7880-2307-1) (printed book $16.95, e-book $14.41) and *If a Sermon Falls in the Forest...: Preaching Resurrection Texts* (978-0-7880-1937-1) (printed book $23.95, e-book $9.95). William was also an *Emphasis*, Charting the Course author in past years for CSS Publishing Company.

Prices are subject to change without notice.

www.ingramcontent.com/pod-product-compliance
Lightning Source LLC
Chambersburg PA
CBHW081800300426
44116CB00014B/2183